Public Speaking

Content and Communication

Sixth Edition

Charles S. Mudd
California State University, Northridge

Malcolm O. Sillars
The University of Utah

WAVELAND
PRESS, INC.
Prospect Heights, Illinois

For information about this book, write or call:
Waveland Press, Inc.
P.O. Box 400
Prospect Heights, Illinois 60070
(708) 634-0081

Photo Credits

The Bettmann Archive xiv, 44

Emilio Mercado/Jeroboam, Inc. 74

Jennifer Ogilvie reverse Parts II and III, 136, 144, 292

UPI/Bettmann 29, 35, 152

Wide World 42, 50, 60, 84, 96, 118, 119, 150, 175, 185, 193, reverse Part IV, 227, 229, 243, 253, 255, 281, 288, 327, 359, 365

Table of Contents

Part IV   Communicating Speeches

Part V   Types of Speaking Situations

Part VI   Evaluating Speeches

Speeches for Study

Preface

As long as there are wars and rumors of wars, courtrooms and corporations, pulpits and families, and legislatures there will be no need to argue the importance of public speaking. Pluralism and democracy are the very essence of American society, and such a society inevitably generates and promotes disagreements, doubts, difficulties, and debates. If the society is to flourish within the bounds of civil order, it must be fostered by a citizenry skilled in rhetoric — the art and practice of effective communication.

College and university students, particularly, must prepare themselves to assume the roles of ethical citizens and skilled public speakers. They must have the ability to construct messages that work; to distinguish between drivel and data; and to speak effectively in any situation linked to their goals.

Toward these ends, *Public Speaking: Content and Communication, 6/E* is designed for college and university students in a public speaking course. The altered title of the new edition emphasizes the central focus of public speaking.

Like all instructors, we insist that the text for a course in public speaking must do more than teach students how to make adequate classroom speeches. Our goal is to prepare students for the demands of the speaking situations they will face throughout life.

The study of public speaking is not only a search for technical skill; it is also a liberal art. As such, it helps students to think well *and* to speak well. Therefore, we have committed *Public Speaking: Content and Communication* to the pursuit of both these goals. As we said in the preface to an earlier edition, our perspective is evident and our biases are clear. We still believe that:

1. The basic assumptions of classical rhetorical theory are applicable and useful today. This edition retains the fusion of classical and contemporary rhetorical theory on which all the earlier editions have been based. Classical rhetoric is the underpinning; contemporary theory is its bulwark. In making this union, we have tried throughout to preserve unity of theme and coherence in development.

2. Clear thinking is prerequisite to public communication. Effective speaking is not the product of simplistic formulas but of mental activity, analytical reading, perceptive listening and critical thinking.

3. Any approach to public speaking must be **audience-centered**. A specific target audience must be foremost in the speaker's mind.

4. Inherently, the subjects of *all* speeches are potentially controversial. Thus the need for reasoning, synonymous with argument, is inescapable. This accounts for our emphasis on the analysis of subjects and audiences. It explains why we stress the importance of speech organization.

5. Every element of a speech—lines of thought, organization, materials, language, delivery—must be based on sound reasoning, linked to values appropriate to the audience, and advanced with convincing credibility.

6. Competence in communication demands not only the intelligent production of effective messages but the intelligent consumption of them as well.

7. Speakers are morally responsible for what they say. This implies not only that they be competent but that they be ethical as well.

Features of the New Edition

An improved design makes the book more readable. Type choice and the spacing of materials make sections and topics more readily identifiable.

Colleagues and students have found the outlines at the beginning of the chapters useful; a list of key terms and a set of exercises appear at the end of each chapter. These three items give a clear indication of where each chapter is going, where it has been, and whether the students have mastered the material well enough to put it into practice.

The organization of the book retains the flexibility of earlier editions and can still be adapted to a one- or two-term course, for either a quarter or semester system. The *Instructor's Guide* suggests a variety of ways to adapt the materials to these different courses. Moreover, instructors may freely deviate from our sequence of the chapters without sacrificing the unity or coherence of the material.

The discussions of rhetorical principles, types of discourse, and practical elements of speech preparation are supported by a large number of examples, sample outlines, and sample speeches. In updating the material we have tried to use selections from actual speeches, or adaptations of them. Whenever possible, we have resisted the temptation to create an example to illustrate a rhetorical principle, even though this is usually much easier than finding a real one. We believe it is better for students to see how real speakers interact with real audiences.

Our purpose has always been to make *Public Speaking: Content and Communication* as current, interesting, and teachable as we can. Therefore, the title is not all that's new. This edition has been newly researched and updated. No chapter has been left unchanged. Each has been closely examined and, in most cases, extensively rewritten. We have made several changes that we think improve this edition.

1. Chapter 1 has expanded the discussion of the classical foundations of rhetoric. The Aristotelian rhetorical proofs, *logos, pathos* and *ethos* are at the heart of our conception of reasonable, effective rhetoric: reasoning, values, credibility.

2. We have put greater emphasis on critical thinking and tied the concept directly into speech skills. Learning to be a competent public speaker reciprocally develops the skills of critical thinking.

3. The chapter on subject analysis and the chapter on audience analysis have been reversed in sequence on the grounds that issues exist only if they are issues for a particular audience. Finding the potential issues in a subject and then deciding which of these will be significant to a targeted audience gives greater emphasis to centering on the audience. Chapter 6, "Analyzing the Audience," has been significantly revamped to emphasize the practical problem of adapting actual speech materials to what is learned from the analysis of audience demographics.

4. The topics of "arguments" and "values" are treated in separate chapters, as they have been in all editions except the fifth. This provides for a stronger development of, and a clearer distinction between, the roles of *logos* and *pathos*.

5. Instead of discussing anxiety in a separate chapter, we have made it a section in the chapter on delivery. This treatment gives less emphasis to a subject that students are too often prone to make paramount. Our approach to the topic of apprehension is unchanged: Think about the audience, not about yourself; be well prepared and trust your preparation. We leave serious psychological disruption to the professionals in that area.

6. In this edition, we have taken more examples from speeches by students. This strikes a better balance between student speeches and those given by people in professional positions. It gives students a clearer picture of what they might expect of themselves in the class and in their later careers.

7. Sample speeches, formerly in an appendix, have been attached to appropriate chapters. They seem more likely to catch the attention of both instructors and students there than in an appendix. For the same reason, we have moved the list of suggested speech subject areas from an appendix to the chapter on speech subjects and purposes.

In addition to the exercises appended to each of the chapters, the large number and variety of sample outlines, and a substantial number of sample speeches, an *Instructor's Guide* is available. It offers a variety of instructional aids including syllabi for various approaches to both quarter and semester courses, evaluation forms, assignment sheets, lists of additional resources, help with special problems, chapter-by-chapter explanations, and essay, true-false, and multiple-choice questions.

Writers inevitably accrue debts of gratitude to many people. We have borrowed much of the time, energy, intelligence, learning, and experience of a large number of our colleagues. We are pleased to acknowledge our obligations to them.

Over the years, we have profited from many suggestions made by both colleagues and students. We thank all of these unnamed friends. More specifically, we extend our sincere thanks to these colleagues who have given more formal help: Dorothy Ashe, West Hills College, California; Ceres Birkhead, University of Utah; Julie Brown, University of California, Davis; Michael Brown, University of Utah; Carl R. Burgchardt, Colorado State University; Ralph E. Dowling, Ball State University; Ann Marie Gill, Colorado State University; David Henry, California Polytechnic State University, San Luis Obispo; Curley Jones, University of Utah; Mary G. McEdwards, California State University, Northridge; Bambi Rockwell, University of Utah; Gerard Schoening, University of Utah; James Stewart, Tennessee Technological Institute; Mina A. Vaughn, California Polytechnic State University, San Luis Obispo; Beth M. Waggenspack, Virginia Polytechnic Institute and State University; Leonard B. Wurthman, California State University, Northridge; Raymond Bud Zeuschner, California Polytechnic State University; San Luis Obispo.

Neil and Carol Rowe have earned our respect for their careful and creative work to make this sixth edition one of the best writing experiences we have had.

With patience and proofreading, Anne Mudd has carried much of the burden. We cannot count the hours Charlane Sillars has spent editing, typing, and making sense of a scribbled manuscript.

Part One

Introduction

The Tradition of Public Speaking

Think about people who always know exactly what to say and how to say it. What are your impressions of them? Do they appear successful, intelligent, and confident? What makes them stand out? Chances are their speech distinguishes them from others who have not yet learned how to communicate as effectively.

What is your image of your own communication? Have you ever been in a group discussion and not volunteered your opinion because you weren't sure you could express your thoughts? Did you try—only to find that your audience misunderstood what you wanted to say? If you have had this or similar disappointments, you're in the right course!

If you lack confidence about how you speak, take heart. As you progress through this class, you will learn the skills of effective speaking. The focus of this textbook is on public communication, but the same principles apply whether you are talking with a friend, presenting an idea to a group of people at work, or delivering a public speech. The skills you will learn are not isolated bits of knowledge useful only while you are in this class.

The Skills of Effective Speaking

- Thinking and listening critically
- Organizing ideas rationally
- Using good evidence
- Explaining clearly
- Developing sound arguments
- Using language appropriately
- Delivering messages effectively

People have studied the art of communication for centuries. This chapter will explore some of those historical foundations. We begin our exploration of public speaking by looking at the rich history of the rhetorical tradition. When we look to ancient Greece, we can see reflections of our times. While they may not be mirror images, we will discover essential elements for our search to improve our speaking.

Effective Communication Is an Ancient Art

We call communication an art because it has been recognized as just that for more than 2500 years. Clever and effective speakers were highly respected by the Greeks. Several of the warrior-heroes of the ''Iliad,'' especially Ulysses, were admired almost as much for their prowess in debate as for their awesome fighting skills.

The Sophists

Significant study of the art of pubic speaking began several hundred years after the Trojan war. Public speaking was first taught professionally in the fifth century B.C. by a group of men called "Sophists." The name sophist is derived from the Greek word *sophistes*, wise men. The Sophists offered their services as teachers of a wide variety of subjects. Taken together, the subjects they taught covered virtually all of the knowledge of the day. "Above all," wrote W.G. deBurge in *The Legacy of the Ancient World*, "they taught rhetoric, the art of public speech . . . its chief importance lay in the training it afforded in the general conduct of public and private life. When Protagoras [a sophist] was asked by Socrates what benefits his young pupil would receive, he answered that he would teach him to speak, and thereby make him day by day a better citizen, more competent to handle the affairs whether of the *Polis* [city-state] or of his domestic household."[1]

The Sophists were much in demand because they offered a crucial service to their society. Democracy spread rapidly in Greece at that time. Since all public business (political and legal) was carried on orally, the ability to speak effectively in the assembly and in the courts was essential, not only as a way of life but as a means of getting, keeping, and using power. In addition, it was the law that everyone had to defend himself (women were not allowed to participate) in either a civil or criminal case. If he or members of his family had a complaint, he had to prosecute the case in court. The sophists became very rich since they alone taught the oral skills necessary to preserve and to promote one's position in Greek society.[2]

The politicians who were active in civic affairs were called "rhetors," that is, speakers. The equivalent word in Latin is "orator." We still give this name to certain kinds of public speakers today. *Rhetors*, then were the public speakers; the theory of public speaking was called *rhetoric*, and those who taught it were (and) are *rhetoricians*.

Enemies of the Sophists

Despite their popularity and wealth, the Sophists were not without enemies. Among the most daunting of these were the philosopher Socrates and his followers. Socrates' star pupil, Plato, was the most powerful enemy. Much of what Plato wrote was an open, deliberate attack on the Sophists and their teachings. His disdain rested on moral grounds. Indeed, he was the first to make ethics and morality a relevant consideration in the practice of rhetoric.

Plato (speaking for Socrates) accuses the Sophists of teaching young speakers to seek victory at any cost—even if they didn't know what they were talking about. For Plato (as for us), this would be a clearly unethical practice. The principal flaw in rhetoric, then, was a problem of knowledge. A speaker must grasp the *absolute* truth of a matter; to persuade others to accept a *probable* truth was immoral. The Sophists had to admit that rhetoric could not supply that knowledge.

Aristotle's *Rhetoric*

One of the great intellects of the fourth century B.C. (and of all time) was the Greek philosopher Aristotle. Rhetoric was among the large number of subjects that attracted his interest. Over the centuries, his book on the subject has been more influential than any other in the history of the discipline. Rhetoricians for hundreds of years have given his *Rhetoric* the respect frequently reserved for the Bible.

Aristotle (the star pupil of Plato) was much more pragmatic than his idealistic teacher about the way rhetoric operates in the world of legal and political debate. He realized that in the majority of day-to-day disputes, the absolute truth was unattainable. Opinions and conjectural arguments were the basis of decision. He also saw that even though rhetoric could be put to bad uses, any fatal flaw was not in the nature of rhetoric itself but in the moral purpose of the speaker.

Even though they differed greatly about the nature and function of rhetoric, Plato and Aristotle did agree on one thing: rhetoric is put to bad use when it helps to bring about bad ends.

The Importance of Rhetoric

Honest, socially responsible rhetoric can flourish only in an atmosphere of free speech. Democracy can flourish only as long as it is nourished by honest, socially responsible rhetoric. For centuries the citizens of Greece and the citizens of Rome enjoyed the freedom to speak, and their audiences enjoyed the right to make effective decisions. Athens in the fourth century B.C. witnessed an unequaled development in the techniques of public speaking. Robert Connor in *Greek Orations* writes "Except for Isocrates none of these men ever thought of himself as a literary figure. They were citizens, advocates, politicians and, in occasional moments of idealism, statesmen."[3]

In the classical periods of Athens and Rome, rhetorical skill was essential to survival for someone who wanted to be a political leader. Losing a debate often meant a great deal more than winning or losing an election. It could cost you your life.

In some parts of the world, losing an election today can still carry as drastic a price. Fortunately, that is not the case in this country. Since we live in a democracy, the need for effective communication and the valuable skill of public speaking is as great today as it was in the democracies of Greece and Rome. If our democracy is to survive, we must be as competent in communication as the Greeks and Romans ever were.

The world today makes great demands on its leaders, but it offers great opportunities and vast rewards for the effective speaker. Radio and television provide potential audiences far greater than any crowd who ever heard the Greek rhetor Demosthenes or the Roman orator Cicero.

The potential danger from an unscrupulous use of rhetoric is as great as the potential good that can come from its ethical use. People misuse guns, automobiles, and alcohol and these are not outlawed. There is no need to abandon rhetoric just because it can be misused. The art of rhetoric has its values. Aristotle pointed out four:

> [Rhetoric] is valuable, first, because truth and justice are by nature more powerful than their opposites; so that, when decisions are not made as they should be, the speakers with the right on their side have only themselves to thank for the outcome. Their neglect of the art needs correction. . . . Secondly . . . [e]ven if our speaker had the most accurate scientific information, still there are persons whom he could not readily persuade with scientific arguments. True instruction, by the method of logic, is here impossible; the speaker must frame his proofs and arguments with the help of common knowledge and accepted opinions. . . . Thirdly, in Rhetoric . . . we should be able to argue on either side of a question; not with a view to putting both sides into practice—we must not advocate evil—but in order that no aspect of the case may escape us, and that if our opponent makes unfair use of the arguments, we may be able in turn to refute them. . . . Lastly, if it is a disgrace to a man when he cannot defend himself in a bodily way, it would be odd not to think him disgraced when he cannot defend himself with reason.[4]

Aristotle was right. His principal point is that even if you're not a lawyer, a salesman, or a politician, you need to know how rhetoric works in order to protect yourself from the con-artists of the world. Another significant point is his injunction against an unethical use of rhetoric—using rhetoric, as he puts it, to "advocate evil."

More significantly, Aristotle says that "the speaker must frame his proofs and arguments with the help of common knowledge and accepted opinions." This insight is the most important element in Aristotle's rhetorical theory—that the proofs in rhetorical argument are probable, not absolute. You'll see just how significant this is when you read Chapter 10.

Everyone Needs Communication Skills

Philosophers don't sit around and think all the time. They tell other philosophers (and anyone else who would like to know) what they have been thinking about. And since their colleagues are highly critical, they must be able to defend their ideas in debate. Social scientists and physical scientists put themselves no less at risk when they express their views and their findings to a skeptical world. They must be able to communicate effectively.

People in business, law and religion have the same need. Politicians, of course, don't survive long in the public arena unless they are good speakers. Let's bring what we're saying about public speaking closer to home.

Communication Is Especially Important to You

You know that speaking skill is a must for people in public life, but it's important for you, too. The ability to speak well is essential to any job you would want. You may never be President or even a city council member, but you will be called upon to speak. When your employer says, ''The board meeting tomorrow morning is at ten o'clock. Could you bring us up to date on the Amex contract negotiations?'' you are going to make a speech.

Vast changes now underway will make communication even more important to your success. ''Technological advances and expanded trade promise to transform work and the American economy in the late 20th and early 21st centuries at least as much as the industrial revolution did in the late 19th and early 20th centuries.''[5] Many existing jobs will be lost and millions of new ones will be created by robotization and computerization. These new jobs will be in white-collar and service areas.[6] They will depend heavily on a set of communication skills and a rhetorical theory that is very like the classical theory studied by the great speakers of Athens and Rome.

Contemporary Teaching Is Based on Classical Theory

The communication principles speakers learn today are not greatly different from those described by Aristotle. One basic assumption, then and now, has been that rhetoric is about making arguments. Whether you are informing the Board of Directors about the Amex contract, presenting an award to the outgoing club president, or persuading your classmates to join an environmental protection activity, you will use arguments to get the responses you want from your audience.

Aristotle's Analysis of Argument

Central to Aristotle's theory of rhetoric was his analysis of proofs. He says that the art of rhetoric ''consists of proofs alone—all else is but accessory.''[7] He identifies three kinds of proofs:

Logos—**rational argument**   Persuasion is brought about by arguments that are meant to give rational proof of the speaker's claim.

Pathos—**appeals to emotion**   Aristotle shows how a speaker can appeal directly to the emotions of an audience. We have ''modernized'' his theory of *pathos* somewhat. We will speak of *pathos* as appeals not to emotion but to values. Think of it this way: instead of using arguments to arouse emotions so that people will act out of love, anger, pity, fear, hate or envy, think of arguments as your way of showing an audience that what you want it to do is consistent with its own beliefs and values. Whatever emotion is aroused in the process is incidental. As we will see in Chapter 4, however, the emotions can be put to both good and bad uses.

Ethos—**speaker credibility**   The speech, by its content and delivery, shows that the speaker is credible—someone who, because of good character, intellect, and good will toward the audience, is worthy of belief.

The Five "Canons" of Rhetoric

The Romans learned rhetoric from the Greeks and carried the subject over into the Latin language. They didn't make significant contributions to Aristotle's basic theory of argument, but in a typically Roman manner they systematized rhetoric just as they systematized everything. They introduced the useful practice of thinking about rhetoric in terms of what are called the five classical "canons" of the art.

The word *canon*, derived from Greek, is used in the sense of a body of laws. In the case of rhetoric, the laws are rules or principles for preparing and delivering effective speeches.

Invention—**discovery of subject matter**   The canon of invention is concerned with the discovery of the subject matter of the speech. This involves principally the finding of evidence and the construction of arguments based on *logos*, *pathos*, and *ethos*.

Disposition—**organization**   The canon of disposition is concerned with the structure of the message, its organization.

Elocution—**language style**   The canon of elocution is the theory of rhetorical style, principally the means of achieving clarity, correctness, propriety, and elegance in the speech.

Delivery—**use of voice and body in speaking**   The canon of delivery tells the speaker how to use voice and body to transmit a message most effectively.

Memory—**mnemonic devices**   Finally, the canon of memory has often been called the "lost" canon because today speeches are not memorized, therefore, elaborate mnemonic systems for aiding a speaker's memory are no longer needed. Moreover, libraries and the memory banks of computers are better storage bins for data than the human brain. Nonetheless, the other four canons, invention, disposition, style, and delivery are very much what they were many centuries ago.

The Canons Are Fundamental to Contemporary Rhetoric

You'll also see in later chapters that the canons of rhetoric underlie everything that is important to effective speaking. Most of the following chapters are directly related to these four canons and the Aristotelian analysis of proofs. The entire message that your speech conveys is made up of those four elements. We introduce all of them briefly in Chapter 2, but each one is discussed in greater detail in subsequent chapters. Three other chapters discuss the significant relationship that listening, ethics, and criticism have to public speaking.

Everything we have said so far has to do with the history and theory of public speaking and the utility of communication skills. But let's ask a more fundamental question, "What are the elements of the public speaking act itself?"

Communication Is a Process and a Transaction

The best way to understand public speaking is to think of it as a process and a transaction. It is a process because it is an ongoing, ever-changing, dynamic activity; it is a single, continuous event rather than being a series of individual, discrete operations. It is a transaction because of the *mutual influence* between speaker and audience, whether the audience is one, few, or many; it entails a constant interaction among all of those who are involved.

You don't get a good picture of communication if you think of it as a series of separate steps. For a long time, people mistakenly believed that making a speech was pretty much the same as following a recipe. First, melt some butter, add some flour, then stir, add milk, and so on. Apply the same notion to speaking. First, say something. Then the audience hears what you say. After that, the audience responds. Next, you get the audience response, and so on.

That is not the way communication works. Instead of being a series of separate steps, it's all of one piece. Look at it as a number of constantly changing variables, always in some relationship with each other. Actually, both you and the audience begin to respond to each other even before you start to speak. And you keep on responding to each other all the while you're speaking.

If you think of a conversation you'll get a much better picture of what goes on. The number of people involved is not important. In a lively situation, everyone actively takes part—giving and getting responses; thinking, speaking, listening; shifting and causing shifts in beliefs and values. The conversation is continuous, flowing, constantly changing. It does not start and stop, nor is it static. Everyone is actively engaged in it all the time.

Any speech you give should display those same characteristics of liveliness, interchange, and flow. The speech doesn't begin when you first stand before the audience. The actual delivery is merely an episode in the on-going life of everyone in the room. Everything you and the audience have ever been, done, read, heard, or seen is a part of the process. And the speech doesn't end when you sit down. The effects of that particular transaction will last long after you have finished.

The interactions of seven closely related variables determine what goes on in the speech transaction: speaker, speech, audience, occasion, channel, feedback, interference.

Speaker—The Source of a Message

There can't be a speech without a speaker. Who and what you are helps to determine what an audience gets out of your speech.

Speech—The Message

Your speech is the sum of all of the devices of invention, disposition, style, and delivery that you use to move the audience to understanding, belief, and action.

Audience—Of One, Few, or Many

An audience is the group to whom your speech is directed. What an audience hears you say (irrespective of what you intend to say) is, in fact, what you do say. The ideal, of course, is for the audience to hear exactly what you mean to say.

Occasion—Surrounding Circumstances

A speech doesn't take place in a vacuum. There will always be an occasion of some kind. Are you engaged in a group discussion, making a sales presentation, involved in a conversation, or delivering a formal speech? Each of these occasions influences the transaction because it helps to determine the subject and purpose of the speech, it establishes the general atmosphere, and it often mandates the physical setting as well.

Channel—Roadway Between Source and Receiver

Ideas don't get poured out of one head and into another and they aren't zapped across time and space by mental telepathy. They need a road to travel on and a vehicle to carry them. Together the road and the vehicle are the channel through which your message is transmitted.

The vehicle is everything that the audience sees and hears when you deliver the speech: language, your use of voice and body, visual aids.

The roadway is the method of presentation. You can talk face-to-face with an audience of one or more, or you can deliver a speech on radio or television.[8]

Feedback—Audience Reactions

Feedback is the response an audience gives you while you're delivering a speech. It can come in the form of sharp attention and obvious

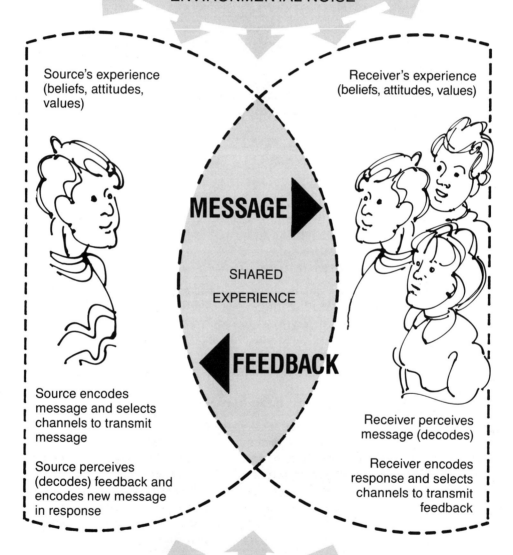

MODEL OF COMMUNICATION

ENVIRONMENTAL NOISE

Source's experience
(beliefs, attitudes,
values)

Receiver's experience
(beliefs, attitudes, values)

MESSAGE ▶

SHARED

EXPERIENCE

◀ FEEDBACK

Source encodes
message and selects
channels to transmit
message

Source perceives
(decodes) feedback and
encodes new message
in response

Receiver perceives
message (decodes)

Receiver encodes
response and selects
channels to transmit
feedback

ENVIRONMENTAL NOISE

understanding, a smile or a laugh, a puzzled frown of disagreement, or clear evidence of boredom. Any of these and more. When you adjust to the feedback, the audience responds to your adjustment, and so on. This kind of interaction between you and an audience is precisely what makes speaking an ongoing process and an interpersonal transaction.

Interference—Hindrance to Understanding

Interference is any kind of "noise" that puts up barriers to the audience's accurate understanding of your message. It may be kids yelling outside the window, a diesel truck passing by, or an airplane coming into an airport not far away. The noise can also come from inside the room where you're speaking: sneezing or coughing, the shuffling of papers or feet, members of the audience talking among themselves.

There can also be psychological noise. If some of the people in your audience are tired, their fatigue acts as a sort of noise to keep them from listening well. Others may be thinking about a test they have just taken or are about to take.

Any of these conditions and any others that make it harder for you to communicate the message to the audience (or for the audience to receive the message) are examples of what we mean by interference. Eliminate interference whenever you have any control over it.

Critical Thinking

You won't be able to develop any of the skills you need without critical thinking. The whole operation depends on it. You have to think critically, not only when you're giving advice to others, but also when you're trying to find out what might be wrong with the information and arguments somebody gives you. The skills of critical thinking are crucial to your development as a good public speaker. Don't expect them only of yourself. Demand them of others as well.

To be a critical thinker you have to be knowledgeable of the subject at hand. This requires you to have the right information. Once you have that, you have to cast it into a reasonable structure. Only then can you expect to build clear explanations and sound arguments. The principal skill of the critical thinker is the ability to identify flaws in the arguments of others and to prevent similar flaws in their own arguments.

Learning to think critically in this course will bring you at least two benefits: you can prepare yourself to give service to your society by being a knowledgeable leader and you can save yourself from unscrupulous manipulation.

Develop Rhetorical Skills

In this chapter, we may have given the impression that learning to speak well is a tough job. Fortunately for all of us, that isn't the case. The truth is, it's a lot easier than it may seem. Look at the huge number of people who have mastered the skills quite well and are very good speakers. Our experience has been that any student who completed the course you are in now made a noticeable improvement in speaking ability.

For one thing, you are coming into the course with a big head start in the game. You've been practicing rhetorical skills almost since you first began to talk. You've been making speeches practically all your life. Look at what's going on in your life right now. When you return a sweater to a department store because you don't like the way it fits, do you sometimes plan and rehearse what you will say? If you have a job and decide to ask for a raise, do you collect your arguments and then present them to your boss? If you want your sorority or fraternity to participate in homecoming, do you give the other members your reasons at the next meeting? In all of these instances, you can recognize subject matter, organization, style, and delivery. In every case, you are making a speech.

Of course, you'll have to develop and practice the skills appropriate to all four canons. But that's why you're in this course. As you move along, your speeches will become more sophisticated and more mature. At the end of the term, you'll be surprised at how much your competence and confidence have grown.

This Is What Public Speaking Is About

- A specific audience must be first, foremost, and consistently in your mind.
- Everything in the speech must associate your purpose with the values of the audience.
- The content, structure, language, and presentation of your speech must appear to the audience to be based on reasonable grounds.
- The effectiveness of your speech is determined by how well reasoning, values, and credibility merge in each argument.

Summary

Competent public speaking is an ancient art. It has been studied and taught for more than twenty-five centuries. It was essential to success in ancient times and is no less significant today.

We have adopted (and adapted) Aristotle's analysis of rhetorical proofs: *logos* (rational argument), *pathos* (appeal to values), and *ethos* (speaker credibility).

The Romans gave us the five canons of rhetoric: invention, disposition, elocution, delivery, and memory. We no longer consider memory a significant part of rhetorical theory, but the other four canons are of central importance. We recognize them today in the form of speech content, organization, style, and delivery.

Communication is best understood as a process and a transaction: a dynamic, on-going, changing activity in which the speaker and the audience constantly interact with one another. The process is made up of seven variables. Their interaction determines what goes on in the transaction: speaker, speech, audience, occasion, channel, feedback, and interference.

Critical thinking is necessary to the development of adequate speaking skill. This means getting the right information, putting ideas in order, building clear explanations and sound arguments, and locating the flaws in arguments and evidence.

Fortunately, effective public speaking is easily within your reach if you develop the skills you have been practicing almost all your life.

Key Terms

Sophists	Transaction
Plato	Speaker
Aristotle	Speech
Canons of Rhetoric	Audience
Process of Communication	Occasion
Invention—argument	Channel
Disposition—organization	Feedback
Elocution—delivery	Interference
Memory	Critical Thinking

Exercises

1. For one day, keep track of the speaking situations in which you find yourself. How many different kinds of situations can you identify? How were you involved? In what sense were they processual? In what sense were they transactions? Compare your findings with others in the class.

2. Observe a public speaking situation (on campus, in class, on TV, etc.). What elements described in this chapter (speaker, speech, audience, occasion, channel, feedback, and interference) can you identify? Based on this situation, how well does the model reflect the public speaking situation? Does the model need to be revised?

3. Write a one-page paper analyzing how an audience you know well might respond to a public speaking situation with you as a speaker.

4. Are the proofs of *logos, pathos* and *ethos* and the five canons of public speaking from ancient times still appropriate today? Discuss your answer to this question with the other students in your class. What current communication conditions make them appropriate or inappropriate?

Notes

[1] W.G. deBurge, *The Legacy of the Ancient World* (New York: Pelican, 1953) 161.

[2] If you're curious about this very interesting group of fellows, see Harold Barrett, *The Sophists* (Novato, CA: Chandler and Sharp, 1987).

[3] W. Robert Connor, *Greek Orations: 4th Century BC* (Prospect Heights, IL: Waveland, 1987) v.

[4] Lane Cooper (trans.), *The Rhetoric of Aristotle* (New York: Appleton-Century-Crofts, 1932) 5-6.

[5] "The Work Force of the Future, *Nation's Business* 70 (1982): 58.

[6] Max L. Carely, "Occupational Employment Growth Through 1990," *Monthly Labor Review* 8 Aug 1981: 43.

[7] Cooper, 1.

[8] Television uses some interesting combinations of both direct and indirect confrontation in programs like "The MacNeil/Lehrer NewsHour" and "The Firing Line." Some of the participants in these programs are in the same studio, while others may be in entirely different cities, but they can all talk together and each one can monitor all the others.

Preparing First Speeches

It takes a combination of theory and experience to make good speeches. Fortunately, almost anybody can learn the theory and gain the experience that's needed. Unfortunately, the question of whether the theory or the practice should come first has never been answered satisfactorily. This is a lot like asking which came first, the hen or the egg. If you don't make speeches until you have a good understanding of theory, your speaking shows a need of practice. On the other hand, if you start making speeches from the beginning of the course, you lack the guidance of theory.

We think it's better to start making speeches as soon as possible. That way, you begin to get the experience you need and you'll pick up the theory as you go along. Even your first speeches need some theoretical background if they are going to be effective. They ought to have some degree of substance, order, coherence, and form; they ought to help the audience see you as a believable and knowledgeable person, and they ought to be well presented.

The speeches you make later on will most likely be longer and more complex. They will be all the better because of the more sophisticated knowledge of theory you'll have when you prepare them. To get you started, we're going to look briefly at the elements of any effective speech: subject and purpose, organization, supporting material, and delivery. We'll discuss each of these topics in greater detail in later chapters.

Selecting a Subject and a Purpose

The first step in preparing a speech is deciding what you want to talk about. This, of course, means choosing a subject and a purpose. The number of available subjects is unlimited, but you can reduce the number of purposes or goals to these three: to entertain, to inform, or to persuade.

There are lots of occasions for making speeches to entertain. After-dinner speeches, for example, are usually intended to be amusing, and masters of ceremonies frequently try to be funny.

Your instructor will probably want you to wait until you are further along in the course before you make a speech to entertain. A speech for any kind of special occasion—and most speeches to entertain fall into this category— seem to require a more developed and sophisticated command of speaking skills. The majority of speeches are intended to inform or to persuade. The purpose of your first speech is likely to fit one of these two categories.

Since the number of available speech subjects is so large, how can you tell which one you want?

1. The subject must be one you are competent to talk about. Ordinarily, the first speech you will make comes along so early in the course that you won't have time to do a great deal of research. Pick a subject you know something about. It will be easier to interest your audience in a topic you already know.

2. The subject ought to be worth talking about, not only because no one likes to waste time on insignificant matters, but also because of the problem of interest. That doesn't mean that you have to tell an audience only what it *wants* to hear. The task is to decide what the audience *needs* to hear and then find ways of making that subject interesting.

3. The subject must be appropriate to the listeners. It makes no sense to ask an audience to listen to something it can't understand or to do something it can't do.

Once you have decided whether your purpose is to inform or to persuade and have identified the subject, the next consideration is the number of minutes you have been allotted for your speech. Fidel Castro talks to Cuban audiences for several hours at a stretch. You don't have that luxury. Limit your subject to the amount of time that is available to you. The subject is then further defined in a statement of specific purpose, which says what you are going to talk about. Here are some examples.

For an informative speech:

General subject: Suicide
Narrowed subject: Youth suicide today
Specific purpose: To inform the audience about the problem of suicide in this city's high schools

For a persuasive speech:

General subject: Capital Punishment
Narrowed subject: The effect of capital punishment on crime
Specific purpose: To persuade the audience that capital punishment is a deterrent to crime

Notice how concrete these statements are. Each points to one specific purpose and excludes any others. Compare them with the following examples that are labelled specific but actually are multiple and diffuse, and therefore poorly constructed.

Specific purpose: To inform the audience about why young people are killing themselves today and whether they really want to die

Specific purpose: To persuade the audience that punishment deters crime and, and as a matter of fact, that severe punishment is effective, even with children at home

Both of these statements of purpose are poor because they don't identify a clear, unified subject. Instead, they convey only vague notions of what the subject might be.

A statement of specific purpose not only says clearly and precisely what the speech is about, it is also useful to you as a guide to choosing the organization and materials of the speech. Every statement and every piece of supporting material should relate directly to your purpose. Exclude any piece of material that doesn't help you achieve your goal.

Limit the Subject in Length

- Select a general subject
- Narrow the scope of the subject so that you can develop it adequately in the time allowed
- Identify the subject precisely in a statement of specific purpose that says exactly what you plan to do

---

Organizing the Speech

Speeches are divided into three parts: an *introduction*, a *body*, and a *conclusion*. Organize the body of the speech first because it carries the principal burden of getting the right response from the audience. You build the introduction and the conclusion after you have developed the body of the speech. The introduction prepares the audience to listen to your speech and the conclusion reinforces what you have said.

Organizing the Body of the Speech

Think of the subject of your speech as a jigsaw puzzle. If you simply dump the pieces of a puzzle out on a table, each piece will have to be searched out and painstakingly put together before the puzzle can become an intelligible picture. But, if you remove the pieces one at a time and in the right order, they will fit together easily and the pieces will become a clear picture.

Organizing a speech is like that. First, find the right way to put together the ideas and supporting materials so that you can see the whole picture yourself; then decide in what order you will hand the pieces to your audience.

To make sure that your listeners see the same picture you do, divide the subject of your speech into a series of main points and organize them in a clear and orderly pattern. These main points, along with their supporting materials, constitute the body of your speech. There are many ways of organizing a speech, but here are four patterns that will help you begin.

Chronological pattern   One way to arrange the main points of a speech is in the order of their occurrence in time.

Specific purpose: To inform the audience about the development of keyboard instruments
  I. The Greeks had a keyboard organ in ancient times
  II. The clavichord appeared in the 14th century
  III. Harpsichords were built by Bartolomeo Christofori in the 18th century
  IV. Steinway, who came to America in 1850, perfected grand and upright pianos

Geographical or spatial pattern   In this pattern, you put the main points of the speech in the same order in which listeners might visualize a map or see themselves moving physically from one to another.

Specific purpose: To inform the audience about some of the uses for which horses have been bred in North America
  I. In Mexico, Spanish Arabian horses were bred for cow sense, stamina, speed
  II. On the East coast, colonists' horses were bred for farming, transportation, racing
  III. Quarter horses of the American west, bred mainly for herding cows, are also used for racing

Topical pattern   When you use this pattern, you break the subject down into its main elements, and then you discuss them in the body of the speech. Added together these elements (or topics) make up the whole idea.

Specific purpose: To inform the audience about financial aid for education
  I. Sources
  II. Types
  III. Eligibility
  IV. Contractual nature of awards

Argumentative pattern   The body of a speech to persuade is organized in what may be thought of as one kind of topical pattern. The main points are the arguments you use to give the audience reason to believe what you're trying to prove.

Specific purpose: To persuade the audience of the need for a cooperative public and private educational program to prevent injuries
  I. One in four Americans is injured every year

II. In 1988, injuries cost $180 million for health
    care, lost wages, disability and death
III. Education can cut those losses
IV. Government or private organizations alone can't
    be successful

Organizing the Conclusion

After you have organized the body of the speech, you plan a conclusion that will pull together the main ideas. A reader can reread a paragraph, a page, a whole book, but a listener cannot rehear any part of a speech that has gone before. For that reason, a brief summary that reminds the audience of your specific purpose and the main points that develop it is often an effective way to close. Of course, not all conclusions are summaries, but you will find them useful in your first speeches.

Organizing the Introduction

The last part of the speech you develop is the introduction. This may seem strange because the introduction is the first thing the audience hears. You prepare it last because, until you have developed the body and the conclusion, you don't know what you are going to say. Once you do know, you'll be able to prepare an introduction that is related to the subject and purpose of the speech.

A good introduction does two principle things. First, it catches the attention of the audience. There are many different interest factors that will help you do the job. Among them are such devices as telling a story, relating an incident, giving a description, making a startling statement, or citing a quotation.

The second thing the introduction does is tell the audience what you're going to talk about. This is done in a subject sentence. The subject sentence is a statement that says in an informal, oral style what the specific subject of the speech is about. In an informative speech, it says what you are going to explain. In a persuasive speech, it tells the audience what you want it to believe or to do. Here is an example of each kind.

For an informative speech:

Specific purpose: To inform the audience about the problem of suicide
in this city's high schools

Subject sentence: In an effort to escape the pressures and problems in
their lives, kids in the high schools of this city are
turning to suicide

For a persuasive speech:

Specific purpose: To persuade the audience that capital punishment is
a deterrent to crime

Subject sentence: The best evidence makes it clear that the threat of death stops many people from committing capital crimes

Supporting the Ideas in the Speech

Examples, statistics, quotations, and arguments all help to make your ideas more interesting, believable, and clear. Always use at least *one* item of this kind in support of each important point in the body of the speech. More often than not, two or more pieces of support are necessary (or at least desirable). These supporting materials will make your ideas more precise and vivid, clarify the subject, add interest, and establish belief. They also help to establish your credibility because they convince the audience that you are worth listening to and you know what you're talking about.

It's quite probable that when you prepare your speech you will make notes of your ideas and supporting details. It is also likely that these notes aren't going to be organized well enough to serve much purpose. The best way to put the content and organization of a speech on paper is to outline it. The outline can also serve as speaking notes. Here's a sample outline format that is suitable for organizing either an informative or a persuasive speech. To make clear how it works, we have included a sample outline of an informative speech that would be appropriate for a first assignment. In a persuasive speech, the main points would be arguments and the supporting material would be evidence.

Introduction	Introduction
I. Interest factor	I. Ask yourself which side of your brain you use
A. Supporting material	A. "Maps don't make any sense. Tell me how to get there"
B. Supporting material	B. "Draw me a picture. I don't visualize very well."
II. Subject sentence	II. To get the most out of our brains we need to understand how the left and right sides work

Body	Body
I. First main point	I. The parts are separate but they help each other out
A. Supporting material	A. They are interactive and interdependent
B. Supporting material	B. They perform different jobs
II. Second main point	II. The "logical" left brain handles time sequences

A. Supporting material	A. Uses words
B. Supporting material	B. Analyzes step-by-step and part-by-part
C. Supporting material	C. Uses reasoning
D. Supporting material	D. Uses numbers
III. Third main point	III. The "artistic" right deals with space relationships
A. Supporting material	A. Synthesizes parts into whole
B. Supporting material	B. Sees analogies, likenesses and metaphors
C. Supporting material	C. Makes intuitive leaps based on hunches and feelings
D. Supporting material	D. Sees overall patterns

Conclusion	**Conclusion**
I. Summary statement including subject and purpose.	I. The more we know about the brain, the better we can use it
A. First main point	A. The left brain takes care of time relationships
B. Second main point	B. The right brain takes care of space relationships

Delivering the Speech

It doesn't make any difference whether you write an essay or deliver a speech, the ideas, organization, and supporting details can be the same. Except perhaps for a few variations in style, what makes the biggest difference between writing and speaking is that a speech must be delivered orally. In fact, it doesn't become a speech until it is delivered. Consequently, good delivery makes a necessary contribution to effectiveness. Delivery is the vital, physical means by which your ideas are carried to the audience.

Your delivery will be best when you look directly at the audience. Then your listeners will know you are really talking to them with interest and involvement in your subject. The kind of speaking that sounds best to an audience has the spontaneous quality of good conversation. *The ideas sound as if they were being spoken for the first time.* When delivery has these characteristics, the physical part (posture, stance, movement and gesture) will come naturally. You'll seem relaxed and in command of the situation. If your voice is loud enough to be heard easily, and if you speak clearly and use pronunciation that is acceptable in your part of the country, your delivery will be quite good indeed.

Don't wait until you have the final draft of the outline to begin working on delivery. The more often you practice during the preparation period, the easier it will be when you deliver the speech to find the words that will get the results you want.

Once you have what you think will be the final draft of the outline, see if you can find one or more friends who are willing to serve as an audience. But *don't* write the speech out and *don't* try to memorize it. If you are familiar with the ideas, you will find that the words will come naturally to mind when you speak. Several generations before Cicero, the Roman orator Cato put it this way. He said, "Get a firm grasp on the subject. The words will follow." Depend on it. If you are prepared, the words will come.

Good Delivery Has these Characteristics:

- It is spoken directly to the audience with good eye contact
- It is spontaneous. It sounds as if the ideas were being spoken for the first time
- It shows your own interest and involvement in the subject
- It is articulate, the words are correctly pronounced, and it is loud enough to be heard easily

---

Summary

Even though you may lack background in the theory of public speaking, it is better to begin speaking early in the course rather than waiting until you know the theory better. The great benefits of practicing the essential skills of organization and delivery outweigh the lack of theoretical knowledge. In preparing your first speeches, keep these four basic steps in mind:

1. Choose a subject that is interesting to you: one that you think you can make interesting for an audience and that you can handle adequately in the allotted time. Formulate a specific statement of purpose.

2. Organize the speech in the pattern that you think will be best suited to your purpose: chronological, spatial, topical, or argumentative. An outline is a great help in organizing your ideas. Prepare a conclusion that summarizes the main ideas, and an introduction that will arouse the interest of the audience. It must include an accurate subject sentence.

3. Find supporting materials that will make your ideas clear, interesting, and reasonable, and that will make your arguments persuasive.

4. Practice delivering the speech. Think in terms of *oral* delivery from the moment you begin to prepare. Don't write out the speech and don't memorize it. If you know the subject, the words you need will come to mind when you speak.

Key Terms

General subject   Spatial pattern
Specific purpose   Topical pattern
Informative speech   Argumentative pattern
Persuasive speech   Support
Introduction   Delivery
Body   Eye contact
Conclusion

Exercises

1. Organize and deliver a three-minute informative speech explaining some local historical place, person, or thing.
2. Listen carefully to a lecture by one of your instructors. Come to class prepared to explain briefly what you noted about the strong points and weak points of the organization, supporting material, and delivery of the lecture. ·
3. Organize and deliver a three-minute persuasive speech that proposes a change in some university policy.
4. Interview a classmate to find out the subject of his or her first speech. Also, ask what qualifications he or she has for speaking on the subject. Prepare and deliver an introduction to the speech of no more than 30 seconds based on your interview.

chapter 3

Listening Effectively

I. The importance of listening

II. The nature of listening
   A. Listening is more than hearing
   B. Kinds of listening
      1. Comprehension
      2. Criticism
      3. Empathy
      4. Appreciation

III. Obstacles to effective listening
   A. Physical obstacles
   B. Intellectual obstacles
   C. Emotional obstacles

IV. Improving listening skills
   A. Overcome distractions
   B. Prepare to listen
   C. Don't judge too quickly
   D. Don't short-circuit your critical faculties
   E. Listen for main ideas
   F. Listen for the full meaning
   G. Listen actively
      1. Summarize
      2. Anticipate
      3. Question

No one can be a competent communicator without the ability to use four essential skills: writing, reading, speaking, and listening. We list them in that order because universities and colleges stress their importance in that order. But notice two interesting facts: (1) this is precisely the reverse of the order in which people learn these skills in childhood[1] and (2) it is probably the reverse of the frequency with which adults use them. Although estimates vary, it is generally agreed that listening occupies by far the greatest amount of your time and is considered the most important skill in work and social settings.[2] Despite this, few people listen well. Tests done at a number of universities show that immediately after listening to a ten-minute talk, the average person remembers only half of what was said and within two weeks loses another 25 percent. In other words, people listen at 25 percent efficiency.[3]

Importance of Listening

Historically, the development of printing and increased emphasis on universal education gave great importance to reading. However, in this electronic age of radio, television, and cable systems, listening is probably the primary means for receiving messages.

For you, perhaps the most obvious importance of listening is in the classroom. You spend several hours a week listening to lectures, discussions, and speeches. If you listen at only the 25 percent level of efficiency we mentioned, you will probably not be as successful as you would like. In a public speaking class, listening is also a courtesy you owe to your classmates. Active participation in the communication process not only sharpens your listening skills but enables you to give honest reactions and advice to speakers. Careful attention to other speeches will help you to improve your own speaking ability. You will discern examples of the do's and don'ts of effective speaking.

The ability to listen well is an important social asset. In *The Devil's Dictionary*, humorist Ambrose Bierce defines a bore as someone who talks when you want him to listen. But listening is more than just the courtesy of letting someone else talk. Communication is the *exchange* of *understood* messages. Because good listeners are willing to work at understanding a message, they help make the communication transaction more successful. When messages are understood, the results are more likely to be satisfactory—on any level. Good listening is an asset in making friends, interviewing for a job, negotiating a contract, or solving social problems.

In a business environment and in political situations, active and efficient listening is another defense against unethical speakers who try to manipulate you. Loaded language and appeals to prejudice can trigger unthinking responses.

In 1990, Teikyo University in Japan purchased Salem College in West Virginia and advertised their purpose to transform "Japanese students into a new breed of bilingual, bicultural 'world citizens' with an open minded, international point of view." When Japanese students began to enroll, some area residents ignored the stated purpose. They listened to those who urged local citizens to "Remember Pearl Harbor," asked "Are those Japs coming in?", and proclaimed, "I can't stand Japs."[4] Although the number of people who let their prejudices block their ability to listen was apparently small, those few provide a good example of not listening carefully and permitting prejudices to control what is heard.

From classroom to business transaction, careful listening is a valuable tool. Despite the gloomy statistics about how ineffectively people listen, you don't need to belong to that group. With average hearing and intelligence you can become a good listener if you want to be one.[5]

The Nature of Listening

Too often people take the skill of listening for granted. The general attitude seems to be that listening is a simple skill and that everyone develops it naturally. The truth is quite the opposite.

Listening Is More than Hearing

Although the hearing mechanism is complicated, it is completely automatic. A normal, healthy hearing mechanism never shuts off and is ready to work 24 hours a day. When sound waves stimulate it, you hear. Otherwise, you don't.

Listening, however, is a complex activity that goes far beyond the mere reception of sound. It involves intellectual, emotional and social factors: who is talking, what is said, when, where, and why one listens.[6] Listening, then, is not only hearing; it is an active intellectual process of decoding, interpreting, understanding, and evaluating messages.

Kinds of Listening

There are several different ways of listening to messages.[7] That is, poems, music, arguments, explanations, or conversations with friends all call for different kinds of listening. Every message gives an audience a reason for listening with some particular purpose in view. Let's examine briefly some of these different kinds of listening.

Comprehension No matter what the circumstances or the context of communication, the *primary* goal of listening is always the same: correct understanding of the message. Because language of some kind (words, gestures, numbers, signs) is necessary to convey any message, the primary need of a listener is to understand the language used. In oral communication, adequate mastery of the grammar, vocabulary and syntax of the language supplies at least the basic tools for understanding. But words don't automatically mean something. Instead, the meaning of a communication grows out of the context in which the words are used and out of the relationship the participants have to each other and to the context.[8] That is, a listener "participates in the development of understanding as he or she encounters the discourse."[9] Thus, to make sense of a message requires a conscious listening effort.

Criticism   People often feel they can't depend on what they hear. They have heard so much about false advertising and the empty promises of campaigning politicians that they begin to look for hidden meanings in messages and hidden motives in speakers. Taken too far, this attitude becomes an obstacle to communication. You should at least hear the speaker out.

As a listener, you have a lot to say about the speaker's meaning. No matter what a speaker has in mind, the audience's perception of the speech is the deciding factor. If a speech seems informative, it is informative. If it seems persuasive, it is persuasive. More important than judging the purpose of a speech is to sort out the good from the bad in what a speaker says, to make sound judgments about what to accept and what to reject.

So, hear the speaker out but listen with a critical ear. Critical listening goes beyond the basic goal of comprehension. Its purpose is to identify the strategy in the message, to distinguish fact from opinion, to understand and evaluate the speaker's reasoning, and to guard against prejudice and propaganda.

Empathy   Empathy is the ability of one person to feel the emotions of another. A familiar example of empathic response is what happens in the theater. The members of an audience can actually feel within themselves all the emotions of joy, sorrow, pain, triumph, or terror portrayed by the actors.

Empathic listening takes place easily and often among friends. Suppose, for example, your brother told you about going to class unprepared for a test because he had forgotten about it. Hearing and understanding him and sharing his feeling of embarrassment would be an example of empathic listening. It's the way a friend will act. Empathy is not the same thing as sympathy because emotions like pity or compassion are not necessarily involved. You might think your brother was pretty dumb to forget the test and that he deserved the bad grade he got, but that shouldn't keep you from sharing his feeling of chagrin.

One reason for empathic listening is that more often than not it has therapeutic value for the speaker. People usually feel better when they share their joys and sorrows with someone they trust. In addition, you learn more about others when you choose, according to a Native American proverb, to "walk a mile in their moccasins."

Appreciation   The goal in listening to a concert, a play, poetry, or a stand-up comedian is the pleasure it gives. Of course, those who know and

A listener participates in the sharing of meaning as he or she hears the message.

understand the music, literature, or whatever are best equipped to listen appreciatively. When the purpose of listening goes beyond the aesthetic pleasure of the experience, expertise is required. The music critic, for example, must be able to analyze a performance, not just admire it.

Two writers on listening have noted the following ways in which appreciative listening can enhance the quality of life:

1. It can increase the enjoyment of life.
2. It can enlarge one's experience.
3. It can improve one's use of language.
4. It can expand the range of what one enjoys.
5. It can decrease the tension of daily living.[10]

It would be a mistake to think that any speaking occasion calls for a single kind of listening. There will be elements of each kind of listening in every situation. Suppose, for example, that you're listening to a debate in the student senate over a proposal to ban certain magazines from the campus bookstore. Even though you are listening for comprehension, you will also give critical attention to the arguments. At the same time, there is nothing to keep you from appreciating the flashes of wit and empathizing with the concerns of the senators.

There is also a temptation to think of one kind of listening as "better" than another. For example, you might be told, "Don't be critical. Try to be supportive." This says that empathic listening is better than evaluating what you hear. In some situations, it is. Even though certain situations call for one kind of listening rather than another, that does not mean that one type is always best.

A change in the context of communication will often call for a different kind of listening. For example, suppose someone who has spent a lot of time in foreign countries is telling you about personal experiences with terrorists. As the conversation progresses, it develops into a debate over whether the United States should use military force against foreign governments that export terrorism. You began by listening for comprehension, but when arguments came into the conversation, the new context required critical listening.

A course in public speaking can sometimes be a hindrance rather than a help in developing listening skills. Speakers are told to be interesting and clear, to command attention, and to use language, materials, organization, and delivery so well that it is virtually impossible for an audience not to listen. In fact, a good way for you to evaluate those elements in your own speech is to imagine yourself as a member of the audience, listening to the speech. If, for example, the language is not interesting to you, consider the possibility that your audience may be similarly bored.

Although the speaker is responsible for the elements in the preparation and delivery of the speech, that does not mean that listening should be passive. Listening is not merely a courtesy given because someone needs to practice on an audience. The audience has a greater share than this in the communication act, and a greater responsibility than passive listening implies. A little later in this chapter we will offer some advice about how to refine and sharpen listening skills. Perhaps the best way to begin is to look at some of the factors that stand in the way of efficient listening.

Obstacles to Effective Listening

Physical Obstacles

As we have said, listening is more than merely hearing, but the ability to hear a message is a necessary part of listening. The most basic obstacle to listening, therefore, is not being able to hear. One obvious hindrance would be an uncorrected hearing loss. Such a problem requires professional help not available in a speech class. Many other times, however, not hearing a message has nothing to do with physical impairment. In these cases, poor audibility is either the fault of the speaker or the result of external distractions. Inattention is probably the most common reason for distraction. Inattention results from physical factors (for example, fatigue) and also from intellectual or emotional causes.

Intellectual Obstacles

Contrary to popular reasoning, listening skill is not a simple matter of intelligence,[11] although there is some connection between the two.[12] A listener must be intelligent enough to see the connections among the speaker's ideas and to see the reasoning behind them. The speaker also bears responsibility to organize the material so that the audience can find the connections. The language of the speech often presents the most basic source of difficulty. Someone who doesn't understand English very well will obviously have trouble listening to a speech in that language. Other listeners can have trouble if they have a limited vocabulary or if the speaker uses a vocabulary that is too technical or too full of jargon. Conversely, subject matter or language at too low a level leads to boredom. The point is that any language difficulty is an obstacle to effective listening.

Your own beliefs and values can also become an obstacle to effective listening. While your strongest attitudes are always present, you can work to prevent them from blocking listening skills. Try to avoid disputing every statement the speaker makes or tuning out a speaker you think is wrong. Reserve your judgment until the speaker has finished and you can weigh all the arguments.

Emotional Obstacles

Audiences have a hard time paying attention even if physical and intellectual factors have been eliminated. Perhaps the worst obstacle to effective listening is the personal baggage that listeners bring with them: a recent conversation, last night's bowling, tomorrow's test. Emotional factors such as worry, stress, unhappiness and excitement make the listener tune a speaker out and miss what is said. To listen effectively, recognize that your emotions can intrude and work to overcome them. As one writer warned, ''Anything that impairs an individual's ability to perceive through listening impairs that individual's ability to function well in society.''[13]

Improving Listening Skills

Except for a hearing loss that can't be remedied, none of these obstacles is inescapable. Rather, the most important factor in becoming a good listener is the development of specific behaviors and listening skills.

Nutritionists tell us that we—quite literally—are what we eat (and drink and breathe). In terms of our physical being, this is true. In terms of our psychic selves, we—quite literally—are what we hear and read and view. As our social systems and structures become more complex, each individual becomes more dependent on the ability to process information effectively. Competence in speaking and listening is central to the achievement of that end. Being a good listener will not guarantee success or happiness or the securing of one's life goals, but, for most, poor listening will stand in the way of their achievement.[14]

—William Work, *Emeritus Executive Director of the Speech Communication Association.*

Overcome Distractions

No matter how perfect the speaking situation, there will always be distractions: someone coughing, a restless child, an airplane flying by, a thunderstorm, workers down the hall. Concentration will force many of these distractions into the background. If there is likely to be external noise, sitting closer to the front will help. Sometimes it is necessary to let the speaker know that he or she needs to speak louder. Focus attention on the speaker. Everything we say in Chapter 17 about the importance of eye contact for the speaker applies to the listener as well. Looking directly at the speaker develops an immediate sense of interaction and makes you a more attentive listener. Seeing attentive listeners reinforces the speaker and contributes to an improved transaction.

Prepare to Listen

Take some time to prepare for what the speaker will discuss. You have probably run from one activity or class to another and sat down wondering where you were and why. "If it's eleven o'clock, this must be sociology." It's a common practice among college students to read the campus newspaper or chat among themselves while they're waiting for a class to begin. This can make listening less effective. Even if you have only a minute, remind yourself of what went on the last time the class met.

Don't Judge too Quickly

What often passes for an inability to listen is merely unwillingness. People miss a great deal if they are willing to listen only to the subjects they already care about. If they literally limit themselves to that degree, they will never learn anything new. Of course it helps to have a real interest in a subject, but the topic may turn out to be important to you some day even if you don't currently have an interest. Be selfish about listening. Develop the attitude, "What's in it for me?" It's advantageous to listen attentively until you can make a reasonable decision about what is significant. In short, you should earn the right to be bored by initially giving the speaker the benefit of the doubt. Be open-minded and flexible enough to give the speaker a fair hearing.

Judge the importance of specific data as you go along. No one listens totally without bias. Everyone weighs information based on what they already know. But resist the temptation to evaluate the overall concept too soon. It's perfectly natural to have preferences, but that doesn't justify turning people off without a fair hearing. "I can't stand that Jesse Jackson." "I'm just not interested in religion." "Health food addicts give me a pain." When you disagree with someone or think a subject will be uninteresting, there is a tendency to establish a negative mind-set that is a major obstacle to improved listening skills.

Don't Short-Circuit Your Critical Faculties

Another kind of listener tends to go along with the views of others in the audience. Many people in a group, because they want to be socially acceptable, are more easily persuaded than they would be as individuals.[15] Attentive listening will not stop this tendency but will help to control it.

Delivery is the most likely element in a speaking situation to dull critical faculties. The less training one has in public speaking, the more impact delivery will have. The great Greek statesman and orator, Demosthenes, is said to have claimed that the three most important elements of speaking are, "Delivery, delivery, delivery."

Delivery can be quite beguiling and can lure a listener away from the substance of a speech. The story is told of a politician writing in the margin of a speech, "Argument weak here. Yell like hell." A listener has to seek the speaker's meaning and not be fooled by delivery. Substance is the only essential element. There's a piece of doggerel that makes the point nicely.

> As you wander on through life, friends,
> Let this be your goal:
> Keep your eye upon the doughnut,
> Not upon the hole.

Listen for Main Ideas

Only about 25 percent of an audience understands the central idea of a speech.[16] Many people do not know how to listen for main ideas. They treat each sentence as if it were as significant as every other. Listeners can often repeat a story they heard in a speech but cannot say what the central point was. When one part of a speech seems to be no more or less important than another, stories will command attention because they entertain the most.

Look specifically for the central idea of the speech and the main points that support it. The central idea may not be completely clear until the end of the speech so you should keep reevaluating the relative importance of individual points. The aim at the end of a speech is to be able to say, "The proposal was that we ought to convert industry to coal because it is cheaper, more abundant in the United States, and a benefit to the economy." If you can remember some of the evidence that supported the points, so much the better.

It is useful to augment your listening for main points with note taking. No one can remember all the main points, so even the most experienced and able listeners frequently take notes. Note taking is an extremely useful skill. Finding the main ideas and noting them in outline form focuses your attention and helps you avoid two common problems. The first is the tendency to record only the most striking, unusual or humorous statements. The second is the attempt to write down every statement the speaker makes. Either one distracts you from listening to the content to identify the main points which support the central idea.

Freshta was giving a speech in class on the basic tenets of the religion of Islam. Robin took notes in a kind of topical shorthand that looked like this:

I. "Islam": Arabic for "surrendering oneself to God"

II. Monotheistic, almighty, compassionate God (Allah)

III. Muhammed as messenger of God

IV. *Koran* — sacred book

    A. Arabic for "lecture"

    B. Length similar to *New Testament*

    C. 114 recorded speeches by Muhammed

    D. Revelations Allah made to Muhammed

This is obviously not a formally correct outline of the kind we recommend in Chapter 13, but it's good enough to help Robin carry on a discussion about what Freshta said. Once you have honed this skill, you will find yourself using it in many situations.

Listen for the Full Meaning

Good listeners do more than simply recall what a speaker says; they try to discover the full implication of the ideas communicated. What makes this speaker's ideas unique? To what extent are they objective observations? To what extent are they biased conclusions intended to persuade? To what extent is emotional language used?

Some subject matter seems ordinary on the surface, but fuller under-standing brings new insights. A speaker may support legalized abortion

Good listeners do more than simply recall what a speaker says; they try to discover the full implication of the ideas communicated.

for a number of reasons: to control overpopulation, to give freedom to women, to avoid dooming unwanted children to poor living conditions. Opponents will have different reasons: Abortion is murder, it is selfish, it violates the standards of Western culture. Recognizing the *values* on which either side bases its position—social well-being, freedom, the quality and sanctity of life, for example—helps to clarify any controversy. When listeners find the values behind the ideas, they can understand more fully how the ideas relate to their own beliefs and values.

Listen Actively

A classroom speaker talks at about 100 words per minute. In general conversation, about 125 words per minute is the average. But one can understand speech as fast as 400 words per minute. Given these conditions, and the additional fact that some sections of a speech do not demand as much attention as others, a listener clearly has more time than is necessary to follow a speaker. This time can be used either effectively or ineffectively. There is the danger, for example, of daydreaming passively. But good listening is not a passive process. It requires a listener to cooperate with a speaker by participating *actively* in the communication transaction.

The kneeling benches in old churches were unpadded, and the hard wood was often slanted a bit. Kneeling was not unbearable, but it was not overly comfortable either. The thinking was that too much ease while praying might lead to drowsing and distraction. The same holds true for listening. Listeners shouldn't be so relaxed that they can't stay alert. Hearing is passive and automatic, but listening always involves tension. Here are some ways to listen actively.

Summarize   From time to time, summarize what has been said. "Now, let's see. The point is that we ought to convert industry to coal and the reason given so far is that coal is cheaper than oil or gas." Summaries like this help to keep the material in mind and make it more comprehensible.

Anticipate   Try to anticipate what will come next. Anticipation can be a great help in critical listening. Even if the predictions are inaccurate, they are an aid to concentration.

Question   Although an audience doesn't usually ask questions until after a speech, bringing them to mind while listening can be an important aid to critical listening because it avoids the danger of blindly accepting the speaker's point of view. The questions can be about such matters as the reasonableness of an idea, its practicality, its possible consequences, or the arguments the speaker uses to support it. But be patient. Don't spend time preparing to attack what you hear until you're sure you understand it.

Summary

Effective listening is one of the four essential skills (writing, reading, speaking, and listening) of communication. It is considered by many the most important work and social skill. Yet most people do it rather poorly. Good listening fosters better interpersonal relations, makes you a more effective student, and improves your speaking.

Comprehension of ideas is probably the most important goal of listening. However, effective listening can also be used to improve criticism, enhance empathy, and increase appreciation. One of the objectives of effective listening is to determine what kind of listening is needed in a particular situation.

Physical obstacles such as a hearing loss, distracting elements in the environment, or a speaker who doesn't talk loud enough interfere with efficient listening. Intellectual and emotional obstacles can also interfere. Recognizing these impediments helps to overcome them.

Effective listening is active, not passive. Here are some ways to make it active and effective:

1. Overcome distractions by concentrating on the speaker.
2. Prepare to listen.
3. Give a fair hearing. Don't judge the significance or interest value of a subject too quickly.
4. Don't let the herd instincts of the audience, the mood of the setting, or the effectiveness of the speaker's delivery dull the critical function of listening.
5. Listen for main ideas rather than trying to retain all the details.
6. Listen for the full meaning the speaker is trying to convey, principally the values underlying the ideas.
7. Make periodic summaries of what has been said, predict what is coming and make a continuing, critical analysis of the message.

Key Terms

Listening   Distractions
Hearing   Critical faculties
Comprehension   Main ideas
Criticism   Full meaning
Empathy   Active listening
Appreciation   Summarize
Physical obstacles   Anticipate
Intellectual obstacles   Question
Emotional obstacles

Exercises

1. When a speaker is first introduced in class, write down what you think the main idea of the speech will be. As the speech goes on, each time you change your mind about what the central idea is, write down your new statement of it. At the end of the speech, compare your various versions with what the speaker intended to communicate. Were any differences caused by the speaker? If your listening was at fault, where did it go wrong? How might it have been improved?
2. Listen to two speakers who address the class on the same day. Afterwards, engage in a class discussion on how successful you were in retaining what each said. If you listened to one more than the other or understood one better than the other, consider why that happened.

3. Listen carefully to a speaker and try to duplicate the speaker's outline. After the speech, compare your outline with the speaker's.

4. For one week, consciously take five to ten minutes before each of your classes to review what was discussed at the last meeting of the class and speculate on what is to be covered that day. Do you see an improvement in the comprehension you have of the class subject matter?

Notes

[1] Andrew D. Wolvin and Carolyn Gwynn Coakley, *Listening Instruction* (Falls Church, VA: Speech Communication Association, 1979): 5.

[2] William Work, "Listen, My Children ...," *Communication Education* 27 (1978): 146; Andrew D. Wolvin, "Meeting the Communication Needs of the Adult Learner," *Communication Education* 33 (1984): 269.

[3] Ralph G. Nichols, "Do We Know How to Listen? Practical Helps in a Modern Age," *The Speech Teacher* 10 (1961): 118.

[4] Bill Steigerwald, "East Meets West Virginia," *Los Angeles Times Magazine* 5 Aug. 1990: 22-27, 37-39.

[5] Larry R. Smeltzer and Kittie W. Watson, "Listening: An Empirical Comparison of Discussion Length and Level of Incentive," *Central States Speech Journal* 35 (1984): 167.

[6] Paul Bakan, "Some Reflections on Listening Behavior," *The Journal of Communication* 6 (1956): 108.

[7] For a more detailed discussion of the question, "Why Do We Listen?" see Wolvin and Coakley, 7-13.

[8] Ronald C. Arnett and Gordon Nakagawa, "The Assumptive Roots of Empathic Listening," *Communication Education* 32 (1983): 374-75.

[9] John Stewart, "Interpretive Listening: An Alternative to Empathy," *Communication Education* 32 (1983): 383.

[10] Ralph G. Nichols and Thomas R. Lewis, *Listening and Speaking* (Dubuque, IA: Wm. C. Brown, 1954) 68-69.

[11] Nichols and Lewis, 8.

[12] Nichols and Lewis. See also Ralph G. Nichols, "Factors in Listening Comprehension," *Speech Monographs* 15 (1948): 8.

[13] Work, 147.

[14] Work, 152.

[15] Walter W. Stevens, "Polarization, Social Facilitation, and Listening," *Western Speech* 25 (1961): 170-74.

[16] Nichols, 158.

The Speaker's Ethical Responsibility

With rare exceptions, people don't live in isolation. They lead their lives in and through the societies they form—educational, professional, political, religious, recreational, and so on. These various societies are formed primarily through the efforts of people to communicate with each other. Without communication, individuals would not find common ground to share and to create such associations.

But communication demands more of people than just talking to each other. There is a need for trust. If the members of society can't depend on each other to be honest and fair, all of the societies they have formed, and society in general, are in grave danger of being destroyed by distrust.[1]

Yet, it's a sad fact that in business, in the practice of law, in selling, in politics, and in many other activities where people must communicate, principles of honesty and fair play don't carry as much weight as they should. That's understandable because, to a degree, we are all children of the Sophists. We want to win: the seller to win the sale, the lawyer to win the case, the politician to win the election.

Rhetoric (the principles of effective speaking) can be put to bad uses as well as good. It can help an advertiser to misrepresent products, a lawyer to corrupt evidence and testimony, or an office-seeker to make empty promises. When people recognize such abuses (especially if they are the victims of the corruption), they give rhetoric a bad name. They visualize charlatans and demagogues who use their skill in speech to manipulate others to their own selfish ends. But that kind of speaking doesn't do society a lot of good, does it? We all acknowledge that there is more to responsible communication than the clever use of speaking skills.

About four hundred years after Aristotle and about a hundred years after Cicero, a rhetorician by the name of Marcus Fabius Quintilianus taught public speaking in Rome. His definition of the ideal orator is often quoted: *Vir bonus paretus dicendi*, "A good man skilled in speaking." Like Socrates, Plato, and Aristotle before him, and many others who have come after, Quintilian believed that good public speaking is measured by more than immediate effect. A necessary element is the ethical responsibility a speaker assumes.

Ethics is the theory of the good and the right. There are many ethical systems and almost as many answers to ethical questions as there are thinkers who look for them. We are not going to campaign for any specific position. Our purpose in this chapter is to remind you of some principles that you already accept and which are universally acknowledged (at least in Western civilization) as the obligation you assume when you speak.

Characteristics of an Ethical Speaker

When Quintilian defined the ideal public speaker, he was thinking of a morally good person. Speakers who meet the following criteria would surely be acceptable to Quintilian.[2] They would certainly satisfy us. An ethical speaker is characterized by knowledge of the subject, truthfulness, sound reasoning, impartiality, and humaneness. Let's think about the terms in this definition.

Knowledge of the Subject

It's easy enough, really too easy, to make judgments based on very little knowledge. For instance, you might argue that convicted murderers should never be given paroles because paroled killers will commit more murders. Even though that statement **sounds** reasonable, you should not use such an argument unless you **know** whether paroled killers have, in fact, committed additional murders. If you discover that **some** paroled killers have repeated their crimes, does that substantiate the argument? What if parole boards can make a distinction between those who will and those who won't?

It's possible, of course, to make an accurate prediction by sheer dumb luck, but that's not the way you want to run your life. It's certainly not the kind of gamble audiences will knowingly take. Stock brokers, financial advisers, lawyers and doctors are only a few of the highly trained professionals who earn good incomes because their clients believe they know what they're talking about.

The decisions people make and the actions they take are based on what they value and what they believe. Values and beliefs, even when they are shared, are very personal. Thomas More was beheaded because he refused to support Henry the VIII's divorce from his queen, Catherine of Aragon. In Robert Bolt's play, More's future son-in-law said to him it was only a theory that the pope is a direct successor in the line of the apostles. Sir Thomas answered, "Why, it's a theory, yes; you can't see it; you can't touch it; it's a theory. But what matters to me is not whether it's true or not but that I believe it to be true, or rather, not that I **believe** it, but that **I** believe it."[3]

Words do things to people. what you say can change their world, for good or ill. You have no right to interfere with their values and beliefs unless you know what you're doing. Because the information and advice you give can have such a profound effect, you are obliged to have concern for the consequences of what you say. In the extreme, you may be asking your listeners to stake their lives if they believe you're right. Out of ignorance, an inexperienced clerk in an auto parts store might persuade you to buy a part that's "just as good and, besides, it's cheaper." Unless you know more than the clerk, you buy it. Because it is not "just as good," your brakes fail. If the clerk had had a greater concern for consequences, the "facts" and conclusions of the sales pitch would have been far less dangerous to you. The least a speaker can do is to be informed. Otherwise, people are vulnerable, not only to charlatans, but to ignoramuses as well. Every member of society is owed—and owes—more than that.

Words do things to people. What you say can change their world, for good or ill.

Truthfulness

Some statements are true and there's no denying them: Pure water is H_2O. A square has four equal sides and four equal angles; if you want to know the area of such a square, you multiply the length times the width. If you understand these statements you can't reasonably say they are untrue. You would contradict yourself if you did. Except for chemical equations, mathematical formulas, and other similar factual examples, you'll find very few times (some say never) when you can know the absolute truth of what you believe.

In Chapter 1 we listed the four values Aristotle attributes to rhetoric. We think the most important is the one that says the speaker must frame proofs and arguments with the help of common knowledge and accepted opinions. This insight is a major element in Aristotle's theory—that the proofs in rhetorical argumentation are probable, not absolute.

But do these limits to your knowledge create an ethical problem? How can you tell an audience the truth if you don't know what it is? Let's examine several scenarios of presenting information to an audience.

1. You believe one thing and deliberately say something contrary to it. That is simply a lie. When it suits your purpose to tell an audience what it wants to hear and not what you think is right, that is also a lie. These instances are called "objective" lies because they are **deliberately** contrary to what you believe are the objective facts. You won't find many people (even if they lie a lot) who will defend or accept that behavior.
2. You can honestly believe what you say. If you're wrong, and if your error is based on careless investigation and sloppy reasoning, you're telling a lie even if you don't mean to. This is called a "subjective" lie. You aren't deliberately lying about objective reality; your subjective misunderstanding of reality is at fault. You can be blamed to the extent that honest effort on your part would bring you closer to the facts.
3. You give an audience your best thinking, and it's based on the best evidence available to you. You're a stock broker. You persuaded several of your clients to invest heavily in Amex Corporation stock because your expert research convinced you the stock was a winner. If the price per share plummets, there is no ethical fault involved. You may lose your job, but you can't be accused of moral wrong. In some situations, the real facts are often not available, but you should give your own opinion based on as much evidence as you can find.

Sound Reasoning

Your code of ethics will lead you to do some things and not to do others. Ideally, it will also give you good reasons for the way you act.[4] Ethical judgments about acceptable or unacceptable behavior are tied to your values.[5] The way you reason privately when you make moral decisions should be the same as the reasoning you use with an audience. In both instances, solid evidence and sound reasoning are the basic tools of ethical communication.

It is unlikely that there will ever be a universally accepted ethical system. You can, however, make sure that your decisions are not contradictory to your personal code. For example, if you believe cheating on exams is wrong, it would not be reasonable to abandon that belief with the justification "but my grades are too low to get into law school." In speech making, there is a clear relationship between reasoning and ethics.

In later chapters we will identify some of the flaws in evidence and argument that make your informative or persuasive speeches unreasonable. If you use any of those errors deliberately to trick an audience, that would be unethical behavior.

Impartiality

Every day you make moral judgments about the rightness or wrongness of what you and other people do. These judgments should be impartial;

there are no double standards for morality. Ask yourself, "In similar circumstances, would I impose the same requirements on myself that I expect of others?"

Another standard of impartiality is consistency. Guide yourself by your ethical norms on all occasions, not just when a particular situation makes it convenient.

Humaneness

The crucial element in this final characteristic of ethical speakers is respect for your listeners as human beings. Respect for others can be defined in terms of the "golden rule." You respect their rights as fully as you would want them to respect yours. Treat them with kindness, sympathy, benevolence, and compassion—as you would like to be treated. People

Abraham Lincoln at the dedication of Gettysburg National Cemetery, November 19, 1863

Audiences are vulnerable; they expect speakers to tell the truth and to be honest.

are not objects for you to use. They are persons with intelligence and dignity. To do anything that subverts their intelligence or robs them of dignity may very well be the ultimate immorality in communication.

Playing by the Rules

There wouldn't be much point to any kind of game if it didn't have some sort of rules. Otherwise, how could you know who wins? And there wouldn't be much point to the game if somebody didn't win. It's the way you go about winning that sometimes causes problems. If winning becomes so important that the rules are ignored, there is an ethical problem. Think about how you feel when players break the rules. Do you respect them?

The notion of playing to win, but winning by the rules, is as relevant to making speeches as it is to playing games. Rhetoric in American democracy has its own set of rules imposed by society. When those who break the rules are caught, society punishes them.

Americans generally consider democracy the ideal form of government. One of the major foundations of our democracy is free speech. Our society zealously guards our rights to express our opinions. This right also entails responsibility. Audiences are vulnerable; they expect speakers to tell the truth and to give honest advice. They face the danger of demagogues who don't play by the rules and charlatans who are more concerned with prestige, power and wealth than with honesty. In less extreme form, competition and the drive to succeed sometimes make it difficult to put aside prejudice, to be straightforward, and to be scrupulously fair. But democracy fails in its purpose if it doesn't promote the self-realization of individuals and the benefit of society as a whole. It's impossible to reach these goals unless the great majority (ideally, all) play a significant and effective role in the process of making free, informed decisions.

Rule 1: Audience Decisions Should Be Free from Coercion

You are much more likely to make a sound judgment when you have a cool head. The same is true for moral judgments. Under the stress of emotion, you can easily be misled. There is ample evidence to illustrate the point: unhappy teenagers who commit suicide, angry adults who dissolve marriages, times when ambition and greed lead to needless suffering.

Speeches can have an equally devastating influence. When they transform an audience into an angry mob, persuade people to mistrust any stranger out of fear, or use arguments to evoke hatred, they are not only unethical, they do a disservice to society.[6] When you make a speech, you owe the audience the right to let it make cool-headed decisions. An audience overwhelmed with anger, hatred, fear, or any other emotion, won't make prudent judgments. A speaker who deliberately treats an audience this way is like a mugger who says, "Give me your wallet or I'll blow your brains out." An audience driven to a decision by threats, coercion, or undue emotion is being mugged by the speaker. It's what Hitler did in Germany; it's what speakers do when they incite a mob to rioting or lynching; it's what happens when any demagogue uses an audience for self-aggrandizement and selfish gain.

Don't misunderstand. Our insistence on rational discourse does not say that appeals to *ethos* and *pathos* are somehow wrong. In the first chapter of this book, we said that every argument is a necessary mixture of all three forms of proof. Audiences can't avoid making judgments about a speaker's credibility, and speakers can't say anything that is unrelated to beliefs and values.

Human beliefs and values lead to emotional involvements. For instance, the family is accorded high importance all over the world. But parents don't say to their children, "I value you." They may not even be aware that their feelings represent a value. What they do say is, "I love you." The feeling is truly there; love is a natural and universal emotion in human nature. People are complex; audiences are not influenced by reason alone. They have values and emotional attachments to these values. These are all part of what it is to be a human being. There is no intrinsic evil in using arguments that appeal to what is natural and universal in nature.

There is nothing ethically wrong in using value appeals that arouse an emotional response. Emotionalizing value appeals becomes ethically objectionable when used intentionally to interfere with the audience's critical thinking. When a speaker plays on the emotions of the audience with the express purpose of exciting an emotional response and preventing any reasonable assessment, he or she treats the audience as less human and more beastlike. Inflaming the emotions of an audience to the point of invoking irrational behavior or introducing emotional appeals irrelevant to the issue being discussed may help you win, but you ultimately lose because you demean not only your audience but yourself as well.

None of these cautions are meant to prevent you from taking a strong stand. If you believe in your position, present your arguments with vigor, even passion. If you believe the opposition is wrong, say so with vigor, even passion. You owe it to yourself and to your audience to use all the available, ethical, and honest means of persuasion possible. No one will accuse you of foul play unless you subvert what could be effective speech to personal gain. If you respect the audience (and yourself), you will not be guilty of manipulating either your speech or the audience. Manipulation is the principal deterrent to free choice.

Rule 2: The Audience Should Make Informed Decisions

Clouded emotional response is not the only cause of bad decisions. The lack of information is another. In spite of its flaws, democracy works as well as it does because information is freely available in the decision making process. The First Amendment is designed to ensure that people can have the information they need for making informed decisions. Democracy protects the right of the media to provide the public with facts and opinions.

Unfortunately, the amendment falls victim to the same kind of abuse that rhetoric does. Sleazy material, misrepresented claims, irresponsible reporting, public examination of private lives, character assassination, and arguable obscenity are printed under the protection of the First Amendment. Publishers of such material claim the right to freedom of speech, freedom of the press, and the right to uncensored artistic expression. Those who are aggrieved have to prove the lies, the violation of privacy, the libel, or the obscenity. That's a hard job. In cases like this, it is the First Amendment that's being mugged. Despite these subversions, the benefits of freely disseminated information far outweigh the discomforts.

We said in the preceding section that the principal barrier to a free decision is manipulation. When decisions are uninformed, the significant ethical problem is misrepresentation.

The most obvious example of misrepresentation occurs when a speaker argues in favor of one position but actually holds an opposing point of view. Lawyers sometimes do this to defend clients to the full extent allowed by law. University debaters argue affirmative and negative cases, and their own beliefs are irrelevant; training in argumentation is their goal. In times of war, hot or cold, governments ''disinform'' other governments. Special cases of this kind aside, when **you** argue for a position **you** don't believe, you're telling a lie. Earlier in the chapter we called this an objective lie. What we called subjective lies also misrepresent, but there's no ethical fault in them unless you are guilty of inadequate research and poor reasoning. Avoiding misrepresentation is not the only requirement for honest speech, but it is the minimum responsibility every speaker should accept.

Telling the truth, however, doesn't mean that you have to be absolutely literal in every respect. For example, to improve your oral style, you can use all of the figures of speech you'll read about in Chapter 15 as long as you don't try to make your audience misunderstand what you mean. Nobody has to tell you when you cross the line between dramatizing a point and misrepresenting it. You know.

Every issue has two sides, and both sides have a right to the strongest legitimate defense available. But you don't have to present the opposition's case. The defense doesn't offer evidence for the prosecution, nor does a prosecutor argue for the defense. Nevertheless, we have to raise a sticky point in this connection. Questions about manufacturing evidence, using phony statistics, or taking quotations out of context are easy to answer. Even a speaker who deliberately does these things knows they are wrong. But what about withholding information? This can be a more delicate matter. Suppose you think the blind date your roommate sets up for you is a self-centered bore. Unless your opinion is vital to someone, nobody will blame you for keeping it to yourself. But you ought to be concerned when you sell your car if you try to hide the fact that the transmission is shot.

Here's a situation that raises the same question. You're arguing for a federal law that would require all firearms to be licensed. While you don't have to argue for the opposition (that would be foolish), is it legitimate to ignore opposition claims that no licensing law has ever been able to keep guns out of the hands of criminals? That federal laws licensing guns would violate the Second Amendment to the Constitution? That the federal government can only control interstate commerce and taxation? In looking for answers, keep these points in mind:

1. If your only defense against the strong points of the opposing case is to ignore them, your failure to admit them openly is a clear case of misrepresentation.
2. If the information you are withholding is crucial to a prudent judgment, the audience cannot make a fully informed decision.

You have to decide what is fair to the audience, to the subject and to yourself. How defensible is your proposal? Is it good for the audience or just yourself? Are you more concerned with winning than with giving the best advice? If the well-being of the audience is not your principal goal, you have no moral right to speak.

Rule 3: Strike a Fair Bargain with Your Audience

When you give a speech, think of making a bargain with your audience. It's an unspoken agreement intended for the mutual benefit of everybody involved. You say, in effect, "If you give critical and thoughtful attention to what I'm going to tell you, in return I'll do my best to make it worth your while." You are making a promise that you will be worth listening to, that your information and advocacy will be reasoned, and that your counsel will be honest.

Classical Proofs in Ethical Communication

Remember (again) that everything you do and say has to be planned with the audience in mind. Therefore, the three forms of proof are relevant here. We have talked briefly about the ethical use of *logos* and *pathos* in communication, but we haven't said anything so far about the relationship between ethics and *ethos*. Therefore, we'll remind you briefly about the proper use of *logos* and *pathos*, and then say a bit about *ethos*.

Logos   A speech may seem reasonable to an audience and still stand on shaky moral grounds if, through ignorance or intent, you deceive the audience with bad evidence or faulty reasoning. But if you know what you're talking about, and if you use solid evidence to support sound arguments, your speech will stand on solid moral ground.

Pathos   Reasoning can't be done in a vacuum. It must have substance and form. They are as inherent in arguments as they are in a speech, a play, a poem, a statue, or a piece of music. The substance of an argument is the *pathos*, drawn from the system of beliefs and values you hold. The specific beliefs and values that comprise your arguments are the ones which your audience analysis tells you that you share with the audience. The *logos*, the reasoning process, is the form.

Appeals to the beliefs and values of an audience can be ethical or not because of the influence emotion has on their moral quality. It's quite obvious that people are emotionally involved with what they value. If you were a Chicago baseball fan in 1989, you believed that the Cubs were long overdue to win a World Series. You didn't hang onto that belief simply because you're stubborn. At least a part of any fan's loyalty is an emotional attachment to the team. Because a woman values the inviolability of her body, rape is the subject of hatred and fear. The man whose value for material goods is abnormal envies those who have more and feels pity for those who have less. The value he assigns his goods leads to selfishness and greed. If you value justice, you are angry when you see injustice done. It takes more than cool detachment to station yourself in a small boat in front of a submarine in order to stop the test of a nuclear weapon. Every value carries along with it some emotional attachment to what is valued.

The persuasive effectiveness of the substance, the *pathos*, of an argument can be enhanced by its emotional content. Let's say you want an audience to distrust the Soviet policy toward the United States. You can base a speech on appeals to the values of peace, self-preservation, the future well-being of the family, and any others that seem appropriate. The emotions of fear and hatred of war (which threatens the loss of peace, life, family) are associated and relevant. Therefore, it's quite legitimate to use value appeals that arouse those emotions with evidence of the death and destruction war brings.

What makes the use of emotion illegitimate is to use it as a blindfold for the eyes of the intellect. One potential pitfall is the danger of getting carried away by your own zeal. Eagerness to reach your goal, whether it is selfish or humane, can lead you to an unethical use of emotion. No ethical speaker considers emotions like greed, envy, and contempt to be enlightened and edifying appeals to what is humane in the audience.

Even though emotional responses are closely associated with values, using value appeals to stir up emotions isn't and shouldn't be what is central to *pathos*. It's a lot more important to understand the audience, its value system and its beliefs, and to recognize the ones that are most relevant to your subject and purpose. Then you can develop arguments that will lead the audience to accept advice that you honestly believe is for its own good and for the good of society as a whole.

Ethos   In the old Greek, the word *ethos* referred to the character of people. Later, Aristotle used it to name the proof that gets its power from the

Jim Bakker was a charismatic speaker who appealed to the beliefs and values of his televangelism audience but was convicted of unethically using funds donated by followers to his PTL ministry.

character of the speaker. When an audience sees in you honesty, knowledge, and good will, your speech will be believable. Today, we call this mode of proof credibility. The obvious way to be unethical in building credibility is to lie about your credentials or about having the best interests of your audience at heart.

There is also a very practical reason for being honest. If you lie, use phony evidence, or try to deceive people in any way, there is a very good chance that someone in the audience will know the facts. Even if your deceit is not immediately detected, it's almost inevitable that in the future the shoddy tricks you used will come to light. In either case, once you have been caught in a lie, your credibility will suffer severe (maybe irreparable) damage. You will find it very hard to be persuasive when you have the reputation of being a liar.

Pragmatic reasons of this sort are only secondary grounds for honesty. Be honest because of self-respect and because you have sincere interest in the well-being of your audience. Your desire to be an ethical speaker should easily meet the obligation to "play by the rules." To do what's right, follow the advice of St. Paul to his protege, Timothy. Paul told Timothy to aim for integrity, godliness, faith, love, patience and a gentle spirit.[7]

Summary

The societies in and through which people live cannot exist without human communication. Because communication has tremendous influence on society, for good or ill, and because many speakers abuse rhetoric, you make moral judgments about how to use it properly. These judgments should be based on your personal ethical code.

An ethical speaker is characterized by knowledge of the subject, truthfulness, sound reasoning, impartiality, and humaneness.

To be knowledgeable you must be able to give an audience the information it needs in order to make informed and prudent decisions.

Truthfulness demands that you advocate only the positions you honestly espouse. Moreover, you must avoid all objective lies and as many subjective lies as you can with responsible investigation of the subject.

Sound reasoning gives you rational grounds for your moral judgments and prevents bad evidence and bad reasoning from making your arguments faulty.

Impartiality requires you to apply your standards to all persons equally and on all occasions, regardless of convenience.

You will be a humane speaker if you are kind, sympathetic, benevolent and compassionate. You must respect your listeners as persons, not things. To subvert their intelligence or to diminish their dignity demeans both you and them.

Our society considers democracy to be the best form of government. But democracy fails if the desire to achieve individual goals, such as money, power, and status, motivates a kind of speaking that prevents uncoerced decisions by informed audiences. This seriously hampers the legitimate self-realization of individuals and the well-being of society as a whole.

Everything you say and do in a speech is intended to influence the audience. Therefore, ethical use of the three sources of proof, *logos*, *pathos*, and *ethos*, is of concern.

The proper use of *logos* is characterized by solid evidence and sound argument. Ethical use of *pathos* concentrates on appropriate values, not on undue use of emotions. Using evidence and arguments that arouse emotional response in the audience is legitimate as long as the emotion is relevant to the value appeal. Your use of *ethos* is ethically acceptable when it marks you as an honest, knowledgeable speaker who has the best interests of the audience at heart. To be untruthful about your credentials, competence, or your desire for the well-being of the audience is the most obvious ethical fault in building your credibility.

There is a very practical, basic reason for using rhetoric ethically. You risk damaging your reputation if audiences discover your unethical behavior. However, your self-respect and an honest desire to give the audience good information and sound advice are even more compelling reasons to be an ethical speaker.

Key Terms

Trust	Probable
Honesty	Objective lie
Quintilian	Subjective lie
Knowledge	Rules
Truthfulness	Free speech
Reasoning	Responsibility
Impartiality	Coercion
Humaneness	Informed decision
Consequences	Fair bargain

Exercises

1. Write a short paper explaining and justifying the most important ethical responsibility you impose on yourself as a communicator.

2. Discuss with others in class what you consider to be your moral responsibility in one of the following situations of moral conflict:

   a. In a class discussion, someone supports your proposal and convinces others that you are right by presenting evidence you know to be incorrect. What should you do? Why?

   b. A good friend of yours is selling a car in order to buy a newer one. A possible buyer comes to look at it while you are there, and your friend says the car has good brakes. Just last week you heard your friend say that one of the reasons for getting rid of the car was that the brakes were bad. What should you do? Why?

   c. No speaker can say everything there is to say on a subject. The speaker must select. Therefore, no matter how hard you try, you cannot give all the "facts" on a subject. What principles do you think should guide you in deciding what facts you should exclude if time is short? For instance, do you have an obligation to explain the arguments against your idea? Should you cut your evidence short to be sure you make all your arguments, or should you cut the number of points you make and develop them more fully? How ethical is each of your choices?

   d. A friend of yours believes that God is the supreme ruler of the universe and that God has decreed that abortion is immoral. In an argument with someone else who favors abortion, but does not believe in God, your friend does not use God as part of the justification for opposing abortion. Is such an omission ethical?

Notes

1 For a more detailed discussion of communication ethics, see Richard L. Johannesen, *Ethics in Human Communication*, 3/E (Prospect Heights, IL: Waveland, 1990).

2 Quintilian would approve because the list embodies all the elements of *ethos*.

3 Robert Bolt, *A Man For All Seasons*, Act II (New York: Scholastic Book Service, 1963) 53.

4 See Karl R. Wallace, "The Substance of Rhetoric: Good Reasons," *Quarterly Journal of Speech* (1963): 239-49; Walter R. Fisher, "Toward a Logic of Good Reasons," *Quarterly Journal of Speech* (1978): 376-84. Neither Wallace nor Fisher is referring specifically to the ethical reasons one has for doing or not doing. Rather, the "good reasons" one gives for doing or not doing are what all of rhetoric is about.

5 E.J. Bond, *Reason and Value*, (Cambridge U P, 1983) 1.

6 Thomas R. Nilsen, *Ethics of Speech Communication* (Indianapolis: The Bobbs-Merrill, 1966) 10, says anything is wrong that reduces the well-being and the happiness of the people in the society.

7 I Timothy 6:11.

Analyzing Speaking
Situations

chapter 5

The Subject and Purpose of the Speech

I. Choosing your speech subject
   A. Your interests influence your choice of subject
   B. The audience influences your choice of subject
   C. Every speech is designed to solve a problem
   D. The subject should be appropriate to the occasion

II. The general purposes of speeches
   A. Speaking to entertain—to give amusement
   B. Speaking to inform—to bring about understanding
   C. Speaking to persuade—to influence belief or action
   D. Distinguishing among the general purposes

III. Identifying the specific purpose of your speech
   A. Speech claims
      1. Factual claims
      2. Value claims
      3. Policy claims
   B. Stating the specific purpose
   C. Formulating a subject sentence

Try to imagine a speech that doesn't talk about anything. You can't, of course. The notion is a contradiction in terms and makes no sense at all. No matter what the context, every communication—speech, play, poem, novel, essay, whatever it might be—either written or oral, has to talk about something. It has to have a *subject.*

Moreover, all voluntary actions have some purpose. If you put your hand on a hot stove, you move it; you don't make a speech about the nature of pain. But when you have some audience-oriented goal, talking seems the appropriate way to achieve it.[1]

There'll be times, of course, when you won't reach your goal. The failure is often blamed on a communication "breakdown." But breakdowns in communication simply don't exist. When the minimal conditions are present (speaker, speech, audience, channel), communication will occur; it cannot fail to occur.[2] A better way to explain what happens is to call it a "failure of purpose." The question is not whether you will communicate, but what you will communicate and whether it will be what you want to say.[3] The first steps toward saying what you want to say are finding the right subject, choosing an appropriate purpose, and phrasing a precise subject sentence. In this chapter, we show you how to do these things.

Choosing Your Speech Subject

In theory, the number of subjects you could talk about is unlimited. On any given occasion, however, the ideal number of subjects you should talk about is only one. It's a lot easier to find the right subject when you look for one that can be interesting to you and to your audience. For reasons we'll explain in just a moment, it should also be aimed at solving a problem of one kind or another.

Your Interests Influence Your Choice of Subject

The assumption that a good speaker can talk well on any subject is wrong. Good speakers are avid readers and investigators; they pursue all kinds of knowledge. But they cannot be expert on everything. Therefore, they usually choose subjects from areas of their greatest competence.

From time to time, however, a subject will come up that you think is important enough and interesting enough to make a good speech subject. The fact that you don't at first feel competent to talk about it doesn't mean that you shouldn't. When you choose a subject, you may know very little about it. If you're interested in the subject and you think it's worth talking about, you can research it until you learn enough to make a good speech. The only requirement is to be competent when you speak.

It's a lot more pleasant for you and the audience when you talk about something that interests you. For instance, any area of study that you like well enough to make your academic major will provide many interesting subjects. But beyond any specific field lies a world of fascinating people, places, and ideas — including hobbies, sports, cultural events, jobs and a variety of social, political, and religious activities.

Many other experiences are potentially good subjects. What you learned on a trip to Mexico could become a good speech on the language, culture, architecture, or art of the country. Having the stereo stolen from your car (as unpleasant as that would be) might motivate you to investigate the problem of crime and to draw a subject from that information.

Reading, talking to people, developing an interest in national and international politics and economics, or getting involved in school and community affairs are all instructive activities. Wide interests and experiences will supply any number of topics suitable for speeches. At the end of this chapter, you'll find a list of general subjects that will give you many ideas for a speech.

The Audience Influences Your Choice of Subject

You choose the subjects of your speeches, but because the audience is central to the entire communication process, its influence plays a crucial role in the choice.

An audience will be interested in your subject if it seems significant. The greater the significance, the greater the interest. For an art major, the fact that the cost of watercolors had doubled is apt to be of much more interest than to an English major who doesn't need to buy paint. A lecture on the Hopi Indians that an anthropology major would go out of the way to hear wouldn't necessarily interest an astronomy student. Many political science students would gladly spend time tabulating returns of a campus election in which many other students didn't even take the time to vote. But all would respond sharply to news that their tuition had increased 25 percent.

If listeners are not aware of how much the topic affects them, they may not have any feeling at all about it. This kind of indifference doesn't necessarily mean that the subject is a poor choice. It means that you must stimulate interest by helping your listeners see how important it is. Otherwise, they'll have no reason to listen to you.

Once an audience sees the significance of what you're saying, it will listen. Then you need a further adaptation — to adapt your speech to the language, beliefs, and values of your listeners. This is necessary because you see the world in a personal, unique way. You have your own beliefs and values about politics, religion, morality, aesthetics, and every other subject. Taken together, your perceptions and judgments about all of these subjects constitute your ''image'' of the world.[4] The same is true for every member of an audience. But because of different levels of intelligence and education, varied cultural backgrounds, and dissimilar experiences, each person is unique. No two share identical beliefs and values.

The function of speechmaking, then, is that "of adjusting ideas to people and of people to ideas."[5] To make the adjustment successful, choose your subject in light of the needs of the audience and its view of what the world is or ought to be.

The only way you can communicate a speech is to channel it through verbal and nonverbal language. But the language symbols you use don't have any meaning in themselves. The meanings are all in the minds of the people who use them. Your listeners, then, will understand your words in light of their meanings. As far as the audience is concerned, its understanding of your subject **is** your subject. You want to keep the audience clearly in mind when you decide what to discuss.

Every Speech Is Designed to Solve a Problem

In Chapter 1, we called communication a transaction. In a sense, the speaker and the audience become a single entity while they cooperate in creating a mutually understood meaning for the speech. This union between the personal interests of the speaker and the needs of the audience is easier to understand if you think of speeches as devices for solving problems. Let's look at a few examples.

For years experts have asserted the inevitability of a major earthquake in California, even more serious than the one that hit San Francisco during the World Series in October, 1989. The question is not whether it will happen, but when. Yet people go about their business without much visible concern. If you were trying to arouse people to the danger, one factor you would have to deal with is a widespread lack of understanding of just what an earthquake is. Despite the death and destruction caused by the 1989 San Francisco quake, people do not understand how earthquakes happen. The obstacle to your goal would be, "They don't understand how complicated the process is." If the speech is successful, you and the audience have cooperated in a communication transaction and the problem is solved.

Kelly is a member of the basketball team. She is concerned about the problem caused by athletes' use of steroids. This is a problem that an informative speech is not going to solve. The subject obviously calls for a persuasive speech. If her speech arguing against the use of steroids gets the response she wants, her transaction with the audience has solved the problem.

Speeches to entertain work the same way. They are aimed at problems of the sort that say, "My audience doesn't see the humor in. . . ."

A common characteristic of all speeches is the ultimate purpose to solve a problem of some kind. The way to identify the subject and purpose of a speech is to get a clear understanding of precisely what problem needs to be solved in your transaction with the audience.

The Subject Should Be Appropriate to the Occasion

There is no such thing as an inherently good or inherently bad subject. There are only good or bad speeches. Your subject will be the right one when it is appropriate to the audience, the occasion, and the response you want.

One very obvious way of making a speech inappropriate for an audience is to choose a response your specific audience *cannot* give. For instance, a speech promoting a candidate you support to an audience not eligible to vote in the election or a speech to solicit financial support for a project to an audience barely able to pay tuition bills would be futile. Mistakes like these are easy to avoid because normally you can see them in advance. A more likely source of problems is the occasion.

Usually, it is a specific occasion that draws people together. When you choose a subject, the occasion will demand some part of your time. For example, a speech delivered on Lincoln's birthday should indicate at least an awareness of the great president's philosophy and deeds. On the Fourth of July, some aspect of patriotism is traditionally included.

When you think there is any likelihood that your listeners may not quickly see the relevance of a subject, make it clear how the subject relates to their interests. A very good speech was made in class on the subject of automobile insurance. At first glance, it might look like an inappropriate subject because any listener who owned a car would probably have insurance. Knowing this, the speaker introduced the subject by saying, ''Even if you're not among the 40% of all drivers who don't have insurance, there's a good chance that you have friends who are. And you can help them.''

The General Purposes of Speeches

The classical orators of Greece and Rome were concerned with only one kind of speaking: persuasion. They were interested in speeches that would convince an audience to believe the claim argued in the speech. This approach to public speaking persisted throughout the Middle ages and the Renaissance into early modern times. A little more than 200 years ago, other goals were recognized and, depending on the writer, these goals—so-called general ends of speeches—varied in name and number.

Through the years, the list of speech purposes that have been mentioned by one writer or another has reached a ridiculous length. It includes (and we're sure there must be others) speeches to inform, define, explain, exhort, advise, command, persuade, convince, actuate, speculate, stimulate, question, analyze, and amuse. Even today, there is not complete agreement on just what and how many of these goals there are. We realize that writers identify whatever speech purposes they think will be useful, but you'll find that any speech you ever make will be directed toward one of these three goals: to *entertain*, to *inform*, or to *persuade*.

Speaking to Entertain—to give amusement

On many occasions, both formal and informal, a speaker will have the sole purpose of entertaining an audience. The purpose of the speech to entertain is to amuse an audience by revealing the humor that it would not otherwise see in a subject. Ordinarily, humor will be the means. In Chapter 20, we'll talk about some of the forms humor takes.

Many comedians use satire as a stock-in-trade. Although they criticize the foibles and incongruities they see in society, their goal is to amuse, not inform or persuade, their audiences. There is an important distinction to be seen here between the use of ideas to create humor and the use of humor to support ideas. A speech to entertain should not be confused with an informative or persuasive speech that uses humor to maintain interest or support arguments.

Speaking to Inform—to bring about understanding

Making something known to an audience, clarifying ideas, giving facts or information is speaking to inform. The purpose of a speech to inform

The purpose of the speech to entertain is to amuse an audience by revealing the humor that it would not otherwise see in a subject. Garrison Keillor has mastered this art.

is to give an audience an understanding it would not otherwise have on a subject. The primary response you want is understanding of an object, an operation, a condition, or an idea. To fulfill a requirement for an informative speech on international affairs, you might give a report on the Russian concepts of "glasnost" and "perestroika." In a report of this kind, you have no immediate concern for the attitude the audience might have toward those concepts or toward the Soviet Union; nor are you directly concerned with what your listeners might do with the information you give them. Understanding and retention by the audience are the criteria of a successful speech to inform.

Speaking to Persuade—to influence belief or action

A speech to persuade gives listeners reasons for changing their behavior in some way. This becomes necessary when speaker and audience hold different opinions. Persuasion can also be necessary even if both hold the same opinion but at different levels of intensity. The purpose of the speech to persuade is to bring about agreement between speaker and audience in areas that are in dispute. Look at the following example.

Irritated by the fact that she can't find adequate and affordable care for her young child while she goes to school and works, Sylvia decides to start a campaign to establish a day care center on campus. She needs to persuade her friends to give active support to the campaign. But even if her friends agree that day-care ought to be available, they may not have the same concern because they do not have children. They have other problems that are more important to them. Therefore, her specific problem in persuasion depends on how involved her friends are with the situation (how much it bothers them). Her task would be to give them reasons for being bothered and for getting involved.

Distinguishing Among the General Purposes

Because every speech in some way changes a listener's thinking, all speeches can be thought of as persuasive. People always differ to some degree in their views about poltics, religion, aesthetics, or any other area where judgments are made. Even when two people generally agree, as they might if both are interested in mathematics, the Chicago Cubs, or rock music, they will disagree on specifics or have different levels of interest in the subjects. They would have to have identical brains and identical experiences to think exactly alike.

Obviously, no one thinks exactly as you do. The humor you find in some subjects might not be obvious to others unless you highlight the comic aspects. An audience might not understand some topics without your clarification. Your position may cause disagreement unless you defend it.

If you could find a subject on which there was universal consensus you would not want to give a speech on it. There would be no problem it could solve for the audience. What speaker or audience would want to spend time on that? Every speech, therefore, is intended to eliminate some difference between the way speaker and audience view the world.

Although every subject is potentially debatable and every successful speech eliminates some degree of difference between speaker and audience, not all speeches are treated alike. A reasonable way to distinguish one general purpose from another is to identify the specific problem your speech is supposed to solve and to determine what type of speech you must prepare in order to reach your goal. How you use your analysis of the audience and the subject differentiates one type of speech from the others.

Audience analysis and subject analysis both show you how to treat disputes so that they won't interfere with your speech purpose. Both types of analysis are so important to the success of your speeches that we have devoted the two following chapters to them.

We stated earlier that your subject *is* what the audience *understands* it to be. Therefore, you must make their understanding as identical as possible to your own. For example, Jennifer left an audience quite unsure of her purpose when she spoke on the subject, "Abstract art is fun!" The listeners had to decide for themselves whether: 1) she meant to give advice: "Try it. You'll like it," 2) to explain how she used it in her own life: "It's a good form of therapy for me," or 3) to persuade them to a higher appreciation of its value: "It has greater merit than most people realize."

Unfortunately, a speaker will sometimes deliberately try to mislead an audience. Lane Cooper says, "Shakespeare's Antony begins by saying that he came to bury Caesar, not to praise him. With his tricky speech he does praise Caesar, but also accuses the murderers, and inflames the mob to violent action against them." [6] Here's how analysis helps you distinguish one general purpose from another and, at the same time, protects you (and any other honest speaker) from ambiguity and saves your audiences from confusion.

When you prepare a speech to entertain, you say to yourself, "I realize that my subject (e.g.: income tax), like any other topic, is volatile. I want to show the humor in some of the contradictions I have found in the income tax law. I don't want the audience's dislike of taxes in general to interfere with my purpose." Analysis of the subject points out the areas that can be treated with humor. Analysis of the audience shows you how to use humor without stirring up immaterial disagreements.

Similarly, you say about an informative speech, "I want this audience to understand the financial problems hospitals face today. I don't want it to think I'm joking about the subject or making a pitch for socialized medicine." The job of analysis in speeches to entertain and to inform is to find ways to suppress inherent controversies, to keep them from turning the audience's thinking away from your purpose.

In a speech to persuade, on the other hand, areas of dispute need to be brought out into the open. In persuasion, disagreements interfere with your purpose when you examine those that are not crucial and leave the crucial conflicts unresolved. Analysis of the subject digs out all of the areas of conflict. Audience analysis tells you which ones have to be faced for this audience, and which ones can be ignored.

Identifying the Specific Purpose of Your Speech

When you find the right subject, it will be one that is of interest to you, adapted to the audience, aimed at solving a problem, and appropriate to the occasion. And, by the time you find the right subject, you'll know whether the general purpose of your speech is to entertain, inform, or persuade. But a general purpose is too broad. Now you have to refine it. To do this, devise a specific purpose for the speech. Without it, neither you nor your audience can know precisely what you want the speech to do. The specific purpose is expressed in a statement called the speech claim. A speech claim is a sentence that clearly and accurately expresses exactly what you want the audience to find amusing, understand, believe, or do.

Speech Claims

A thoroughly dependable way of creating an accurate speech claim is to identify precisely what problem you want your speech to solve. The solution you propose is your speech claim. Claims of *fact* and *value* assert that something is. A *policy* claim says that something ought to be.

Factual claims   A factual claim is *an assertion that certain specified conditions could be observed in the real world.* That is, the specified conditions are said not to exist merely as attitudes in somebody's mind but as realities that can be experienced in the physical world. For example:

1. There is a disparity among the divorce laws of the several states.
2. Before the year 2000, a woman will be elected President of the United States.

The first example talks about conditions that can be observed here and now. In the second example, no amount of investigation at the present time will justify the claim. It is a prediction about the future. But it is still a factual claim because it says that a specified condition some day could (at least theoretically) be observed. And this kind of claim is a legitimate factual speech claim.

Value claims   Because of its form, a value claim can easily be mistaken for a factual claim. Yet the two are different in a very significant respect. A factual claim says that something in the physical world could (given the right conditions) be observed. In other words, it says something about the actual existence of the object referred to. Divorce laws throughout the United States either are or are not uniform; in the year 2000 there will either be a woman president or there will not. A value claim, on the other hand, does not make a verifiable statement about the physical world. Instead, it expresses an attitude that exists only in somebody's mind.

A value claim is *a statement expressing a judgment about the goodness, rightness, quality,* or *merit of something.* For example:

1. Drug abuse is the most serious problem we face today.
2. The American educational system is superior to the educational systems of Europe.
3. A woman would make a better president than a man.

Policy claims   You make decisions every day about how to conduct your life. Moreover, it is often useful to ask others to believe or to do something; to change their lives in some way. In such a case, the expression you use is called a policy claim and it says something about how you think the world ought to be.

A policy claim is *a statement that identifies a course of action (a policy) and calls for its adoption.* For example:

1. The Associated Students should establish a day-care center for children of students.
2. All the states should adopt uniform divorce laws.
3. A woman should be elected President.

It is not always easy to know what kind of claim a statement expresses. We have already said that it is sometimes difficult to tell a factual claim from a value claim because the two look as if they make the same kind of statement. On the other hand, it should be easy to recognize policy claims even though they can be phrased in a wide variety of ways. For example, there are several ways of saying that the states should adopt uniform divorce laws:

"The states ought to. . . ."
"It would be the best course of action (or the best policy) for the states to. . . ."
"The states have to. . . ."
"What we need are. . . ."

And so on. But no matter how the claim is worded, it always implies the notion of "should" or "ought."

Despite the clear-cut criteria for distinguishing one kind of claim from another, it is easy to confuse them if you classify them according to whether you believe them or not. The imaginary conversation that follows shows the kind of trouble this can cause.

"What kind of claim is this? Everyone should give good value for money received."

"That must be a factual claim because it's true."

"No, it's a policy claim because of the kind of proposal it makes. It identifies a policy, that is, a course of action, or a mode of conduct, and calls for its adoption. And the fact that you believe it doesn't make it true.''

''What kind of claim is this? There's no life anywhere in the universe except on Earth.''

''That must be a value claim because it's only your opinion.''

''No, *all* claims are expressions of opinion. This claim identifies a condition that could, at least theoretically, be observed in the physical world. For that reason it is a factual claim.''

We have stressed the importance of correctly identifying each kind of claim because the differences among them are significant. Not to identify each one correctly makes for fuzzy thinking and blurred notions of what you need to say. It is particularly important in preparing a persuasive speech to know whether you are supporting a claim of fact, value, or policy.

Stating the Specific Purpose

Before you can organize a speech, or even begin to gather materials, you must make a clear statement of precisely what response you want from the audience. A common procedure is to formulate an infinitive phrase which specifies the subject and purpose of the speech. This is called a *statement of specific purpose*. For example:

To **entertain** the audience with a description of my first experience with college registration (*a factual claim*).

To **inform** the audience about the effects of steroid use (*a factual claim*).

To **persuade** the audience that there is extraterrestrial life (*a factual claim*).

To **persuade** the audience that attitudes toward Vietnam veterans are unfair (*a value claim*).

To **persuade** the audience that the Associated Students should provide day care for the children of students. (*a policy claim*).

The statement of purpose is your guide in speech preparation. It helps to determine what material belongs in the speech and what does not. There are always temptations to include interesting but irrelevant pieces of material. The problem is one of selection: using the items that are essential and rejecting those that are not. Sometimes even the most interesting material must be omitted in order to preserve the unity of the speech. Once formed, the statement of purpose should be a rigorous standard to judge what materials to use.

Formulating a Subject Sentence

A statement of purpose helps you keep your goal in mind while you prepare your speech and it guides your decisions about the materials you should and shouldn't use. Its style, however, is not suited to good oral communication. Therefore you won't use it in the speech. Instead, you will use a subject sentence. This, in effect, is the statement of purpose phrased as a brief, clear, graceful sentence that says exactly what the speech is going to be about.

For a speech to entertain:

Specific purpose: To amuse the audience with an experience I had as an insurance salesman

Subject sentence: I started my job as an insurance salesman with great enthusiasm—my parents had to throw me out the front door.

For an informative speech:

Specific purpose: To inform the audience about how a color photograph becomes an illustration in a magazine

Subject sentence: I've appreciated the pictures in full-color magazines a lot more since I learned how they are made.

For a persuasive speech:

Specific purpose: To persuade the audience to support my campaign for a day-care facility on campus

Subject sentence: All students, whether they have children or not, would profit from a day-care center on campus.

When you've completed the steps we've described in this chapter, you're well on your way toward preparing what will most likely be a very good speech.

Summary

Every speech has a subject (the topic under discussion) and a purpose (the reason for giving it). Several factors influence your choice of subject. When you find the right one, it will be of interest to you, adapted to the audience, aimed at solving a problem, and appropriate to the occasion.

The reason for giving any speech is to solve a problem of some kind: the audience's need for amusement, information, or advice. The solutions you propose are best thought of in terms of the three general purposes of speaking: To entertain—to give amusement; to inform—to bring about understanding; to persuade—to influence belief or action.

Because all speeches change the way a listener sees the world, they are in that sense persusive. Even so, they are not all treated as persuasive speeches. In order to tell whether the speech for a given occasion ought to entertain, inform, or persuade, you must identify the specific problem you want the speech to solve. Audience analysis and subject analysis help you to achieve your speech goal.

Your proposed solution to the problem you want your speech to solve is expressed in a sentence that states one of three kinds of speech claims:

A factual claim says that certain specified conditions could (at least theoretically) be observed in the physical world. A value claim makes known the speaker's attitude toward something. A policy claim identifies a course of action and calls for its adoption. If you don't make correct distinctions among these three kinds of claims, you won't have a clear picture of the needs of the audience and the demands of the occasion.

The statement of specific purpose identifies the general end of your speech (to entertain, inform, or persuade) and makes clear exactly what you want the audience to laugh about, understand, believe, or do. This statement helps you decide which of your materials belong in the speech and which don't. For oral delivery, the statement of purpose is phrased as a sentence in good oral style.

Key Terms

Audience oriented	Value claim
Problem solving	Policy claim
Occasion	Subject sentence
Entertaining	Speaker interest
Informing	Audience influence
Persuading	Appropriateness
Differentiating purposes	Statement of purpose
Factual claim	Retention

Exercises

1. Phrase a factual claim and a value claim from the same general subject. Explain, by using them as examples, the difference between claims of fact and value. What policy claim might be based on these factual and value claims?

2. Select one of the audiences below or one assigned by your instructor and make a list of five speech subjects you believe would interest that audience:
   a. A church group to which you belong
   b. An assembly of the high school from which you graduated
   c. An organization to which your parents belong
   d. A meeting of the students in your major department

3. Make a list of three general subjects on which you believe you are qualified to speak. Form a specific purpose for an entertaining, informative, and persuasive speech from each general subject.

Speech Subject Areas

The following list is intended to simulate your thinking about the choice of a speech subject. It merely suggests some of the broad general areas of discussion from which you can draw topics. You won't find a specific speech subject here, but the list may help you think of one that is significant, appropriate, and interesting to you and your audience.

Education

Admission tests
Alcohol on campus
Athletic scholarships
Campus politics
Cheating
Community colleges
Counseling
Drop-outs
Ethnic quotas
Financial aid
Grading systems
Graduation requirements

Honors programs
Impacted programs
International students
Large vs. small colleges
Private vs. public education
Progressive education
ROTC
SAT scores
Student government
Teacher preparation
Tuition
Vocational education

World Politics

Human rights
England-Ireland relations
Espionage
Foreign aid
Foreign trade
Iran
Iraq
Israel and the Arabs
Nuclear disarmament

OPEC
Persian Gulf
South Africa
Soviet Union
Terrorism
Underdeveloped countries
United Nations
U.S. military strength
U.S.-Soviet relations

National Politics

Balancing the federal budget
Campaign reform
Capital gains tax
Central Intelligence Agency
Civil disobedience
Cold war
Congress
Constitutional interpretation

Military budgets
National health insurance
Political parties
Postal service
Presidency
Reforming income tax law
Socialized medicine
Star Wars

Deficit spending
Funding political campaigns

Stealth bomber
Supreme Court

Science

Acid Rain
Computerized TV commercials
Controlling the medfly
Curing AIDS
Destruction of ozone layer
Geothermal energy
Global warming
Magnetism
Nuclear power

Organ transplants
Predicting earthquakes
Psychiatry and psychology
Safe insecticides
Solar energy
Space travel
Subatomic particles
Telescope in space
Weather

Humanities

Abstract art
Can art be pornographic?
Commedia dell' arte
Dadaism
Funding the arts
Gospel music
Heavy metal
Is history true?
Japanese NO drama

Novels and novelists
Pantomime
Political poetry
Pop music
Rock concerts and mob behavior
Rock groups
Satanism in song lyrics
Shakespeare's sonnets
Theater of the absurd

Society

Abortion
Advertising
American Civil Liberties Union
Capital punishment
Child molestation
Civil rights
Crime
Divorce
Energy shortages
Environment
Euthanasia
Fairness of media reporting
Freedom of speech

Homelessness
Joblessness
Labor Unions
Natural resources
Oil spills
Pollution
Poverty
Professional sports
Race relations
Small farm depression
Teenage alcoholism
Television advertising
The drug war

Religion

Denominational schools
Druids
Education of the clergy
Election of the pope
Evolution vs. divine creation
Fundamentalism and the Bible
Great preachers
Islam
Mysticism
Native American religion

Oriental religions
Politics and religion
Religion as a business
Religious persecution
Religious war in Ireland
Science vs. religion
Separation of church and state
Taxation and religion
Television evangelism
Varieties of Judaism

Definitions

Capitalism
Communism
Conservatism
Demagoguery
Dictatorship
Ethics
Feminism
Individualism
Liberalism

Loyalty
Marriage
Morality
Propaganda
Religion
Rumor
Socialism
Success
Superstition

Notes

[1] For a definition of the kind of situation to which speech is an appropriate response, see Lloyd F. Bitzer, "The Rhetorical Situation," *Philosophy and Rhetoric* 1 (1968) 5-6.

[2] Dennis R. Smith, "The Fallacy of the Communication Breakdown," *Quarterly Journal of Speech* 56 (1970): 343-46.

[3] Lee Thayer, *Communication and Communication Systems* (Homewood, IL: Irwin, 1968) 111.

[4] Cf. Kenneth E. Boulding, *The Image* (Ann Arbor: U of Michigan P, 1956). See especially his "Introduction."

[5] Donald C. Bryant, "Rhetoric: Its Function and Its Scope," *Quarterly Journal of Speech* 39 (1953): 413.

[6] Aristotle, *The Rhetoric*, trans. Lane Cooper (New York: Appleton-Century-Crofts, 1932) xxix.

Analyzing the Audience

Our basic theme throughout this book has been (and will be) that effective public speaking is audience-centered. The communication transaction we call a speech is a shared venture between you and your audience. Competent speakers select, develop, and present their ideas with the desired audience response in mind. To do this they must ask themselves: What is this audience like? What must I do in the speech to achieve my goal? These two questions and the relationship between them are the subject of this chapter.

What Is an Audience?

Audience analysis is a basic requisite of successful public speaking. It therefore seems paradoxical that an *audience exists only as a concept in a speaker's mind.* A collection of individuals who live in the real world comprise a group. But the group is not an audience until a speaker has defined it as an audience. "Audience," then, is a word used to name a group of people in a communication situation defined by a speaker as the "target" of a message. A communication situation can be as varied as a State of the Union Address, an after-dinner conversation, or people listening to a street corner vendor. The persons involved in a communication situation do not lose their individuality; no audience shares a collective mind. The concept of an audience is no more than an *approximation* of a composite of all the individuals in it. To make the approximation useful, audience analysis must account for the knowledge and cohesiveness of the audience.

Audiences Vary in Knowledge

What an audience knows about the subject will influence the way it responds to your speech. Audience members with limited knowledge of a complex subject will quickly become irritated by too many words they don't know. A speaker who mistakenly assumes that the audience understands complicated concepts will confuse and alienate the listeners. Equally annoying is a speaker who underestimates what the listeners know and tediously explains basic information.

The problem of determining the level of knowledge of the audience is compounded by the fact that not only do audiences differ from one another in their knowledge of subjects, but individuals within any given audience will differ as well. In your classroom audience there are skiers and non-skiers, tennis players and non-tennis players, the mathematically sophisticated and the mathematically naive, those who have been to Europe and those who haven't. You must analyze the audience and adapt your speech to accomodate the level of knowledge about the subject of as many audience members as possible.

Audiences Vary in Cohesiveness

Some groups have very specific reasons for meeting, and the members share very definite beliefs and values. Other groups are not significantly united. Consider the difference between a church congregation and the crowd at a shopping center. Both groups have reasons for being where they are, but the former is a much more cohesive audience because its members probably have more in common.

However, degrees of cohesiveness differ. A congregation may be quite cohesive in church but a lot less so when they invite two candidates for mayor to debate the issues of the campaign at an open forum. People who join the Kiwanis, Rotary, or Lions clubs solely to make business contacts or who go to church "for the children" don't add to the cohesiveness of the group. Some people are even hostile to a group in which they find themselves. You have probably been disgruntled at having to sit through a required course that you would never have chosen on your own.

Ask yourself, for example, how cohesive is a typical college speech class? Here is a group of people who come from a variety of social and ethnic backgrounds and from different economic levels. They represent a number of religions, have different academic majors, and cover a broad spectrum of political preferences. There may be little agreement among them on how to handle crime, whether abortion should be subsidized for the poor, whether tighter restrictions should be placed on strip mining, or whether the President of the United States is doing a good job.

The members of this group, no matter how diverse they may be, also have much in common. By and large they are young, have similar kinds of ambitions, have had many comparable experiences, have taken several subjects in common, and have either elected or been required to take the class.

You can make a very good estimate of the degree of cohesiveness in an audience by examining its interests, its central tendency, and the particular beliefs that are salient for it.

Interests   Some groups have obvious interests. People join the Ski Club because they like skiing, the Photography Club because they enjoy photography, a church because they are religious, the PTA because they care about education, the Chamber of Commerce because they are interested in business. When the subject of your speech appeals to some strong interest of the audience, you improve the likelihood that it will listen to what you say.

Central tendency   When people meet as a group, if only for a single occasion, there is some mutual interest or some common problem to solve: a lack of information, a desire to be amused, a need for advice. Whatever the interest is, it identifies a central tendency. Think of central tendency as any set of common denominators that gives the audience a collective "momentum" toward some goal. The goal is unspecified until your speech puts it into focus.

Think of central tendency as any set of common denominators that gives the audience a collective momentum toward some goal.

But this momentum doesn't automatically move everyone in the audience in the direction you want because, no matter how precisely you tailor the materials of a speech to fit your analysis of the audience, you can expect that someone will disagree with you. What you seek, therefore, is a maximum of approval and a minimum of disapproval. You cannot, in one speech, respond to all the possible attitudes audience members may have. Design your speech to appeal to the majority of the group. What Abraham Lincoln said about not being able to fool all of the people all of the time can just as well be applied to pleasing them.

Salience   The central tendency of the audience gives you a *general* target at which to aim. But its salient beliefs—those *specific* beliefs that are most immediately relevant—will give you a more precise target. Suppose you want to convince your listeners that a certain candidate should be elected. You know the audience admires hard work. But if the audience believes the candidate is corrupt, that belief, because it is immediately relevant, will carry more weight than evidence that the candidate is a hard worker.

No matter how strongly a belief is held, if it does not apply at the moment, it will have no effect. Political beliefs, for example, are not usually salient in discussions of food, music, or sports. To be salient, a belief must not only be important to the listener, it must also be considered relevant to the immediate communication situation.

Composition of Audiences

You'll come to understand a lot about how a particular audience is likely to respond if you examine its "demographics": the interaction of its gender, age, economic position, social background, and group memberships.

Gender

Recent years have seen great changes in our society's assumptions about the differences between men and women. The feminist movement has made us aware that men and women, particularly of the educated, upper middle-class, are much more similar than we previously thought in their beliefs and values concerning professions, political activities, social action, and the like. Any student speaker today who characterizes women as husband-hunters and sees their potential only as housewives is bound to get an argument. Yet most middle-class, middle-aged men and women still see real differences in self-image and in role.

A 1988 poll of preferred sports activities revealed some interesting similarities and differences among American men and women.

> Not surprisingly, participation in many of the activities tested was greater among men than women. Hunting, for example, was engaged in by 23 percent of men but only 3 percent of women. And while the percentage of women who went fishing last year (17 percent) was large enough to make it their fifth-ranking pastime, fishing was the leading sporting activity among men, with 41 percent participating. By the same token, weight training appears in the top 10 of both sexes, but the proportion of men who worked out with weights was about twice that of women, 26 percent to 12 percent.
>
> Four of the leading leisure activities, however, were equally popular with both sexes: swimming, bicycling, bowling, and running or jogging. Only aerobics was markedly more popular among women (23 percent) than men (5 percent).[1]

Women seem to be more concerned than men about neighborhood crime, to be less satisfied with the national condition, to be less interested in space exploration, and more interested in having the government provide child-care services.[2] Personal crime and child care may be examples of what are called "women's issues" along with abortion and equal pay for equal work. However, you should note that the differences between men and women even on these issues are not always great.

As we have said, the self-image of an audience is salient. If you are addressing a group with a reasonable number of working women with children, you know that their belief in better child care and the family values salient to their situation will differ from those of the average male and perhaps from those of many other women. When self-image is not an immediate factor, as with young women without children, the potential of child rearing might be used as a basis of their interest and persuasion.

Age

In the late 1960s and early 1970s, young people seemed to be more socially concerned, even more radical, than their parents. Some observers predicted a broad change in the nation's values because of the controversy over racism and the war in Vietnam. The college students of the 1980s and 1990s seem to be strongly oriented toward practical success and financial security. Between 1970 and 1984, for instance, the percentage of entering freshmen who identified themselves as liberal declined from 37 percent to 22 percent. While the percentage identifying themselves as conservative increased little. The middle-of-the-road category gained from 45 percent to 57 percent.[3] Traditional interests in athletics and in the "Greeks" have revived. But a kind of activism can still be found in student interest in rape crisis centers, peer counseling, and opposition to nuclear power. Although active concern for religion has seemed to increase among young people in recent years, there is still a smaller percentage of church membership among them than in other age groups.

It is not surprising that young people are more likely to be rock 'n roll fans. Fifty-eight percent of 18-29 year olds identify themselves as fans, as do 40 percent of 30-49 year olds, while those 50 and older identify themselves as fans only 6 percent of the time.[4] But, on a number of social issues age provides a variety of responses. Here are some 1989 examples:[5]

Age	Members of a Church or Synagogue	Favor Increased Government Support for					
		Financial Aid for Students	Aid to Farmers	Provide Child Care	Environmental Protection	Increase Social Security	Programs for the Elderly
18-29	56%	54%	57%	48%	37%	50%	56%
30-49	65%	43%	48%	44%	43%	49%	50%
50+	76%	38%	43%	32%	36%	41%	45%

As you can see by examining these figures, there are some age differences. There are also significant similarities. While younger people are less likely than older groups to be church or synagogue members, there are still more than 50 percent of them who are members. Also, on a variety of social issues, they are more likely than older people to favor increased governmental support including increased programs for the elderly. In this instance, they are more supportive than the age group most likely to receive such services. But when this poll was taken in 1989, they were less likely to favor environmental protection than 30-49-year-olds.

Economic Position

It will come as no surprise that the greater one's wealth, the more conservative one's economic doctrine tends to be. Proposals to increase taxes (larger welfare payments, more parks, better pay for teachers) are generally considered less acceptable to those who pay the largest share of the taxes.

Statistically, more well-to-do people are Republicans and fewer affluent people are Democrats. But don't push the generalization too far, because there are, of course, poor Republicans and wealthy Democrats. Further, some recent studies indicate that willingness to pay taxes is more related to other interests than just income. People with a household income over $50,000, for instance, are more likely to support environmental protection, research on AIDS, scientific research in general, and funds to combat the drug problem. They are less likely than those with lower household incomes to favor increases in social security and payments to the elderly.[6]

Past economic experience is often more important than present economic position. People who grew up in poverty, in the ghetto, the barrio, or a poor white neighborhood, often respond as if they were still poor even though they are now in a higher economic class.

Yet it is easy to give too much significance to economic position. "Economic determinists" consider all reactions to be economically motivated, but this is only one of a number of factors that influence people's judgment.

Social Background

The past conditions of people's lives—the way they grew up and the kinds of beliefs and values their parents had—make up the social background of an audience and have a significant effect on how it will react to your ideas. You can easily imagine that the views of one group might differ from the views of any other. Does an audience meet as a group of Polish Americans? Of Japanese Americans? Of African Americans? Of Southerners? Of Methodists? Of Sons or Daughters of the American Revolution? Most people find it impossible to escape their background completely. Thus, being a Mexican American, a white Anglo-Saxon Protestant, or a Jew may often be more indicative of a listener's response than being wealthy, a woman, or 20 years old.

Group Memberships

The sex, age, economic, or social background of an audience tells you much about it, but knowing the affiliations of its members will pinpoint your analysis more sharply. The fact that an audience includes a substantial percentage of Democrats, American Legionnaires, or members of the National Organization of Women, gives you a clear indication of a number of likely responses.

People usually join groups with ideas and goals similar to their own. The group further reinforces them. The American Farm Bureau, Chamber of Commerce, or Communication Workers of America represent recognizable social and economic values. Service clubs, such as Rotary, Kiwanis, and Lions, all have projects that are important to them. Religious auxiliaries— B'nai B'rith, the Knights of Columbus, the Women's Club of the First Baptist Church—have distinctive approaches not only to questions of faith and morals, but to many other subjects as well. Political clubs have their obvious partisan views.

Many groups compose "mission statements" that specify their ideals and goals, and these are not difficult to find. Therefore, if you can identify the group memberships of an audience, you can tell much about its beliefs and values and associate your subject with them.

Identifying the Target Audience

The fact that an audience is made up of individuals doesn't mean that it has no cohesion. The fact that the people have come together suggests that they have something in common. As an audience, they interact with and influence one another. People in groups tend to respond alike more than they would if they were separated from the group. Nonetheless, there are differences among them even when they are in groups. Not all Democrats are enthusiastic about all Democratic Party policies or candidates. Not everyone at a travel lecture cares about the Amazon basin. Not everyone has an interest in sailboarding, skiing, fishing or bluegrass music. There are some people who will not be persuaded, informed, or entertained, no matter what you do. There are others who have varying degrees of interest in and support for your claim.

It is impossible to address all of the countless differences among any group of individuals. Therefore, you must identify a target audience in the group, that is, the ones who are most likely to be influenced by what you say. Somewhere amidst all of the similarities and differences in their beliefs and values they will have a central tendency. And a demographic analysis will help you discover what it is. Once you discover the central tendency of the audience you will have a better insight into who the target audience is and the means of influencing it. The best you can do for those who intractably reject your claims is to try not to offend them or make them even more negative. Concentrate on the target audience—those you can move in your direction.

Dave was well aware of the problem of cancer. His mother and his uncle had each had serious bouts with it. He wanted to talk to his public speaking class about the symptoms and causes of cancer because there are many misconceptions he believed he could counter. It would be an informative speech. No one is in favor of cancer. But many people are uninformed, misinformed, or uninterested. What would he do to define and analyze his target audience? What he had learned from the demographics of his audience and from information available from government and private sources including the American Cancer Society, helped him to classify it this way:

Audience Characteristics	This Audience	Attitude Toward Cancer
Gender	About equal men & women	Women tend to be more aware and concerned than men. More men die from cancer than do women.
Age	Mostly young—18-25 yrs. of age. Three are 30-40 yrs. old.	Young people are less likely to be concerned about cancer. But most college students are about to enter the age group (25-34) when death from cancer more than doubles over earlier ages.
Economic Position	Most of the students at this university come from lower middle class families and have to work to support themselves in school.	The less affluent people are, the less likely they are to be aware of available options or to seek help with cancer.
Social Background	Most of the students are caucasian. 3 are Mexican American, 4 African American and 1 is Chinese. Several are Catholic, like him, and the Chinese may be Buddhist but religion probably doesn't matter on this subject.	Dave believes that these differences are not as important as the other factors. However, it might be worth noting that African Americans and Mexican Americans are more likely to get cancer and die from it than are others.
Group Memberships	On this subject the most salient group membership factor is that they are students. About half are business majors and none that he knows of are preparing for a health profession.	Students tend to see themselves as learning and preparing for a more affluent future. As college students they will be more informed than many people. He will have to be careful not to be too elementary on the subject.[7]

There are people in this audience, who, like Dave, think cancer symptoms and causes are quite important, but the prevailing attitude toward the subject is probably one of indifference. There may be a bit of hostility: ''Oh, no! Not another crusader against smoking!'' How can he aim his speech at this target audience of indifferent people? How can he adapt his speech to the indifference? He will have to mention smoking; lung cancer is the only cause of cancer death that is increasing and it has more than doubled in twenty years. But there are other ways to adapt. Use examples of young people who have had cancer. Emphasize causes that are specifically relevant to their lives: the effect of freeway smog in urban areas or pesticides in rural areas. Or, ''Did you know that the paints you use in art class may contribute to cancer?'' Young people like to ''catch a few rays,'' to get a good suntan in the summer. Do they know about how the sun can cause cancer? And for students, particularly those who carry on a full schedule of school and work deadlines, how about stress—another source of cancer?

The demographic analysis of a group will help to identify the target audience. That target audience is characterized by an attitude (like indifference, curiosity, hostility, interest) toward the subject. That attitude can be addressed by a speaker who highlights the beliefs and values that respond to it.

Beliefs and Values Influence Audience Response

Audience response is significantly influenced by the beliefs and values that people hold. Understanding what those beliefs and values are, how they influence an audience's views of the world, and how you can use them will help you make your speech claims amusing, understandable or persuasive.

A *belief* can be understood as "any simple proposition, conscious or unconscious, inferred from what a person says or does, capable of being preceded by the phrase, 'I believe... .'"[8] What follows the phrase, "I believe," is a claim of fact, value, or policy.

Beliefs are virtually infinite in number. You believe that the world is round, the Rockies are high, it is a mile from home to the city hall, candy is made with sugar, and so forth. You may also believe that home videos are funny, the Oakland Athletics are the best baseball team, America is a great country, swimming is fun, and the Toyota is the most economical car. Likewise, you might believe that we should ban arms sales to foreign countries, join a church, buy a Buick, and so forth. Such specific statements, whether fact, value, or policy, are belief claims.

Values, on the other hand, are "abstract ideals, positive or negative, not tied to any specific attitude, object, or situation, representing a person's beliefs about ideal modes of conduct and ideal terminal goals."[9] Your values constitute broad bases for your behavior; you may value hard work, truthfulness, cleanliness, love, strength, or all of them. Values are general conceptions of what individuals and a society or culture regards as good or bad.

Beliefs and values function together in value systems. People do not live their lives by a single value or a single set of beliefs. Someone may judge freedom to be the most important value. But it is unlikely to be his or her *only* value. Other values, such as family, financial security, health, and self- respect would also help predict audience response, and associated with these values are countless beliefs consistent with them.[10] You can associate your claim with these other beliefs and values of your listeners as well as with those that are most salient.

In any value system there are far more beliefs than there are values. "An adult," says Milton Rokeach, "probably has tens or hundreds of thousands of beliefs . . . , but only dozens of values.''[11] Thus, it is most practical for you to base your discussion on audience values. It would be impossible to catalog all the beliefs of even one individual, and yet you can discover the most salient beliefs and the few relevant values of a target audience in the particular speaking situation. Your speech should utilize the most relevant value-belief system.

A Gallup poll taken in 1986 investigated the relative importance of eight social values (see table).

What's Important to Americans?	
(Percent rating importance very high or high)	
Having a Good Family Life	89%
Having a Good Self-Image	85%
Being in Good Physical Health	84%
Having a Sense of Accomplishment	69%
Working to Better America	67%
Following a Strict Moral Code	60%
Having an Exciting, Stimulating Life	50%
Nice Home, Car, Etc.	41%

Although the list does not constitute a complete catalog, it does give an indication of what we mean by values and some indication of their relative importance in contemporary American society.[12]

Four areas of analysis will help you to assess an audience. You want to know what beliefs and values they have about your subject, about you the speaker, about the occasion, and about themselves.

Beliefs and Values about the Subject

Generally, you have considerable leeway in deciding what to say. If you want to show how amusing campus politics can be, explain how an internal combustion engine works, or persuade an audience that a president should be elected for a single six-year term, most people will listen even though they aren't much interested in your subject. The internal combustion engine may be boring to them. "I'm no engineer," someone will think. "Why should I care?" But the same person may take pride in his or her car. To take advantage of that fact you might say, "Knowing how the engine works will help you to enjoy your car better, know when it has problems, and how to save money on repairs."

The subject, however, is yours. It's what you want to talk about, and you shouldn't reject it because of an audience attitude. You don't have to find a subject your audience agrees with or in which it is vitally interested. Instead, knowing what beliefs and values the audience is likely to associate with the subject can help you adapt your speech to the audience for greater interest and effect.

Beliefs about the Speaker

Sometimes it's really tough to make an adequate analysis of the beliefs an audience has about you. Scottish poet Robert Burns put it neatly:

> O wad some Pow'r the giftee gie us
> to see ousels as others see us!
> It wad frae monie a blunder free us
> And foolish notion. . . .

One natural but erroneous assumption is that others see you as you see yourself. The fact is that audiences use pretty much the same system to classify speakers as speakers use to sort out audiences. To an audience, speakers are engineering majors, football players, professors, or what have you. Nonetheless, you want to know as much as you can about what an audience thinks of you, no matter how erroneous its view may be.

A Gallup Poll in 1988 showed sharp differences among Americans in how they rate members of 25 professions on honesty and ethical standards.[13] Speakers need to consider such attitudes in preparing to speak.

Honesty and Ethical Standards — Overview			
	Very High and High		*Very High and High*
Druggists, Pharmacists	66%	Senators	19%
Clergymen	60	Lawyers	18
College teachers	54	Business executives	16
Medical doctors	53	Congressmen	16
Dentists	51	Local officeholders	14
Engineers	48	Labor union leaders	14
Policemen	47	Real estate agents	13
Bankers	26	Stockbrokers	13
Funeral directors	24	State officeholders	11
Journalists	23	Insurance salesmen	10
TV reporters, Commentators	22	Advertising practitioners	7
Newspaper reporters	22	Car salesmen	6
Building contractors	22		

An element of what makes you believable is your reputation with the audience. You can enhance your credibility during the speech (see Chapter 12) if you know the audience's opinion of you before you begin.

Beliefs about the Occasion

The way you handle a speech subject is strongly influenced by the way the audience perceives the speech occasion. Chapter 20 deals more specifically with the kinds of special occasions that demand a particular kind of speech such as welcomes, farewells, eulogies and commendations. If the occasion has some special meaning for the listeners, you can build interest by identifying your subject with it. Holiday speeches invariably do this. The speaker at a Labor Day meeting may talk about world affairs, but the subject will also relate to the aspirations of workers. At religious meetings, people expect certain values to emerge. Even if you don't share those values, you still have to recognize that they are a strong influence on the lives of the audience. Other occasions may not demand the same degree of adaptation. For instance, a sermon requires more adaptation than a speech at a church picnic.

Beliefs about Itself

What listeners think about themselves affects how they respond to a speech. Consider two men sitting side by side at a lodge meeting. Although one is a Democrat and the other a Republican, on this occasion they think of themselves as lodge members. For the present, they submerge their political differences and think of themselves as "brothers." Although their religious convictions, political loyalties, and economic stations are dormant for the time, they are still factors. You can arouse these associations to your own advantage or disadvantage.

Beliefs about self will also be related directly to beliefs about a message and about the speaker. A political science professor stops on campus to chat with the lead cellist of the university symphony; they discuss music. Beliefs and values about oneself on this occasion are considerably different from attitude toward self when comparative government is being discussed in the classroom.

Speakers who affront the beliefs of others do so at their own risk. An extraordinary instance of insensitivity was highly publicized in 1983. In part, it cost Secretary of the Interior James Watt his job. In a misguided effort to show how free of bias he was, the Secretary forgot that minority group members, women, and the handicapped resent being labelled a group rather than as individuals with singular qualifications for the job. He gave this description of a committee he had appointed: "We have every kind of mix you can have. I have a black, I have a woman, two Jews and a cripple. And we have talent." [14]

Speakers who affront the beliefs of others do so at their own risk, as James Watt quickly learned.

Applying Audience Analysis

It's impossible for you to say all there is to say on any subject. What you do say should be influenced by your audience analysis. The information you uncover will help you adapt to the audience not only in preparing the speech but during and after the speech as well.

Audience Analysis in Speech Preparation

After you have analyzed the audience, the next step is to decide how to use the information. At this stage you have time to adapt your speech in all the facets of preparation: selecting appropriate claims, speech organization, supporting material, values, credibility, language, delivery.

Claims you need to prove Not all of the claims you make will have to be proved, because the audience will accept some of them without question. Others are at issue. Returning to our example of federal licensing of all firearms, your sub-claims would probably include these two: "Gun-related crimes are a serious problem,'' and ''Federal licensing of guns is constitutional.'' The first of these two claims is widely accepted and need not be argued at length. The constitutional claim is clearly controversial and needs support.

It is also true that controversial claims need different amounts of proof. For instance, some listeners may have little interest in technical arguments about constitutionality but may be quite concerned about losing the protection they feel they get from a gun. Your analysis of the audience helps you decide not only which claims are controversial but also which of them require more extensive proof.

Speech organization   There are many methods of organizing a speech. You will select the one that seems best suited to your subject and to the occasion. If you were explaining how to tune an automobile engine, a chronological step-by-step organization would probably be the most useful. In addition, your audience's knowledge of the subject would help you decide which points to emphasize most. In a persuasive speech, the extent to which the audience accepts or rejects your claim would influence how you might organize the speech. If you favored gun registration and you thought your audience was opposed, you might want to deal with the least controversial claims first and delay the more controversial ones until later.

Amount of supporting material   The amount of material needed to clarify or prove a specific point varies in relation to audience need. In a speech to inform, for example, you will need few specific details if you think the audience will quickly understand a given point. The keynote speaker at a political convention, delivering a persuasive speech, judges the amount of evidence needed to support arguments knowing that the members of the convention already agree with virtually all of the points to be made. When allocating student body funds to various campus activities, the student council may cut the budget for the opera program based on the lack of student interest in classical music. A speaker who is asking for more money for the opera program may need to give a great deal of evidence to the group.

Kind of supporting material   When you collect material for a speech, you will find more than you can use. Your selection from the pool of information you have gathered is made in light of your audience analysis. You will choose quotations not only because they say exactly what you want to say but also because the authorities you quote are respected by your audience. You will draw illustrations from the experiences that will make the most sense to your immediate audience. In a talk on the peaceful uses of atomic energy, you will need a different and simpler kind of material for students who have never had a physics course than would be the case if they had some knowledge of the subject.

Targeting appropriate beliefs and values   The most useful aspect of audience analysis is the help it gives you in deciding what beliefs and values concerning your subject are most salient to the target audience. For example, suppose you are talking to your sister about the rehabilitation and punishment of criminals. She has high humanitarian values and assumes that people are essentially good. She very likely might believe that severe punishment such as long mandatory prison terms or the death penalty is unacceptable. These are the salient beliefs and values for her in this situation. If your view is that vocational training and work-release for criminals is the best policy, her salient beliefs and values will work for you. But if you want to argue for prison terms for drunken drivers, you will have to emphasize other beliefs and values that she might hold in order to help her see the situation as you do. You might emphasize the success of stronger punishment in recent years on curbing DUI or the danger of having such persons on the road.

Credibility Credibility is the quality which gives an audience the confidence to believe that you know what you are talking about and can be trusted to tell the truth. It is not something that is inherent in you; rather, it is *ascribed* to you by your listeners. So, when your listeners expect you to dress up, speak in formal English, and provide evidence from intellectual sources, your decision to do or not to do these things will influence your credibility with them.

Language The kind of language you would use in speaking to a labor union local might be quite unsuited to a board meeting of corporate directors, even though the subject matter could be substantially the same. The principal difference between the two groups—as far as language is concerned, at any rate—is in the differing levels of education you would expect to find among the listeners. What we said earlier in the chapter about the different levels of knowledge among audiences is relevant here.

Delivery Like language, delivery can be too elaborate for an audience. Queen Victoria said of her prime minister, "Mr. Gladstone always addresses me as if I were a public meeting." The level of intensity in voice and physical action appropriate to an occasion is dependent on the audience. Your audience analysis will suggest whether to use a vigorous delivery or to be calm and relaxed.

Audience Analysis during the Speech

While you may do a lot of careful audience analysis before the speech, there are several additional steps you can take in the actual communication situation. When you are invited to speak at a meeting of a group you do not know, be sure to go a little early, talk to the leader, and if possible, some of the members in advance about their group. Ask them about themselves and others in the group. Check out your predictions about their beliefs and values. Look for specific references you can make to identify with this audience.

While you are giving the speech, be alert to the reactions you get. If the audience responds quickly to a claim, you will know the claim doesn't need much support. If the audience seems to be knowledgeable, you can give more complex explanations than you had planned. Remember, your speech is a shared venture between you and your audience. Respond to your listeners' feedback.

To be useful, audience feedback must not be unduly colored by what you *want* it to be. That is, make sure that you don't attribute your own beliefs and values to the audience. It can be disastrous to assume that others understand or believe things in the same way that you do.

Audience Analysis after the Speech

Learning to be an effective speaker is not a one-time experience. It is an ongoing process. So, when you make mistakes in a speech, you can avoid them in the future. Take a few moments after a speech to remind yourself what your assumptions were about the audience; make a list of the main ones. Then check them against the responses you got during the speech and afterwards. In cases where you were in error, think how the error came about and decide how best to avoid it in the future.

Summary

A speech is a transaction between you and your audience. A group is only a collection of people. It becomes an audience as a concept in a speaker's mind. The speaker has to define the target audience of the speech. Individual members will have different interpretations of a speaking situation and their role in it. Audiences vary in knowledge, and their level of knowledge helps to determine how they respond to the subject. They vary in cohesiveness depending on their interests, central tendency, and salience.

It is easier to discover a target audience if you look at five demographic factors: gender, age, economic position, social background, and group memberships. These won't tell you everything and sometimes you can be fooled, but they will help to give you a general understanding of the group.

You need to identify your target audience by noting how its demographic factors relate to the subject of your speech. This shows you the attitudes of your target audience. From this you can determine what you must do to make your speech effective.

The beliefs and values of an audience are probably most important in influencing audience responses. Beliefs are simple propositions that are virtually infinite in number. Values are abstract ideas contributing to a conception of the ideal mode of behavior or terminal goals. Beliefs and values function together in systems and influence responses to speeches.

It is useful to know the kinds of beliefs and values an audience has about your subject, you as a speaker, the occasion, and about itself.

Your audience analysis can help you to determine the amount and kind of material you need, which claims you need to prove, your speech organization, audience values, how to enhance your credibility, and what language and delivery will be appropriate. During the speech you can test your analysis by the reactions you receive. Afterwards, it is wise to check your original analysis against actual reactions to avoid future errors.

Key Terms

Audience	Gender
Group	Age
Knowledge	Economic position
Cohesiveness	Social background
Interests	Group membership
Central tendency	Target audience
Salient beliefs	Beliefs
Demographics	Values

Exercises

1. Write a brief paper (no more than three double-spaced, typewritten pages) in which you explain what you need to know about one of your parents or a brother or sister before you ask a favor. You will probably find it easier to write this paper if you select a specific favor to ask. Your purpose in this paper is to make an "audience" analysis of that one person, so do not write about the techniques you would use to get the favor. For instance, what do you need to know about your father's ideas and attitudes in order to successfully ask him to let you use his car for the weekend?

2. Select any one of the five demographic factors in the composition of an audience (gender, age, economic position, social background, and group membership). Also select for consideration some specific question of current news interest. How do you think the attitudes of any two groups of people within the classification (for example, men and women, teenagers and middle-aged people, well-to-do people and poor people, African Americans and Caucasians) would differ *generally* on the question? What limitations do you see in this generalization? If you believe that there are no differences on the question you have chosen, explain why you believe so.

3. Make a careful and honest assessment of yourself as an "audience" for a speaker on a specific subject. What do people who wish to communicate with you on that subject, have to know about you?

4. Conduct a discussion in class with four or five other students about the following subjects and audiences. Which demographic factors are most important, and what beliefs and values will come into play in each of the nine possible combinations?

Subject	Audience
• To inform the audience about the training of a fashion model.	► Young Mexican American women college students from urban areas.
• To persuade the audience to support the university football team.	► Mostly white Protestant men of at least 40 years of age who own small businesses.
• To persuade the audience to support an immediate reduction in federal taxes.	► Mostly white students of both sexes at a Roman Catholic college.

Do certain factors seem less important than others? Which are most difficult for your group to analyze? Do some factors immediately give you some clues as to how you ought to prepare your speech for maximum effectiveness? What is each audience's attitude likely to be toward you?

5. With four or five classmates, develop an analysis of the class as an audience for a speech on a specific subject selected by your instructor. Share your findings with the class. Do they agree with you? What factors did you analyze correctly? On which did you miss?

6. For one of your classroom speeches assigned by your instructor, turn in a one-page analysis of how your speech is adapted to the audience.

7. For one of your classroom speeches assigned by your instructor, turn in a one-page analysis of how you might change the speech if you were to give it to a different audience.

Notes

[1] "Swimming, Fishing, Bicycling are Top Sports Activities," *Gallup Report* 281 (Feb. 1989): 28.

[2] "Public Supports Higher Taxes for Domestic Program: Education Drug War Leads the List," *Gallup Report* 289 (Oct. 1989): 10; "American Patriotism Running High," *Gallup Report* 249 (June 1986): 15; "Fear of Crime Pervasive, But Trend Appears Stable,"*Gallup Report* 282-83 (Mar./Apr. 1989): 7.

[3] "Why It's All Quiet On The Campus Front," *US News And World Report* 31 Jan. 1984: 44-47; Terry W. Hartle and John Taylor, "What's Big on Campus," *Public Opinion* 8 (Aug./Sept. 1985): 50.

[4] "20 Years Later, Woodstock Era Gets Mixed Reviews," *Gallup Report* 287 (Aug. 1989): 32.

[5] "Public Image of TV Evangelists Deteriorates," *Gallup Report* 288 (Sept. 1989): 19; "Public Supports,": 10; "Proposals to Trim Aid to Elderly Meet With Stiff

Public Opposition,'' *Gallup Report* 284 (May 1989): 20-21.

6 ''Proposals,'' 20-21.

7 The information in this example is taken from a variety of sources including *Vital Statistics of the United States 1986*, U.S. Department of Health and Human Services (Hyattsville, MD: 1988) 336; American Cancer Society, *Cancer Facts and Figures — 1987*; ''Winning the Battle Against Cancer,'' *Black Enterprise* 19 (Oct. 1988) 76.

8 Milton Rokeach, *Beliefs, Attitudes and Values* (San Francisco: Jossey Bass, 1968) 113.

9 Rokeach, 124.

10 Richard D. Rieke and Malcolm O. Sillars, *Argumentation and the Decision Making Process* (Chicago: Scott Foresman, 1984) 109-10.

11 Rokeach, 124.

12 George Gallup, ''Public Holds Moderate Values on Social Issues,'' *Gallup Report* 249 (June 1986): 22-23.

13 ''Honesty and Ethical Standards,'' *Gallup Report* 279 (Dec. 1988): 3.

14 ''James Watt Strikes Again,'' *US News and World Report* 31 Jan 1984: 44-47; Steve Goldzwig, ''James Watt's Subversion of Values: An Analysis of Rhetorical Failure,'' *Southern Speech Communication Journal* 50 (1985): 305-26.

chapter *7*

Analyzing the Subject

I. Analysis in speech preparation

II. Analyzing the subject of a speech to entertain

III. Analyzing the subject of a speech to inform

IV. Analyzing the subject of a speech to persuade
   A. Issues defined
   B. Analyzing policy claims
      1. Finding the issues
      2. Phrasing the issues
      3. Reducing the number of issues
      4. Using stock issues
   C. Analyzing claims of fact and value

V. The five possible sources of issues
   A. Need for a change
   B. Criteria
   C. Relative importance of the criteria
   D. Meeting the criteria
   E. Evidence

VI. How to use the analysis
   A. To indicate lines of argument
   B. To determine emphasis
   C. To group arguments

At the beginning of Chapter 5 we asked you to imagine a speech that has neither a subject nor a purpose. You can't, of course. Now try something equally unlikely. Imagine delivering a speech when you don't care whether the audience understands what you say. Silly, isn't it? You always want your audience to understand your subject. That's true for speeches of any type in any context.

The principal reason you have to make the audience understand is that a speech is meant to solve some problem for the audience. A speech can't do that unless you give the audience a clear understanding of what the subject is all about. But you also want to be understood in the sense you intend. In this chapter, we are going to examine the concept of subject analysis. This is a set of procedures that will help you make the audience understand correctly.

Analysis in Speech Preparation

Recall what you read in Chapter 5 about the different general purposes of speaking and the type of speech you construct in order to attain each of these goals.

General purpose (goal)	Speech type
To amuse the audience ——————————	A speech to entertain
To bring about understanding ——————	A speech to inform
To influence belief or action ——————	A speech to persuade

You will always know whether you plan to entertain, inform, or persuade. The audience, however, has to discover your intention from what you say. But even though your listeners don't know in advance what you're going to talk about, they bring with them a "mind-set," formed by whatever beliefs and values they have about your subject.

In Chapter 6 we addressed the question, "What do I know about the mind-set of the target audience that can help me reach my goal?" Audience analysis answers the question by telling you what the beliefs and values of that audience might be and how those influences affect the way a listener tends to react. In this chapter, we ask, "What approach to this subject will best help me reach my goal?" A more precise way of putting the question is, "How can I handle this topic so that I can defuse or resolve any disagreements that exist between me and my audience?"

It's pretty obvious that in persuasive speaking, disagreements are easy to find. If there weren't any, there would be no need for persuasion. But what kind of disagreements would you find in a speech to entertain or to inform? Audiences shouldn't object to being amused or being given a new understanding, so how could such claims be controversial?

The fact is, though, that all subjects are controversial. For example, think of such topics as the origin of the earth, abortion, the death penalty, and sexual values. They are surrounded by all sorts of disagreements, not only between you and the audience but among the listeners themselves. These varying opinions grow out of the preexisting beliefs and values of the people involved.

Look at it from the listener's point of view. Someone makes a speech to entertain, poking fun at the way the county board of supervisors handles the disposal of toxic wastes. But something happens in the speech to make a listener say, "I don't think toxic waste is funny." On another occasion, a member of the audience responds to a straightforward description of the disposal sites for toxic wastes by saying, "How can you defend those polluters?" In a third example, a speaker argues for safe disposal sites but gets the reaction, "Sure, your plan would do the job, but you never told us how to pay for it." Here too, something has clearly gone wrong.

These are not necessarily cases of poor listening or confused listeners. Instead, the speakers should re-evaluate their identification of the target audience. In every case, the audience analysis failed to recognize the listeners' beliefs and values. In the first instance, the humor simply didn't get through, perhaps because it seemed to poke fun at the wrong thing — to make light of the problem, or to deride those who are concerned. In the next case, perhaps the listener's strong negative feelings on the subject make even an informative speech on the topic seem argumentative. As a result, a speech that doesn't present an outright defense of the listener's position is perceived as an attack on it. In the third example, although the proposal for solving a recognized problem is admittedly attractive, the arguments fail to answer one of the listener's serious concerns.

In all three of the examples, what the listener understands comes into conflict with what the speaker means. The speaker's approach to the subject somehow missed the point. Therefore, the speech failed to solve any problem for the audience.

In making a speech to entertain or inform, you have to find a way to prevent conflicts from interfering with your purpose. In speaking to persuade, you must know what conflicts must be resolved. The problem is, "How?" Analysis of the subject is a necessary part of the solution.

Analysis is *the activity of dividing something into its parts to get a better understanding of the whole.* Speakers aren't the only ones who use analysis as a method of investigation. Among others, philosophers, mathematicians, chemists and linguists use some form of analysis in their work.

When you prepare a speech, you'll use analysis in several different ways. In the previous chapter, you discovered how audience analysis helps you find your target audience and adapt to it — finding the beliefs and values that are salient to a discussion of any particular topic. In this chapter, we will show you how to analyze a specific subject in order to link your speech claim to the beliefs and values of the target audience.

Let's turn now to the kinds of subject analysis you use in speeches to entertain, to inform, and to persuade.

Analyzing the Subject of a Speech to Entertain

Many people seem to think that speeches to entertain have only one purpose—to make the audience laugh. That will usually be the principal goal, but it's relatively rare for a speaker to have the sole intention of amusing people. Of course, all speeches should be entertaining—otherwise, no one would listen to them. But the speech to entertain has the special goal to make the audience laugh and uses humor as the principal support for ideas.

Mark Twain was a humorist, but he wasn't just looking for laughs. He was a surgeon, trying to cut out the foibles of society and using humor as his scalpel. The same is true of many other speakers and writers—George Bernard Shaw, Will Rogers, Art Buchwald, and Dick Cavett, for example. In other words, speeches to entertain are not the sole property of stand-up comedians and after-dinner speakers. With the probable exception of funeral orations, virtually any subject or occasion can produce a speech to entertain.

An entertainment and a speech to entertain are different in the way a comic strip differs from a political cartoon. Both can be funny, but they use different kinds of humor to achieve different goals. Think of speaking to entertain as an approach to a topic that would (except for the fact that amusement is the principal goal) be a speech to inform or persuade. Let's return to our earlier example. On one occasion, you can discuss current methods of nuclear waste disposal and be very serious about it. The goal of that speech is to inform, to make the target audience understand. At another time, you can speak on exactly the same subject but talk about the funny things that happened on the way to the dump. In both cases you may be quite serious about the problem, but in the second instance, your primary purpose is to make the audience laugh—not at the nuclear waste, but at the way it is handled, the dumb things that happen to it, or perhaps at the society that creates it.

Read the following paragraph from a speech of welcome delivered by Mark Twain in Hartford, Connecticut at a dinner to honor a visiting Englishman, Cornelius Walford. Hartford was and is a center for the insurance business, and the general subject of the speech is insurance. Twain's purpose is to amuse his audience by satirizing the insurance industry.

> There is nothing more beneficial than accident insurance. I have seen an entire family lifted out of poverty and into affluence by the simple boon of a broken leg. I have had people come to me on crutches, with tears in their eyes, to bless this beneficent institution. In all my experience of life, I have seen nothing so seraphic as the look that comes into a freshly mutilated man's face when he feels in his vest pocket with his remaining hand and finds his accident ticket all right. And I have seen nothing so sad as the look that came into another splintered customer's face when he found he couldn't collect on a wooden leg.[1]

Without Twain's special brand of satire, the subject would be quite ordinary. Although Twain himself was a director of an accident-insurance company, he saw the opportunity to spoof insurance companies in general.

When you prepare a speech to entertain, your analysis should point out areas of the subject which you can make the audience see as comical, quaint, absurd, or droll. Your analysis of the audience suggests how to avoid controversies related to the audience's attitudes toward the subject. Don't let the audience be diverted from your purpose by disputes that are irrelevant to it.

Analyzing the Subject of a Speech to Inform

The method of analyzing an informative speech subject is very much like the one you use when you prepare a speech to entertain, but it has this significant difference. In a speech to entertain, your analysis looks for areas of the subject where you can amuse the audience. When you prepare a speech to inform, a successful analysis brings to light the elements of the subject that will help your audience understand it clearly and correctly.

One of the ways people sort out the physical world is by dividing it into classes of objects: animal, vegetable, mineral. The United States Government can be divided into its legislative, executive, and judicial branches. The parts of a symphony orchestra are the string, brass, woodwind, and percussion sections. In all these examples, the important question is: What are the significant and reasonable parts of the subject? Here too, keep in mind that you want to discuss the subject in a way that will avoid controversies stemming from the beliefs and values of the listeners if those influences are irrelevant to the subject.

You will see a special case of this objective when your purpose is to inform an audience about a controversy. Suppose, for instance, that you want to explain the debate over disposing nuclear waste in the caverns of the southwestern United States. You would use the same kind of analysis you would for a persuasive speech. But, rather than trying to persuade the audience to favor or to oppose the plan, you would only explain the conflicting positions. Giving the impression that you preferred one side or the other would generate an unnecessary and irrelevant challenge from those who held the opposite view.

Look again at the section in Chapter 2 that discusses the body of the speech. You'll see several examples of how speech subjects are analyzed into parts that will make the topic clear. Incidentally, when you read that section, and again when you read about the different types of speeches in Part V, you will see how strongly analysis of the subject influences the way you organize the body of a speech.

So far, we have promoted the utility of analysis as a method of *avoiding* a clash between speaker and audience. Any such dispute would stand as a barrier to the speaker's goal. The function of persuasive analysis, on the

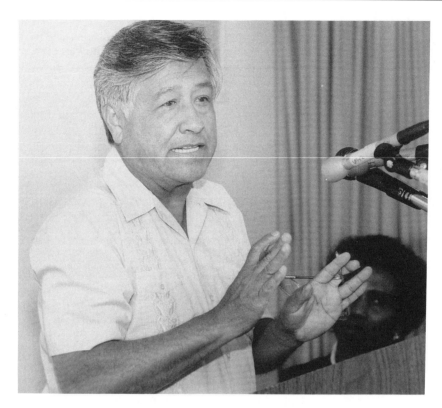

The subject of every speech is a claim of fact, value, or policy that asks the audience to make a change in how it views the world.

other hand, is to find the areas of disagreement. The purpose of persuasive speaking is to resolve them. Consequently, the method of analyzing a subject for persuasion is significantly different from the ones we have looked at so far. The rest of this chapter will explore the various elements in a persuasive speech topic.

Analyzing the Subject of a Speech to Persuade

The subject of every speech is a claim of fact, value, or policy that asks the audience to make some kind of change in how it views the world, what it believes, or how it acts. Reasoning is inherent in all speeches, of course, but in persuasion you use it to build arguments that prove your claim. To accomplish this, you have to understand issues, because success in persuasion depends largely on arguments that address the issues.

Issues Defined

Today, conditions in a number of foreign countries are driving hundreds and thousands of their citizens to look for political refuge and economic opportunity in the United States. But they don't have visas, nor have they applied for citizenship. The Federal government at one time offered amnesty to illegal aliens who met certain conditions. If you supported the amnesty plan, how would you persuade other people to approve it? You could argue that historically the United States has given refuge to victims of tyranny and starvation. You could also argue that these people make up a much-needed labor pool to do work that most American citizens won't do. Or you could emphasize practicality and economics: it's impossible to keep them out; it's too difficult and too expensive to find them, arrest them, and deport them.

Even though your arguments seem reasonable, the audience might refuse to support you. Why? Ask them. They might say, "Look, I'm as sympathetic as anyone to the needs of the illegal immigrants. But don't you see what's happening? They're putting too heavy a burden on our welfare system."

This is a serious objection to the plan you're supporting. You may believe that their thinking is all wrong, but that's no answer. If you want to persuade them, you have to find the right answer to this question: Do illegal immigrants put too much burden on the welfare system? That question is a precise example of what we mean by an *issue*. Issues are *questions that must be answered yes or no and which identify the point of dispute between opposing claims*. In this case:

Claim	Counterclaim
The immigrants put too much pressure on the welfare system	The immigrants do not put too much pressure on the welfare system

Issue

Do the immigrants put too much
pressure on the welfare system?

Unless you know what issues stand between you and your listeners, your arguments will answer their objections only by sheer luck. But you don't want to depend on luck when you're trying to justify a claim that's important to you. It doesn't matter whether the claim is one of policy, value, or fact, analysis of the controversy is the method you use to find issues.

Analyzing Policy Claims

Policy claims are more complicated to analyze than claims of fact or value. Moreover, they are analyzed by a different method. Here's an example of analysis based on the well-known flag-burning controversy.

No matter which side you take, here is how you would analyze the policy claim "The Constitution of the United States should be amended to give

Congress the power to regulate and protect the use, dignity and integrity of the flag.''[2]

Finding the issues   First draw a line down the center of a sheet of paper. On the left side, list all the claims you can find that support the proposal. On the right side of the page, list the claims that oppose it. Match the opposing claims by pairing them against each other. For instance;

For the amendment	Against the amendment
This vital and wellprepared proposal demands immediate attention.	The proposal is an emotional reaction that needs further thought before we take action.

Sometimes the same claim can be made by both sides:

For the amendment	Against the amendment
The flag holds a unique place in our national life.	The flag holds a unique place in our national life.

Assertions undisputed by either side are called waived matter. Anyone debating this subject would accept as waived matter statements such as, ''Burning a flag is a form of protest against the government,'' and ''Not all forms of self-expression are protected by the First Amendment.''

Sometimes you will find an argument that has no opposition, at least none that you have seen.

For the amendment	Against the amendment
It is inconsistent to permit flag-burning (a form of obscenity) when obscenity is not protected.	No apparent argument

An unopposed argument automatically constitute waived matter. The very fact that an argument is offered suggests the existence of an issue. To make the analysis complete, construct an argument that will clarify the dispute.

For the amendment	Against the amendment
It is inconsistent to permit flag-burning (a form of obscenity) when obscenity is not protected.	There can not be an inconsistency because burning a flag is not an obscenity.

When you have eliminated waived matters and have set the opposing arguments up against each other, your analysis sheet will look something like this:

For the amendment	Against the amendment
This well-prepared proposal demands immediate attention.	The proposal is a hasty and emotional reaction that needs further thought before any action is taken.
It is inconsistent to permit flag-burning (a form of obsenity) when obsenity is not protected.	It is not inconsistent because burning a flag is not an obscenity.
This amendment would reinforce law and order in the nation.	The amendment would lead to the kind of lawlessness the country experienced during prohibition.
Patriotism is more important than letting someone destroy our country's most cherished symbol.	Patriotism is important, of course, but if it comes to a choice, fostering patriotism has to take a back seat to protecting freedom of expression.
The flag has never been desecrated by anyone who can be called a true patriot.	The act of burning the flag has often been a call to high patriotism.

Phrasing the issues   After the analysis sheet has been prepared, it is much easier to see where the arguments conflict. The next step is to phrase each clash as a yes-or-no question. Those questions are the *issues*. For example:

For the amendment	Against the amendment
It is inconsistent to permit flag-burning (a form of obscenity) when obscenity is not protected.	It is not inconsistent because burning the flag is not an obscenity.

The Issue
Is the act of burning the flag an obscenity?

Be sure all of the issues are properly stated. This is *not* an issue: "How serious is the threat to freedom of speech today?" It isn't a yes-or-no question; it presents no clash between two *clearly opposed* points of view. Moreover, it assumes that there is a threat to freedom of speech when in fact that point itself is in dispute.

Reducing the number of issues   Some issues need not be argued because the audience would consider them trivial.

For the amendment	Against the amendment
The flag has been desecrated more often by women than by men.	That's not true, but who wants to argue over a minor point like that?

Some issues need not be argued because they are *irrelevant*.

For the amendment	Against the amendment
Desecration of the flag is the result of the attitudes of the "me generation."	That claim is both simplistic and untrue, but in any event it has nothing to do with the case at hand.

Whenever possible, combine issues that overlap. At first glance, the two issues that follow seem to identify two separate points of conflict.

Issue: Would amending the Constitution create a threat to the stability of the nation?

Issue: Is there danger that a new amendment would bring back evils like the days of prohibition?

In fact, however, the second question is only a narrowing and a specification of the first, not a separate issue.

When the job of analyzing the claim is finished, you'll have a list of issues that would very likely include many of these:

Issue: Has the proposal for a constitutional amendment been well thought out?

Issue: Is criticizing the government by burning the flag a form of obscenity?

Issue: Would the amendment reinforce respect for law and order?

Issue: Is patriotism more important than freedom of expression?

Issue: Can anyone who burns a flag be patriotic?

Using stock issues   Some issues, as we have shown, are irrelevant or trivial. Instead of arguing these insignificant points, it is more important to discover the crucial, specific issues that will actually decide the case in a listener's mind. The so-called stock issues are helpful in doing this.

To prove any policy claim, your arguments have to persuade the audience to say "yes" to three questions that are inherent in every policy dispute. (That's why they're called stock issues: they apply to all policy debates.) These questions identify the general areas where the crucial, specific issues are found.

1. *Is there a need for a change?* When you advise an audience to vote for legislation or a candidate you support, or to invest money or time in your project, or to adopt **any** course of action you propose, you're asking them to change their lives in some way. People aren't easily motivated to change. If they are satisfied with their world as it is, they

won't feel a need to change. They might say, for instance, "Flag-burning isn't a big problem. Why should we bother to stop it?" A new policy will be attractive only when it is presented as the solution to a felt need.

2. *Is the proposed new policy desirable?* A proposal will be appealing only when it promises an overall improvement on the present situation. Even then, it will be attractive only if the audience is dissatisfied with the *status quo*.

3. *Is the proposed new policy workable?* When the plan is unworkable (for example, the cost is prohibitive, or the political climate makes it unacceptable), the audience won't approve it.

The stock issues identify the general areas that have to be decided in policy disputes, but they don't define the specific issues you must resolve in order to prove your claim. The crucial questions are related to the stock issues, but they are much more specific. People ask:

"Does permitting desecration of the flag lead to the destruction of patriotism?" (first stock issue).
"Has this proposal been well thought out?" (second stock issue).
"Could such an amendment be enforced?" (third stock issue).

A speech that fails to satisfy an audience in the general area covered by any one of the stock issues is sure to fail with a critical audience. Any issue that is not essential to deciding one of the stock issue questions is either irrelevant or trivial.

Analyzing Claims of Fact and Value

A policy claim says that something should be done. Its proof is based on claims of fact (assertions about actual conditions) and claims of value (statements that assign levels of virtue and vice).

Claims of fact and value consist of two parts, a subject term which refers to something or someone, and a judgment term which in a word, phrase, or clause asserts something about the subject term. The claim alleges that the judgment term can reasonably be attributed to the subject term. "Flying saucers are real," is a factual claim. It says that the saucers are not just imaginary, that they actually exist. "*Star Trek* is the best television series ever made," makes a value claim. It says that the quality of being "best" can properly be ascribed to *Star Trek*. Like all other claims that aren't self-evident to an audience, they are debatable. Analyzing them brings to light the issues that make them controversial.

The first step in this kind of analysis is to define the judgment term. In the on-going dispute over proposals to permit prayer in public schools, proponents claim that participation in the prayer will be totally voluntary. Here the subject term is "participation in the prayer" and the judgment term is "totally voluntary." How should we define a voluntary act? It is "something done by one's own free choice—willingly undertaken without force or threat." The act is "totally" voluntary if outside pressures are completely absent.

If this definition of the judgment term is acceptable, it will be a criterion for measuring the quality of the evidence that supports the claim. A criterion is a standard for making a judgment. That is, to prove that participation will be "voluntary," the evidence must show that it will meet the criterion of "a complete absence of force or threat." If an argument persuades the audience that a particular plan has these characteristics, it will accept the claim that any participation in a school prayer would be voluntary.

In analyzing the subject of a speech to persuade, we have discussed a general definition of issues and how that definition helps us identify the issue in both policy claims and claims of fact and value. Let's explore the subject of issues more specifically and then conclude with how to use the analysis.

The Five Possible Sources of Issues

Understanding issues isn't nearly as complicated as it sounds. Every issue you find will evolve from one or another of five possible sources. Understanding which is the actual source of an issue will tell you what kind of argument you must use in order to resolve it.

1. Is there a need for a change?
2. Do you have the right criteria, acceptably defined?
3. Are the criteria given the proper relative importance?
4. Does the proposed plan meet the criteria?
5. Is the evidence correct?

Need for a Change

The most basic question in a policy dispute is the first stock issue: "Is there a need for a change?" Are the problems of the *status quo* severe enough to demand a new policy?

When Willard C. Butcher, Chairman of the Chase Manhattan Corporation, spoke to the World Affairs Council of Orange County, California, his purpose was to offer a solution to the trade deficit of the United States. He said, "Before I propose that solution, however, let's see if we agree on the urgency of the problem."[3] He knew that it would do no good to offer a plan until his audience was aware of the need for a new policy.

Look again at the proposal to protect the flag with a constitutional amendment. This question never became an actual issue in the Congressional debate because so few government leaders agreed with the Supreme Court decision. If you were in favor of the amendment, then, it would have been a waste of time to insist that we have to do something to protect the flag. That claim was acknowledged. The argument, therefore, missed the point because what Congress had to decide was not whether something needs to be done, but whether amending the constitution was the best thing to do.

Criteria

The only reasonable way to judge a proposal is to have a set of standards (criteria) for evaluating it. For two reasons, the criteria themselves are a potential source of issues.

First, there can be disagreement over how to define the judgment term of a claim. You'd never maintain that Abraham Lincoln was a "great" president because, (1) he was more than 6 feet 3 inches tall, (2) wore a stovepipe hat, and (3) was in office during a time of war. Lincoln met all of these criteria, but they are a silly way to define a great president.

In the case of flag desecration, everyone would agree that any proposed constitutional amendment must be consistent with the First Amendment. In other words, freedom of expression is an undisputed criterion. But proponents of the amendment argue that burning a flag is profane, therefore it is an obscenity and not protected by the First Amendment. Opponents answer with the counter-argument that burning a flag is protected by the First Amendment because, even if it were a profane act, to say that a "profane" act is "obscene" is utter foolishness. The issue, then, is whether it makes any sense to define a profane act as an obscenity.

Secondly, even when a criterion is acceptably defined, it can generate an issue. For example, the claim, "The administration of such an amendment would be too costly for the taxpayers" might draw the response "We shouldn't even consider cost when we're protecting the dignity of our flag." The issue to be decided becomes "Is cost a relevant criterion for making a judgment in this dispute?"

Relative Importance of the Criteria

Even when there is agreement on what the criteria should be and how they should be defined, there can be disputes over what rank order of importance they should have. To maintain patriotism and to protect free speech are both desirable goals, yet the two can come into conflict.

> "In my book, patriotism is more important than any law that lets you destroy our country's most cherished symbol. That would be like having open season on the bald eagle."

> "Patriotism is important, of course. But if it comes to a choice, fostering patriotism has to take a back seat to the protection of free speech."

The issue is clear. "Is patriotism more important than freedom of expression?"

Meeting the Criteria

Even if fostering patriotism is judged less (or more) important than protecting freedom of expression, even if both goals are agreed on and acceptably defined, issues can arise over whether these (or any other) criteria have been met.

> "The amendment will motivate young people to volunteer for military service."
> "Is that your idea of how to promote patriotism?"
> "It will give them the courage to beat up on people who desecrate the flag."
> "Is that how you want to preserve freedom of expression?"

If these disputes arise, they represent issues: Does motivating people to enlist in military service promote patriotism? Does beating up on people who burn flags preserve freedom of speech? Disagreements like these raise the argument, "Hey, wait a minute! We've agreed that any amendment we approve should foster patriotism and preserve freedom, but an amendment that would breed actions like those does not meet the standards we've established."

Evidence

Every argument must ultimately rest on some kind of evidence. Yet, it's also true that disagreements over the evidence can give rise to important issues. Look once more at the flag-burning controversy. What evidence supports the claim that most Americans do in fact value the flag as something more than "just another symbol?" Is there statistical evidence in the form of a survey? Is it the President's opinion? Are there examples of Americans protesting in State capitals and in Washington? Once you have found the facts and used them as evidence, you can expect to find such issues as, "Does the survey tell us about more than just a temporary feeling?" "Is the President's opinion authoritative?" "Do the numbers and kinds of protesters represent national consensus?"

How to Use the Analysis

By the time you complete your analysis, you will have made several long strides toward successful persuasion. You will know what the issues are and, because you know what their sources are, you will know precisely what kind of arguments you must have. In addition to this, the analysis will help you in several other ways.

To Indicate Lines of Argument

Analysis of a subject not only reveals the issues, it also points out the waived matter. Undisputed ideas can be helpful too. The reason the waived matter is undisputed is that you and the audience share certain beliefs and values. They serve as a common ground between you, and they suggest a path that some of your arguments might follow. Here's a case in point:

You're a candidate for treasurer of the student council. You're recognized on campus as an honest, intelligent, and trusted member of the student body. But you're not an accounting major and other students ask, "Can you handle the books well enough for the job?" Since the other students don't deny your honesty, intelligence, and dependability, you can build a line of argument claiming that those qualities balance your lack of training in accounting. By giving a more complete picture of your qualifications, a line of argument built on the waived matter helps to establish the probability that you would be the best treasurer even though your opponent is an accounting major. In this sense, then, both issues (Can you keep good books?) and waived matter (Nobody denies your good qualities) can point out useful lines of argument.

To Determine Emphasis

Speaking time is always limited. You can use it more efficiently if you know what you need to emphasize for the greatest effect. You'll base your final decision about which issues to emphasize on your analysis of the audience. Analysis of the claims exposes areas of agreement (waived matter) and disagreement (issues). Analysis of the audience suggests which issues identify specific areas of controversy for this audience.

A *potential* issue cannot become an *actual* issue until the *audience* becomes aware of an area of disagreement. Issues do not exist until they are issues for the *audience*.

To Group Arguments

Analyzing the subject helps you to organize a speech because it suggests a reasonable order for grouping the arguments. Every argument is intended to attack some specific issue. Important issues (those neither trivial nor irrelevant) will be related to one of the three stock issues. Arguments that show the severity of the problem, or the inadequacy of the present system to cope with it, all support the need for a change. They should be grouped together and they should be presented first. Arguments that show the desirability of the proposal should be grouped in the same way and presented second. Arguments that show the proposal will work are presented last.

There are good reasons for this sequence: There is no point in showing that a plan will work until you convince the audience that it's a *good* plan. And no plan is any good until the audience believes there is a need for a change. Besides being the most reasonable order, this sequence offers a number of other valuable benefits—all of which add to your credibility.

1. It shows the thoroughness of your speech preparation.
2. It avoids giving the impression of careless organization.
3. It gives the impression of having blocks of firm argument and evidence.
4. It makes transitions easier.

Summary

Since no two people have precisely the same beliefs and values, every speech subject can be controversial. Your task, then, is to keep the disagreements that are inherent in the subject from interfering with your purpose. Analysis of the subject helps you to accomplish this. Analysis is the *activity of dividing something into its parts to get a better understanding of the whole.*

The principal purpose of a speech to entertain is to amuse. Analysis of the subject, therefore, should point out areas of the subject which you think the audience will consider comical, quaint, absurd, or droll.

When you prepare a speech to inform, a successful analysis identifies elements of the subject that will help your audience understand it clearly and correctly.

In persuasive speaking, the purpose of analyzing the subject is to bring to light the issues. Issues are yes-or-no questions that identify the point disputed by opposing claims.

In policy debates, reduce the number of issues you have to argue by eliminating waived matter, combining issues that overlap, and eliminating those that seem trivial or irrelevant.

Three questions are called stock issues because they are inherent in every disputed policy debate: (1) Is there a need for a change? (2) Is the proposed change desirable? (3) Is the proposed change workable? The stock issues don't disclose the specific issues that must be argued in any particular case, but they are valuable because they identify the minimum requirements for proving a policy claim.

To find the issues in a claim of fact or value, define the judgment term of the claim. This definition is used as a criterion for deciding whether the available evidence will justify the claim.

Every issue arises from one of five possible sources: (1) a dispute over the need for a change; (2) a dispute over the criteria; (3) a dispute over the relative importance of the criteria; (4) a dispute over whether the criteria have been met; and (5) a dispute over the adequacy of the evidence. Knowing the source of an issue tells you what kind of argument is needed to resolve it.

The relative importance the audience attributes to the issues suggests the most efficient way to use your speaking time.

Grouping arguments as they relate to the stock issues suggests an effective way to order them in a speech. This kind of grouping provides several benefits, including an enhancement of your credibility: (1) It indicates a thoroughness in your speech preparation; (2) It avoids the impression of having scattered arguments; (3) It gives the impression of having ordered blocks of firm argument and evidence; and (4) It makes transitions easier.

Key Terms

Analysis	Subject term
Finding issues	Judgment term
Phrasing issues	Meeting criteria
Reducing issues	Relative importance
Stock issues	Evidence
Need for a change	Lines of argument
Desirability	Emphasis
Workability	Grouping arguments

Exercises

An issue in the United States in 1990 was a proposal to amend the Clean Air Act. In 1989, President George Bush recommended legislation that would tighten auto emission standards, encourage the use of alternate fuels, limit emissions that are believed to cause acid rain, and reduce up to 90 percent toxic industrial chemicals that could be released in the air. The *Congressional Digest* summarized the disagreement as follows:

> Those who favor strengthening the law warn that unless improvements are made in air quality, severe public health and environmental consequences will result, and that such improvements will not be made without the force of Federal regulations. They believe that the global threats of inaction far outweigh any concerns relating to increased costs, altered lifestyles or job loss. They point to the health care costs associated with air pollution, and maintain that the more modern equipment and technology that businesses would have to invest in would be to their advantage in the long run, making them more efficient.

> Those opposing more stringent clean air laws argue that industries are already bearing too much of the cost of cleaning up the atmosphere, and that the new proposals would require them to spend billions more. They say that these costs would result in higher prices for consumers, cause many companies to go out of business and diminish the ability of many others to compete on an international level. They also point out that the technology currently does not exist to comply with many of the proposed restrictions and that the deadlines for meeting goals are unrealistic.

Using that summary and the following statements,

1. Identify the major arguments on each side.
2. Identify the issues they establish.
3. Identify the most important stock issue.
4. Identify the most important source(s) of issues.

Pro: Senator James M. Jeffords, Democrat of Vermont.

S. 816 and S. 196 seek to put in place reasonable and effective regulations for toxic air emissions, municipal incinerator emissions and incinerator ash disposal. These rules are important for our country and can serve as a model for other nations of the world.

In drafting these bills, we have not lost sight of the ultimate goal of assuring healthy, breathable air to all Americans. We remain convinced that of all rights important to our citizens, the right to a clean and healthy environment is paramount.

S. 816, the Toxics Release Prevention Act of 1989, eliminates ambiguities that have spawned reams of litigation each time the EPA sought to move or stand still. This circus of legal challenges has thwarted the effectiveness of past legislation, and as a Nation we have suffered as our air has become more toxic. The bill we consider today lists the priority pollutants that EPA shall regulate, and it establishes clear guidelines for doing so. No longer will Americans be denied protection from pollution while courts entertain arguments over the intention of Congress and the parameters of pollution.

The bill establishes a realistic time frame for industries to install the best of available control technologies. It gives clear authority to the administrator of the Environmental Protection Agency to order further controls or management changes if emission levels remain too high. This bill requires that any facility that does not meet strict criteria for toxic emissions be shut down.

We recently learned that U.S. industries annually emit billions of pounds for every individual in the country. Some people are more vulnerable than others, due to such factors as geographic location and physical sensitivity.

Because it has proven impossible to regulate pollutant-by-pollutant, we have devised a method by which major sources of pollution are categorized by inherent similarities, and we have required each source in a category to install controls equal to the toughest that have been achieved in practice. If this does not assure an adequate margin of safety for those people who are most exposed to the emissions, then EPA must order stricter controls until such safety level is assured.

S. 196, the Municipal Waste Combustion Act of 1989, sets forth much needed national rules for an increasingly popular method of solid waste handling. As local decision-makers contemplate incineration as part of their solid waste plan, it is imperative that Federal regulations be clear, comprehensive and provide safeguards for air emission and ash disposal. New incinerators must meet the best available technology standards that have been achieved in practice, and existing sources are given a realistic time period to match these standards.

The Environmental Protection Agency is required to set numerical standards for particularly important pollutants and to put forth standards to ensure efficient combustion.

The bill requires that comprehensive solid waste management plans, consistent with RCRA (Resource Conservation and Recovery Act) and including a 25 percent recycling goal, be developed before an incinerator may be permitted. The facility must also demonstrate an ability to dispose of its ash for a period of at least five years before its permit is approved. Emissions must be monitored and permits must be renewed and periodically upgraded.

For disposal of incinerator ash, a new section requires the EPA to promulgate regulations for all phases of handling and disposal. Preference is given to disposal in a facility with two liners, leachate collection and ground water monitoring. A monofil with one liner may be used if the fly ash is pretreated to remove hazardous constitutents. Sanitary landfills may be used if the fly ash is neutralized and tested and not found to be hazardous. Reuse or recycling of ash may be considered only after complying with new standards to be issued by EPA.

Con: William F. O'Keefe, Vice President and Chief Operating Officer of the American Petroleum Institute.

API shares the goal of the Congress, the Administration and the American people to reduce concentrations of hazardous air pollutants. API plans to continue its active participation in the debate over legislation that fulfills this goal, keeping in mind other goals that the American people desire — such as the expansion of economic growth and opportunity.

We believe that the legislation proposed thus far must be refined in order to achieve all of these goals simultaneously. Improvement can be made by adopting provisions in the legislation for reasonable technology-based controls for those sources found to be significant emitters of toxic air pollutants, and by targeting residual risk control requirements for any remaining facilities that pose an unreasonable risk after implementation of technology-based control requirements.

Successful implementation of a hazardous air pollutant control program will depend, in part, on focusing the program towards control of the sources of greatest concern first. To ensure that controls are first implemented on the sources of greatest concern, the criteria used to select and rank source categories for regulations should include substance toxicity, population exposure, quantity of emissions, geographic location of facilities and current degree of emissions controls. These criteria should focus on protecting public health, and not attempt to address environmental effects. Public health is the primary concern over air toxics, and should remain as the central focus of air toxics legislation. Furthermore, we believe that control requirements to protect public health will also protect the environment, while avoiding difficult and uncertain attempts to assess impacts on the environment.

Recent data collected under SARA (Superfund Amendments and Reauthorization Act) Section 313 indicate that large volumes of chemicals are released to the atmosphere from manufacturing facilities nationwide. While this information raises legitimate concern about toxic releases, the data do not indicate the degree of exposure that these emissions contribute to overall population or environmental risks. For example, benzene is listed in the toxic air pollutant inventory as one of the top 25 chemicals released.

Total Exposure Assessment Methodology (TEAM) from EPA indicate that industry emissions account for only about 14 percent of the total releases of benzene to the atmosphere. The TEAM data further emphasize that industry emissions account for only about three percent of total human exposures to atmospheric benzene. The EPA TEAM data underscores the conclusion that emission data do not provide a direct measure of human exposure. It should also be recognized that controls established under existing law have led to significant progress in reducing toxic emissions. The current National Ambient Air Quality Standards (NAAQS) controls also reduce toxic air emissions. For example, measures to reduce volatile organic compounds (VOCs) for control of ozone already control many of the VOCs addressed in the proposed legislation for air toxics. Particulates are controlled in the NAAQS program with technologies that reduce emissions of hazardous metal coumpounds.

We believe that while air toxics is an issue that requires continuing effort, toxic air emissions do not pose a nationwide public health crisis. For example, EPA has estimated that the risk of cancer from lifetime ambient exposure to hazardous air pollutants ranges from 5 to 7.4 cases per million people annually. To put this in perspective, the annual risk of electrocution in the U.S. is of a similar magnitude (5.3 [per] million people per year). Reasonable progress should be the goal of air toxics legislation, not draconian measures that could severely impact our economy and standard of living.

The material for this exercise is taken from: "Clean Air Act Amendments," *Congressional Digest* 69 (Mar. 1990): 65, 74-77.

Notes

[1] Mark Twain, *Mark Twain's Speeches* (New York: Harper and Row, 1951) 249-51.
[2] This example is based on materials drawn from "Flag Desecration Legislation," *Congressional Digest* (Aug./Sept. 1989): 193.
[3] Willard C. Butcher, "Action Time for the Trade Deficit," *Vital Speeches of the Day* 15 Feb. 1990: 273.

Part Three

Preparing Speeches

chapter 8

Types of Supporting Material

I. Clarity and interest

II. Definition
    A. Types of definitions
        1. Classification and differentiation
        2. Function
        3. Example
        4. Figure of speech
        5. Usage
        6. Etymology
    B. Using definitions
        1. A dictionary definition is not always the best
        2. Use terms your audience understands
        3. Differentiate biased from unbiased definitions
        4. Don't insult your listeners

III. Statements about facts: examples
    A. Types of examples
        1. Real examples
        2. Secondary examples
        3. Hypothetical examples
        4. Extended examples
    B. Using examples for clarity and interest
    C. Using examples to prove
        1. Are the examples representative?
        2. Are there enough examples to support your point?
        3. Are negative instances accounted for?

IV. Statements about facts: statistics
    A. Using statistics for clarity and interest
    B. Using statistics to prove.
        1. Check the currency of the data
        2. Check the reliability of the source of the statistical data
        3. Be sure the statistics measure what they appear to measure

V. Opinions about facts: testimony
   A. Using testimony
   B. Evaluating testimony
      1. The authority should be competent.
      2. The authority should be trustworthy.

VI. Comparison and contrast

The meanings you and your listeners have for the words you use will never be precisely the same. Therefore, you must help your listeners understand what you say as precisely as possible. Concrete, specific, vivid details help them to visualize your ideas in terms of their own experiences and clarify your ideas for them.

All supporting materials are designed to help you convey your ideas effectively, but these materials are not things; except for some visual aids, they are statements about things. They carry meaning for the listener because they refer to something in the listener's experience: things, people, thoughts, ideas, beliefs,values. We speak of giving evidence to support a point. But you can't give "facts"; you make statements about facts. Gravity is a fact; the law of gravity is a statement about a fact. A definition of global warming is a statement about global warming. A college president's opinion on the pass/no-pass system of grading is a statement about that system. Your purpose in using supporting material is to increase your listeners' understanding of what you believe reality to be. You are not giving them facts.

Clarity and Interest

In choosing the supporting materials of your speech, you need to search for a balance between two qualities: *clarity* and *interest*. Your materials need to be clear so that they will convey your message accurately. They need to be interesting so that the audience will listen. Achieving this balance requires thoughtful selection; qualities of clarity and interest are somewhat antagonistic. Clarity increases as the listener becomes confident about predicting your meaning. Interest increases with novelty and change—which are far less predictable.

Clarity without interest will produce a speech that is dull and difficult to listen to. Actuarial tables, for example, can be extremely clear, but they do not make good listening! On the other hand, using interesting materials that are unrelated to your purpose is equally harmful to a successful speech. A major factor in all communication is striking a careful balance between what is dull but accurate and what is exciting but misleading. Try to find the point where your supporting materials strike a balance between clarity and interest—where your meaning is both interesting and clear.

Supporting materials may be classified into four categories. Definitions are used to clarify your meaning for words or concepts that may be unfamiliar, obscure, or ambiguous (your definition might differ from the definition of your listeners). Statements about facts are details found in the forms of examples and statistics. Opinions about facts occur in the form of the testimony of others. Comparison and contrast establish a relationship for the listener between the known and the unknown.

Definition

A druggist labels a bottle of medicine so that there will be no confusion about the contents or the dosage. In a similar sense, language provides labels for ideas. The labels put on ideas, like the labels on bottles of medicine, should be recognizable, clear, and precise. But language is not always easy to use in speaking about complex or abstract ideas. "Democracy," "communism," "ecology," or "feminism" are not "seen" in the same sense as "aspirin" or "vitamin C." When you use words like "aspirin" or "vitamin C," listeners recognize your simple denotative meaning, even though they may not have full insight into the exact chemical components. "Democracy," "truth," and "honesty," however, are abstract terms. These labels imply a greater variety of meanings than do those of material objects. Listeners are often confused because they do not understand the labels in the same way that you use and understand them. Consequently, an abstract, unfamiliar, or obscure term will need to be defined.

Types of Definitions

We will explain six types of definitions which should be useful in establishing exactly what you want your listeners to understand: definition by classification and differentiation; by function; by example; by usage, etymology, or history; by figure of speech. Depending upon your audience and the particular concept you want to clarify, choose the most appropriate method to meet the requirements of a good definition: (1) indicate the sense in which you use a term and (2) bring your meaning within the scope of your listeners' experience.

Classification and differentiation   The most common method of definition—the primary one your dictionary uses—is definition by classification and differentiation. The thing or idea to be defined is put into a class with which the listener is already familiar. Then, to specify the meaning and eliminate ambiguity, the definition differentiates the thing defined from all other members of that class. For example, Vladislar Krasnov, a scholar from the Soviet Union, defined *perestroika* [the term to be defined] as a "restructuring of the Soviet economy [classification] so as to replace rigid central planning with greater respect for local management, profit incentives, and market forces [differentiation]."[1]

Function   You can define a term by explaining the use or function of what the term names. "The differential gear in an automobile divides the driving force of the engine between the two rear axles and lets the axles turn at different speeds."

George Gerbner, former Dean of the Annenberg School of Communication, speaking at a symposium on Television and Children, set the persuasive basis for his speech "Children's Television: A National Disgrace" with this definition of television by its function:

> What are some general features of the world of television? For the first time in history children are born into a symbolic world that does not originate with parents, church, or school, and requires no literacy. Television has replaced most stories told by parents, and has either replaced or reorganized what we learn in school or in church. It has become the norm, the standard to which we all have to relate. We use it as a measure of our own behavior and of the behavior of people around us. We use it as a way of defining ourselves. Even if you don't watch television, you get it through other people who do.[2]

Such a definition reveals clearly Dean Gerbner's opinion of television's function in our society. It illustrates, moreover, that not all definitions are uncontroversial. Frequently, definition is used to forward the speaker's persuasive goal.

Example   Dennis Taylor, a student at Marshall University in West Virginia, began his speech "Terrorism — American Style" with a series of examples that defined his topic: vigilantism.

> At 8:00 every evening, men calling themselves New Texas Rangers head for the U.S.-Mexican border. Bearing guns and ammunition, they promise to use any means necessary — including murder — to keep aliens from entering this country.

> After a white police officer is killed in Mobile, Alabama, a pair of Ku Klux Klansmen abduct Michael Donald, an innocent black bystander, and hang him as revenge for the crime.

> In February of this year, two Detroit residents burned down a house reputed to be a haven for drug dealers in their neighborhood. Both confess to the crime, saying that other neighbors had chipped in money for the gasoline.

> What do these three cases of Terrorism-American Style have in common? Each is an example of vigilantism, "a largely unrecognized cancer" which, according to a report released earlier this year by the national Council of Churches, is "eating away at our communities."[3]

Figure of speech   In most cases, you will be concerned primarily with the clarity and precision of definitions. However, they can add interest value to what you are saying, and, as in the definition of "television," they are not always solely denotative. Sometimes definitions can be connotative as they clearly are in these examples of definition by figure of speech.

Carl Sandburg defined slang as "language that takes off its coat, spits on its hands and goes to work."[4] One speaker defined situation ethics this way: "Ethics, therefore, may seem to vary depending upon the situation. As Mark Twain once remarked, 'An ethical man is a Christian holding four aces.'"[5]

Usage   A dictionary always reports the usage of a term, as in the following example.

> **showdown**, *n*. 1: In poker, the play in which the hands are laid on the table face up. 2: Any action or disclosure that brings an issue to a head.

Etymology   Earlier we cited Vladislar Krasnov's definition of *perestroika* as an example of definition by classification and differentiation. In that same speech he defined *glasnost* through the etymology of the word. "Glasnost," he said, "derived from the Russian word for 'voice,' does not mean abolition or censorship but offers a greater opportunity for Soviet citizens to voice their opinion."[6]

Using Definitions

As you can see, the varieties of definition discussed above are quite different, although they all help to clarify terms. Here are some general principles to consider in choosing what type of definition to use.

A dictionary definition is not always the best   Beginning public speakers frequently turn to the dictionary for definitions. "Webster says . . ." is an often-repeated phrase used to introduce a definition. If you are interested in explaining how something works, for example, a functional definition would be much better. Even when a dictionary definition is appropriate, it may be more useful if you adapt it to your audience. "Intersession" is defined by one dictionary as "the time between two academic sessions or semesters." If you are speaking to a college class, you could alter the definition to "the period in January between the autumn and spring semesters when the University provides a number of special short-term courses for credit." This definition is much more specific for your audience.

Use terms your audience understands   Definitions that use terms the audience doesn't understand can be more confusing than no definition at all. If you have more knowledge about your subject than your audience, you have to find terms they understand. The specialized vocabulary of any field (engineering, medicine, literary criticism, etc.) should be used only for those who understand it.

Differentiate biased from unbiased definitions   Definitions used for persuasive purposes, such as George Gerbner's definition of "television," are not appropriate when your aim is to be informative or when your audience is likely to view the definition as unfair. In short, such definitions are fine for listeners who generally agree with your point of view, but not for others.

Don't insult your listeners   Frequently, you will be confronted with a problem. Some of your listeners may not understand what a term means, but many will. Avoid comments such as, ''I know that you don't understand this term, so let me define it for you.'' If your listeners do not understand the term, you don't need to remind them! Put the responsibility on yourself: ''To make myself clear, let me point out that by *materialistic*, I mean valuing wealth over ideals.''

Statements about Facts: Examples

Examples are the product of experience and observation — either yours or someone else's. Colorado State University is in Fort Collins. The Salinas Valley is an agricultural area in California. The Alaskan Gold Rush began in 1896. The Berlin Wall was torn down in 1989. All of these are statements about facts that may be used as examples to illustrate some point.

If you want to become a truly effective speaker, learn to use examples well. Think of the interesting speakers you have heard, whether on a public platform or in your own living room. What kind of examples did they use to illustrate the subjects they discussed?

Types of Examples

Examples may be real, secondary, or hypothetical. They vary in length from brief to extended.

Real examples   An example is a statement about an incident, person, or thing that you use to illustrate a point. A real example refers to something that actually exists and is known to both you and your listener. It is real to you — you are familiar with it from first-hand experience.

> ''. . . a really great football team like, say, the San Francisco 49ers.''
>
> ''When you visit a National Park — Yosemite, for instance.''
>
> ''A liberal politician such as Ted Kennedy. . . .''

Governor Mario Cuomo of New York in his Keynote Address to the Democratic Party Convention in San Francisco in 1984 extolled his party's history with historical examples. He chose to reflect his political point of view, but they were real cases with which his audience was familiar.

> Now for 50 years, for 50 years we Democrats created a better future for our children . . . Roosevelt's alphabet programs, Truman's NATO and the GI Bill of Rights and the nearly miraculous Camp David Peace Accord.[7]

Secondary examples   Because the personal knowledge that any speaker and any listener bring to the communication transaction is necessarily

Governor Mario Cuomo described his political point of view using real examples familiar to his audience.

limited, many of the examples you will use are not drawn from your own experience. You accept them as accurate because you trust the reliability (credibility) of your source. Not everyone can personally testify to starvation in an African nation, brutality in a foreign jail, or the beauty of the French countryside. On all historical subjects except the most recent, you must use examples you obtain from others. Even if they are real to you, they will frequently not be to your listener. While your personal experience in the French countryside may supply you with vivid examples to make the area *seem* more real to your listeners, it is secondary to the audience because it must depend on you as the source.

Congresswoman Helen Delich Bentley of Maryland spoke in 1989 to the Maritime Institute on the costs of doing business in the new technological areas. Although some of her listeners were probably familiar with the technology, most would not have known of this dramatic secondary example:

> The acceptance by the world's banking systems of electronic blips as money allows the emptying of a nation's tills with lightning speed, leaving not even the time of a bookkeeper's notation for defensive action. A case in point would be the run on Continental Illinois in the mid-80s.

In 8 days, reserves in excess of 25 billions of dollars were withdrawn electronically from as far away as Tokyo and Bonn and even though the bank's officers had been part of the electronics business age and seemingly understood the system, interviews with them afterward proved they still didn't comprehend the true liquidity of electronically held assets.[8]

Hypothetical examples   If an example describes an incident that has not actually occurred—but is possible—the example is hypothetical. Heidi Hinds, a student at Mankato State University, introduced a speech on ''Testing Prescription Drugs for the Elderly'' with this hypothetical, and yet very realistic, example:

An elderly man, we'll call him Sam, enjoys a relatively healthy lifestyle. He is taking Tenormin for moderate high blood pressure and has developed a nagging wheeze. Sam decides to go to his doctor to see about alleviating the problem. Instead of switching Sam's medication, his doctor prescribes theophylline, an asthma medication which upsets Sam's stomach and makes him so jittery he can't sleep. To treat his stomach his doctor prescribes Tagamet, which makes Sam confused and disoriented. To treat the jitteriness and the insomnia, his doctor prescribes Valium. In addition to causing mental confusion, Tagamet also increases the level of Valium in Sam's blood system thus making the drug more toxic. So Sam has Tagamet causing confusion, and higher

Since the audience was unlikely to have had personal experience with her topic, Congresswoman Helen Bentley used a secondary example to help them understand.

levels of Valium causing disorientation. His condition continues to deteriorate and he is eventually diagnosed as having senile dementia: senility. Feeling at the end of his rope, Sam decides to go to another doctor and inquires if his medication could have anything to do with his problem? Absolutely.[9]

Extended examples   Sometimes you will want to develop an example at greater length and in more detail than the brief form the example ordinarily takes. Such illustrations are called extended examples and may be hypothetical, real, or secondary. In the following extended example, Thomas P. Pike tells of his own experience to illustrate how serious a problem alcoholism can be in the "executive suite":

> I had my first drink and got drunk when I was seventeen in 1926. I continued to drink heavily, but in a relatively controlled manner, and with no serious problems until I was 27. Then, in 1936, I had the insanity to resort to morning drinking in a futile attempt to cure my King-size hangover with a bit of "the hair of the dog that bit me."
>
> This was when I unknowingly crossed that invisible line from heavy drinking to uncontrolled drinking and became an alcoholic. Alcoholism had sneaked up on me like a thief in the night and seized me in its death grip. I became a compulsive drinker . . , and suffered frequent blackouts. I got fired in 1937 when my lost weekends grew into lost weeks. This is now called excessive absenteeism. My employer, unlike some of you, had no enlightened employee alcoholism program. Instead of being counseled and referred to help, I was given the "old fashioned treatment" and summarily canned. It was a miracle that I didn't lose my wife, my sanity, and the new drilling company I had started after being fired.
>
> Finally, in 1946, at the age of 37, after repeated hospitalizations and futile attempts at so-called controlled drinking, I became a hopeless alcoholic. I was bankrupt, mentally, physically, and spiritually. I had lost all my confidence and self-esteem. I loathed myself. A thousand nameless fears possessed me, and I was in a state of total demoralization and despair.
>
> Then, the miracle happened. With the faith and loving help of my wife, Katherine, and the guidance of the late blessed Dr. John Doyle, I found a new and better way of life in the fellowship of Alcoholics Anonymous. I learned the facts and the truths about alcoholism which freed me from the bondage of booze (and believe me, this is another instance in which the truth can make you free).[10]

Using Examples for Clarity and Interest

In using examples there are some rules to remember:

1. Use extended examples only when detailed knowledge or appreciation is essential to understanding the point. Be sure the detail is essential. In most cases, brief examples are sufficient and preferred.

2. Use the best example you can find for the particular idea you are discussing. Unless examples are precisely relevant, the listener is thrown off track. After a few such instances, the audience may well give up listening.

3. Be sure that the necessary value characterizations are given with the example: The San Francisco 49ers are not just *any* football team, they are a *great* one; while the Cottonwood High School Colts are a "typical high school" team.

4. Your own good judgment will tell you when to use more than one short example for a specific point. A single example might enlighten part of the audience and not the rest, or may only partly enlighten the audience as a whole. A greater number and variety of examples will often clarify or prove when one example might fail and, incidentally, help to lend interest at the same time.

5. Real examples would seem to be preferable to use if good ones are available. But no matter whether examples are real, secondary, or hypothetical, they should all seem as real as possible. Use the kind of detail that will bring them close to a listener's experience. Notice the detail, for instance, in the hypothetical example used by Heidi Hinds about prescription drugs for the elderly.

Using Examples to Prove

When you use examples to support an argument, you not only choose illustrations for their value in achieving clarity and interest, you also select instances to meet three further criteria. If the answer to all three of the following questions is "yes," the examples will be useful.

Are the examples representative? Examples must be typical, not exceptions to the rule.

Heidi Hinds, for instance, after she told her story about Sam, made sure her listeners realized that this was a typical case. She added, "Unfortunately, contends Dr. Joe Graedon, author of *50 Plus*, Sam's situation is not an isolated case."

Are there enough examples to support your point? The number of instances that will be necessary is not the same in every case. One may be enough if it meets the needs of the target audience. Usually, more than one is needed to prove a point to an audience. Even if a single example might be persuasive, several will frequently make your point more persuasive and more interesting. Marion Wright Edelman, speaking on "Educating the Black Child," wanted to emphasize the significance of African Americans in our society. She used nine short examples to do it.

> Bill Cosby is America's favorite Daddy and Micheal Jackson and Whitney Houston dot the top ten charts. Black leadership has permeated

a range of mainstream institutions. Bill Gray heads the House Budget Committee, Frank Thomas heads the Ford Foundation, and Cliff Wharton heads TIAA-CREF. A. Barry Rand is in charge of marketing at Xerox. Anita DeFrantz is America's representative to the Olympic Committee, and Richard Knight is the city manager of Dallas.[11]

Are negative examples addressed? You cannot get rid of negative instances, but in one of two ways you can put them in perspective for your listeners. (1) You can show that they are not representative. Thus you might say, "Although there have been a very few cases where a particular ski binding had to be replaced after one season, the vast majority of those bindings gave long-term service." (2) You can show that the negative instances aren't important. Henry A. Wallace, a former Vice President, had developed a strain of feed corn with more kernels to the ear than other strains. When experts complained that some of his corn had irregular rows of kernels, he said, "What's looks to a hog?"

Statements about Facts: Statistics

Statistics are not just numbers. You may say, "There are 21 students in my public speaking class." While that is a correct number, it has no particular significance until it is quoted in relation to something else. For example, you might note that the number is greater than the 17 students per class average at your university or it totals one/tenth of the 198 students in Biology 101. Statistics showing relationships among numbers are ordinarily used to segment large numbers of things, events, or people into some working relationships.

John E. Jacob, President of the National Urban League, used this statistical comparison to indicate the severity of the problems facing African Americans:

> Our concern is with winning racial parity so that being black in American no longer means you're twice as likely to be a dropout and be out of work...no longer means you're twice as likely to be homeless or without health insurance...no longer means you're three times as likely to be poor...no longer means that black infants are twice as likely to die in their first year and black adults live 6 fewer years than whites....Parity is the opposite of the gross inequality we have today, when every statistic that matters shows that African Americans lag far behind the white majority.[12]

Using Statistics for Clarity and Interest

When you use statistics in large numbers (roughly four or more digits), it is wise to round the numbers off. You will note that in the statement above, John Jacob has not only made a comparison statistically between

African Americans and Caucasian Americans, he has simplified the statistics. The actual statistics are undoubtedly more complex than what he used. He rounded the complex numbers to "twice as likely," "three times more likely," and "six fewer years." Such rounding is much easier for the listener to remember. Just be certain that the statistics remain relevant and accurate.

Statistics can be used for interest by combining an unexpected measure with a more common description. For example, an article in the *Chicago Tribune* referred to an average patient at a headache clinic "downing 5.4 pounds of aspirin a year..., an average of 13 aspirin a day."[13]

Percentages, fractions, and proportions all help to put statistical examples into a clear relationship with other facts. Statistics can add clarity and interest if you round the numbers off and, by using comparisons, show relationships.

Using Statistics to Prove

When statistical data are used as evidence to support a claim, they must be accurate and meaningful, as well as interesting and clear. Remember, your primary goal is to help the audience understand. Statistics can reveal a lot of information, but they can also conceal important facts. For instance, a recent analysis showed that SAT scores in Illinois increased 4 points overall, while national scores declined. Before using such a statistic to prove that Illinois schools are doing a better job of educating their students, more investigation is necessary. How many students took the SAT's nationally? In Illinois? Since many schools in the Midwest require ACT scores only 16 percent of Illinois high school seniors take the SAT compared to 40 percent nationally.[14]

Similarly, if you wanted to use statistics to prove that the economy in a certain city was improving, you might do research to find that unemployment figures showed a drop of 1.5 percent. You should not stop there, however. What is the state average? If your city's unemployment rate had been 16 percent, a drop of 1.5 percent would result in a 14.5 percent unemployment rate. If the state average is 5.8 percent, the economy is, by definition, improving but the audience deserves to know that the city has a long way to go!

Keep the following cautions in mind when you use statistics.

Check the currency of the data   The date the statistics were compiled is one of the first things to ask about some statistical information. Recency is not relevant, of course, in matters that change very little. A statement of the number of times a human heart beats per minute need not be questioned today even though the subject was studied years ago. If, however, you see a report on the number of jet fighter planes that Iraq has, you need to know when the count was made. Statistics such as this change rapidly and require up-to-date research to be useful.

Check the reliability of the source of the statistical data Accurate reporting depends on the reliability of sources. You must ask: "Who made the statistical study?" "Did the information come from sources that may be intentionally misleading?" Will my audience accept the source of the statistics I use as trustworthy?

Certain governmental agencies, such as the Bureau of Labor Statistics, are generally accepted as a source of honest reports. The Brookings Institution is a private economics research group that has earned general acceptance. But, as any television viewer can tell you, many so-called independent agencies are nothing more than support for special interests. If the source is unfamiliar to you, investigate its background. The audience may be familiar with the source and may know if the "statistics" have been used as propaganda.

Be sure the statistics measure what they appear to measure The most commonly used statistical measure is an average. You may want to know the average age of the student body, the average income of the members of a particular profession, or the average annual value of the agricultural production of Iowa or Illinois. But when you find such statistics, it is a good idea to ask how the term "average" is used. There are three kinds of averages: the mean, the median, and the mode.

The *mean* is a simple arithmetical average. To find it, add together the quantity of each item in a series and divide by the number of items. The *mode* is the figure that appears most frequently in a series. The *median* is the middle number—half the items are greater than the median and half are less.

According to 1988 estimates, 15 states have a population of 5 million or more. In the list below,[15] the numbers have been rounded to a hundred thousand persons:

California	27.7M	Michigan	9.2M
New York	17.8M	New Jersey	7.7M
Texas	16.8M	North Carolina	6.4M
Florida	12.0M	Georgia	6.2M
Pennsylvania	11.9M	Massachusetts	5.9M
Illinois	11.6M	Virginia	5.9M
Ohio	10.8M	Indiana	5.5M
		Missouri	5.1M

In this case the mean (add all totals and divide by 15) is 10.7M—a population that Ohio most closely matches. The median (seven states have greater numbers, seven have less) is 9.2, the figure for Michigan. The mode is 5.9 (it appears twice—all others appear only once), the population of Massachusetts and Virginia. Statistical measures demand scrutiny and interpretation. Try to imagine how the mode in the list above would be useful. While it may be interesting that two states have the same population, how would you use that information to establish a relationship among all

15 states in the list? The saying that "figures don't lie" is a generalization that should be questioned, although the remainder of the saying, "but liars figure," is unfortunately true!

Opinions about Facts: Testimony

Often the supporting material you find will contain statements by an expert on the subject. Such statements are called testimony—expert opinions about facts. The strength of the testimony depends on the credibility of the expert.

Fred Wertheimer of Common Cause, a nonpartisan citizen-action organization, spoke to the national Press Club in Washington, DC in 1983. His subject was one that still troubles many people: the influence of political action committees on members of the Congress. He argued that,

> More and more, Members of Congress have been publicly expressing their concerns.
>
> Senator Robert Dole of Kansas, for example, said, "When these political action committees give money they expect something in return other than good government. It is making it much more difficult to legislate. We may reach a point where everybody is buying something with PAC money. We cannot get anything done."
>
> Senator Dale Bumpers of Arkansas said, "Money is the number one political problem our country is facing. . . . You can't have a sensible debate about how much is enough for defense when those PACs are contributing so much."
>
> Representative Barber Conable of New York said, "I'm scared. These new PACs not only buy incumbents, but affect legislation. It's the same crummy business as judges putting the arm on lawyers who appear before them to finance their next campaign;" and
>
> Representative Jim Shannon of Massachusetts said, "The problem of money in politics isn't an obsession of mine, but it's becoming one now. . . . There has been too much discussion around here about how what we do in the House and on our committees is going to affect our ability to raise money. I mean, people aren't embarrassed about saying this anymore." [16]

You should note that the testimony he uses comes from both Senators and Congressmen, Democrats and Republicans, they come from different areas of the country, and all are prominent. Even with testimony from experts, there is strength in making sure the persons chosen are representative and important.

Using Testimony

Using testimony in a speech makes it possible for you to tap the resources of generations of thought and expression. All that has been written and said becomes a vast reservoir from which you can draw authoritative testimony of expert witnesses. You add clarity and interest to your own attitudes and opinions with the thoughts and feelings of other people your audiences know, respect, and admire.

The privilege of using testimony in a speech is one that brings certain obligations. Honesty demands that you identify ideas and language that you have taken from someone else. This is not merely a moral injunction against plagiarism; two other considerations are involved. First, by failing to identify your source, you pass up the opportunity to add the credibility of someone else to your own, and second, if a listener recognizes that the statement is not your own, it will diminish your credibility as a trustworthy person.

To gain the best results from the use of testimony, you must identify the qualifications of the person you wish to quote. When you quote a well-known person such as Thomas Jefferson, most adult audiences already identify him as the author of the Declaration of Independence and third President of the United States. But what about someone not so well-known?

Benjamin Beringer, a student at Wabash College in Indiana, supported his claim about the developing resistance of bacteria to antibiotics with a quotation from a person many in the audience wouldn't know. He explained why his source qualified as an authority by identifying the profession and honors received: "'If we don't do something soon,' says Harvard University Professor Walter Gilbert, a Nobel prize winner in chemistry, 'there may be a time down the road when 80 to 90% of infections will be resistant to all known antibiotics.'" [17]

Using direct quotations as testimony in a speech requires special care in your delivery. Stating "quote" to signal the beginning of the quotation and "unquote" to signal the end would be awkward. Instead, identify the source of your material as thoroughly as the situation requires, and then let your voice (through pause, change in tempo, or other means) indicate which words are yours and which belong to your source.

When you use testimony, direct quotations are not always necessary. Expert opinion can be presented in your own words, with an added identification of the source. If words of the authority are particularly clear and appropriate for your audience, you may decide to quote the source directly. In general, putting the idea into your own words will help keep a uniform level of language in your speech.

Regardless of the form, testimony is always opinion about facts, not fact itself. Consequently, the best use of testimony will show how your authorities arrived at their conclusions. Testimony that merely states an opinion asks listeners to accept the conclusion simply because they trust the source. It is much more convincing to support this trust with the facts and reasons behind the judgment.

Evaluating Testimony

Before you decide to use a piece of testimony, ask yourself two questions about it: Is the source qualified? Is the source trustworthy?

The authority should be competent   To be qualified, the persons whose opinions you use as supporting material should be speaking about their area of expertise. For example, your audience would question a theologian's opinion about biology. Similarly, Lee Trevino, the professional golfer, would be a much more credible source if he endorsed Ram golf balls instead of Bridgestone tires. Look for sources whose competence will be clear to the listener. When you cite less well-known authorities, it is necessary to give the audience evidence of their competence.

The authority should be trustworthy   Even a competent authority may not be considered thoroughly trustworthy. William F. Buckley, Jr., a conservative columnist and lecturer is regarded as a knowledgeable and intelligent person, but his strong conservative biases make his opinions less trustworthy for many people. Biases, whether real or only imagined by the audience, will decrease the credibility of testimony.

Comparison and Constrast

Comparison and *contrast* are useful for the general clarification of ideas. Although they can be treated separately, they are essentially two aspects of the same process. Comparison shows how one thing is *like* another; contrast shows how things are *unlike*. David P. Gardner, President of the University of California, spoke about American education; he contrasted it with education in "all other industrial societies."

> Compared with all other industrial societies, the U.S. has an extraordinarily nonselective educational system. In the United States, and virtually nowhere else until very recently, it is possible for a mildly persistent but singularly untalented student to complete high school, to attend a two-year college, and to transfer to some four-year institution and obtain a bachelor's degree. Virtually every other society places a series of checkpoints along this path so as to screen out the less able or uncommitted student. In Britain and France a series of examinations makes it unlikely that such a student would achieve a university place, and even in the unlikely event that it occurred, examinations at universities would screen out the student before graduation. In Germany, where as late as the mid-1960s only 9 percent of the relevant age group graduated from upper secondary school as compared with 75 percent in the U.S., this hypothetical student would probably not be admitted to the academic preparatory secondary school and, thus, would have no chance to go on to higher education.[18]

Summary

Effective speaking is interesting and clear. Supporting materials supply clarity and interest by helping the audience visualize ideas concretely and accurately. There are four types of supporting materials used by speakers:

(1) definition, (2) statements about facts—examples and statistics, (3) opinion about facts—testimony, and (4) comparison and contrast.

Definitions are necessary to clarify abstract, unfamiliar, or obscure terms. The most common method of definition, the one most used in the dictionary, is definition by classification and differentiation. In this form, the thing to be defined is put in a general class and differentiated from other items in the class. You can also define by explaining the use or function of the thing being defined, by giving an example of it, by figure of speech, usage, and etymology.

In defining terms, remember that a dictionary definition is not always the best. Use terms close to your audience's understanding, differentiate biased from unbiased definitions, and put the burden of explanation on yourself, not the audience.

Examples can be used to illustrate statements about facts. Examples may be first-hand experiences for you and your audience, or they may be *secondary*—ones you have learned about without personal experience. *Hypothetical* examples are useful when a good real or secondary example is not available. Any of these types of examples can be used in an *extended* form. Examples are used to provide clarity and interest, and they are used as proof.

Statistics are also statements about facts. Statistics compact large numbers of examples for easier use. Numbers should be rounded off and should show a relationship to other ideas. Statistical data should be current and reliable. The measure used, such as the mean, median, or mode, should be carefully weighed to determine its relevance to your purpose.

Testimony advances the opinions of others in support of your ideas; testimony is an *opinion* about facts. In using testimony you need to identify the ideas of others. Sometimes you will also need to clarify for your listeners who your authority is. Testimony can be paraphrased as long as you are careful to maintain the original intent. Testimony should come from an authority who will be regarded by the audience as trustworthy and competent.

Comparison and contrast can each be used alone or in combination with the other. Comparison and contrast clearly distinguish for the audience how something is like and/or unlike something else.

Key Terms

Clarity	Facts
Interest	Real examples
Classification	Secondary examples
Differentiation	Hypothetical examples
Function	Representative examples
Example	Negative instances
Figure of speech	Statistics
Usage	Testimony
Etymology	Comparison and contrast

Exercises

1. Develop a one-point speech in which you support that point with at least three different types of supporting material.

2. From one of the other classes you are enrolled in, select a term you have never heard before. Define that term in a brief definition by classification and differentiation and by three other methods of definition. Decide which of the four methods has given the clearest explanation of the term. Decide which method was the least clear. Why do you think one method is better than the others for defining this term? What audience do you have in mind?

3. Survey the opinions of several groups of students on campus. For instance, what do the men at the Sigma Chi fraternity house think about rock and roll? What generalization can you make from the statistics?

4. Develop three hypothetical examples, each of which has "the characteristics of a real example," to support a claim.

5. In one of the speeches in Chapters 13, 18, 19, or 20, see if you can find examples of:
   a. Functional definition
   b. Extended examples
   c. Testimony
   d. Statistics
   e. Comparison and contrast

6. In one of the speeches in Chapters 13, 18, 19, or 20, see if you can find places where the speech would be strengthened by additional supporting material. Explain in class what kind you would recommend and why.

Notes

[1] Voladislav Krasnov, "The Soviet Union and the Asian-Pacific Region in the 1990s: Coordination of Policies," *Vital Speeches of the Day* 1 Jan. 1989: 164.

[2] George Gerbner, "Children's Television: A National Disgrace," *Representative American Speeches 1985-86,* ed. Owen Peterson (New York: Wilson, 1986) 143.

[3] Dennis C. Taylor, "Terrorism—American Style," *Winning Orations* ed. Larry G. Schnoor (Mankato, MN: Interstate Oratorical Association, 1988) 110.

[4] Quoted in *Life* 15 Dec. 1941: 89.

[5] Ben H. Warren, "Constant Values in a Changing World," *Vital Speeches of the Day* 1 Jan. 1980: 183-4.

[6] Krasnov, 164.

[7] Mario Cuomo, "Keynote to the Democratic Convention," *Contemporary American Speeches,* ed. Richard L. Johannesen, R.R. Allen, Wil A. Linkugel (Dubuque, IA: Kendall/Hunt, 1988) 314.

[8] Helen Delich Bently, "U.S. Competition in Emerging Technology Areas: Fines—Just the Cost of Doing Business," *Vital Speeches of the Day* 15 Oct. 1989: 2.

[9] Heidi Hinds, "Testing Prescription Drugs for the Elderly," *Winning Orations* ed. Larry G. Schnoor (Mankato, MN: Interstate Oratorical Association, 1989) 53.

[10] Thomas P. Pike, "Alcoholism in the Executive Suite," *Vital Speeches of the Day* 1 Jan. 1980: 166-67.

[11] Marian Wright Edelman, "Educating the Black Child: Our Past and Our Future," *Representative American Speeches,* 1987-88 ed. Owen Peterson (New York: Wilson, 1988) 107.

[12] John E. Jacob, "Major Issues Facing African-Americans: Drugs and Supreme Court Decisions," *Vital Speeches of the Day* 15 Oct. 1989: 8.

[13] The *Chicago Tribune,* September 23, 1990, Section 2, page 3.

[14] The *Chicago Tribune,* November 4, 1990, Section 5, page 1.

[15] The USA and Canada (London: Europe Publications Limited, 1989) 6.

[16] Fred Wertheimer, "It's Time to Declare War on Political Action Committees," *Contemporary American Speeches* eds. Richard L. Johannesen, R.R. Allen and Wil A. Linkugel (Dubuque, IA: Kendall/Hunt, 1988) 188.

[17] Benjamin P. Beringer, "Health and the Hubris of Human Nature," *Winning Orations* ed. Larry G. Schnoor (Mankato, MN: Interstate Oratorical Association, 1987) 34.

[18] David P. Gardner, "Excellence and Equality of Opportunity: Education and Society," *Vital Speeches of the Day* 1 Jan. 1983: 173.

Finding Supporting Materials

To be a competent public speaker you must demonstrate to your audience that you know what you are talking about. To a significant degree, your competence is revealed through the kinds of supporting materials you use. Since you can't know in advance precisely what you will need to adapt to a target audience, you should gather (and be familiar with) as much supporting material as you can find. From a large store of examples, statistics, and testimony you can select those that best suit the audience and your subject and purpose. You will find supporting material in a variety of places discussed in this chapter, including nonpublished sources. We will also talk about how to use the library and a method of recording the information you discover.

Using Nonpublished Sources

A good library is a valuable asset to a public speaker, as we will discuss later in this chapter. There are other resources that can also be used to advantage. They will sometimes shorten your research time because they are easier to use. These resources include personal experience, the knowledge of experts and information you get from radio and TV.

Personal Experience

The most obvious place to begin looking for information is in your own personal experience. Don't let this information go to waste. Anyone who has, for example, worked on an assembly line has absorbed countless minute details. Vivid recollection of such details can provide a spark of realism that diligent research alone would lack.

Personal experience should, however, be treated like any other source of information. Do not assume that you can talk about a familiar subject without much preparation. As you think about the speech, make notes about any personal experiences that might be used as examples. After you have looked elsewhere for additional information about the subject, you will have a full set of data from which to work. With notes available, you will be less likely to forget something important in preparing your speech outline.

Interviewing an Expert

One of the most important ways of finding information is to ask someone who knows the subject. Acquaintances, friends, and family members are all potential sources, or they may suggest possible alternatives. You may have a friend who knows a lot about Yellowstone National Park, skiing, the effect of exercise, or growing corn in the Middle West. Frequently, someone in your own family can help you get information. Your mother or father may be a member of a profession or trade (lawyer, stockbroker, electrician, or teacher) that deals with the problem you are going to discuss.

One of the best ways to learn information is to interview an expert.

You may be surprised to discover how willing an expert is to grant you an interview. Faculty members or people in the business community, for example, are usually pleased to find their fields of specialization of interest to others. Since you will be asking these experts to spend their time, plan the interview carefully. Gather as much information as you can in the least amount of time.

Planning the interview Before an interview, learn as much as you can about the subject. Interviews are not intended to gain the basic information that is easily available elsewhere. If you don't already know something about the subject from experience or study, you can't ask good questions. The most valuable interview will give you details not easily available elsewhere. There is no point in spending the interviewee's time—or your own—on questions that are easily answered with a little research at the nearest library.

You should be familiar enough with the subject to know in advance just what kind of information you need from the interview. After you have determined this purpose, ask for an appointment. Explain what information you want and why. This will give the person you interview some time to think about the subject and your particular needs.

In advance of the appointment, prepare eight or ten specific questions that cover all the essential areas in which you are interested. Write them on sheets of paper with enough space for notes after each question. If you use one question per sheet, you can easily rearrange the order of the questions depending upon the flow of the conversation.

Make sure that you know the essential information about the person you are interviewing: name, occupation, title, important accomplishments. It may seem unnecessary to mention these steps in your preparation, but they are essential. Interviewers who omit this crucial information seem grossly unprepared to the person they interview. Don't allow an oversight to detract from your purpose.

Conducting the interview   When you come for your appointment, be on time and be prepared to take notes. You may want to use a cassette recorder. Most people won't object to it, but be sure to ask whether there is any objection. Some people are initially nervous when confronted by a recording device, but most soon forget that it is there. Even if you use a cassette recorder, take ample notes. Use the recording to check your notes or to get specific figures, stories, or quotations. The recording is to insure accuracy. If you don't take notes, playing back and searching through the tape afterwards will be too time-consuming.

Ask your questions one at a time and let your respondent answer fully. If the question doesn't get the response you expected, try rephrasing it or asking a more specific subquestion. If a question seems unclear to the interviewee, use other, more general, questions and return to the unclear one later. Remember, even with careful preparation beforehand, it will take a while for you and the person you are interviewing to be comfortable with one another, and the initial questions are more likely to be confusing than later ones will be.

In the questioning, keep your objective in mind. You want to gain information. Don't argue with the person you interview. If you want a reaction to an opposing point of view, don't state it as your opinion (even if it is!). Say, "Some people say that offshore oil drilling is inevitably damaging to the environment. What is your opinion?"

You will discover that if you prepare carefully, the questions you ask will provide much of the information you want. You may also discover new topics cropping up. *If* they pertain to your subject, you should pursue them with questions you didn't plan beforehand.

Don't overstay your welcome. If your appointment was half an hour, try to finish in that length of time. If you find yourself running out of time, look over your list of questions and turn quickly to the most important ones. Before you leave, find out whether the person objects to being quoted in the speech. Most will not, but you should respect the wishes of those who do not want to be quoted. You can gracefully avoid naming your source by saying, "The vice president of a local bank told me . . . ."

After the interview   Review your notes and your tape as soon as possible after the interview. They will be much clearer then than two or three days later. Select the material you can use and organize it along with the other information you will use in your speech.

Radio, Television, and Public Lectures

In many instances, radio and television programs offer data that would otherwise be unavailable. it isn't likely that a college student could approach the President of the United States, for instance, and ask him for his views on federal aid to education or continued support of Medicare. Yet the President's views are often communicated to the nation over radio and television. Some statements made under these circumstances will not appear in print, because most newspapers do not report the complete text of a broadcast speech or press conference. Accurate note-taking of statements in such broadcasts can provide information not available elsewhere. Be sure to identify the source including time and date. Public lectures at local museums or events are another valuable source of information. Unlike the interview, however, you can't always ask questions. And, unlike printed sources, you can't reread the material if you don't understand. To use this source you must be a careful listener. Review Chapter 3 on listening effectively. The principles explained in that chapter will be useful when you gather materials from any nonpublished sources.

Using the Library

By far the richest source of speech materials (indeed, of knowledge of all kinds) is a well-supplied library. Yet for many students a library is an untapped gold mine of fabulous wealth. They want the gold and are willing to work to dig it out, but they can't find the mother lode. A few nuggets fall into their hands by chance, but the real riches are never uncovered.

Each library has a systematic method of cataloging and arranging materials. Become familiar with your library system. If you do not understand the online access system, the card catalog, the use of indexes, or the numbering system in your library, librarians will gladly explain them to you. They are professionally trained teachers. They will help you find specific pieces of information and help you familiarize yourself with the resources of the library.

The next section of this chapter will give a general overview of the online access system or card catalog which indexes the books in the library. Then we will look at the special reference tools that you can use to find frequently needed information: facts, statistics, brief articles, extended articles, biography, dates, and quotations.

Online Library Access System

Most college and university libraries now have a computerized system to help you find books, periodicals, audio-visual materials, government publications, maps and music collected in that library.[1] If you have a modem and a personal computer, it may be possible to access your library online system from your home. Some smaller libraries still rely on the card catalog. For some individuals, the catalog is not as easy to use as the computerized system, but it contains essentially the same information. Most universities and colleges have both the computer based system and the card catalog. If one of the methods causes confusion, you can use the alternative.

Most computerized systems have their own designation. For instance, the University of Utah system is called UNIS (University of Utah Network Information System) and the University of Iowa system is called OASIS (Online Access System for Information Sources). Whatever the system is called at your school, it will be essentially the same as others and probably based on NOTIS (Northwestern Outline Total Integrated System) developed at Northwestern University. Let's see how you can best use your system.

First of all, be sure you know just how much information your library system contains. It may not yet have government documents in it, for example. If the content of your system is not clearly posted, ask a librarian to help you.

A second step is to learn the basic commands for the system. You need only a few. The "help" menu in the program will give you information for the type of search you need.

There are three basic search strategies. They correspond to the kinds of cards in the card catalog: author, title and subject. Which one you use will depend on how much you know about the subject. If you know the name of an author who writes on the subject, you can start with that. If you have heard of a book title, you can use it as a starting point. If you only have your subject—start there.

> *Subject*: Type S = [subject] (return)
>
> *Author*: Type A = [author's last, first name] (return)
>
> *Title*: Type T = [title] (return)

The list of authors includes, in addition to individual authors, what is called corporate authors such as The American Society of Civil Engineers, The American Management Association, or The Speech Communication Association.

The title search may also be used to discover whether a periodical is available in the library and where it is shelved. So you might ask: T = *Argument* and *Advocacy* (return) to find what issues of that journal are in the library and where they may be found.

The computer will respond in three steps: *Guide*, *Index*, and *Bibliographic Record* to any of your inquiries. The *Guide* will list all of the possible choices from which you can select the Index you want.

Guide

```
UNIS SEARCH REQUEST: S = COLLECTIVE BARGAINING
  SUBJECT HEADING GUIDE — 285 HEADINGS FOUND, 1 - 10 DISPLAYED
   1  COLLECTIVE BARGAINING
   2  —ACCOUNTING
   3  —AERONAUTICS -UNITED STATES
   4  —AERONAUTICS -UNITED STATES -CONGRESSES
   5  —AEROPLANE INDUSTRY -GREAT BRITAIN -CASE STUDIES
   6  —AFRICA -CONGRESSES
   7  —AFRICA SUB-SAHARRAN
   8  —AGRICULTURE -CALIFORNIA
   9  —ARGENTINA -HISTORY
  10  —AUTOMOBILE INDUSTRY -CASE STUDIES
  11  —AUTOMOBILE INDUSTRY -GERMANY WEST
  12  —AUTOMOBILE INDUSTRY -UNITED STATES -HISTORY
  13  —BIBLIOGRAPHY
  14  —BOOK-MAKING BETTING -MICHIGAN
  15  —BRITISH COLUMBIA
  16  —CALIFORNIA -CONGRESSES
  17  —CALIFORNIA -SAN FRANCISCO
  18  —CANADA
TYPE m FOR MORE SUBJECT HEADINGS. TYPE LINE NO. FOR TITLES UNDER A
HEADING. TYPE r TO REVISE, h FOR HELP, e FOR UNIS INTRODUCTION.
TYPE COMMAND AND PRESS RETURN = ▶
```

If you wanted general information on the subject of "collective bargaining," you would touch the number 1 and return for the following index.

Index

```
UNIS SEARCH REQUEST: S=COLLECTIVE BARGAINING
  SUBJECT/TITLE INDEX — 108 TITLES FOUND, 1 - 16 DISPLAYED
COLLECTIVE BARGAINING

 1 collective bargaining in Industr  (1987)MR stks:HD6971.5 C64 1987
 2 management of collective bargain  (1987)MR stks:HD6971.5 S57 1987
 3 collective bargain               (1986)LW law,main:HD6483 .C48 1986
 4 collective bargaining: how it wo  (1986)MR stks:HD6971.5 C66 1986
 5 collective bargaining by objecti  (1985)MR stks:HD6971.5 .R53 1985
 6 employer bargaining objectives 1  (1985)MR gref:HD6971.5 .E55 1985
 7 issues in management-labour rela  (1985)MR stks:HD6971.5 .P45 1985
 8 labor guide to negotiating wages  (1985)MR stks:HD6971.5 .D36 1985
 9 man mismanagement                (1985)MR stks:HD6971 .F643 1985
10 collective bargaining: a respons  (1984)MR stks:HD6971.5 .C64 1984
11 debate sindical nacional e inter  (1984)MR stks:HD6530.5 .D43 1984
12 general survey on the applicatio  (1983)MR stks:JC607 ,I67 1983
13 bargaining power tactics and out  (1981)MR stks:HD38 .B17
14 how to calculate the manufacture  (1980)MR stks:HD4909 .S89
15 promotion of collective bargaini  (1980)MR stks:HD6483 .I64 1980
16 unions rights to company informa  (1980)MR stks:HD6483 .0738
TYPE LINE NO. FOF BIBLIOGRAPHIC RECORD WITH HOLDINGS
TYPE m FOR MORE TITLES.
TYPE g FOR GUIDE. TYPE r TO REVISE, h FOR HELP, e FOR UNIS INTRODUCITON.
TYPE COMMAND AND PRESS RETURN = ►
```

The index gives you a list of the books the library has on the subject. In this case, it is a list of books on collective bargaining. From the index you can select the Bibliographic Record card you want. It gives you complete information on the publication including the call number of the book so you can find it in the stacks of the library.

Bibliographic Record

```
UNIS SEARCH REQUEST: S=COLLECTIVE BARGAINING
  BIBLIOGRAPHIC RECORD — NO. 7 OF 107 ENTRIES FOUND
Peitchinis, Stephen G.
   Issues in management-labour relations in the 1990s / Stephen G. Peitchinis.
New York : St. Martin's Press, 1985
   xii, 177 p. : 22 cm.
   Bibliography: p. 170-172.
   Includes index.
SUBJECT HEADINGS (Library of Congress: use s = ):
     Collective bargaining.
     Industrial relations.

LOCATION: LC BOOKS, LEVEL 4
CALL NUMBER: HD6971.5 .P45 1985
     Not charged out. If not on shelf, ask at Circulation Desk.

TYPE m FOR NEXT RECORD. TYPE i FOR INDEX, g FOR GUIDE.
TYPE r TO REVISE, h FOR HELP, u FOR UNIS INTRODUCITON.
TYPE COMMAND AND PRESS RETURN = ►
```

Note that the Bibliographic record is laid out in order: Author, Title, Subject. If you need to use the card catalog you will find that each book is listed alphabetically by at least three cards—one headed like the bibliographic record illustrated above (the author card), another is filed by the title, and at least one other is filed by subject.

Most online systems have one or more terminals connected to a printer so that when you find the display you want to preserve you can push the *print* key for a copy of it.

Search Hints[2]

Type h (return) for help at any time. If you are in a search sequence, the help screen gives hints for your type of search.

Use hyphens but omit all other punctuation. Using other kinds of punctuation in a search term may cause a NO ENTRIES FOUND response.

If you get a NO ENTRIES FOUND response, try some other possibilities. Did you misspell an author's name? Is the title wrong? Is there an alternative way of stating a subject?

An article, such as "a," "an," or "the," at the beginning of a title may or may not be used in the title. "And" may be treated as "&" or "+" or "and" in an entry. If unsuccessful, try it a different way.

Abbreviations may or may not be successful—try it both ways.

A search term is read from left to right. This feature can be useful if you are unsure of your search term.

Example: s = luna (return) retrieves:
luna juan de
lunacharsky anatoly vasailierich
lunar craters
lunar theory

Special Reference Tools

Libraries differ on the amount of material in the online computerized system. Periodical articles usually are not referenced. The online computer system at your library will probably tell you whether the library has, for instance, the *International Encyclopedia of Communications*, *Forbes*, or the *Los Angeles Times*. It probably won't tell you what specific articles are in the periodicals.

New search procedures for information are constantly being developed. CD-ROM (compact disc-read only memory) is a system of compact discs capable of storing up to 275,000 printed pages of information on one 5 1/4'' disc. They are expensive and many libraries do not have them or have only a few. The CD-ROM system discs contain citations and abstracts of articles in a variety of fields including: MEDLINE, which stores information in the health sciences; PsychLIT, which stores psychological abstracts; Newsbank, which indexes articles in some 400 newspapers. System disks also include the Humanities Index, the Social Science Index and ERIC (Educational Resources Information Center), a wide-based source for education-related topics.

Info-Trac is another very useful system which covers many of the subjects you might choose as speech topics. It indexes current articles and abstracts from the more popular periodicals. It is based on indexes such as the *Reader's Guide to Periodical Literature* for the previous three years. If your university or college does not have Info-Trac, CD-ROM, or the particular index you need, that index is also available in printed form.

Before using any of these computer-based systems or printed indexes and reference works, you need to select the most appropriate reference work for your research. They differ from one another in the kinds of information they provide. In the following pages, we have organized reference sources according to the kinds of materials you might need.

For basic facts and statistics   The *World Almanac*, the *Information Please Almanac*, and a number of other such volumes provide a vast amount of specific, up-to-date information. The *Statistical Abstract of the United States* provides quantitative summary statistics (usually covering 15 to 20 years) on the political, social, and industrial organization of the United States. The *Statesman's Yearbook* gives statistics and facts on the government. *World Statistics in Brief* covers similar data for 163 countries. *Facts on File* is a weekly synopsis of world events. Its index supplies a ready reference for a variety of information. The *Congressional Quarterly* gives a synopsis of federal legislation and the voting records of Senators and Representatives.

For dates   Dictionaries supply many of the dates you will need. The *World Almanac* has a chronological listing of the events of the year previous to its publication. The *New York Times Index* provides the dates of events reported in the newspapers.

For quotations   John Bartlett's *Familiar Quotations* is the best-known source of short quotations. It is arranged chronologically by author and has a fine index of topics as well. Another source of quotations, Burton E. Stevenson's *Home Book of Quotations*, contains more entries than Bartlett's book. It is arranged by topics.

For biographies   *Current Biography* is a publication that gives short, useful biographies of living persons. A wide variety of *Who's Who* books give brief biographical sketches. Webster's *Biographical Dictionary* contains very brief biographies of many distinguished persons. The *Dictionary of American Biography* sketches the lives of historically prominent Americans, and the *Dictionary of National Biography* does the same for historically notable British citizens. The *Biographic Index* is helpful in locating more extended biographies. It is cross-referenced according to profession or occupation as well as the name of the persons listed; it indexes biographical periodical articles as well as books. In addition, the encyclopedias discussed in the next section also contain biographies.

For brief, authoritative articles   For an introductory discussion of a subject, you should go first to an encyclopedia. General encyclopedias such as the *Britannica* and the *Americana* give information on all phases of human knowledge, and their articles usually include references for further study. The *Britannica* is widely considered the best general reference in the humanities, whereas the *Americana* is thought to be stronger in science and technology.

Specialized encyclopedias are available for more thorough treatment of a subject. *Religion and Ethics, World History, Banking and Finance, World Arts and Sports,* Van Nostrand's *Scientific Encyclopedia, The International Encyclopedia of the Social Sciences,* Grove's *Dictionary of Music and Musicians,* and the *Dictionary of American History* all supply information in the specific areas their titles name.

For more extensively developed articles   Although the basic sorts of information we have discussed so far can be found in reference books such

There are numerous reference sources with information on almost any subject that you choose to research.

as almanacs and encyclopedias, more extensively developed articles will be found in magazines and scholarly journals. Such publications will be useful only if you know how to use CD-ROM, Info-Trac, or their equivalents in a printed index.

Periodical indexes are arranged by subject. The subject headings are often the same as those in the online library access system or card catalog. If you understand those systems, you should be able to find items in a periodical index. Remember, however, that indexes cover specific periods of time. The most common index of magazines is the *Reader's Guide to Periodical Literature*. It indexes a large number of popular periodicals from 1900 to the present.

Except for the online library system, the *Reader's Guide* is probably the most used index in the library, but its limitations are too frequently overlooked. It indexes only popular magazines. It is excellent for current, less technical articles. However, it is of limited usefulness in investigating more specialized topics. There are too many specialized indexes to list them all here, but we will name some that should prove useful. The *Social Sciences Index* and the *Humanities Index* are author and subject indexes to the scholarly journals in the social sciences and humanities. The *Business Periodicals Index* lists articles on business administration, public administration, and economics. The *Public Affairs Information Service* indexes a wide variety of books, periodicals, public documents, and mimeographed material in government, sociology, and business. The *Biological and Agricultural Index*, the *Education Index*, the *Art Index*, the *Music Index*, and the *Applied Science and Technology Index* catalog periodical literature in special fields.

When you have found the author, title, periodical, volume, page, and date of an article from the index, CD-ROM, or Info-Trac, you will want to check to see whether your library subscribes to the periodical in which it appears. This information can be found in your online library system or in separate guides to periodicals in your library.

The *New York Times* is an especially useful source of information on current events. This newspaper prints complete texts of many speeches and documents of public interest. Its treatment of news items is ordinarily more extensive than that found in many other papers and in news magazines. Most libraries subscribe to the paper and keep it on microfilm. The *New York Times Index* locates specific items in the paper and is an excellent reference tool. It can be used to find news items in other papers also, because most newspapers cover a story at about the same time. There are also indexes to major newspapers such as the *Chicago Tribune* and the *Los Angeles Times*.

Remember too that the United States government is the largest publisher in the world. You may want to look into the government documents in your library. They are probably indexed in your online library system. If not, there are special indexes which your librarian can provide. Government documents cover a wide variety of current topics and an amazing array of statistical information.

Methods of Recording Information

The information you collect should be recorded on cards or paper. You can cut 8 1/2" X 11" sheets of paper into four pieces and use these, or you can buy cards at any stationery store. Four items of information should be entered on these cards: (1) a label to identify the material, (2) the author, (3) the information you plan to use, and (4) the necessary bibliographical data. If you record these four items accurately, you will need to check the original source only *once*. Figure 9.1 shows an example of a note card made from the book in the bibliographic record on page 139.

Because the information you gather from all the sources we have listed eventually finds its way into the outline of your speech, you will want to make it as easy as possible to handle. Putting each item on a separate card makes it easy to rearrange the sequence of cards without excessive rewriting

Figure 9.1

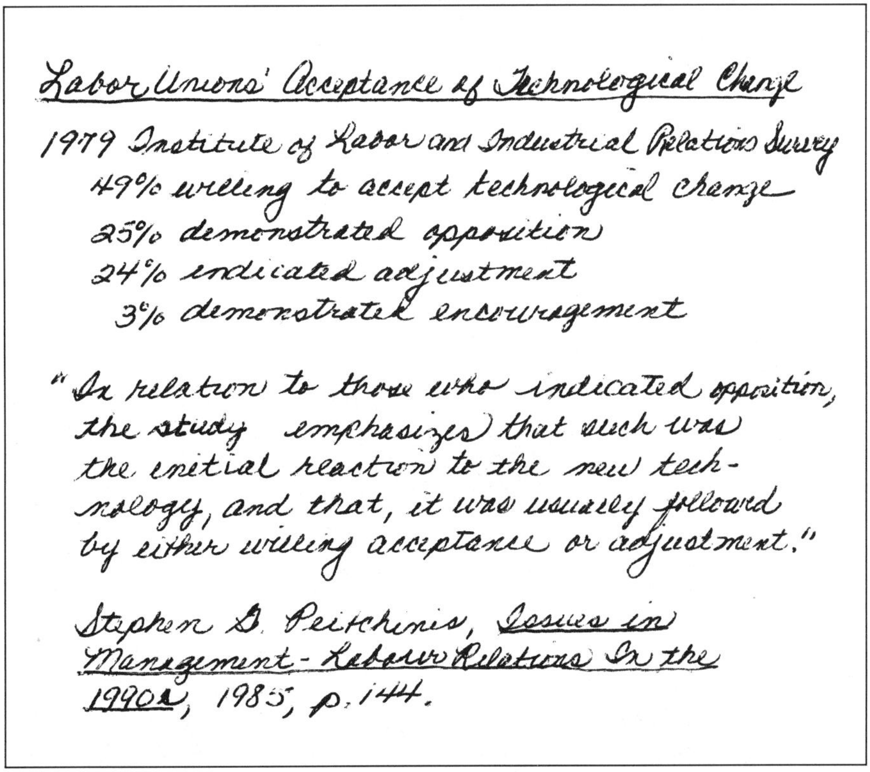

Labor Unions' Acceptance of Technological Change

1979 Institute of Labor and Industrial Relations Survey
    49% willing to accept technological change
    25% demonstrated opposition
    24% indicated adjustment
    3% demonstrated encouragement

"In relation to those who indicated opposition, the study emphasizes that such was the initial reaction to the new technology, and that, it was usually followed by either willing acceptance or adjustment."

Stephen G. Peitchinis, *Issues in Management - Labour Relations In the 1990s*, 1985, p. 144.

The use of note cards to record the information you gathered makes outlining the speech much easier.

or constant re-reading of your notes. When the rough draft of your outline has been prepared, you can decide where the data on each card fits into the outline. When you use note cards in this manner, much of the work of preparing an outline is done automatically, painlessly, and easily.

Summary

An often overlooked source of supporting material is your personal experience. Frequently you have valuable knowledge and experience that others don't have. Use that experience when it is relevant.

Information can also be obtained by interviewing an expert on your subject. Plan the interview and select questions in advance. Do some research to be sure you have some essential information before you go to the interview. During the interview be prepared to take notes or ask if you can use a tape recorder. Don't argue with the person you interview and don't overstay your welcome. Review your notes as soon after the interview as possible. Radio, television, and public lectures can provide good information. Like interviews, they require careful note-taking.

The library is probably the richest source of information. The online system indexes by author, title, and subject all the books in your library and tells you where to find them. There are also special computerized (CD-ROM and Info-Trac) and printed reference works and indexes that will help you to find information. These will give you basic facts, statistics, dates, quotations, biographies, and brief authoritative articles. All the necessary information should be collected on cards so that it can be easily integrated into your outline. If you record the bibliographic information carefully you won't have to go back to check the original source.

Key Terms

Personal experience	CD-ROM
Interviewing	Info-trac
Radio and television	Facts
Lectures	Statistics
Online Library Access System	Dates
Card catalog	Quotations
Guide	Biographies
Index	Authoritative articles
Bibliographic record	Recording information

Exercises

1. Before you begin your next speech assignment, select two or three subjects and make a list of each to compare:

   a. the amount of personal experience you have with the subject.

   b. possible interviews for further information.

   c. radio or TV programs on the subject.

   If you had only these sources of information to draw on, which subject would you know best?

2. If you are not knowledgeable about your library, go there and take a tour to learn about the various resources and where they are found.

3. On one of your speech assignments, use the online library access system or card catalog to find three books pertaining to your subject.

4. On one of your speech assignments, use each of the six types of special reference tools and find one piece of information of each type. Turn in the list of what you found to your instructor.

Notes

[1] Much of the material in this section has been adapted from: Ceres Birkhead, Dennis Isbell, Juli Hinz, Mark Spivey, and Robin Reid, Library Literacy, (Salt Lake City: Marriott Library, U of Utah, 1990).

[2] The Online Catalog (UNIS), U of Utah, n.d. unpub. 2-3.

Arguing Reasonably

As a preamble to his novel *Cardinal of the Kremlin*, Tom Clancy wrote, "A number of very bright people were struggling to find the Truth—the scientific kind that did not depend on human opinion." The struggle to find truth rests on the assumption that there *is* truth. In that case, we only have to find it. Once found, the truth becomes a touchstone for evaluating judgments in political, economic, and social affairs—or any other arena of human action where decisions are made.

Aristotle had a more pragmatic attitude toward the making of decisions. He assumed, just as Clancy's truth-seekers did, that there is knowable truth. He also called it scientific knowledge. He said, however, that some people cannot be persuaded with scientific knowledge. True instruction in those cases is impossible.

In rhetoric, arguments must be based on general opinions. Think of a general opinion as a widely held belief rather than certain knowledge. Since a belief of this kind can never be more than a probability, claims based on opinions can themselves never be more than probabilities. By a probability, we mean something that can be reasonably believed on the basis of available evidence, although it is not proved or certain. That is the nature of decisions in everyday human affairs. People debate disagreements in science, psychology, religion, politics, law, etc. The claims they ask an audience to accept must always be considered no more than *probably* wise or just.

Both Clancy and Aristotle understood that decision makers do not have the comfort of certain truth. That makes sense. If you already knew the truth about the theory of continental drift, whether Vietnam veterans have been treated fairly, or whether it would be best to reelect Susan Reynolds to the Student Senate, you wouldn't need to make a decision at all.

Before you accept a judgment on any issue, you want to test it. The method of testing is called argumentation. Argumentation is a process of advancing reasons to accept or reject any claim. The reasons for deciding one way or the other are called arguments. When you persuade others to accept your point of view, you give them arguments—reasons to believe the probability of your claim.

The word argument itself is frequently troublesome. In addition to being the same as "quarrel" for most people, it also suggests mathematical and philosophical arguments—and these are scary.

> "Argument" is a word with a bad reputation. On the one hand it reminds us of siblings' quarrels or of battles conducted across a courtroom. On the other, it recalls mathematical arguments, which many of us find more fearsome than any personal fray. Arguments, it seems are something to avoid.
>
> But such a reading is clearly reading in. "Arguments" need not mean anything contentious or mathematical either. Really, the term refers broadly and neutrally to reasoning in order to make decisions or test the truth of claims. We neglect such reasoning only at our own hazard.[1]

Audiences are persuaded by the three elements inherent in any rhetorical argument. That is, an audience is persuaded when it accepts your *logos* (is convinced that your arguments are reasonable); your *pathos* (understands that your claim is consistent with its own beliefs and values), and your ethos (believes that you are knowledgeable and trustworthy). In this chapter, our concern is with effective *logos*; we will show you how to construct reasonable arguments.

Arguments and Proof

In a speech, you ask an audience to make some kind of change in attitude or behavior, such as understanding something new or understanding it differently, accepting a new belief, abandoning an old belief in favor of a new one, or strengthening an already held conviction.

Audience response to the change in attitude or behavior you ask for is influenced by the fact that in our culture people are taught to expect understandings, beliefs, and actions to be reasonable. Every claim you make, then, must be justified. Even though you firmly believe that something is reasonable and wise, merely voicing the belief does not necessarily justify it for an audience. "I don't believe that—prove it to me," is a common, expected response. Be sure you understand what you are saying when you talk about "proving" a claim. In geometry you prove the claim that every angle of a triangle has to be less than 180 degrees. You argue that: (1) the total of all the angles in a triangle is 180 degrees; (2) there are three angles in every triangle; (3) no single part of anything can be as great as the total of all the parts. Therefore, each one of the three angles must necessarily be less than 180 degrees. Your argument proves the claim so strongly that there can be no doubt. Anyone who tries to deny it lands right in the middle of a contradiction between the two axioms.

You won't be making speeches to prove mathematical theorems. Instead, your subjects will be claims of fact, value, and policy that grow out of interest or necessity.

Look at the following examples. You can see that all of them are debatable because of unresolved issues that cause disagreements.

Since 1951 the number of women who work outside the home has increased by 200%. How can you prove this factual claim to an audience? Clearly, you cannot show that like the angles of a triangle it is necessarily true and that denying it would therefore create a contradiction. The best you can do is give the audience enough acceptable evidence and reasonable argument to make it seem the most probable position to take.

The absence of the woman from the home is detrimental to the stability of the home. Like any other value claim, a judgment in this case will be based on the beliefs and values of the audience. Beliefs and values, however, are neither true nor false. People simply have them or they don't. For example, your preference for vanilla ice cream doesn't make it better

Phyllis Schlafly would endorse the value claim The absence of the woman from the home is detrimental to the stability of the home. *Others would disagree.*

than chocolate. Your choice is based on personal taste. It is very much like the idea that beauty is in the eye of the beholder. If you ever watched the television series *Beauty and the Beast*, you might have wondered how the young Assistant District Attorney could find anything lovable about the Beast. Given her beliefs and values, she could and did. When you support a value claim, the most your arguments can "prove" is that there is no contradiction between your claim and the beliefs and values of the audience.

The working member of a family should pay the one who stays at home a salary commensurate with the work required to run the household. Like claims of fact and value, a policy claim is merely an expression of beliefs and values. Remember what we said in Chapter 5: policy claims are supported by resolving issues of fact and value. Again, arguments will not prove that the claim is true; they can only show that it is probably a correct solution because it is consistent with the beliefs and values of the audience.

In public speaking, instead of arguing that a claim is true, think in terms of winning the agreement of the audience. The function of *logos* is to persuade the audience that your claim is the most reasonable position to take.

We said earlier that people are taught to expect arguments to make reasonable inferences. The formal method of testing inferences is logic. Even though people are generally reasonable, most of them know little or nothing about the rules of formal logic. Reasonableness you are born with; logic you have to learn. Instead of using formal logic in making arguments, human beings have a system of informal logic, a method of practical reasoning to justify the claims they make in their everyday affairs. The skills of critical thinking that we discussed in Chapter 1 are an informal logic of this kind.

To be a critical thinker, you must be knowledgeable about the subject at hand; you have to have the right information. Once you have that, you need to organize it into a reasonable structure. Only then can you expect to build clear explanations and sound arguments. The principal skill of critical thinking is the ability to identify flaws in the evidence and arguments of others as well as in your own.

The best way to insure that your arguments are reasonable justifications for your claims is to understand how arguments work. Let's begin by looking at a diagram that is useful both for constructing arguments and for evaluating them.

The Toulmin Model of Argument

Near the middle of this century, an English philosopher named Stephen Toulmin observed that in day-to-day public debate, disputes arise in areas such as science, psychology, religion, politics, and law. Toulmin also observed that arguments do not strictly follow the rules of formal logic. Nonetheless, they are reasonable; people have reasons for what they believe or say or do. He also noticed that there is some system to how they argue. With these ideas in mind, Toulmin developed a model to demonstrate the system people actually use. Our model, adapted from Toulmin's, illustrates arguments so they can be evaluated.[2]

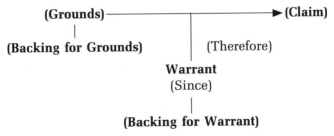

Let's go through the major elements of this model and see how easily it can be used to analyze an argument.

You have a claim you want to prove. To justify the claim you need some evidence on which to ground your claim—some fact or principle that will serve as a basis for the argument.

John F. Kennedy and Richard M. Nixon were the first presidential candidates to appear in a televised debate (October, 1960). Political debates are now common in many political campaigns.

(Grounds) ──────────	──────────► **(Claim)**
Day-care centers for employees' children would increase the corporation's profits.	(Therefore) Corporations should maintain day-care centers.

The argument must also show how the relationship between grounds and claim is reasonably justified. That is, the argument must show *why* the grounds warrant the claim. So, let's add the warrant (justification) to the diagram.

(Grounds) ──────────	──────────► **(Claim)**
Day-care centers for employees' children would increase the corporation's profits.	(Therefore) Corporations should maintain day-care centers.

(Warrant)

(Since) All corporations want to increase profits.

Sometimes the grounds and/or the warrant of the argument will need to be strengthened before the audience will accept it. In that case, you must introduce whatever supporting material is needed: further evidence, your own credibility, or some appropriate belief or value held by the audience. Although Toulmin does not include backing for the grounds as part of his diagram, you may need to use it in some audience situations.

(Grounds) ⎯⎯⎯⎯⎯⎯⎯⎯⎯⟶ **(Claim)**

Day-care centers for employees' children would increase corporation profits.

(Therefore) Corporations should maintain day-care centers.

(Backing for Grounds)

Corporations get tax breaks for supplying day care. Turnover rates decrease among employees with children. One company saved more than $40,000 in retraining costs.

(Warrant)

(Since) All corporations want to increase profits.

(Backing for Warrant)

One CEO said, "The only reason we're in business is to make money."

Toulmin's model of argument is an analytical tool. It does not tell you the best order (or any order) of parts in an actual argument. What it does tell you is how to lay out arguments (yours or anybody else's) to see whether they are reasonable.

The principal value of the Toulmin model is to help you diagram and test your own arguments before you present them to an audience. Using the model will improve your argumentation in at least three significant ways: first, it will help you discover weaknesses in the arguments you hear; second, you can use it as a framework for constructing your own arguments, and third, it points out the sections of the argument where weaknesses lie. To find the flaws in any argument, lay it out and then ask: "Does it have adequate grounds?" "Does it need backing (substantiation) to make the grounds believable?" "Is the warrant acceptable?" "Does it need backing to give it greater strength?" "Is the claim a reasonable inference from the grounds and warrant; that is, does the warrant justify the inferential leap from grounds to claim?" If the arguments pass these tests, you can feel assured that with respect to *logos* the arguments are sound. Testing your arguments will help you avoid errors like these:

> "I put a new set of Bridgestone tires on my car because Lee Trevino says they are really great. You can feel the difference when you drive."

> "Sure he can afford to contribute to the program. When a fellow owns a car like his, it's a sure thing he has plenty of money."

> "You ought to read my book on self-confidence. Right after I finished it, I made a pile of money on my next trip to Las Vegas."

> "I'll never trust you again. You lied to me when you told me you would pay me back on Thursday."

> "That diet won't help you lose weight. I tried it last summer."

Before we talk about what causes errors in arguments, we'll examine the five forms rhetorical arguments take.

The Five Forms of Argument

Any argument falls into one of five different forms: argument from authority, argument from sign, argument from cause, argument by generalization, and argument by analogy. Each of the forms can be diagrammed and tested by using Toulmin's analytical model.

Argument from Authority

An argument from authority says that a claim should be accepted because it is the opinion of a knowledgeable and trustworthy source. If your audience accepts the authority as credible, the claim will be warranted.

Richard Lamm, former Governor of Colorado, said to the Colorado Bar Association:

> Derek Bok, President of Harvard University, has pointed out that 40 percent of our Rhodes Scholars go to law school and he has quoted the Japanese: "Engineers make the pie grow larger; lawyers only decide how to carve it up."

> Derek Bok charged that our American legal process is the most expensive in the world yet it does not manage to protect the rights of most of its citizens. He stated, "The blunt, inexcusable fact is that this nation, which prides itself on efficiency and justice, has developed a legal system which is the most expensive in the world."[3]

We will discuss credibility at greater length in Chapter 12. In this case, however, you can see that unless the audience of lawyers accepted Bok as a credible authority on the legal system, it would not accept Lamm's claim.

An argument from authority is diagrammed this way:

(Grounds) ————————————————▶**(Claim)**

| Derek Bok says our legal system is the most expensive in the world. | (Therefore) The American legal system is the most expensive in the world. |

(Warrant)

(Since) Derek Bok is an authority
on the American legal system.

(Backing for Warrant)

He was the dean of the school
of law at Harvard University.

Argument from Sign

In an argument from sign, you observe directly some fact or condition. Using this as a basis (grounds), you make the claim that some other fact or condition, not immediately observable, exists.

Mikhail Gorbachev, then Prime Minister of the Soviet Union, spoke to the United Nations in the winter of 1988. In his speech he used this argument from sign:

> Profound social changes are taking place.
>
> In the East and in the South, in the West and in the North, hundreds of millions of people, new nations and states, new public movements and ideologies have advanced to the foreground of history.
>
> The striving for independence, democracy and social justice manifests itself, in all its diversity and with all its contradictions, in broad and frequently turbulent popular movements. The idea of democratizing the entire world order has grown into a powerful social and political force.
>
> At the same time, the revolution in science and technology has turned economic, food, energy, ecological, information and demographic problems, which only recently were of a national or regional character, into global problems.
>
> The newest techniques of communications, mass information and transport have made the world more visible and more tangible to everyone. International communication is easier now than ever before.[4]

You can diagram the argument this way:

(Grounds) ───────────────	► (Claim)
There are new nations, movements and ideologies.	(Therefore) Profound social changes are taking place.
Democratizing the entire world is now a social and political force.	
Revolutions in science technology have caused global problems. International communication is easier than ever before.	

(Warrant)

(Since) These events are definite signs of social change.

Argument from Cause

When an event is the direct result of a preceding event, the relationship between them is said to be that of cause and effect. The earlier one that brings about the later event is said to be the cause. The later one, that exists as a direct result of the first, is said to be the effect. You can develop an argument from causal reasoning in one of two strategic forms: *from cause to effect or from effect to cause.*

Argument from cause to effect   The moral and ethical issues that surround the question of prolonging human life by medical means are staggering. Eva M. Skinner is a member of the Board of Directors of the American Association of Retired Persons. In December 1988, she spoke to the physicians who make up the membership of the Forum for Medical Affairs in Dallas, Texas. Skinner used this argument from cause to show her audience the nature of the problem society faces:

> We are proud that better health care, better nutrition and advances in medical science enable us to live longer than every before. But those advances increase the possibility that most of us will need some kind of assistance later in life—either care in our home or in a nursing facility, or prolonged care in other settings as the end of life approaches.[5]

Here is how the argument looks when it is diagrammed:

(Grounds) ───────────────	► (Claim)
People are living longer.	(Therefore) We will need help in our old age.
(Backing for Grounds)	
Better care, better nutrition and medical advances help extend our lives.	

(Warrant)

(Since) A longer life increases the need for care.

Argument from effect to cause　The second kind of causal reasoning moves backward in time. It identifies the probable cause of an observed condition. Medical diagnosis reasons from effect to cause. Your symptoms are directly observed conditions that are caused by the illness the doctor wants to identify. Your fever (effect) is caused by an infection (cause) of some kind. Other symptoms that are the effects of the illness, will show your doctor specifically what disease is causing you to be sick.

To prove her claim that testing procedures for AIDS are inadequate, Pam Espinoza, a student at Regis College in Colorado, used this argument from effect to cause.

> The College of American Pathologists concluded that for people at low risk for AIDS, 9 out of 10 positive findings is a false positive, indicating infection where none exists. On the other hand, however, for people at high risk for AIDS, 1 out of every 10 negative findings is a false negative, meaning that people are told they are not infected with the AIDS virus when they actually are. Now, the College of American Pathologists concluded that in this case, the laboratories weren't at fault. Therefore, the error had to lie within the test itself.[6]

Diagrammed, the argument looks like this:

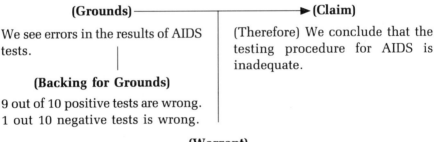

(Grounds) ──────────────▶ **(Claim)**

We see errors in the results of AIDS tests.

(Therefore) We conclude that the testing procedure for AIDS is inadequate.

(Backing for Grounds)

9 out of 10 positive tests are wrong.
1 out 10 negative tests is wrong.

(Warrant)

(Since) The tests are the source of the error.

(Backing for Warrant)

The labs (the only other source of error) are not at fault.

Reasoning from effect to cause can be confused with reasoning from sign. Distinguish between them this way: If the claim is the cause of the grounds, the argument is from effect to cause. If not, the argument is from sign. We can make the difference clear with an example. When you have a fever, you can infer from this effect (grounds) that the cause is an illness (claim). When you come home from a ski trip with a cast on your ankle (grounds), your friends can infer by argument from sign that you broke it (claim). The cast is neither a cause nor an effect of the broken ankle, but it is a good sign that your ankle is in bad shape.

Argument by Generalization

A generalization makes a claim about all of the members of some class or group. What kind of group it is doesn't matter. It may be people ("liars never prosper"), objects ("sports cars are the most expensive automobiles to maintain"), or events ("exams are a pain in the neck"), or anything else that can be classified. The inference is made this way: "I can always be sure of getting a good bargain when I go to a U-Save store. I've been to three of them and every time I've found good stuff at a very decent price." The argument says that what is true of all the observed examples of an event (grounds)—"I've always found good bargains at U-Save," will be true of the whole class of events, including those not observed (claim)—"I can always be sure of getting a bargain at U-Save." The warrant, of course, is the belief that what is true of the examples—"My own visits to U-Save," will be true of the class—"all visits to U-Save."

In a speech supporting his plan to help college athletes get a better education, Steven P. Poessnecker, a student at South Dakota State University, used this argument by generalization. First, he sets the background for the argument:

> *Each year*, former college athletes go out into the world expecting to find a job in professional sports. Unfortunately, they can find employment only in dead end minimum wage jobs, if they're lucky. Why? Because they simply don't have the education for anything better. A recent victim is former University of Arkansas basketball center Dean Tolsen who entered college in the 1970s amid promises and assurances that he had what it takes to go all the way to the pros. But he did not graduate from college. In *Sports Illustrated*, May 30, 1988, Tolsen related how he had 38 credit hours of Fs and a 1.43 GPA. After playing professional basketball for 10 years, he jumped from job to job. Nothing ever materialized into a permanent position. Tolsen said, "When my career was over, I was worth $3.50 an hour. That's all."[7]

Then Steven makes the argument itself:

> Dean Tolsen is not an exception. Another example of a student who didn't get an education while being a college athlete is Kevin Ross. According to the January 30, 1989, *Newsweek*, Ross was admitted to Creighton University, played basketball for three years and left the school functionally illiterate. Ross is now suing Creighton University for failing to educate him. As Ross's lawyer reports, "Kevin couldn't even figure out what the score of the game was. He just knew if they were ahead or behind." Chicago educator Marva Collins, who taught Kevin Ross after college, found that he could read at the second-grade level, [could] print and that school secretaries had typed his papers.[8]

The argument is diagrammed this way:

(Grounds) ————————————————➤ **(Claim)**

Dean Tolsen can't hold a job. Kevin Ross left school almost illiterate.	(Therefore) Colleges are turning out illiterate athletes.

(Warrant)

(Since) what is true of these athletes will be true of colleges athletes in general.

Your audience will probably already believe many of the generalizations you make. If not, you have to prove them. The proof lies in the examples and statistics you use as evidence. Remember that statistics act as a series of compacted examples. The amount of support you need to make a reasonable generalization will vary with the audience and the subject. If Steven's listeners believe that the two examples he gives are not enough to justify the claim, they will reject his argument as a hasty generalization. Chapter 8 shows you how to select examples or statistics that will do the job.

Argument by Analogy

An analogy clarifies a new idea with another one that has similar characteristics. The reasoning is, "What is true of the first instance will also be true of the second because they are essentially alike." "We all know," said Ralph Waldo Emerson, "that as the human body can be nourished by any food, though it were boiled grass and the broth of shoes, so the human mind can be fed by any knowledge."

In an analogy you predict that because two things are alike in certain known respects, they will be alike in other respects. Thus, you might argue that legalizing marijuana in Holland was successful so legalization would work well in the United States. The difference between an analogy and a generalization is that a generalization infers a claim about an entire class, whereas an analogy draws the comparison between two individual members of the same class.

The Manhattan Maritime Project was established to investigate the potential of the earth's oceans to contribute to the economic and physical needs of the world's population. In 1988, Gilven M. Slonim, President of the Oceanic Educational Foundation, used this argument to support the project.

> The massive drive to unlock the "secrets of the ocean" will attract the Nation's finest maritime minds. Here, an analogy can be drawn to Prince Henry the Navigator's Ocean Institute at Sagres Point, Portugal in Columbus's day. In the final years of the 15th Century, this brooding prince congregated the top navigators, cartographers, mathematicians,

the talented men in all aspects of seafaring for a breakthrough to the great global sea. He marshalled conceptual thinkers, scientists, scholars from every field of oceanic endeavor, every scientific discipline to his maritime "think-tank." What this oceanic brain-trust unleashed upon the sea changed our world forever!

The "Manhattan Maritime Project," conceived to foster a comparable role within the modern world, promises unprecedented contribution again for all mankind.[9]

You don't have to forecast your analogy as bluntly as Slonim does unless you think it will give your argument greater effect. For example, if the analogy you use is not immediately obvious, you need not automatically abandon it. Instead, tell your listeners it is coming. Their increased attention can make it easier for them to see the comparison. Here is a diagram of Slonim's argument"

(Grounds) ──────────────────────────┐──────────► **(Claim)**

Henry's Oceanic Institute did great things for the world. │ (Therefore) The Manhattan Maritime Project will also be beneficial.

(Warrant)

(Since) The two projects are essentially alike.

The chief benefit of argument by analogy is that it lets you profit from experience; the chief danger comes when some important difference has been overlooked. For example, even if the audience accepts the grounds that legalizing marijuana in Holland is a success, a similar program can be expected to operate successfully in another country only if the two countries are similar in important respects. For an argument by analogy to be effective, the listener must believe that the similarities outweigh the differences. Holland is like the United States. It is a western nation, has farms and industry, seaports, large cities, and so forth. But it is also different. It is smaller, less populated, less industrial, and ethnically homogeneous. The crucial problem in analogy, therefore, is to identify for the audience a set of "significant" similarities and "insignificant" differences.

Avoiding Errors in Argument

The primary reason for diagramming an argument is to discover any errors in it and, by correcting them, to make the argument more effective.

There may be many things "wrong" with an argument. An audience can reject your argument simply because it doesn't like the way you deliver your speech. What we mean by an "error in argument" is any flaw in the *reasoning* that lays the argument open to attack. Such errors are frequently called *fallacies*. These errors can be identified and eliminated through the analytical model.

Claim Errors

A claim should be a clear statement to which a listener can give an unambiguous response. Sometimes, however, a claim, whether it is justified by the argument or not, can make one of two serious errors: it can beg the question or ignore the issue.

Begging the question   A claim begs the question when the argument is circular: "I predict that before the snow flies we are going to have compulsory rationing of fuel oil in this country because as soon as it turns cold, the government is going to tell us all just how many gallons a month we can burn."

In this case, the claim that we will have rationing of fuel oil this winter is quite clear but the reasoning is circular because the grounds merely repeat the claim. The argument begs the question. For a claim to be reasonable it must go outside itself for grounds.

Ignoring the issue   This error is sometimes called *irrelevant conclusion*. It occurs when the claim that is supported by an argument is beside the point. Suppose you don't do well on a test and you go to the instructor to argue for a higher grade. You might say that some of the questions were ambiguous, that the instructor misunderstood your answers, that one or more of your answers were worth more points than they were given, or even that the instructor didn't add correctly. All of these arguments are at least to the point. But if your reason is that you studied hard, the instructor will say that your argument is irrelevant. "The issue is not whether you studied, but whether you knew the material."

Grounds Errors and Backing Errors

The grounds and backing in an argument are the evidence from which you expect an audience to infer the claim of the argument. Obviously, they must be acceptable to the audience. If an audience doesn't believe (Grounds), "There is a shortage of oil," there is no reason it should accept (Claim), "Rationing is necessary." The same principle applies to backing for both grounds and warrant. The backing must be accepted by the audience or the argument will fail. To avoid errors in grounds or backing, review the tests for supporting materials in Chapter 8.

Warrant Errors

The only reason for an audience to believe, "Given the grounds, therefore the claim," is that some condition justifies (warrants) the inference. A weak warrant will not give the audience enough incentive to believe that the claim is a reasonable result of the grounds. Warrants can be weak for one (or both) of two reasons: First, a warrant might justify the inference from grounds to claim, but the audience will not accept the warrant as true.

For example:

(Grounds) ─────────────────────────► **(Claim)**

Volvo and Mercedes are foreign cars. | (Therefore) Volvo and Mercedes cost less than American cars.

(Warrant)

(Since) All foreign cars cost less than American cars.

The inference is clear, yet the argument will fail because no knowledgeable audience would accept the warrant. Second, even if a warrant is accepted as true, it might not justify the inference from grounds to claim. For example:

(Grounds) ─────────────────────────► **(Claim)**

Kansas is a wheat producing state. | (Therefore) Kansans should get a break on their income taxes.

(Warrant)

(Since) Wheat is the staff of life.

In arguments from sign, the sign relationship you allege in the warrant is the crucial point. To test for errors you need to examine the warrant in the light of three questions.

Is there a reliable relationship between the grounds and the claim?   There may be a remote correlation between the number of smogless days in Los Angeles and the number of days of rain in Phoenix, but a smogless day in Los Angeles is nonetheless a poor sign of rain in Phoenix. Perhaps you have heard it said that the birth of more boys than girls in any year is a sign of impending war. Such a condition is about as trustworthy a sign of war as left-handedness is of superior intelligence.

Do changed circumstances of time or place make the warrant less reasonable?   In the first half of the nineteenth century, the fact that a Southern farmer was wealthy would be a very reliable sign that he was a slave-owner. Today, such a relationship would be meaningless.

Is the claim supported by the concurrence of other signs?   To say that someone who was in the vicinity at the time of a burglary is guilty of the crime is a weak argument. But to show, in addition, that the person was seen leaving the burglarized home with stolen articles is to offer further and more substantial signs of guilt.

When you test causal arguments, ask these questions about the warrants:

Is there a believable causal relationship?   A cause always precedes its effect in time. This one characteristic is often an occasion of the error called *post hoc, ergo propter hoc* — "after this, therefore on account of this." The fact that one event follows another does not necessarily mean that the second is the result of the first. Superstitions are good examples of faulty causal reasoning of this sort. "Oh, you broke a mirror. Seven years bad luck!" "I sprained my ankle when I stepped off the curb because I walked under a ladder just before it happened."

Even when a causal relationship might reasonably be expected, you may fail to notice that other causal factors intervene. Having the engine in an automobile overhauled should result in improved performance and economy. But if you try to economize further by using paint thinner for fuel, you introduce another factor that will keep the engine overhaul from having the effect you want.

Is the cause and effect relationship oversimplified? Rarely, if ever, is cause and effect reasoning found in a simple one-to-one ratio. Most often, an effect has a whole series of contributing causes. It is quite common to say that a President *caused* a depression or a war. The nature of social ills is complex and oversimplification is both a temptation and a danger. If, however, you can show that a President's policies made a *substantial* contribution to certain events, you are on more reasonable ground.

Not only must a warrant account for the presence of multiple causes, it must also account for the fact that a cause generates, or at least influences, multiple effects. If you argue that juvenile delinquency results from television violence, you may be ignoring the possibility that TV violence gives some people relief from tension, reduces aggressiveness for others, and has additional positive effects.

It is as important in an argument by generalization or by analogy as it is in arguments from sign or cause to have credible warrants. Suppose you were arguing in defense of socialized medicine. If you pointed out a number of specific places where it has worked well and then claimed that it would therefore work well everywhere, that would be an argument by generalization. But unless the audience believes that programs of socialized medicine are pretty much alike, you can't use other nations' experiences as a warrant for the argument. Nor will that warrant justify the argument by analogy that because socialized medicine has worked well in Sweden it will be successful in the United States.

Summary

In our society you are expected to give reasons when you ask someone to believe as you do. A successful argument will give the audience acceptable evidence and good justification for believing that your claim follows from it. Adequate grounds and a credible warrant (with whatever backing they need) give you the materials for building responsible arguments. The claims of arguments used in everyday debate are never more than probable.

There are five forms of argument. Argument from authority justifies a claim by associating it with a person who is considered an expert. Argument from sign argues that one set of conditions points to another. Argument from cause may move from cause to effect and from effect to cause. Both are based on a belief that one of two conditions is caused by the other. Argument by generalization is grounded in examples that are believed to justify a general claim. Argument by analogy is a prediction that two things that are alike in certain known respects will be alike in another unknown respect.

It is quite useful to be able to recognize errors in the arguments of your opponents and to avoid them in your own speeches. Claim errors and backing errors are characterized by violations of the tests of evidence discussed in Chapter 8. Warrants are weak when an audience will not believe them or when they do not justify the claim even if they are believed. Depending upon the form of the argument used, there are specific tests that can be applied for warrant errors.

Key Terms

Truth	Warrant
Opinion	Backing
Probability	Authority
Proof	Sign
Reasoning	Cause to effect
Argumentation	Effect to cause
Justification	Generalization
Toulmin model	Analogy
Grounds	Testing arguments

Exercises

1. Examine one of the speeches at the end of Chapter 19. Find and evaluate arguments from sign and analogy.

2. In the editorials of a news magazine or newspaper, find samples of argument from sign and argument from cause. Diagram the arguments in the format of the Toulmin Model. Supply any missing part and assess the arguments.

3. Collect examples of arguments you hear in conversation and evaluate them as in Exercise 2. Here are some samples of what you might listen for:

   a. "I didn't think you were at home. I didn't see your car in the driveway."

   b. "My eyes are bothering me. I must have been studying too much."

      c. "Don't make so much noise; you'll wake your mother."

      d. "All the best television-viewing times are filled with crime dramas. Look at Saturday night's schedule."

Tell what kind of argument is used in each of the examples you find. Using the Toulmin model, explain how you would counter each of these arguments if you disagreed.

Notes

[1] D.N. Perkings, *Knowledge as Design* (Hillside, NJ: Lawrence Erlbaum, 1986) 155.

[2] The actual model introduced here is taken from Richard D. Rieke and Malcolm O. Sillars, *Argumentation and the Decision Making Process* (Glenview, Ill.: Scott Foresman and Co., 1984) 66-70. For the original diagram see: Stephen Toulmin, *The Uses of Argument* (Cambridge: University Press, 1964) 94-113.

[3] Richard D. Lamm, "Lawyers and Lawyering," *Vital Speeches of the Day* 15 Jan. 1989: 207.

[4] Mikhail Gorbachev, "U.S.S.R. Arms Reduction," *Vital Speeches of the Day* 1 Feb. 1989: 229.

[5] Eva M. Skinner, "The Prolongation of Life," *Vital Speeches of the Day* 15 Feb. 1989: 271.

[6] Pam Espinoza, "Medical Testing: A Prescription for Error," *Winning Orations* ed. Larry Schnoor (Mankato, MN: Interstate Oratorical Association, 1989) 12.

[7] Steven P. Poessnecker, "Athletes in Academia," *Winning Orations* ed. Larry Schnoor (Mankato, MN: Interstate Oratorical Association, 1989) 102.

[8] Poessnecker, 102.

Applying Values

"Is marriage on the rocks? Recent surveys suggest that . . . the percentage of married people who said they were 'very happy' declined substantially from 1972 to 1986. . . . In 1981 there were 2.4 million marriages and 1.2 million divorces.'' Some argue, therefore, that the divorce rate in this country is now at 50 percent. Pollster Louis Harris counters that "only one in eight marriages ends in divorce, and fully 89% of those surveyed say their relationships with their partners are satisfying.''[1]

Here is an issue for our society to consider: "Is marriage a failing institution?'' Alarming statistics have been used by some people as grounds for a number of policy claims that call for requirements such as premarital counseling, a waiting period before marriage, and stiffer divorce laws. Others find in the statistics a sign of serious moral breakdown in society. Still others are not alarmed by these conflicting statistics. "Dogs and cats love their offspring but they don't bother with marriage and frogs don't seem to care!''

The reason people argue about the divorce rate, or even generate statistics about it, is that a large portion of our society values the institution of marriage. "Stability in marriage protects the family and the economic and personal security of children,'' they say. Others claim, "A strong two parent family structure is important to the stability of the society.'' Some use divine law as a reason for objecting to divorce with statements like "What God has joined together let no man put asunder.'' Others say that a complex and troubled society like ours has tensions that make it difficult to maintain a marriage. "It is better for both children and adults,'' they say, "to end a marriage than to keep it going despite their unhappiness.''

Whether an audience would accept any of these claims (or any others you may have thought of) depends, in part at least, on what values the speaker identifies with the claim. One person believes that marriage provides *"stability,'' "family''* and *"security.''* Another wants a marriage to survive only if there is *"happiness.''* Still another wants to be sure that the society reflects divine law. *"Stability, family, security, happiness, divine law''*—these terms all represent values that are, as we said in Chapter 6, "a person's beliefs about ideal modes of conduct and ideal terminal goals.''[2]

As you can see, values are abstract concepts to which people attach importance. Milton Rokeach called them terminal and instrumental values and identified eighteen of each. His lists are probably not exhaustive, but they provide you with an understanding about what concepts constitute people's values. Terminal values identify what goals or *ends* people have and instrumental values are the *means* they consider admirable in the day-to-day conduct of their lives.[3]

Terminal Values	
1. A comfortable life	10. Inner harmony
2. An exciting life	11. Mature love
3. A sense of accomplishment	12. National security
4. A world at peace	13. Pleasure
5. A world of beauty	14. Salvation
6. Equality	15. Self-respect
7. Family security	16. Social recognition
8. Freedom	17. True friendship
9. Happiness	18. Wisdom

Instrumental Values	
1. Ambitious	10. Imaginative
2. Broadminded	11. Independent
3. Capable	12. Intellectual
4. Cheerful	13. Logical
5. Clean	14. Loving
6. Courageous	15. Obedient
7. Forgiving	16. Polite
8. Helpful	17. Responsible
9. Honest	18. Self-controlled

The Nature of Values

All arguments are supported by values. Audiences accept the claims of speakers when the claims are developed so that a system of values compatible with the audience's values is identified with a specific claim. Those abstract concepts (e.g.: "stability," "family," "security," "divine law") are made specific by being identified with specific claims ("Marriages should be preserved to protect the stability of society"). Values may be found in any element of an argument: claim, grounds, warrant or backing. Of course, you won't often see an argument that states only values with no supporting materials such as definitions, statistics, examples, or testimony. But, such an argument is possible. Here is an extreme example of an argument where each statement is a value claim.

(Grounds) ──────────────────────────▶ **(Claim)**

Friends trust you more when they | (Therefore) You should always be
know you are honest with them. | honest with your friends.

(Warrant)

(Since) Maintaining the trust of
friends is necessary and desirable.

(Backing for Warrant)

Trustworthiness and friendships
are good.

Even though values may appear anywhere in an argument, their primary responsibility is to support the warrant. It is the warrant that justifies the movement of the argument from grounds to claim. Sometimes the warrant will be stated by the speaker. At other times it will only be implied. Look at the example above. If the warrant were not expressed, you could surmise it from the grounds and the claim. The warrant is always implied even if it is not stated.

The warrant of an argument, stated or unstated, need not be a statement of value like the one cited above (Maintaining the trust of friends is necessary and desirable). It may be a belief statement. Daren, in a classroom speech, argued in support of President Bush's plan to control acid rain. In one subargument he said:

> The burning of fossil fuels in industrial plants and automobiles each year produces an estimated twenty-five to thirty tons of sulfur dioxide and fifteen tons of nitrogen oxide. In the atmosphere these combine with water to produce sulfuric and nitric acids. These return to the earth and raise the acidity level in lakes and streams which kills the fish. As a result, thousands of lakes in eastern Canada and the Adirondacks are fishless or almost so.

His argument is from cause to effect and the warrant is that acid rain kills fish.

(Grounds) ──────────────────────────▶ **(Claim)**

SO2 and NO combine with H2O to | (Therefore) Lakes in Canada and
produce sulfuric and nitric acid | the Adirondacks are fishless.
(acid rain).

(Warrant)

(Since) Acid rain kills fish

(Backing for Warrant)

Nature, recreation.

The warrant is a factual claim that does not explicity state a value. But in light of the total argument, it has one or more unstated values that back it—nature and recreation, for instance.

Not all parts of an argument need to be stated because an audience will intuitively supply the missing part. This is particularly true of a value warrant. Consider the example: "Parents of small children should not divorce because divorce damages a child's sense of personal security." The warrant (personal security is valuable) is unstated. However, there is no question that the argument rests on the value of personal security. As a speaker, you must find what values in your subject are most salient to your target audience. You can then use those values in your argument to support your claim.

Even in informative speeches, or portions of persuasive speeches that audiences will accept as noncontroversial, values are at least implied. Here is an example from a speech delivered in 1988 by Lauro E. Cavazos, former Secretary of Education. This section of the speech will be seen by most people as noncontroversial and its values are not stated. But, the values of education and equality are clearly implied. Without them there is no sense in making the argument:

> I'm sure you agree, the general level of science and math achievement among many students in this country is dismal. But the problem is even worse among minority youngsters. When compared with Anglo juniors in high school, only half as many black and Hispanic juniors can perform junior high school level tasks in mathematics, such as calculating the area of a rectangle or estimating 87% of 10.
>
> The ethnic gap is even wider in science. Only about half of the Anglo juniors can evaluate experiments, interpret texts and graphs, and understand basic principles of physical science. But fewer than 15 percent of black and Hispanic juniors can do these things.[4]

Values may be stated either positively or negatively. Freedom, for instance, has many words associated with it like "free," "freely," "independent," and "liberty." You recognize its negative opposites in terms like "slavery," "dictatorship," "control," and "restriction." As a public speaker you use words with positive value implications to tell your audience what values you associate with your claims. You use words with negative value implications to tell them what values are violated by the claims to which you object.

Values may be abstract or concrete. Abstract values are "rules, valid for everyone and for all occasions, such as justice, truthfulness [and] love of humanity . . . ."[5] Concrete values are attached to particular people, groups, institutions, or objects:[6] the flag, the family, the Constitution, the cross or the star of David. Whether terminal or instrumental, abstract or concrete, positive or negative, values are general principles. They become specific when applied to a specific argument. Earlier in this chapter we pointed out positive and negative abstract values in statements such as these:

"*Stability* in marriage protects the economic and personal *security* of children."

"It is better to end a marriage than to keep it going despite *unhappiness.*

"The ethnic gap *[inequality]* is even wider in science."

And a concrete value of divine law is reflected in:

"What God has joined together let no man put asunder."

In speech preparation, discovering the values of your audience and identifying them with your arguments does not mean that you must alter your own beliefs. Such a tactic would be unethical and foolish. Your beliefs are important to you and should not be surrendered for immediate popularity. Fortunately, such a practice is also unnecessary. It is unnecessary because an audience has a variety of values with which you can identify your claims.

Think again about the marriage and divorce issue that opened the chapter. While arguments about "stability," "family," and "security" may be used to support a rejection of divorce, all might also be used to support divorce as a sensible option: "It is better for the children if parents live separately than for them to be forced into an unhappy, unstable family unit." Such an argument would be based not only on the personal value of the well-being of the children but also on the very values of happiness and stability used to warrant the opposite claim. Therefore, you have options in selecting a cluster of values that the audience will see as appropriate to the subject.

Values Are Stated or Implied in Every Aspect of a Speech[7]

- In positive terms—*freedom, truth, logic, nature.*
- In negative terms—*waste, dirt, filth, undemocratic.*
- Implied in claims that do not state them—Health: "Crest tooth paste prevents cavities" or "Cigarettes cause cancer."
- In style—"Liberty and Union, now and forever, one and inseparable."
- In the sources cited—Edward Kennedy, Albert Einstein, Gloria Steinem, William F. Buckley, Barbara Bush.
- In proportion—What values get the most emphasis?

Value Systems Relate Your Claims to the Audience

A single sentence may have only one stated value. Consider, for instance, the claim "Cigarettes damage your health." The claim states a belief about cigarettes and in so doing makes specific the value "health." But, a speech will have more than one claim ("Cigarettes damage your health," "Cigarette smoking bothers others," "Cigarettes are an expensive luxury," etc.) with more than one value. The values implied by these claims ("health," "courtesy," "expense") are used together to support the claim "You should stop smoking." Values are not just a heap of disorganized concepts; they combine to form value systems.

Milton Rokeach in his study of values in American society identified three dozen values, as we discussed earlier. Only a few of those values apply to a particular claim like "Parents of small children should not divorce," or "You should stop smoking," or "Science instruction should be improved for black and Hispanic children."

From the values *potentially* relevant to a given claim, you must select those that will identify your claim with the value system of the audience. Such values as "family," "health," "self-respect," "happiness," and "freedom" will be considered important by most people. The question you have to ask is: "Which ones will determine how the audience judges my claim?"

Selecting a cluster of appropriate values is not the only basis for winning audience approval. A value system is also characterized by the relative importance of one value to another. Any two values looked at by themselves can be shown to be inconsistent. For instance, "freedom" and "security" are highly valued in American society. In order to get financial security you need to have a job, but a job restricts your personal freedom. To understand their relationships, values have to be "graded." "A particular audience," says Chaim Perelman, "is characterized less by what values it accepts than by the way it grades them." If you think of an audience's values in isolation, independent of interrelationships you "may neglect the question of their hierarchy, which solves the conflicts between them."[8]

In order to resolve the apparent conflict between financial security and personal freedom, you might argue, "A good job brings security and with security comes more freedom to do the things I want to do, to live my life the way I want to live it." In short "security" insures "freedom." That phrase forms the basis of a value system that will justify your claim for the audience. If the value system that underpins the argument is consistent with your listeners' values, your argument will seem reasonable to them. Therefore, you use a value system to arrange a cluster of values in the order of relative importance to achieving a desired audience response.

You and your listeners have literally millions of beliefs and as many as three dozen values. It would be impossible to sift through all of them to determine the value system most appropriate to your speech. Luckily enough, you don't need to. The subject matter and the audience will limit the possibilities to a relative few.[9]

In the claim of Daren's speech on acid rain, we identified two values: "nature" and "recreation." The whole speech on acid rain reflects several additional values including the economy ("damage to crops and forests") and health ("damage to drinking water in reservoirs"). But it doesn't suggest 20 or 30 values. Your speech, like Daren's, should feature a half dozen or fewer values. Those values in hierarchical order—a value system—can serve as warrants for arguments.

Of course, no argument is accepted as a proof simply because it makes an appeal to appropriate beliefs and values. As we said in earlier chapters, an argument implies all three varieties of proof: (1) the contention that the claim is a *reasonable* conclusion from the evidence; (2) the intention that it be consistent with the *beliefs* and *values* of the audience; and (3) the suggestion that the speaker is a *credible source*.

Values serve as the motivating force of the proof, but they do not stand alone. They must be integrated into systems and reflected in the materials of the speech. The following sections of this chapter offer suggestions and cautions about how to use values in your speeches.

Use Values to Dampen Controversy

There are times when you can't appeal to an audience on the basis of a specific belief. Frequently, the speaker and the audience do not share specific beliefs, but they do share value systems. Martin Luther King, Jr.'s famous "I Have a Dream" speech (delivered August 28, 1963 at the Lincoln Memorial in Washington, D.C.) was a major triumph for the extension of civil rights to African Americans. That speech played down the specific beliefs that could have been controversial (busing, job preference, integrated housing) and centered on more universal values. In this relatively short speech, the Reverend King used the words "freedom" and "free" twenty-six times including this impressive conclusion:

> From every mountainside, let freedom ring, and when this happens . . . when we allow freedom [to] ring, when we let it ring from every village and every hamlet, from every state and every city, we will be able to speed up that day when all of God's children, black men and white men, Jews and Gentiles, Protestants and Catholics, will be able to join hands and sing in the words of the old Negro spiritual, "Free at last! Free at last! Thank God Almightly, we are free at last![10]

Even though some members of his audience might disagree with him on some specific beliefs, they would find it difficult to reject the warrant, based on freedom, that dominates all the arguments of the speech. The value of freedom is deeply imbedded in the American consciousness.

Martin Luther King, Jr. focused on universal values rather than controversial beliefs in his ''I Have a Dream'' speech.

Relate Values Directly to Speech Claims

Some listeners, unless they see clearly that the particular action you propose is consistent with their values, may take an action you do not desire.

Thomas R. Donahue, Secretary Treasurer of the AFL-CIO, addressed the City Club Forum Foundation of Cleveland, Ohio, an organization of community leaders usually oriented to a management perspective. He needed to make his case for maintaining the workers' standard of living without seeming to be selfish. He did this by justifying his claims with the idea of "work" as a central value explicity stated and linked to his claim.

> American workers should not — and will not — accept cuts . . . . in the standard of living they have worked so hard to secure. Moreover to "compete" in this way [by cutting American workers to third world wage scales] would threaten a basic premise of our society: that every productive citizen should have a fair share of what should be a general prosperity.
>
> It is, after all, work which binds most adults to the rest of society. It makes them economic participants. It is through work that a large part of each of us is defined. So, America's future is linked inexorably to full employment.[11]

How explicit you need to be in making the value clear will depend on the knowledge and preconceptions of your listeners. You cannot assume that they will figure out what you mean, and you cannot leave the values to chance. Therefore, it is best to clarify the relationship of value and claim.

Provide Your Audience with Personal and Social Values

It is quite unusual for a single value or belief to be used as a general warrant throughout an entire message.[12] Multiple values in a unified value system are useful in meeting the problem of possible differences within audiences. Some audience members will respond strongly to a social concern such as family security. Others will be impervious to that appeal but will put a high value on their own self-respect. One appeal reaches one listener and a second reaches another, and so both listeners may be persuaded.

Debbie wanted to inform her classmates about the problem of illiteracy that affects approximately twenty million adults in the United States. She argued:

> Not only does illiteracy lead to lower paying jobs, a poorer standard of living and social stigma for the illiterate person but it has consequences to the economy as well. Such workers are a liability to their employers. They require more time and supervision. They are more

likely to make mistakes because they don't understand instructions.
These problems expanded through many individuals costs the society
in productivity.

She has based her argument on both the personal value of a better life for
the individual and the social value of the cost to the employer and the
society. The two values working together appeal to different parts of the
audience.

Let the Materials of the Speech Develop the Values

Values are most effectively developed through the details of the speech,
not by merely naming them. The old dictum applies well here: "Show,
don't tell." The more concretely you establish a warrant, the greater its
capacity to serve as a justification for an argument. Select the examples,
statistics, comparisons, and contrasts with which your listeners can most
readily identify.

Here are four ways in which you can use the materials of your speech
to develop values.

By Direct Argument.

When Mikhail Gorbachev addressed the United Nations in December of
1988 he argued that "Soviet Democracy" was developing on a sound legal
basis.

> ... with the highest standards from the point of view of insuring human
> rights. . . . People are no longer kept in prison for their political and
> religious views. The draft [of] new laws propose[s] additional guarantees
> to rule out any form of persecution on these grounds. Of course, this
> does not apply to criminal offenders or those guilty of crimes against
> the state (spying, subversion, terrorism, etc.) no matter what their
> political views or their world outlook.[13]

The value of human rights is defined by the promised guarantees against
persecution, but the negative values of "subversion" and "terror" still
deserve punishment as criminal acts. His value warrants are made clear
by the specific applications expressed in the argument.

By Emphasizing the Severity of the Problem

Even when the audience recognizes a need, the need will frequently not
be strong enough to provide a basis for action. In such a case, the need
must be amplified in the listeners' minds.

Pei-Lin Kao, a student at Linfield College in Oregon, spoke on the
problem of illiteracy in the United States. The following paragraph from
the speech is a portion of the analysis of the problem. Notice how the

specific details emphasize the severity of the impact of illiteracy in areas of personal and social value.

> What are the specific problems caused by illiteracy in the society? I was asking myself that same question and found the answer in *Science* and *Time*. Since 1974, there has been an illiterate class in the U.S. that is expected to grow throughout the remainder of this century. This illiteracy contributes to problems in two major areas: the day-to-day functioning of human beings and the economic well-being of society. Topping the list, we have the human aspect which takes its toll in many ways. Millions of American citizens are unable to follow written instructions, study a driver's manual or take a written driver's test, check classifieds for helpwanted ads, use a phone directory or understand emergency signs. These Americans are socially handicapped because they lack the abilities to communicate clearly, to gather information, to reason and to analyze issues. Experts label this handicap as "the new work place illiteracy." These people often become parents who are unable to provide their children with the basic knowledge and capabilities needed for success in school. Illiteracy does not end with the individual but is passed on indirectly to future generations in a vicious circle that can only be broken by people like you and me who have a genuine concern for these people and also for future generations.[14]

By the Choice of Examples

On July 17, 1984 the Reverend Jesse Jackson, then a presidential candidate, addressed the Democratic National Convention. In his speech he used a series of hypothetical examples to develop the values of self-respect and optimism for slum youth:

> I told them [the youth] that like Jesus, I too was born in a slum. But just because you're born in the slum doesn't mean the slum is born in you, and you can rise above it if your mind is made up. I told them, in every slum there are two sides. When I see a broken window, that's the slummy side. Train some youth to become a glazer. That's the sunny side. When I see a missing door, that's the slummy side. Train some youth to become a carpenter: that's the sunny side. And when I see the vulgar words and hieroglyphics of destitution on the walls, that's the slummy side. Train some youth to become a painter and artist: that's the sunny side. We leave this place looking for the sunny side because there's a brighter side somewhere.

By the Choice of Words

If the language you use is intense, the audience will perceive that your conviction is intense. Such intensity, if not overdone, will tend to make your listeners more conscious of the warrant and how it relates to your proposal. There is no doubt that the words you choose can reinforce the warrant you want to develop from your values.

Norman Lear, the creator of such television shows as *All in the Family*, *Maude*, *Mary Hartman, Mary Hartman*, *One Day at a Time*, and *Archie's Place*, spoke to the Institute of Politics of the John F. Kennedy School of Government at Harvard University in 1987. He used his own industry and then others to illustrate his point that America's failure was in the short-term persuit of success. Note how he argues, using intensely negative words such as, "mindless," "suicide," "refused," "surrrendered," and "bitch-goddess," that America's values are being destroyed.

> But despite the encroachment of cable TV, syndication, video cassettes, backyard satellite dishes and other technologies, the networks frittered away their franchise by puttering around with the same tired formats, adding more sex here and more violence there—more mindlessness—in an effort to grab the jaded viewer's attention quickly. In 1978, many of us were saying that if the network chiefs were standing in a circle with razors to their own throats, they could not be committing suicide more effectively.
>
> We know the results now. Their share of prime-time audiences has slipped from 92% in 1978 to less than 78% today. ABC has been acquired by Cap Cities and is still in trouble. NBC has been acquired by General Electric, and the once pre-eminent CBS, even after laying off hundreds, is struggling to keep its head above water.
>
> I would suggest that the fate of the networks befell another Big Three many years before—the Big Three automakers. As has been documented they failed to heed the handwriting on the wall and refused to innovate, to build small fuel-efficient cars; refused to sacrifice a current quarterly profit statement to invest in the future and meet the threat of imports from abroad. There is the ailing steel industry, which refused to modernize and invest in its future. There are the labor unions in both industries, which fought only for added wages and benefits—and declined to fight to modernize and to protect the members' jobs in the long term. There is the U.S. consumer electronics industry, which surrended the compact disc technology to Japan and Holland, who were willing to make long-term investments in the fledgling technology.
>
> In playing the Common*wheel* of Fortune, what matters most are the numbers. Who can amass the highest sum? Who can become Number One? We worship at the altar of the numerical bitch-goddesses: the Nielsen ratings; the Dow-Jones index; opinion polls; and cost benefit analyses. Politicians give more credence to opinion polls than their own gut instincts. Students surrender their self-image to SAT scores. And on and on.[15]

Don't Overuse Value Appeals

In one sense, this principle is a contradiction in terms, because an overused value is of no value. The member of the college club or fraternity who sees all small crises as major catastrophes and the politician who sees every occasion as a time to defend "home, flag, and mother" lose effectiveness because listeners soon begin to discount what they say. When a case does indeed demand powerful motivation, these speakers, like the boy who cried "wolf" too often, will be ignored. When your objective is to get a substantial intellectual commitment, strong values designed to arouse the most basic emotions such as fear can actually *reduce* the attention listeners give to the message and turn their attention to the personal characteristics of the speakers. Such appeals can have a negative or boomerang effect.[16]

To a significant extent, the problem of overusing values is a matter of selecting inappropriate ones. If you give values more intensity than the audience can accept, you are not likely to be effective. You are also not likely to be effective if you appeal to values that are too powerful for the particular situation. Humans are motivated to their own self-preservation, but not all claims will make sense if they are linked to this value.

Frequently, the audience will not be concerned about self-preservation even if it is a relevant factor. This is particularly true of younger people. Arguments about the health dangers of smoking are less persuasive with younger people than arguments highlighting the values of social esteem or acceptability to peers. Perhaps you have seen the television advertisements addressed to teen-aged smokers that emphasize the possibility of social rejection rather than death from lung cancer or heart disease. We would expect self-preservation to be a stronger motive than social rejection, but a hierarchy of values is not determined on some abstract principle. Rather, it is determined by the value system of the audience. Using a value just because it is powerful will make your appeal seem overdone if that value is not seen as relevant by the target audience.

Summary

Values are concepts people hold about ideal modes of conduct and ideal terminal goals. These are stated or implied in an argument, particularly in the warrant. Values may be stated positively to support claims or negatively to attack the claims to which you object. They may be abstract (justice, truth, freedom) or concrete (the flag, the constitution, the family).

Seldom will you find an argument supported by only one value. These values are related to one another in systems. By selecting a cluster of values and relating them to one another you can see how values that might be inconsistent in some cases will make sense to the target audience. The value system is an intimate part of the argument structure, the support and language used, and the credibility of the speaker.

Values are useful to dampen controversy when the specific beliefs advocated may be controversial but the values are shared by speaker and audience. They should be related directly to the speech claims so that there is no confusion. Claims should be supported by arguments based on both personal and social values. The materials of the speech should develop the values through direct argument, emphasizing the severity of the problem, choosing the most value-communicating examples, and selecting words that communicate the value concepts. You should be careful not to overuse values by implying or stating a value connection to your claim that will not be acceptable to the audience.

Key Terms

Terminal values   Relating to claims
Instrumental values   Personal values
Positive values   Social values
Negative values   Direct argument
Abstract values   Emphasize a problem
Concrete values   Choice of examples
Value systems   Choice of words
Dampen controversy   Overuse of values

Exercises

1. Examine one of the speeches in chapters 13, 18, 19, or 20 and come to class prepared to discuss the following:
   a. What are the most salient values of the speech?
   b. To what extent are they linked to specific beliefs? Explicitly stated? Positive or negative?
   c. How do these values relate to one another in a value system?
   d. How effective do you think these value appeals would be with an audience such as your class?
   e. Could they be improved upon?
2. Examine one of the speeches in chapters 13, 18, 19, or 20. Imagine it was given to two quite different audiences. Write a short paper analyzing how its values might have been received by the two audiences.
3. What values and beliefs are likely to be held by people like yourself? Discuss with your class the differences and similarities among you and why.

Notes

1 Norval D. Glenn, "Marriage on the Rocks" *Psychology Today* Oct. 1987: 20-21; "One in Two? Not True," *Time* 13 July 1987: 21.
2 Milton Rokeach, *Beliefs, Attitudes and Values* (San Francisco: Jossey Bass, 1968) 124.
3 Milton Rokeach, *The Nature of Human Values* (New York: Free Press, 1973) 28.
4 Lauro E. Cavazos, "The Huge Problem in American Schools" *Vital Speeches of the Day* 1 Feb. 1989: 236.
5 Chaim Perelman, *The Realm of Rhetoric* (Notre Dame: University of Notre Dame Press, 1982) 28.
6 Chaim Perelman and L. Olbrechts-Tyteca, *The New Rhetoric; A Treatise on Argumentation* (Notre Dame: University of Notre Dame Press, 1969) 77.
7 Adapted from Richard D. Rieke and Malcolm O. Sillars, *Argumentation and the Decision Making Process* (Glenview, IL: Scott Foresman, 1984) 113-14.
8 Perelman and Olbrechts-Tyteca, 81-82.
9 Malcolm O. Sillars and Patricia Ganer, "Values and Beliefs: A Systematic Basis for Argumentation," *Advances in Argumentation Theory and Research* eds. J. Robert Cox and Charles A. Willard (Carbondale: Southern Illinois University Press, 1982) 187.
10 Martin Luther King, Jr., "I Have A Dream" *Three Centuries of American Rhetorical Discourse* ed. Ronald F. Reid (Prospects Heights, IL: Waveland, 1988) 726.
11 Thomas R. Donahue, "Worker Dignity on the Job," *Vital Speeches of the Day* 1 May 1989: 424.
12 Sillars and Ganer, 188.
13 Mikhail Gorbachev, "U.S.S.R. Arms Reduction" *Vital Speeches of the Day* 1 Feb. 1989: 234.
14 Kao, Pei-Lin, "Illiteracy" *Winning Orations* ed. Larry Schnoor (Mankato, MN: Interstate Oratorical, 1989) 88.
15 Norman Lear, "Cashing in the Commonweal for the Common*wheel* of Fortune," 1987 address to the Institute of Politics of the John F. Kennedy School of Government at Harvard University. Reprinted with permission of Norman Lear, Act III Communications.
16 Mary John Smith, *Persuasion and Human Action* (Belmont, CA: Wadsworth, 1982) 230-32.

chapter 12

Enhancing Credibility

I. The nature of creditibility

II. Credibility factors
   A. Trustworthiness
   B. Competence
   C. Dynamism
   D. Relationship among factors

III. Kinds of credibility
   A. Reputation
   B. Direct credibility
   C. Secondary credibility
   D. Indirect credibility

IV. Establishing credibility
   A. Analyze your potential credibility
   B. Be temperate but show your competence
   C. Link your proposal to audience interest
   D. Speak with genuine conviction
   E. Sometimes use candor to disarm a hostile audience

Aristotle said that he would "almost affirm" that credibility "is the most potent of all the means to persuasion." [1] Some researchers have argued that credibility is the "dominant factor" in persuasion. [2] The media frequently report on image, charisma, personality, and charm—all of which refer to some aspect of credibility.

"Mario Cuomo's image"
"Michael Jackson's charisma"
"Barbara Bush's personality"
"Burt Reynolds' charm"
"Joan Rivers' abrasive style"

Thus, popular notions are added to ancient theory and modern research to say that the message of a person who is perceived as credible is more likely to be accepted.

The Nature of Credibility

Every time you believe something because you hear it on the 6 o'clock news, you are giving credibility to the newscaster and the news team. Chances are that when you accept what a professor tells you or believe something you read, you are accepting the ideas because you trust the source from which they came. When you reject an idea because it comes from someone you don't trust, a lack of credibility is the basis of your negative judgment. Credibility is, therefore, the image the audience has of a speaker which makes what the speaker says believable. Reread that sentence carefully. *It says that the speaker's image is in the mind of the listener*. Credibility is not something a speaker *has*; it is what an audience *gives*. Credibility is assigned by the audience.

In the summer of 1990, 72-year-old Nelson Mandela made a triumphant tour of the United States, speaking to large crowds in cities across the nation. This leader of the African National Congress, who had been imprisoned in South Africa for 27 years, was called "one of the most honored and respected men alive." [3] Still several communities were skeptical about Mandela. The Miami Cuban community attacked him for his favorable statements about Fidel Castro who had supported the African National Congress. Because of his support of Castro, he lost credibility with that potential target audience. Nelson Mandela's experience shows that credibility is a function of the audience.

Note also that credibility does not stand alone. It is not personality alone that makes Mandela persuasive. It is also the claims he supports, the arguments he makes, the values he espouses, and the way in which he presents his case. What is true of major world figures such as Mandela, is also true of you. The process is self-supporting. People will see you as credible if you have values like theirs, have done the kinds of things they consider important, and speak in ways they consider most appropriate. The audience's estimation of your credibility is affected by its reactions

Nelson Mandela's credibility is established by the claims he supports, the arguments he makes, the values he espouses and the way in which he presents his case.

to what you say and how you say it, and your effectiveness is influenced by your listener's estimation of your credibility.

An ancient term, *ethos*, was used by Aristotle to name this phenomenon. We mention it now because you will frequently hear it used even today. For Aristotle *ethos* meant the credibility a speaker generated through what was said in a speech. In this chapter, we will also consider the prior reputation of a speaker as a source of credibility. As a student speaker, you will find *ethos* in the classical sense the most relevant. You cannot change your reputation with your classmates very fast; indeed, you may not yet have a reputation with them. You can, nonetheless, improve what you do in your speeches to maximize your credibility. In this chapter we will identify the factors that contribute to credibility, discuss the different kinds of credibility, and show you how to enhance your own credibility.

Credibility Factors

There has been considerable research in recent years to identify those factors that cause audiences to give a speaker credibility.[4] Although research has identified a variety of factors, two are predominant. In fact, trustworthiness and competence have been recognized ever since Aristotle first defined the factors of *ethos*. A third, less important, element is dynamism.

Trustworthiness

Listeners tend to give credibility to people they feel can be trusted. Obviously, the characteristics that are signs of trustworthiness will vary with audience and subject. What characteristics cause you to trust someone? Sincerity? Church affiliation? Income? Age? Experience? While some broad characteristics, such as sincerity, are valued in society, they are difficult for an audience to judge.

Certainly you should be sincere in your desire to provide your listeners with useful information and to help them find solutions to their problems. But frequently, audiences are unable to judge sincerity. Just being sincere isn't enough. In addition, you will need to build the idea of trustworthiness through what you say in your speech.

There are several ways to develop an image as a trustworthy person. One is to identify with the audience by linking the arguments and appeals of the speech with the beliefs and values that are important to the listeners. Another is to use language the audience considers appropriate. Adapting delivery, physical actions, and even dress (characteristics that fit the audience's image of trustworthiness) may also have a positive effect.

Competence

Listeners tend to believe speakers they feel are competent. Even if listeners have every reason to believe that someone is trustworthy, they may not see that person as competent on a particular subject. You may trust a friend to be competent about where to get a good hamburger but not competent to advise you on an algebra test. You may find your mother completely trustworthy and competent on financial matters but not competent to advise you on music.

Judgments of a speaker's competence will frequently vary from one audience to another. One audience may find the person who engages in manual labor competent, whereas another sees competence as a function of higher education. Any audience must perceive you to be competent before it will consider you a credible speaker.

Listeners expect a speaker to demonstrate competence on the subject — at least to know more about it than they do. That is why it is important to make a thorough study of the subject and why there is a need for well-developed supporting material. Without the support of reputation, an audience can only judge competence on the basis of what a speaker says.

Dynamism

A third factor has been identified by a number of researchers. Dynamism is represented by intensity in language, voice, and physical activity. However, unlike trustworthiness and competence, it can be viewed as negative.[5] What may be "dynamic" to one person is "pushy," "brassy," or "loud" to another. The overly aggressive salesperson is a good example of the negative quality of dynamism. You probably can't imagine saying, "I didn't like him because he was too trustworthy," or "She's competent, so she must be wrong." But you might remark, "I don't trust him, he's too pushy."

Relationship among Factors

In addition to the variety of definitions of each of the factors of credibility, there is variability in the relationships among them. Suppose an audience finds you highly trustworthy but not particularly competent, or vice versa. This is not an unusual situation, and it illustrates again the complexity of credibility. Credibility is not a simple matter of respecting and trusting someone in general. Credibility emerges from the listener's perceptions of all of the elements of the communication situation: speaker, occasion, subject.[6] In addition, impressions of competence and trustworthiness may change during the course of the speech, depending on the subject you are discussing and how you approach it.

Trustworthiness, competence, and dynamism (especially the first two) are characteristics that are admired by audiences. Your problem, as a speaker, is to utilize your past experience and your present knowledge to create for the audience an image of believability. Before we look at how you do this, however, let's consider the different ways you can convey your trustworthiness, competence, and dynamism to an audience.

Kinds of Credibility

There are four ways in which you can generate credibility: by your reputation, by direct statements about your competence, by associating your proposals with credible secondary sources, and through indirect means.

Reputation

Although the three kinds of credibility we will discuss subsequently are all part of the speech you deliver, reputation is not. Aristotle specifically excludes reputation from his concept of *ethos*. Reputation is the credibility which speakers have *before* they begin to speak and is based on their past actions. Reputation may be altered by the other forms of credibility, but only over time. At the beginning of a speech, you are stuck with your reputation—and it can play a large role in determining your effectiveness.

Chances are that when you address your class, you don't have a reputation with them. There are probably groups, however, to which you are known and with which you can draw on your reputation. Perhaps your club, church group, or a small number of close friends will accept what you say because you have a good reputation with them. Individuals in your class may believe you because they know you. But for many in the class, you have no reputation. When you speak to them, you will need to build other forms of credibility.

Direct Credibility

Some speakers will make direct references to themselves to gain credibility. They will tell their listeners about aspects of their character that should make them believable: "Listen, I wouldn't cheat you," "You ask Sam, he will tell you I'm a right guy," "I promise you I will do everything in my power to see that you are happy."

Stephen E. Ewing, President of Michigan Consolidated Gas Company, faced a difficult problem in speaking on child care before a Child Care Coordinating Committee in that state. How could he speak to them authoritatively on the subject? He began his speech by acknowledging his problems but added statements that directly attested to his credibility on the subject.

> I'm very flattered to be asked to be here today. And as I stand here I truly find myself in an awkward position of being an amateur speaking to experts. For anyone who looks into the topic of child care very quickly comes across the long-time experts in the field—Carol Quarterman—Lynn Bankes—and organizations like the Child Care Coordinating Council. So, I don't hope to give you any really new information, but I do hope to offer a different perspective on child care that you can integrate into your own thinking on the matter.
>
> As some of you know, I have a strong personal interest in child care matters. My wife and I balance two careers and have raised two daughters who are now—or soon will be—entering the workforce. I know how difficult it can be to balance work and family commitments. I also had the opportunity to be the primary parent for a year or so, and I wouldn't trade that experience for anything.
>
> But those life experiences didn't make me an expert on child care, and frankly, they didn't bring me here today. I'm interested in child care today for very practical business reasons.
>
> I'd like to stand before you and tell you that my company—MichCon—is way ahead of the pack in implementing child care programs. The fact is, we're not. At MichCon, many of our female workers—approximately one third of our workforce—from executives to our support personnel—must arrange for—and worry about, child care

centers, babysitters, or latch key programs. So, no—MichCon is not where we want to be on child care.

At the same time, we, along with many American corporations are beginning to realize that child care is an area we need to be involved in *now*—and actively involved.

Why? The workforce is changing—and changing dramatically. Our labor pool *is decreasing*—while we face an increasing need for qualified, well-trained people. White middle aged men are relinquishing their dominance in the labor pool. By the year 2000, only 15 percent of the new entrants into the labor force will be white males.[7]

Mr. Ewing cannot get by on his reputation as a business leader. He must show this audience how and why he is qualified to speak on child care even while admitting that he is not an expert.

Secondary Credibility

The strength of secondary credibility depends on the trustworthiness and competence an audience ascribes to the person you link with your proposal. Would you quote someone whom your audience distrusts? If the audience doesn't value your source of information, your own credibility may suffer.

Ernest Boyer, President of the Carnegie Foundation for the Advancement of Teaching, is a recognized authority on the problems of education. For that reason, he was invited in February of 1990 to speak to the National Governor's Association on America's "Educational Goals." Despite his own credibility, he associated himself with a wide range of others for secondary credibility. These references are scattered through the speech at crucial points:

> . . . for a very long time governors have been at the very heart of school reform. Years ago, Governors Jim Hunt, Lamar Alexander, Bill Clinton, Dick Riley, Tom Kean, and others, called for better schools, ... Just a month ago, President Bush made a decisive move when he announced six ambitious goals for the nation's schools, ... Winston Churchill said that putting milk into babies is the finest investment a community can make, ... Harvard psychologist Howard Gardner reminds us that children have not only verbal intelligence, they also have spatial intelligence, intuitive intelligence, aesthetic intelligence, and social intelligence. . . . Thirty years ago, John Kennedy inspired the nation's youth to serve in the Peace Corps overseas. Why not challenge *this* generation to serve in inner cities and rural districts here at home?[8]

Indirect Credibility

In developing indirect credibility, speakers do not directly associate their proposal with their own or someone else's qualifications. Instead, credibility is enhanced by anything in the speech that identifies the speaker with arguments, values, and salient beliefs in which the audience has confidence. Even the use of language the audience admires or impressive delivery techniques add to a speaker's credibility.

Everything you do in your speech affects your credibility indirectly. If your audience wants specific evidence and you give them only opinion, that will hurt your credibility. If they see a problem as complex and you say it is simple with a simple answer, that will hurt your credibility. If your speech is disorganized, it will hurt your credibility.

Reverse all these negatives and make them positive. If you meet the expectations of the audience with a thorough analysis and a well-organized and supported speech, it will aid your credibility. It may well be the crucial factor in strengthening your credibility and, therefore, your effectiveness with an audience.

Establishing Credibility

There are, of course, many ways to use credibility, and different audiences and situations will call for different approaches. But here are five general principles for enhancing your credibility:

1. Analyze your potential credibility.
2. Be temperate but show your competence.
3. Link your proposal to audience interests.
4. Speak with genuine conviction.
5. Sometimes use candor to disarm a hostile audience.

Analyze Your Potential Credibility

One of the reasons you need to analyze your audience carefully is to discover possible links between you and it that will make you more credible. Consider possible similarities of ethnic background, home town, school ties—in short, experiences that create a bond between you and your audience. The references you make to experiences you have had need not call attention to the similarity—they need only draw on it.

"When I was growing up on a farm we learned . . . ."
"I learned a lot from high school sports . . . ."
"Inner-city life can be very rewarding . . . ."
"Because my mother was such a good cook I learned to love Jewish food . . . ."

Be Temperate but Show Your Competence

These kinds of references can be developed if you take careful stock of your experience, knowledge, beliefs, and values. Even when you do not have a strong reputation because your audience does not know you, by taking stock you can find areas in your own background where you can strengthen your credibility.

Direct, heavy-handed attempts to impress listeners with one's own qualifications or denials of any personal advantage from a proposal (like the salesperson who keeps denying any personal reason for making a sale when the customer knows about commissions) can be injurious. Avoid any statements which hint to your listeners that you mean to manipulate them or which imply you are what your listeners know you are not.

It is difficult to tell an audience directly that you are trustworthy, but competence can and should be shown.[9] After you have made an analysis of your potential credibility, look for ways to build it into your speech. Investigate the topic thoroughly and let your audience know about your research:

> "My study of this problem shows . . . ."
>
> "There are over 50 references to this in the online library
>   system."
>
> "I was working at Mammoth Hot Springs when the worst
>   recorded fire in the history of Yellowstone Park started."
>
> "Five years in the insurance business convinces me. . . ."

Of course, you have to be temperate about presenting such information.

Humor can frequently be used to soften the possible negative impact of direct credibility statements. There is also some evidence that humor makes a speaker seem more dynamic. Dennis Sanderson was giving a speech on football strategy. He began with a story of his high school football experience:

> In my sophomore year in high school I didn't get to play much football. As a matter of fact I spent the year on the bench. There was an incident late in the year that raised my hopes. There had been a lot of injuries. As a matter of fact, at one point it came down to eleven players on the field and me — on the bench. Then someone got injured. I knew it was my chance. I waited calmly as the coach approached me. He looked at me and said, "Get up Sanderson, I'm sending in the bench."

> Well, you know, you can learn a lot about football by by riding the bench if you pay attention to the strategy of the game.

Link Your Proposal to Audience Interest

Credibility can be best built indirectly if you *show* rather than *tell* your listeners that you are credible. This means that you must establish common ground with them. Prepare thoroughly, organize carefully, use the secondary credibility of people your audience admires. Find the common ground in the beliefs and values the audience knows.

All the factors of the speaking situation work together. Credibility helps to make argument, evidence, and value appeals more believable and thus more persuasive. Conversely, when you organize clearly, support reasonably, and use language well, you strengthen your audience's image of your competence. Your trustworthiness, for example, can be enhanced by revealing shared experience, religious background, social origins, or friendships better than by a direct claim that you and your listeners are alike. Even though you may have the experience on which to build credibility, you can still make sure you have carried on adequate study and research. Use the results of that research to demonstrate your competence.

Common ground is also developed by the way you dress, use your voice, and act physically. In general, you should behave and dress in a way that will not be seen as odd to the audience (unless, of course, oddness is your credibility objective). It is a small concession to a conservative audience that you dress conservatively in order to establish credibility with them.

Speak with Genuine Conviction

We noted before that audiences admire sincerity but that it is sometimes difficult to know who is insincere. Many times an insincere speaker will fool an audience. That does not take away from the general principle that you should speak with genuine conviction. Choose subjects you believe in; be honest about your beliefs. Such an approach will help you to be more self-assured and to maintain better eye contact.

It is true, as Abraham Lincoln said, that ''you can fool all of the people some of the time, some of the people all of the time, but you can't fool all of the people all of the time.'' Sooner or later, insincerity is discovered and the negative consequences to the speaker are significant. It is best, therefore, to concentrate on the positive. Speak with genuine conviction and avoid the long term consequences of insincerity.

Sometimes Use Candor to Disarm a Hostile Audience

So much emphasis is placed on not offending hostile listeners that you may think it is always best to hide your true views from them. Many speakers are very successful through candor, and this technique should be explored. Sometimes the audience knows your views in advance; to hide them would be foolish. It is best in such circumstances to be candid. Senator Edward M. Kennedy is regarded by conservatives as the epitome of the liberalism they reject. On October 3, 1983, he spoke to the students of Liberty Baptist College. The Reverend Jerry Falwell, leader of fundamentalist Christian conservatives who opposed Kennedy's views is the President of Liberty Baptist. To disarm his hostile audience, Senator Kennedy used candor about his differences with Reverend Falwell:

I have come here to discuss my beliefs about faith and country, tolerance and truth in America. I know we begin with certain disagreements; I strongly suspect that at the end of the evening some of our disagreements will remain. But I also hope that tonight and in the months and years ahead, we will always respect the right of others to differ—that we will never lose sight of our own fallibility—that we will view ourselves with a sense of perspective and a sense of humor. After all, in the New Testament, even the disciples had to be taught to look first to the beam in their own eyes, and only then to the mote in their neighbor's eye.

I am mindful of that counsel. I am an American and a Catholic; I love my country and treasure my faith. But I do not assume that my conception of patriotism or policy is invariably correct—or that my convictions about religion should command any greater respect than any other faith in this pluralistic society. I believe there surely is such a thing as truth, but who among us can claim a monopoly on it?[10]

Edward Kennedy used candor and humor to build credibility when he addressed Jerry Falwell and the students of Liberty Baptist College.

Candor in that case built credibility, contradicting the all-too-prevalent notion that a politician is one who skirts the issues. There are grave dangers in hiding your biases. When a listener discovers that there is covert bias, that is the time when the most damage is done to your credibility.[11]

Summary

Credibility, the image an audience has of a speaker, is an important part of making what the speaker says believable. It works together with the arguments, the beliefs, and the values in any speaking situation.

There are three factors of credibility: trustworthiness, competence, and dynamism. These factors will be perceived through different characteristics, however, depending on the subject and the situation. Also, it should be realized that dynamism, unlike the other two, is not always positive. A dynamic speaker may be perceived negatively, as too pushy.

There are four kinds of credibility that convey the credibility factors of trust, competence, and dynamism. Reputation is the credibility you have before the speech. The other three are generated during the speech. Direct credibility occurs when you tell your listeners specifically about your trustworthiness and competence. Secondary credibility occurs when you associate yourself with the credibility of others. Indirect credibility is the credibility you gain by the way your audience responds to the arguments, values, language, and delivery of your speech.

There are many ways to develop credibility in specific situations. Five general principles are discussed in this chapter: Analyze your potential credibility, be temperate but show your competence, link your proposal to audience interests, speak with conviction, and sometimes use candor to disarm a hostile audience.

Key Terms

Ethos	Secondary credibility
Trustworthiness	Indirect credibility
Competence	Potential credibility
Dynamism	Enhancing credibility
Intensity	Temperance
Reputation	Personal conviction
Direct credibility	Candor

Exercises

1. Consider some prominent public speaker you have heard recently. In what way did the speaker's reputation affect your reception of the ideas? What did the speaker do in the speech to confirm or deny your opinion of the speaker? Write a short paper explaining your reactions.

2. Which do you consider more important to a speaker's effectiveness: credibility or the ability to use value appeals? Why?

3. Examine one of the speeches in Chapters 13, 18, 19, or 20. How well does the speaker develop credibility according to the principles discussed in this chapter?

4. Choose one of the following well-known persons and write a short paper explaining what factors in that person's reputation would influence your classmates positively or negatively.

George Bush	Michael Jackson	Mikhail Gorbachev
Roseanne Barr	Meryl Streep	Bruce Willis
Edward Kennedy	Robert Redford	Madonna
Lee Iaccoca	Elizabeth Dole	Jesse Jackson

Notes

1 Aristotle, *The Rhetoric* trans. Lane Cooper (New York: Appleton-Century-Crofts, 1932) 9.

2 James C. McCroskey, *An Introduction to Rhetorical Communication* (Englewood Cliffs, NJ: Prentice-Hall, 1978) 67; Mary John Smith, Persuasion and Human Action (Belmont, CA: Wadsworth, 1982) 221, 225.

3 Julie Johnson and Scott MacLeod, "The Burden of Being a Superstar," *Time* 25 June 1990: 20-21; "Living Inside a Hero's Mantle," *U.S. News and World Report* 2 July 1990: 8-99.

4 Kenneth Andersen and Theodore Clevenger, Jr., "A Summary of Experimental Research in Ethos," *Speech Monographs* 30 (1964): 59-78; Kenneth Andersen, *Persuasion: Theory and Practice* (Boston: Allyn & Bacon, 1978) 238-42; Kim Giffin, "The Contribution of Studies of Source Credibility to a Theory of Interpersonal Trust in the Communication Process," *Psychological Bulletin* 68 (1967): 104-20; McCroskey 68-71; Jack L. Whitehead, Jr., "Factors of Source Credibility," *Quarterly Journal of Speech* 54 (1968): 59-63; Gary Cronkhite and Jo Liska, "A Critique of Factor Analytic Approaches to the Study of Credibility." *Communication Monographs* 43 (1976): 91-107.

5 Velma J. Lashbrook, "Source Credibility: A Summary of Experimental Research," Speech Communication Association Convention, San Francisco, Dec. 1971; Gerald R. Miller and John Basehart, "Source Trustworthiness, Opinionated Statements and Responses to Persuasive Communication," *Speech Monographs* 36 (1969): 1-7; W. Barnett Pearce, "The Effect of Vocal Cues on Credibility and Attitude Change," *Western Speech* 35 (1971): 176-184.

[6] Jesse G. Delia, ''A Constructivist Analysis of Credibility,'' *Quarterly Journal of Speech* 62 (1976): 361-75; Jo Liska, ''Situational and Topical Variations in Credibility Criteria,'' *Communication Monographs* 45 (1978): 85-92.

[7] Stephen E. Ewing, ''Nourish Thy Children,'' *Vital Speeches of the Day* 15 June 1990: 517.

[8] Ernest L. Boyer, ''Education Goals,'' *Vital Speeches of the Day* 1 June 1990: 495-97.

[9] Lawrence R. Wheeless, ''Effects of Explicit Credibility Statements by More Credible and Less Credible Sources,'' *Southern Speech Communication Journal* 39 (1973): 33-39.

[10] Edward M. Kennedy, ''Tolerance and Truth in America.'' Text provided by Senator Kennedy.

[11] Judson Mills and Elliot Aronson, ''Opinion Change as a Function of a Communicator's Attractiveness and Desire to Influence,'' *Journal of Personality and Social Psychology* 2 (1965): 173-177.

Organizing and Outlining Speeches

When you were born, your understanding of the world was severely limited by your lack of experience and by the fact that your nervous system was not yet well developed. As time passed and you gradually began to sort out and to classify people, objects and events, you gained two important perceptions. First, there were individual "things" separate from you and distinct from one another. Second, the similarities and differences among these things showed that they belonged to groups or classes. That is, you began to reason. Fundamental to any kind of reasoning is the ability to see relationships.

Relationships and Organization

The number and kind of relationships you assign is limited only by your ability to see them. Some things are taller, shorter, or longer than others in size; above, below, right or left in space; sooner or later in time. People too can be classified according to their relationships to each other: employee-employer, teacher-student, parent-child. And there are many other sorts of relationships as well: example-explanation, proof-claim, evidence-argument. All of these relationships and countless others are important to people because they help to bring a degree of orderliness into the world. In speech making, the process of identifying relationships among a set of otherwise disconnected details is called organizing.

Because the ability to organize is fundamental to reasoning, it is also a major factor in making successful speeches. For one reason, audiences expect it. Random events are unpredictable and, in order to be comfortable, people need to make predictions that seem reliable. Thus, they look for order in their world. They will certainly look for it in the speeches they hear. One way of defining a speech is to call it a *device for giving an audience an orderly set of relationships upon which they can depend.*

There is a direct connection here with our observation in Chapter 5 that all speeches are meant to solve some kind of problem. Given any audience and any subject, the problem can be thought of as the audience's need to understand a new and different set of relationships among the elements of the subject. Then it will be able to see the humor in a subject, to understand an explanation, or to accept an argument.

Organization is also important since the subject matter of a speech cannot be communicated all at once. It has to be broken down into single ideas that can be delivered one at a time— without bewildering the listener.

Even carelessly grouped ideas have some kind of organization. Although we can think about substance (subject matter) and form (organization) as separate entities, it is impossible to separate them in reality. For example, you cannot create a statue without giving it some kind of shape—whether beautiful or ugly. In the same sense, you cannot construct a speech without automatically imposing on it some kind of organization—whether confusing or clear. But an accidental structure will not guarantee that the audience gains a proper understanding of your subject. To keep the ideas distinct and at the same time make their relationships clear, you need something more than just haphazard organization.

Ideally, the organization of a speech will give your listeners a clear and accurate perception of how all the elements of the speech relate to one another. This is a major step toward making your humor, explanations and arguments effective.

Moreover, when the audience understands the subject and purpose correctly, silent distractions that might arise will be largely, if not entirely, avoided. Here again you can see that analysis of the audience and of the subject are significant because they will help you decide what the best organization for a specific subject is likely to be.

In this chapter we have two objectives: to discuss the elements of good speech organization and to explain the principles and methods of outlining your speeches. Good organization will help you sort out the relationships among the ideas in your speech so your audience will understand. Outlining is important because it helps you discover an effective way of structuring the speech, represents the organization of your speech, and can be used as speaking notes.

Elements of Good Organization

We have said that the world makes no sense if people, objects, and ideas are perceived as isolated, random events. Rather, they must be seen in relation to other individual events. The significant task of speech organization is to make these relationships instantly clear to an audience. Remember, hearing a speech is not like reading a book. If your listeners do not understand what you say when you say it, they cannot rehear it the way they can reread an obscure page. Unity and coherence of ideas present significant relationships clearly and accurately in a speech. It is the principal task of organization to insure that a speech has both of these attributes.

Unity

Unity is a feature of a message whose parts fit together to form a consistent whole. A speech possesses this necessary and desirable quality when all of the ideas are related to each other as members of a single entity. This implies, of course, that every piece of material in a speech—each idea, claim, definition, statistic, example, quotation, no matter what—should have some significant relationship to every other element. If any item has no specific and clear relationship to the others, it should not be in the speech at all.

In addition to omitting items that have no important bearing on your purpose, there are two other effective ways of insuring the unity of a speech.

The first is to be sure you have no more than one subject to discuss. For example, look at this statement of purpose:

> To inform the audience about nuclear energy as an alternate source of power and some of its serious drawbacks.

This purpose would require two speeches: one informative, to explain the use of nuclear energy as a source of power and the other persuasive, to prove the value claim that it has serious drawbacks. Given the right audience and the right occasion, either of those two speeches could be very good, but one speech that tried to accomplish both purposes at the same time would lack unity.

Look at another example. Many automobiles have air bags that automatically inflate in case of a collision. These air bags could be the subject of any number of speeches: to describe how they work, to show their life-saving capabilities, to explain the controversy over their value, to argue their superiority over conventional seat belts, and to persuade the audience to buy them, to name only a few. Some of these potential speeches, moreover, would be informative, others persuasive, some even to entertain. Any of these subjects and purposes would do perfectly well given the right audience and the proper occasion but a speech that tried to handle two or more of them at the same time would likely cause a listener to think, "Now I wonder what that was all about."

The second principal way to maintain unity in a speech is to avoid digressions. All speakers are tempted to insert material that is interesting even though it has no real bearing on the subject. You must fight that temptation. Digressions from your immediate purpose hurt the effectiveness of your speech. It makes no difference whether the digression is ad lib ("That reminds me of a story") or whether the material is deliberately included when the speech is prepared. The result is the same — the unity of the speech is impaired.

Unity alone does not guarantee that the audience will see the relationships among your ideas correctly. The speech must be coherent as well.

Coherence

A group of individual elements has unity if all of them are related to a single entity. But to be coherent, they must fit together in a clear and meaningful pattern. When a pair of dice stops rolling, they will be in some spatial and numerical relationship to each other. But this kind of order is random and accidental. It would be like trying to build a watch by shaking up the pieces in a sack. The resulting jumble would have unity because all the parts belong to the watch, but it would have no coherence whatsoever.

Relate the notion of coherence to speaking. No matter how badly garbled a message may be, it will still communicate something. It is even possible that the audience will understand it correctly. But when sense-making is the result of chance, it is inherently unpredictable. Speakers need to be as sure as possible that they will get the response they want. If an audience has only a few minutes to understand a speech that has taken days or even weeks to prepare, an organization that ties all of the ideas together into a coherent package makes it much more likely that the audience will understand it accurately.

Moreover, the efficiency of your communication will be increased because it is easier for the audience to listen when a message is coherent than when it is garbled. The easier it is to understand a message, the greater the chance that interest will be maintained and that the audience will be willing to listen.

The sequence of ideas in a message is the principal means to establish coherence. That is, a speech will seem coherent when all of the parts follow one another in an appropriate order—one that makes the individual elements of humor, explanation, or argument work together to carry the ideas through clearly to the audience. In a coherent speech, the ideas not only fit together, they work together to establish a continuity of ideas. This makes for a systematic movement—first from one idea to another and then, when considered as a whole, all the ideas march with force, precision and clarity toward the final goal.

Outlining a speech is an effective way to discover the most appropriate organization to strengthen both the unity and the coherence of your speech.

Purpose of the Outline

An outline is the blueprint of a speech. The way the outline is put together shows the sequence of ideas and the relationships among them. A well-constructed outline groups related materials in a way that makes clear the unity and coherence of your ideas. As a supplementary benefit, the process of making the outline helps you to determine what the organization of the speech ought to be.

In addition to helping you organize a speech, an outline is useful in delivering it. It helps to insure against the danger of omitting anything significant and, at the same time, it preserves unity and coherence by discouraging the temptation to ramble.

Types of Outlines

There are several different kinds of outlines and each is helpful when used for the right purpose. But only one is of interest to us and, therefore, we will mention the others only briefly.

Scratch Outlines

A scratch outline is a "laundry list" of random notes related only vaguely to each other and to the subject and purpose of a speech. Nonetheless, on occasion, it can be useful. For example, if you are called on unexpectedly to speak, and you have only a little time to prepare, jotting some notes in the form of a scratch outline can serve a useful purpose. It can also be useful for writing down ideas about a topic in the early stages of preparation. The final outline should be better developed. For the most part, a scratch outline invites inadequate analysis and poor development of the subject. It also provides a poor set of notes for delivery.

Briefs

The most elaborate of all outline forms is called, strangely enough, a brief. A brief is an argumentative outline and contains all of the arguments that a speaker can discover, both for and against a claim. It is most useful in situations like debate, where speakers confront many of the opposing arguments. Preparing a brief helps to insure complete analysis of a claim.

Rhetorical Outlines

A brief suffers, in a somewhat different sense, from a problem of the scratch outline. Because of its all-inclusiveness, it is a sophisticated sort of laundry list. A rhetorical outline, on the other hand, contains only the materials needed to accomplish the specific purpose of the speech—to entertain, to inform, or to persuade. A rhetorical outline is by far the most useful in both preparation and delivery.

All three kinds of outlines vary in completeness of content. Rhetorical outlines also vary in the amount of language they contain. This ranges from the sketchiest kind of "topic" outline to the "complete sentence" outline that is virtually a manuscript of the speech.

Complete sentence outlines A complete sentence outline avoids one of the biggest problems with scratch outlines—inadequate development of ideas. Writing a complete sentence requires thinking an idea through before setting it down in final form. A significant disadvantage is that a complete sentence outline is likely to become a manuscript of the speech. Delivery from such an outline is much less likely to be spontaneous.

There is a useful compromise between the advantages of developing your ideas thoroughly in a complete sentence outline and the danger of losing spontaneity in delivery. It is called a topic outline.

Topic outlines The headings of a topic outline are no more than a few words that call to mind the ideas to be discussed. There are several factors to weigh in judging the usefulness of either form. Complete sentence outlines promote thorough analysis of ideas but tend to make delivery less spontaneous. Topic outlines, on the other hand, encourage spontaneity, but require a firmer grasp of materials and may tempt you to memorize the speech since there is much less text to reassure you.

Instructors generally prefer one or the other of the two forms and will tell you which one you ought to use. Whichever it is, both forms are identical in the way they show the unity and coherence of the speech. For example, here is part of the outline of an informative speech discussing the problem of unemployment among young people between 16 and 19 years of age.[1] This part of the outline shows the extent of the problem among a number of ethnic groups.

Complete Sentence Form	Topic Form
I. Employment rates differ among ethnic groups	I. Ethnic groups differ
A. White teenagers have an unemployment rate of 14.4%.	A. Whites 14.4%
B. The unemployment rate among young African Americans is 34.7%.	B. African Americans, 34.7%
C. Young Hispanics have an unemployment rate of 22.3%.	C. Hispanics, 22.3%

One final note. There is no absolute rule that forbids making a proper rhetorical outline in either of the two forms we have described and then, in addition, preparing a separate set of notes to use in delivery. Your instructor will tell you what is required.

Techniques of Outlining

No matter what form of outline you use, the techniques for preparing it are the same. One way to be sure that your speech will contain both unity and coherence is to understand the techniques of outlining and to use them properly.

Parts of the Outline

All well-organized speeches have three identifiable parts: a beginning, a middle, and an end. In a speech outline they are called the introduction, body, and conclusion.

The introduction   The introduction catches attention and arouses interest in the subject. It also contains a subject sentence that says what the speech is going to be about, and it includes any necessary background information.

The body   The body of the outline follows the introduction. It contains all the subject matter of the speech necessary to your purpose to entertain, inform, or persuade.

The conclusion   In the conclusion, you bring the speech to an appropriate close.

In skeleton form, an outline looks like this:

Specific Purpose: _____

Introduction
  I. [Attention and interest material]
 II. [Subject sentence]
III. [Background material, when required]

Body
  I. [First main heading]
     A. [Supporting material]
     B. [Supporting material]
 II. [Second main heading]
     [And so on]

Conclusion
  I. [Summary, if used]
 II. [Concluding remarks, as needed]

Showing Relationships

The symbol that marks each heading (I, II, A, B, 1, 2, or the like) shows the relationship of that heading to others in the outline. The symbol used and the degree to which a heading is indented indicates its superior, subordinate, or coordinate rank.

Symbols of subordination and coordination   The symbols used to show subordination and coordination are purely arbitrary but the following pattern is widely used.

  I. First main head
     A. Support for I
        1. Support for A
           a. support for 1
           b. further support for 1
        2. Further support for A
     B. Further support for I

 II. Second main head
     [and so on]

Subordinate ideas   If one heading is used to explain, prove, or otherwise support another, it is subordinate to the other. That is,

I. A main head is superior to its supporting subheads
   A. Each subhead is subordinate to the main head it supports.

Both the indenting of the subhead and the use of a different symbol series to label the headings at different levels indicate the subordination to the eye. In the outline, supporting materials are **always** subordinate headings. They **always follow** the heading they support.

Wrong

I. Supporting material

[therefore]
  A. Main idea

I. The U.S. postal service contributes significantly to the budget deficit.
[therefore]
  A. The U.S. postal service should be abolished.

Right

I. Main idea

[because]
  A. Supporting material

I. The U.S. postal service should be abolished.
[because]
  A. The U.S. postal service contributes significantly to the budget deficit.

Coordinate ideas If two or more headings support the same larger heading, they are said to be coordinate. In the following illustration, headings A. and B. under I. are coordinate with each other, and so are A. and B. under II. Note also that I. and II. are coordinate because they both support the speech claim.

Speech Claim: All handguns should be registered with the federal government.

I. First main head

  A. Support for I.

  B. Further support for I.

II. Second main head

  A. Support for II.

  B. Further support for II.

   [And so on]

I. Owning a handgun is more a danger than a protection.
  A. Having a gun is an occasion for crimes of impulse or "passion."
  B. Nearly all burglaries are committed when no one is at home, making a gun useless.
II. The restriction would be constitutional.
  A. The right to "keep and bear arms" refers to a "well-regulated militia."
  B. The Supreme Court supported this position in 1939 and again in 1980.
   [And so on]

Checking the Outline

As the outline develops, check it frequently for accurate subordination and coordination, for formal correctness, and for content completeness.

Accurate subordination and coordination Since the major purpose of making an outline is to show how the ideas are related, accuracy in subordination and coordination is an absolute requirement.

I. Teen-age unemployment rates differ among ethnic groups.
   A. The unemployment rate among young African Americans is 34.7%.
   B. White teenagers have an unemployment rate of 14.4%.
   C. Young Hispanics have an unemployment rate of 22.3%.
   D. Teenagers don't work as hard as adults.

This outline says that D. is subordinate to I. and helps to support it. But the idea that teenagers don't work as hard as adults does nothing to explain ethnic differences in unemployment rates. It is not a proper subheading of I.

Formal correctness   Making sure that the speech outline is formally correct will eliminate many of the problems of subordination and coordination. The formal correctness of any speech outline can be checked by a simple and mechanical method.

To check the formal correctness of a persuasive speech outline, add a connective such as "for," "since," "because," "for the reason that" at the end of each heading *that is followed immediately by a subordinate point*. Add the word *and* to each heading *that is followed immediately by a coordinate point or by a superior heading*. The skeleton looks like this:

The speaker's claim should be accepted *for the reason that*:

I. Argument I. helps to prove the claim. [Argument I. should be accepted *for the reason that*]
   A. Helps to prove I. [Point A. should be accepted *for the reason that*]
      1. Helps to prove A. *and*
      2. Also helps to prove A. *and*
   B. Along with A. also helps to prove argument I. [B. ought to be accepted *for the reason that*]
      1. Helps to prove B. *and*
      2. Also helps to prove B. *and*
II. Argument II. along with argument I. also helps to prove the speech claim.
   [Argument II. should be accepted *for the reason that*]
   [And so on]

Checking an outline by the method of adding connective phrases is quite simple. For instance, it makes very good sense to say:

I. It is difficult for teenagers to find jobs [*for the reason that*]
   A. They have little work experience [*and*]
   B. They are less responsible than adults

But within the context of this argument, it makes no sense at all to claim that:

I. It is difficult for teenagers to find jobs [*for the reason that*]
   A. They have little work experience [*and*]
   B. They are less responsible [*and*]
   C. There is less unemployment in rural areas.

The formal correctness of an informative speech outline is tested by mentally adding such connective phrases as "*for example*" and "*that is* to say'' in front of subordinate points. For coordinate positions, use such words as "*moreover,*" "*furthermore,*" and "*in addition.*"

Speeches to entertain frequently do not seem to be as tightly organized as informative and persuasive speeches. This is because they often use disorganization as a part of their humor. However, you will want the organization to show exactly what you are doing. To whatever extent you want the speech to have a formal structure, you can apply the same test you use for an informative or persuasive speech outline.

When speech outlines are tested this way and they make sense, you can be reasonably sure that they are formally correct.

Content completeness of informative outlines   In addition to checking its formal correctness, an informative speech outline can also be tested by a system of "adding" ideas. Coordinate headings taken together should add up to no more and no less than their superior heading. Here is an example in skeleton form.

Specific Purpose: To inform the audience about _____

I.
   A.
   B.
      1.
      2.
II.
   A.
   B.

Now, "add up" the ideas contained in the above headings:

I.B.1 + I.B.2 = I.B.
I.A. + I.B. = I.
II.A. + II.B. = II.
I. + II. = Specific purpose

Let's see how this works in an actual example:

Specific Purpose: To explain the operation of the electoral college

  I. Alexander Hamilton's mistrust of the common man
 II. Method of selecting electors determined by states
III. Number equal to each state's Congressional delegation
IV. Electors nominated by parties
 V. Electoral College injustices

"Adding up" the headings shows that this outline is faulty for two reasons. In the first place, the five points of the outline add up to *less* than the specific purpose because the speech does not explain the operation of the Electoral College. Secondly, because the first and last points are not part of an explanation of how the College operates, they make the outline add up to *more* than the specific purpose. This example pertains to the relationship of main points to the specific purpose. The same principle applies to lower levels of subordination as well.

Important Technical Principles

Applying certain technical principles will not only make it easier to construct well organized outlines, it will make the speeches they represent work better. At the same time, technically correct outlines will help to avoid a number of problems that would plague the speech if the principles were ignored.

Each Heading an Assertion

Each of the headings in an outline should express an assertion. This means that a heading should not be a question. The trouble with questions in an outline is that there is no clear relationship between a question and either a subordinate or a coordinate point. Because a question makes no definite claim, it cannot be proved and it cannot be used as supporting material to clarify or to prove. An outline should answer questions, not ask them.

Wrong: How serious is traffic congestion in Los Angeles?

Right: Traffic congestion in Los Angeles is at a breakdown point.

Rhetorical questions are an effective element of style and Chapter 15 shows how they can be used. We do not mean to deny that. The point here is one that we made in discussing traditional rhetoric in Chapter 1. "Disposition" (organization) and "elocution" (style) are different functions of language. The outline should reflect the *organization* of the speech (the relationships and sequence of its parts). It is not intended to mirror the *style*. Style (of some sort) is inevitably a feature of every communication, even the outline itself, but it is not a significant factor in the outline; it is important only in the language of the speech.

Each Heading a Single Assertion

An outline should show the relationships among the *individual* ideas. It cannot do this correctly unless each of the headings makes one and only one assertion.

Wrong

I. Legislation requiring student athletes to maintain a "C" average to be eligible for sports ignores the inevitable contradiction between raising grade requirements and lowering standards to meet the requirements.

Right

I. Legislation requiring student athletes to maintain a "C" average to be eligible for sports ignores an inevitable contradiction.
   A. Grade requirements will be raised.
   B. Grading standards will be lowered to meet the new requirements.

Only One Symbol per Heading

To label a single heading in the outline both I. and A. or both A. and 1. suggests that a subordinate point is its own main head, which is *clearly* impossible. When a double symbol is used, it ordinarily means that the speaker has recognized a series of points that seem coordinate and senses that they need a common superior heading but hasn't decided what it is.

Wrong

  I. A. The unemployment rate among teenaged African Americans is 34.7%.
    B. White teenagers have an unemployment rate of 14.4%.
    C. Hispanic youth have an unemployment rate of 22.3%.

Right

  I. Rates of unemployment differ among ethnic groups.
    A. The unemployment rate among teenaged African Americans is 34.7%.
    B. White teenagers have an unemployment rate of 14.4%.
    C. Hispanic youth have an unemployment rate of 22.3%.

No Overlapping Headings

An outline is of no use unless it expresses accurately the relationships you see among the ideas. One of the ways it can fail to do this is to show coordination where there is none. The outline not only says that each heading represents a *separate* idea, it also says that each heading represents an idea that is *different* from any other coordinate heading.

  I. Reuniting East and West Germany will bring great benefits to the East Germans.
    A. They will have new economic advantages.
    B. They will be free from political repression.
    C. There will be a great new growth of democratic spirit.
    D. They will be free from military domination.

Notice that C. overlaps both B. and D. Instead of being coordinate with C., both B. and D. are subordinate to C. because they are evidence to show why C. is true. When they are outlined correctly, they will look like this:

  I. Reuniting East and West Germany will bring great benefits to the East Germans.
    A. They will have new economic advantages.
    B. There will be a great new growth of democratic spirit.
      1. They will be free from political repression.
      2. They will be free from military domination.

Revising the Outline

The first outline of a speech is usually little more than a scratch outline of ideas that seem to have some bearing on the subject and some relationship to each other. In beginning to think about a subject, you usually lack enough detailed information to see clearly the best way to relate the ideas. But as information and ideas grow, new relationships develop and less useful ones are discarded. A constant examination of the outline will be necessary, even to the actual moment of speaking.

Summary

Good organization makes clear the relationships among the ideas, arguments and supporting materials. It also determines the sequence in which they will be presented. Good organization is characterized by unity (a harmonious oneness among the parts) and coherence (a rational ordering of the parts).

An outline is a blueprint for a speech. There are several different kinds of outlines, each of which has its proper use, but a rhetorical outline is the one that will usually serve best.

The parts of an outline reflect the parts of the speech. There is an introduction, a body, and a conclusion. The introduction serves to catch attention and to arouse interest, to tell the audience what the subject and purpose are, and to give them any necessary background material. The body of the outline organizes the subject matter of the speech. The conclusion brings the speech to an appropriate close.

Structurally, an outline uses subordination and coordination to show the relationships among the elements of the speech. Subordinate headings clarify or prove some other (superior) heading. Headings are coordinate when they support the same superior heading. Subordination and coordination are shown by the use of symbols and indentation.

The quality of an outline can be tested by checking it for accurate subordination and coordination, formal correctness and, (in the case of informative speech outlines) completeness of content.

Keep these technical principles in mind:

1. Each outline heading should make an assertion.
2. Each heading should contain no more than one assertion.
3. Use only one symbol for any one heading.
4. There should be no overlapping among the headings.

Frequent revision of the outline will be necessary until the speech is actually delivered.

Key Terms

Relationships	Sentence outline
Unity	Topic outline
Digressions	Introduction
Coherence	Body
Sequence	Conclusion
Continuity	Subordination
Scratch outline	Coordination
Brief	Formal correctness
Rhetorical outline	Content completeness

Exercises

1. Two sample speeches appear at the end of this chapter (beginning on page 212). The first has been outlined for you.

2. Read the speech "Ritalin" by Ryan T. Siskow on pages 216-219. State the specific purpose of the speech. Determine the introduction, body, and conclusion. Outline the speech.

3. Write a short paper in which you evaluate the organization of the speech "Ritalin." Could the organization be improved? If so, how? If not, why not?

Notes

[1] The data used in this example are drawn from the Statistical Abstract of the United States, 1989 *(Washington, D.C.: U.S. Department of Commerce, 1989) and from the Handbook of Labor Statistics* (Washington, D.C.: U.S. Department of Labor, 1989).

Speeches for Study

"Sewage: Swamped in our Waste"
Margaret E. Heffernan
University of Wisconsin, Madison

Introduction

I. Boston Tea Party members were heroes for dumping tea into the harbor
II. Today, Bostonians are still dumping
   A. 50,000 gallons of human waste per second
   B. Since 1900 enough to cover state chest deep
III. Happening all over the country
   A. Bays, rivers, lakes becoming cesspools
   B. Effects on our environment, our health, our quality of life
IV. (Subject Sentence) We will examine three areas to understand the seriousness of the problem
   A. The damage improper sewage disposal does
   B. Why this happens
   C. Ways to improve efficiency of treatment facilities

Body

I. Oceans, lakes, rivers have incredible cleansing powers
   A. Have succeeded for centuries
   B. Now 10 billion gallons a day is too much to handle
   C. Too much for aquatic fish and plants

II. Nutrients greatest threat: *New York Times*, phosphorus and nitrogen
   A. Fertilize aquatic plants creating massive algae blooms
   B. Algae dies suffocating fish and shellfish
   C. Dead zones found in waters off every city: *Newsweek*
     1. Dead zone of 3,000 square miles at mouth of Mississippi
     2. EPA—will be years before zones will support life again

1 During our nation's struggle for independence, the citizens of Boston were hailed as heroes for dumping British tea into Boston Harbor. Not to be outdone, modern day Bostonians are also dumping things into the harbor; 5,000 gallons of human waste every second. The New England Aquarium in Boston states that since 1900, Bostonians have dumped enough human sewage into the harbor to cover the entire state of Massachusetts chest deep in sludge. Unfortunately, Boston isn't alone. All over the country bays, rivers and lakes are literally becoming cesspools. Improper sewage disposal is having widespread effects on our environment, our health and our quality of life. In order to better understand how serious these effects are we'll first look at the damage that improper sewage disposal causes to our environment and to us, why this damage is occurring; and finally, ways we can improve the efficiency of our sewage treatment facilities. Examination of these areas will reveal the extent of this problem and the urgent need that it be solved.

2 Our oceans, lakes and rivers have incredible cleansing powers and for centuries they've been able to withstand the onslaught of billions of gallons of waste. However, the Environmental Protection Agency states that the total amount of sewage effluent has doubled in the last decade to ten billion gallons each day. The volume of sewage that is pumped into the water is simply too much for aquatic fish and plants to bear.

3 The *New York Times* of September 13, 1988, explains that the greatest threat posed to waterlife from sewage is the nutrients found in the sewage, namely, phosphorous and nitrogen. Once introduced into the water these nutrients fertilize the aquatic plants, creating massive algae blooms. When this algae dies and decomposes it robs the water of oxygen, suffocating fish and shellfish. These oxygen depleted waters are appropriately called "dead zones." *Newsweek* magazine of August 1, 1988, states that these dead zones can be found in the waters off

every major city on each coast and at the mouth of the Mississippi there is a dead zone measuring 3,000 square miles. According to the Environmental Protection Agency, once a water area becomes oxygen depleted it can be years before it's able to support life once again.

III. Increasing amounts of dead and diseased fish
   A. New York and New Jersey—Dump Site 106: *Time*
      1. Found by fishermen from New England to So. Carolina Hake and tilefish with rotting fins and red lesions
   B. Rarely seen before dumping began

4   Sewage is also thought to contribute to increasing amounts of diseased fish. *Time* magazine of August 1, 1988, states that since 1986 New York and New Jersey have dumped ten million tons of sludge in an area known as Dump Site 106. Located 106 miles from New York Harbor, this dump site is having wide-reaching effects. Fishermen all the way from South Carolina to New England have been catching increasing amounts of hake and tilefish with rotting fins and red lesions on their bellies. Before the dumping began, such deformities were rarely seen.

IV. Fish not alone to suffer
   A. Assaults human sensibilities

      1. William Gordon saw jellyfish—human fecal matter

5   The fish are not the only creatures to suffer. Aquatic sewage dumping assaults human sensibilities and more importantly, human health.

6   William Gordon, a resident of a Boston suburb, was jogging along the Boston Bay shore when he noticed what appeared to be a beached jellyfish. Upon closer inspection, this jellyfish turned out to be clumps of human fecal matter covered in grease.

      2. Scuba divers in San Francisco Bay—clouds of toilet paper and half-dissolved feces

      3. Santa Monica and San Diego have closed beaches

7   Up and down the East and West Coasts and along inland shorelines the story is the same. Scuba divers in the San Francisco area report swimming through clouds of toilet paper and half-dissolved feces. Beaches in Santa Monica and and San Diego have all had to be closed within the past year due to sewage pollution.

   B. Sewage threatens our health
      1. USDH: human sewage carries typhoid, cholera and bacteria

      2. Diseased fish are sold and eaten: *Time*

8   In addition to its assault on our senses, sewage also threatens our health. The United States Department of Health asserts that human sewage is alive with pathogens capable of killing us. It is a known carrier of typhoid, cholera and several strains of harmful bacteria. Sewage's health threat can also be indirect. Many of the fish that are caught in areas such as Dump Site 106 wind up on our dinner tables. *Time* of August 1, 1988, states that due to a lack of fish inspection, many fishermen sell their diseased fish along with the rest of their catch.

V. Technology is available to solve
   these problems
   A. Equipment available to remove 95%
      of the impurities: *NY Times*

   B. EPA: 40% of the facilities have
      problems
   C. 150 Communities dump raw
      sewage
   D. Older communities use outdated
      systems
      1. Boston and New York over 100
         years old
      2. Built for half the population

VI. Government all show and no go

   A. 1977 Clean Water Act
      1. Set higher guidelines
      2. Decade later half the nation has
         unsafe sewage disposal:
         Newsweek

   B. 1988 Bill with fines for ocean
      dumping: *CS Monitor*

      1. Flawed—cost of alternate
         dumping greater than fines

      2. Sally Ann Lentz, Oceanic
         Society: Bill "will not bring an
         end to ocean dumping. It just
         raises the price tag."

VII. Quick and vigorous action must
    be taken

   A. In homes: low flow plumbing
      fixtures
      1. Cut toilet flush from 6 to 2
         gallons
      2. Low flow shower heads

9   The most frustrating aspect of these problems is that the technology available to us is more than adequate to solve these problems. The *New York Times* of September 18, 1988, states that existing sewage treatment equipment is capable of removing 95% of the impurities from our waste water. Unfortunately, this technology is simply not being implemented. The Environmental Protection Agency reports that 40% of the nation's sewage treatment facilities have public health and water quality problems and 150 communities simply dump their raw, untreated sewage into the nearest waterway. Furthermore, many older communities such as New York and Boston rely on sewage treatment equipment that is more than 100 years old and built for populations half the cities' current size.

10   So far, our government's reaction to our sewage disposal problem has been all show and no go. In 1977, Congress passed the Clean Water Act. One of its functions was to set guidelines for the level of impurities that could be present when water was discharged from a treatment plant. A decade later, *Newsweek* of August 1, 1988, states that close to half of the nation disposes of its sewage in an unsafe manner. Last October, the government decided to get tough once again. According to the *Christian Science Monitor* of October 31, 1988, Congress passed a bill stating that anyone caught dumping sludge in the ocean would be fined. However, as the *Monitor* points out, the legislation is severely flawed. The cost of alternative disposal is much higher than the cost of the fines. As a result, ocean dumping is still the quickest and the cheapest way to dispose of waste. Sally Ann Lentz, an attorney for the Oceanic Society states the bill will "not bring an end to ocean dumping. It just raises the price tag."

11   Clearly, quick and vigorous action must be taken to solve our sewage disposal problems. We have to stop burdening Mother Nature with our waste. The best place to begin our efforts is right in our own homes.

12   Households can dramatically cut the amount of waste water they generate by installing low-flow plumbing fixtures. The average toilet flush can be cut from six gallons to two gallons and low-flow shower heads are also available. These devices are easy to install and many cities offer incentive programs for

their use. The logic behind the devices is simple. The less water we get dirty, the less water we have to clean, the less strain on our sewage treatment facilities.

B. Cities and towns, use alternate treatment

  1. Clayton Country, Georgia irrigate forest land
    a. forest serves as a filter

    b. trees are harvested and burned
    c. solid waste sold as fertilizer

  2. Seattle, WA: timber companies buy sludge

  3. Milwaukee, Wisc. sells sludge under tradename Milorganite

C. EPA claims such programs operate at half the cost

D. Present legislation must be enforced
  1. Citizens put pressure on local, state and federal government

  2. William Gordon sued Boston and Boston is being forced to clean up

E. Build better treatment facilities
  1. EPA: it will cost billions

  2. Worth paying for health and quality of life

13 Cities and towns can also contribute by learning to rely less on conventional treatment and more on alternative treatment such as land application programs. For example, rather than dump its primary-treated waste water into the nearest lake or stream, Clayton County, Georgia, uses it to irrigate forest land. The forest is fertilized by the nutrients it would take a treatment facility millions of dollars to remove and the soil of the forest serves as a massive filter, both protecting and purifying groundwater. Trees from the forest are then harvested and burned to help fry the solid waste, or sludge, that has been separated out. This is then sold as fertilizer, helping to offset operating costs.

14 Clayton County isn't the only community to benefit from such a system. In Seattle, Washington, timber companies are lining up to buy city sludge, claiming it makes their trees grow twice as fast. Milwaukee, Wisconsin, sells its sludge under the trade name Milorganite with similar success. The Environmental Protection Agency claims that such land application programs can operate at half the cost of a conventional treatment facility and in some cases, may even turn a profit.

15 As I've mentioned, we have legislation to regulate sewage disposal. It is now a matter of getting this legislation enforced. Citizens can put pressure on their local, state and federal governments by making phone calls, writing letters and in some cases, filing lawsuits. William Gordon, the jellyfish jogger, sued the city of Boston on behalf of his community and as result of his action and similar action by other citizens, Boston is slowly being forced to clean up its act.

16 Finally, new and better treatment facilities have to be built. The Environmental Protection Agency cannot give an exact estimate on how much a national overhaul will cost, only that it will be billions of dollars. However, when we weigh this against the value we place on our health and quality of life, it becomes a price that we must be willing to pay.

Conclusion

17   In examining our nation's sewage disposal problems we've seen the environmental and the human damage that we're suffering, why this damage is occurring; and finally, ways that we can improve our sewage treatment systems. Examination of these areas has hopefully made us realize how important it is that we take action because for Boston Harbor and the rest of our environment, the party's over.

Reprinted with permission of the Interstate Oratorical Association from *Winning Orations* ed. Larry Schnoor (Mankato, MN: Interstate Oratorical Association, 1989) 114-17.

"Ritalin"
Ryan T. Siskow
University of Northern Iowa

1   Nine-year-old Casey Jesson complained of headaches and stomach cramps. He also showed signs of insomnia and loss of appetite. His parents took him off the medication that produced these negative side effects yet school officials continually pressured the Jessons to put Casey back on the medication. Finally, school authorities gave the Jessons an ultimatum: put Casey back on the medication or he could not attend classes.

2   Casey Jesson has attention deficit disorder, more commonly known as hyperactivity. Casey and nearly one million children are being given the new "wonder drug" of the '80s, Ritalin. But this new "wonder drug" is being overused and it is creating a controversy that has parents, state regulators and school administrators up in arms, and more importantly, is jeopardizing the health of countless children.

3   In order to better understand the ramifications of Ritalin overuse, we need to look at what Ritalin is and the potential dangers associated with it, examine how it is becoming a forced issue in the American classroom, investigate why it is being overused; and finally, identify some alternatives that may help alleviate the Ritalin conflict.

4   The January 11, 1988, issue of *U.S. News and World Report* stated that over 5 million pre-adolescent children suffer from hyperactivity. Hyperactivity, or attention deficit disorder, refers to a complex range of behavioral disorders which are characterized by inattentiveness and impulsive behavior.

5   Ritalin, the trade name for methylphenidate, is the most common form of drug therapy used in the treatment of hyperactive children. According to a June, 1988, *Nightline* telecast, over 800,000 children are currently using the drug.

6   *Perceptual and Motor Skills* magazine of 1986 reported that researchers do not know what causes hyperactivity or how Ritalin works to sedate hyperactive children. *Newsweek* of February 15, 1988, stated that Ritalin is

not a cure for hyperactivity. It is simply a chemical mask that hides the symptoms of the disorder.

7   Furthermore, the United States Drug Enforcement Agency lists Ritalin as a schedule two narcotic, which puts it in the same class [as] amphetamines, barbiturates and cocaine. The depressing effect of Ritalin is very similar to that of a cocaine induced high. It is used to slow down the mental and physical processes of hyperactive children. While the drug is approximately 70 percent effective, the side effects associated with it make its use even more questionable.

8   The Fall, 1981, issue of *Adolescence* lists side effects of Ritalin that include insomnia, weight loss, nervousness, headaches, skin rashes, increased blood pressure, as well as increased heart palpitations.

9   For those children who are not hyperactive, the effects of Ritalin can be even more dramatic. The *New York Times* on May 5, 1986, reported that the effects of Ritalin on children who are not hyperactive can be potentially fatal. Because Ritalin is intended to bring down the activity levels of overactive children, its effects on otherwise normal children induces a state of deep depression. This depressed state brings some of the side effects mentioned earlier as well as hallucinations and suicidal tendencies.

10   Even though the origins of its medicinal effects are unknown and its negative side effects have been well documented, the *New York Times* reported on February 12, 1988, that the prescription rate of Ritalin doubled over the last two years. When Ritalin is used correctly it can be very beneficial; when it is used needlessly, the drug becomes dangerous. The Ritalin debate is more prevalent in our nation's schools. Critics charge that school administrators are using Ritalin to curb classroom difficulties which may not stem from hyperactivity.

11   *Psychology Today* of December, 1984, reported that an alarming 10 to 15 percent of students in some school districts are taking what one official says are "potentially dangerous drugs, namely Ritalin." What's even more surprising is that Ritalin is prescribed by a family doctor and very frequently at the urging of school authorities.

12   In Georgia, state legislative hearings were prompted by an Atlanta parents' group who complained that teachers were pressuring them to put their children on Ritalin. LaVerne Parker testified that teachers pressured her to put her ten-year-old son, who is not hyperactive, on the drug. She said the Ritalin caused him to suffer hallucinations and made him suicidal.

13   One of the most publicized cases of Ritalin in the classroom is the one involving young Casey Jesson. In June of last year, New Hampshire's Department of Education ruled that the school system did have the right to require medication as a condition for Casey to receive public education. For the moment Casey is in public school with his own private teacher, but the solution is only temporary.

14   The struggle of Casey Jesson and his family epitomizes the Ritalin problem in our nation's schools, but to fully understand this issue we need to investigate why it is being overused.

15   Parents, psychologists and state regulators fear that the drug is being

used on children whose unruliness and school difficulties result from family problems, emotional difficulties, or inadequate instruction, not the disorder.

16   Dr. Paul Weber, a psychiatrist at the University of Utah and a recognized authority on hyperactivity, attributes the wider use of Ritalin to the tendency to generalize all overactive and disruptive behavior as hyperactivity. He asks the question that many people are thinking, "Are we using Ritalin intelligently, or are we using it to cure a large variety of psychological ills for which it may not be appropriate?"

17   The Citizens Commission on Human Rights has voiced its concern that attempts to find more effective therapies have been abandoned for a drug that does not cure hyperactivity, but only masks its symptoms.

18   Dr. Robert Slayder, an Atlanta Psychiatrist, has also raised questions about Ritalin. He is worried that some see Ritalin as a way to help a classroom teacher settle an unruly student. Slayder best sums up the problem of Ritalin overuse in our nation's schools by saying, "Not every troubled student is hyperactive, and parents and teachers need to realize that."

19   Increased awareness about hyperactivity has resulted in an increased use of Ritalin, and has subsequently resulted in its overuse. Dr. Sid Wolfe of the Citizens Health Research Center says there is no question that Ritalin is being overused. He criticizes those who turn to Ritalin before more creative solutions to a child's problems are even investigated.

20   Creative solutions do exist and there are measures we can take to rectify this conflict. The first step needs to simply address better diagnosis and then we can look to other alternatives for those children who are truly hyperactive.

21   The core of Ritalin overuse stems from hastily made diagnosis. Parents should seek second and even third medical opinions before beginning a treatment program for a hyperactive child. By taking the extra time and precaution we can avoid much of the tension created by the prescription of Ritalin.

22   Once we can eliminate those children who are not hyperactive, we can focus on those children who truly are. Alternatives to drug therapy need to be identified and made more accessible to those children and parents who cannot benefit from the drug or choose not to administer the drug in light of its negative side effects.

23   Behavior modification is one such alternative. The Summer 1982, *Journal of Applied Behavior Analysis* reported that behavior modification provides a feasible alternative to drug therapy. In a Florida State University Study, the group receiving behavior modification showed greater improvement in on-task behavior and academic performance than their counterparts who received Ritalin. Research is not yet complete, but so far the results are very encouraging.

24   While behavior modification would be the preferred method of treatment, we must acknowledge its limitations at the present time. Until research is complete and comprehensive plans for behavior modification are set forth, other alternatives need to be explored. Dr. Jerry Weiner, President of the Academy of Child Psychiatry, believes that a combination of drug therapy and behavior modification is the best plan of action at the moment. According

to Weiner, drug therapy should be used in combination with special educational approaches.

25   Expanding on Weiner's proposals, we must consider the right of teachers and other students to have an educational environment free from distractions. Special programs for hyperactive children would help relieve this problem. Just as there are programs designed to assist mentally and physically handicapped children, children with learning disabilities, as well as those with exceptional abilities, programs designed to assist hyperactive children should be implemented within our school systems.

26   Clearly, medication is easier to administer and does not require the extra effort that behavior modification does. But equally clear is the fact that Ritalin carries with it an armament of potential dangers and that children continue to experience academic difficulty or do not respond positively to psychostimulant medication. Thus, effective, easy to use behavior modification will continue to be required in the future.

27   The safety and well-being of our children is nothing to take lightly. As parents and educators, it is our responsibility to look out for the well-being of children like Casey Jesson. We can take the easy way out and opt for the utility of Ritalin, or we can first investigate our options and then make an intelligent decision for both us and our children.

Reprinted with the permission of the Interstate Oratorical Association from *Winning Orations* ed. Larry Schnoor (Mankato, MN: Interstate Oratorical Association, 1989) 36-39.

Part Four

Communicating
Speeches

chapter 14

Introductions, Transitions, and Conclusions

I. Introducing the speech

    A. Catching attention
        1. Ask a rhetorical question
        2. Use a quotation
        3. Tell a story
        4. Make a striking statement
        5. Use humor
    B. Stating the subject
    C. Eliciting good will
    D. Establishing credibility
    E. Supplying background material

II. Holding attention
    A. Show the importance of the subject and occasion
    B. Create suspense
    C. Dramatize conflict
    D. Repeat significant ideas
    E. Express ideas vividly

III. Using transitions to maintain clarity

IV. Concluding the speech
    A. Summarize the main points
    B. Restate a proposed course of action
    C. Tell a story
    D. Use a quotation
    E. Ask rhetorical questions
    F. Develop an analogy
    G. Call for action

The body of a speech carries the main burden of communication. Before the body of the speech can begin its work, however, the audience must be enticed to listen. To maintain the listeners' interest, the speech must be constructed so that the audience can easily follow the main points. Finally, to insure that all the time and effort that went into preparing the body of the speech is not wasted, the key information must be summarized so that the audience is left with a memory of a clear, interesting, and effective speech. Introductions, transitions, and conclusions play vital roles in the success of a speech by helping the audience focus on the speaker's intentions. Let's review some specific techniques for preparing these three important parts of the speech.

Introducing the Speech

The first function of the introduction is to catch the attention of the audience. Your introduction must also include a *subject sentence* that tells the audience what the speech is about. Depending upon the demands of the occasion, the introduction may or may not have to perform three other functions. In some circumstances, you may have to overcome hostility or disinterest by cultivating the audience's good will. If the audience doesn't know you, the introduction gives you the opportunity to establish your credibility. Finally, the introduction supplies background material when it is needed.

Catching Attention

Human senses receive stimuli constantly. Conscious intelligence, however, is not alert to every stimulus. People perceive the world in a selective fashion. They see and hear some things and not others. To be clearly aware of something at any given moment is to give it attention. *Attention is a preparedness to perceive a selected set of stimuli.*

Attention Can be Caught and Held by Building in Attention Factors
• Intensity—Intellectual energy in idea, value, language
• Change—Variation in the direction of argument or thought
• Familiarity—Prior knowledge of the subject
• Novelty—Newness or strangeness of subject matter
Attention Factors Should Be:
• Emphasized in the introduction
• Apparent throughout the speech
• Pertinent to the subject
• Appropriate to the audience

It is easy to catch attention. Just yell. That advice is obviously facetious but we wanted to capture *your* attention. The most important point to remember is that you need to attract your audience and to make sure that your attention-catching device is related to the purpose of the speech. For instance, you could certainly attract notice by dropping a handful of marbles on the floor. The audience's attention would be directed to the bright, flashing colors of the marbles as they bounced noisily around the room, but not to the subject of the speech. Attention is best used when it compels the audience to focus on your subject. Here are some of the ways you can get the audience's attention *and* focus it on your speech.

Ask a rhetorical question   A rhetorical question is one that is directed to an audience, although no direct response is expected. When you ask a question, rhetorical or otherwise, the instinctive reaction of the audience is to try to answer it. This introduces an abrupt change that takes the audience away from passive reception. It makes the audience think, and thinking draws attention to your subject. A successful method of getting attention, then, is to ask one or more rhetorical questions in the introduction. Insurance executive Gerald D. Stevens said to an audience,

> Let me start with a question: If you had the magic power to change the environment in which we operate and improve our ways of doing business, what would our industry look like five years from now and in the year 2000?[1]

Use a quotation   A striking quotation will catch attention, especially if the source is well-known. Bryan Ciyou, a student at Indiana-Purdue University at Indianapolis, argued for mandatory birth control as an approach to the problem of starvation in third- and fourth-world countries. He opened his speech with this quotation from the Apocalypse:

> And before me was a black horse! Its rider was holding a pair of scales in his hand. Then I heard what sounded like a voice among the four living creatures, saying, "A quart of wheat for a day's wages, and three quarts of barley for a day's wages, and do not damage the oil and the wine!"

> As predicted nearly 2000 years ago by Jesus' disciple John, Famine, the Third Horseman, is now riding upon the earth.[2]

A startling statement commands attention. If the statement is a quotation from a well-known person, or source, the interest level intensifies.

Tell a story   Stories can be used anywhere in the speech—*if* they are pertinent to your topic and clearly illustrate the point you want to make. Stories draw on the attention factors of novelty and familiarity. Both the familiar and the novel invite attention. When ideas are unfamiliar, listeners' minds may wander to more comfortable thoughts, but if a speaker identifies something familiar to them, they are more inclined to concentrate on the speech. Novelty may inspire initial attention because it provokes curiosity. However, the speaker will have to establish how the novel idea relates to the normal experience of the audience. In the presidential address to the 1987 Speech Communication Association convention, Patti P. Gillespie discussed the failure of affirmative action to establish sexual and racial equality among college faculties. To dramatize her point, she told this story:

> As some of you know, I try to spend part of every other summer camping in Kenya. During my last trip in Ambesoli, I was awakened just before daybreak by the sound of furiously pounding hooves that grew closer and closer to my tent. there was a horrible cry that intermingled with growls until both seemed within a few feet of where I was lying. Suddenly the cries and growls stopped, and all I heard was a very deep vibrating sound, not unlike [a] soft growl, or perhaps — ominously — a soft purr. Not daring to open the tent to look out — that one-sixteenth of an inch of canvas being all that protected me from whatever was going on right next to me — I tried to decide what I had heard, what had happened.
>
> Gradually, as I thought about it, the sequence became clear to me. A zebra had been fleeing a lion, who had caught it just outside my tent and was now feasting on it. The five of us in the camp would remain hostage in our tents until the heat of the day when the lion, sleepy and satisfied, would move away from us. Very well, I thought, I will try to calm down and wait. I waited. I had only begun to regret my last night's beer when I heard what sounded like human footsteps — yes, they were human because I next heard the unmistakable sound of pots and pans. The cook was out of his tent. Thinking him slightly mad, I dressed hastily, looked out carefully, and then joined him hurriedly at the fire. "Where was the lion's kill?" I asked in butchered swahili. "No lion," he said, "hyena fight."
>
> Embarrassed as only a tourist can be, I resolved not to make such a silly error again. A couple of weeks later, on a hillside outside Maralal, I was awakened to hear a replay of those same noises, again quite close to my tent: pounding hooves, loud growls, low purrs. This time I remained proudly unafraid. Athough the cook seemed a bit late in rising, as soon as I heard him up, I joined him at the fire for coffee. "Hyena," I said confidently. "No," he said, pointing not very far away, "Lion kill."
>
> This tale is cautionary: things may not be as they seem; things may not be as we hear them to be. And indeed, some things are not as we hear them to be in higher education.[3]

Make a striking statement   When an audience is not fully aware of the details of an important situation, you can call its attention to the subject with an intense or novel statement of the facts. Rear Admiral Ronald J. Kurth, President of the U.S. Naval War College, spoke to executives of the Raytheon Corporation on January 11, 1990. He began his speech by saying:

> Politically, we are living in exciting times. Communism has gone belly up in a way and with a speed which nobody came close to predicting. In Eastern Europe the pace has been frenetic, in each country a political

revolution. In *Time* magazine's brief paradigm, what took 10 years in Poland took 10 months in Hungary, 10 weeks in East Germany, 10 days in Czechoslovakia and 10 hours in Rumania.[4]

Use humor   Some speakers take pride in their ability to tell jokes. They should. Good storytellers have an enviable talent. An aptitude for humor is rewarding to speechmakers. It is even better when it brings novelty to familiar settings or to experiences that the audience might have had. For example:

> A friend of mine had a crush on one of the prettiest women in the freshman class. He was in two courses with her but could never find the right moment to introduce himself. One day in the cafeteria he ended up standing in line right behind her. Because he felt so self-conscious, his voice froze, and as they moved along the serving counter he felt yet another opportunity slipping away.
>
> Suddenly the girl turned to him and pointed at a selection. "Do you know what this is?" she asked.
>
> "Y-yes," he replied, "that's Don MacKensie. Hi, I'm macaroni salad."[5]

A good joke will always draw attention. Use it in a speech, however, only when both the substance and the mood of the joke illuminate the subject and purpose of the speech. Otherwise, the attention it arouses will not be useful. If the joke is intrusive, it damages the unity of the speech. Chapter 20 explains more about the use of jokes and humor in general.

Stating the Subject

One of the first things you do when you prepare a speech is to create a statement of purpose such as this one:

> To inform the audience about the caste system in India.

A statement of purpose is a useful guide in preparation, but it is not a part of the speech as you deliver it. Instead, you rephrase the statement of purpose into a sentence you could use in conversation. For example:

> We can get a better insight into the culture of India if we understand how the caste system works in that country.

This is the subject sentence that tells the audience what your speech claim is.

Eliciting Good Will

A part of the classical concept of *ethos*, as it was described by Aristotle, is the speaker's indication of good will toward the audience. The listeners must feel that the speaker has their best interests at heart. In the speaker-audience relationship, you want the giving and earning of good will to be a two-way street. You hope the audience will return your show of good will by being kindly disposed toward you.

Ancient rhetoricians were well aware of the need for a speaker to arouse a feeling of good will in the audience. It was quite common for the defendant in a law suit to begin a speech with arguments somewhat along these lines:

> If I seem to stumble, it is not because I am lying, but because I am only a naive youth, not experienced in the law. I have never been in court before, but my wily and experienced opponent is always suing somebody or other. Please listen to me with an open mind. I will tell you the truth of the matter.

On occasion, you will meet the same demand for eliciting good will today but probably with a more subtle attempt to achieve it! Your goal in the introduction is to make the audience set aside whatever prejudices it might have against you.

If, on the other hand, you are known to the audience and don't face strong disapproval, the audience's perception of you as competent will ordinarily be enough to win you a fair hearing.

Establishing Credibility

Chapter 12 says that credibility is the audience's belief that you are worth listening to because you are competent and trustworthy. In the introduction you have your first chance to show the audience that you know what you are talking about.

In 1988 historian John Hope Franklin was the first African American to deliver the Commencement Address at Louisiana State University. In the introduction to his address, he tells the audience about his connection to LSU. In the course of that exercise in good will, he tells the audience enough about his background to demonstrate that he is a competent scholar.

> First of all, permit me to say that it is a great honor and pleasure for me to be here and to participate in the commencement exercises of this great institution. I have been in and out of Louisiana State University for more than forty years. I did research here, for the first time, in 1945; and I have returned to use the rich resources of the library and archives on several occasions. In 1972 I delivered the Walter Lynwood Fleming Lectures here, and the Louisiana State University Press has graciously published my works from time to time. In several divisions and departments of the University, there are personal and professional relationships that I greatly cherish. Indeed, in the city, and at Southern University, I have friendships and associations that have been sustained for more than fifty years. For many reasons, therefore, I am delighted to be here.[6]

Supplying Background Material

When your listeners are not familiar with your subject, it is necessary to orient them to it. On July 3, 1988, Carl Sagan (Pulitzer Prize author and professsor of astronomy at Cornell University) was the principal speaker at the rededication ceremonies of the Eternal Light Peace Memorial at Gettysburg, Pennsylvania. Sagan gave his audience this background material of little known facts that were prelude to the Battle of Gettysburg — an event he calls a "doleful and instructive milestone in world history."

> Fifty-one thousand human beings were killed or wounded here, ancestors of some of us, brothers of us all. This was the first full-fledged example of an industrialized war, with machine-made arms and railroad transport of men and materiel. This was the first hint of an age yet to come, our age; an intimation of what technology bent to the purposes of war might be capable. The Spencer repeating rifle was used here. In 1863, a reconnaissance balloon of the Army of the Potomac detected movements of Confederate troops across the Rappahannock River, the beginning of the campaign that led to the Battle of Gettysburg. That balloon was a precursor of air forces and strategic bombing and reconnaissance satellites.[7]

Background material should be no longer than a few sentences. Sagan says what he wants to say in six. If your audience needs a great deal of

When your listeners are not familiar with your subject, be sure to provide enough background material so that they will feel comfortable listening your presentation.

background, it would be better to revise your purpose and make the background material the subject of the speech.

Even though an introduction performs all its tasks well, that is not enough to insure that the audience will continue to listen. You must hold the attention of the audience so that it will want to keep on listening.

Holding Attention

When you say a speech held your attention, you probably mean that it was interesting and clear. You knew and enjoyed what the speech was about. Your reaction implied the speech was well organized and the transitions from one segment to another insured clarity. Later in this chapter we will show you how transitions play their part in this. When a speech is interesting and clear, it comes alive for an audience, and it is easy to follow. Holding attention (developing interest) is an important part of the process.

It is easy to hold the attention of an audience when you are talking about its favorite subject: horses, football, classical music—whatever the audience values. Your subjects will not always fit this description. This does not mean you have a poor subject. It means that to hold attention you must find ways to associate your subject with the value system of the audience.

Each decision you make is determined by one or more of your values: honesty, justice, power, success—to name only a few. A professor who tells the accounting class "This material is going to be on the midterm exam," offers an easily identifiable appeal to the values of the class.

Offered the right incentive, the audience will listen because it wants to realize its values. Given the opportunity for a good grade, the students will pay attention to the lecture. The desire for the actualization of values is an incentive for action.[8]

If you offer an audience the opportunity to substantiate one or more of its values in an attractive speech that captures and holds attention, you are giving them an incentive to listen. The audience will be more likely to pay attention to your information or your arguments. The same methods for catching attention can be used to sustain it. Anything that prompts the audience to look forward to what is coming, either with joy or dread, tends to arouse interest. In addition, you can use the following methods to give your audience incentives to listen.

Show the Importance of the Subject and Occasion

People will listen to a discussion of something they think is important more readily than they will to what they consider trivial. If you think the audience doesn't know enough about your subject to understand its significance, let your introduction make it explicit. Marcia began a speech on acid rain this way.

> Rain can be a real inconvenience to any of us. It might cut short a softball game, eliminate a tennis date, ruin our hair or sop up our clothes. But, there is a kind of rain falling in the United States and Canada which may have a devastating impact on our environment and on our future. It's called acid rain.

When President George Bush told the American people about his plans to combat the drug problem in the United States, he first made sure that his audience understood the importance of the subject. He introduced his speech of September 5, 1989 this way:

> This is the first time since taking the oath of office that I felt an issue was so important, so threatening, that it warranted talking directly with you, the American people. All of us agree that the greatest domestic threat facing our nation today is drugs.
>
> Drugs have strained our faith in our system of justice. Our courts, our prisons, our legal system are stretched to the breaking point. The social costs of drugs are mounting. In short, drugs are sapping our strength as a nation.

George Bush used the introduction of his speech to stress the importance of his subject matter.

Turn on the evening news, or pick up the morning paper and you'll
see what some Americans know just by stepping out their front door.
Our most serious problem today is cocaine, and in particular, crack.[9]

Create Suspense

Monkeys, cats and children are not the only creatures with curiosity.
Everyone is inquisitive to some degree. In human beings, curiosity is
evidence of a desire to learn. You can use this fact to maintain interest in
what you have to say. Curiosity is what makes suspense as useful to
speakers as it is to writers of mystery stories and spy novels. Listeners want
to know how the story ends, so suspense heightens the willingness to listen.

In December 1989, Willard C. Butcher, Chairman of the Chase Manhattan
Corporation, talked to the World Affairs Council of Orange County,
California about the great and growing trade deficit of the United States.
"We spend more and more money buying from foreign countries than we
get from selling our goods to them."

He uses suspense over the first ten paragraphs of the speech. The
suspense lies in making the audience wait to hear the promised solution.
As you will see in Chapter 19, delaying a proposed solution is a
conventional method of structuring a persuasive speech. Butcher does that
but adds suspense when he implies throughout, "I'm going to make you
wait to hear the part of my speech that you are most interested in." Here
is how he does it:

> My approach will be to make you three promises at the outset—then
> do my best to fulfill them. Promise number one: I won't try to persuade
> you, as some economists do, that our trade deficit is not a
> problem.... [Butcher then develops the claim that the large and
> growing deficit is a serious problem.]
>
> Promise number two: I'm *not* going to propose a raft of protectionist
> measures that the United States should impose to straighten out our
> major trading partners.... [After Butcher says what, in his view, is
> wrong with retaliatory tariffs he goes on,]
>
> Promise number three: I won't leave you today with a detailed account
> of a U.S. trade deficit problem—and no solution.... Before I propose
> that solution, however, let's see if we agree on the urgency of the
> problem.[10]

Dramatize Conflict

Conflict has an inherent attractiveness. The interest factor in dramatic
situations of any sort is always some kind of conflict. Sports are competitive
and competition is conflict; hence the popularity of sports. The more
obvious the competition is, the greater the interest becomes. Anything that
suggests a fight draws a crowd—whether a schoolyard scrap, professional
boxing match, or even a chess game. Your speeches will create interest

in the same way when the materials you use suggest conflict or struggle.

Shannon Dyer of Southwest Baptist University spoke on the dilemma of "whistleblowers" —employees who complain about conditions that they believe are dangerous or illegal. Shannon dramatized the conflict between these "troublemakers" and their employers. (Note that when Shannon used the *Newsweek* quotation she assumed her audience was familiar with the name Karen Silkwood.)

> Judith Penley paid the price of a clean conscience with her life. Immediately after taking part in an outside investigation of her employer . . . several attempts were made on her life. Scared and confused, Judith told investigators she knew of no one who would ever want to hurt her. The next day, Judith was brutally gunned down as she waited for a friend. With echoes of Karen Silkwood, *Newsweek* reports that investigators drew an obvious connection.[11]

Some conflicts are always brutal. Wars are. Gang fights are. Boxing is. Killing people who seek remedies for dangerous conditions is a brutal way to end a conflict. Other conflicts are not. A game of golf is not brutal, but it can be dramatized to emphasize the conflicts among the players. If you watch the Masters Golf Tournament on television you will see that this is exactly what the commentators are doing. Your subject, purpose, and audience will determine how you paint the picture of the conflict you describe.

Repeat Significant Ideas

Audiences have short attention spans. They are continually attracted by stimuli that turn their attention away from your speech. Consequently, your ideas need to be reinforced. Skillful speakers periodically rephrase and restate key words and phrases to keep their listeners constantly aware of their subject and purpose. The repetition performs two important tasks: it helps to maintain attention and it reinforces the audience's memory. To be sure that the audience knows you are restating an idea, give it a language signal like "that is," "to be clear," "to put it another way," and "what I mean is."

The repetition of words, phrases or sounds can also be a stylistic device. This lends a rhythmic and poetic feeling to the speech. A well-known example is the closing words of Lincoln's Gettysburg Address. "That government of the people, by the people, and for the people shall not perish from this earth." Turn to Chapter 15 for an example of the way the Reverend Jesse Jackson used the stylistic figure of repetition (*anaphora*) in his speech to the 1984 Democratic National Convention.

Too much repetition or the wrong kind, however, will draw attention *away from* important ideas. Unconscious repetition of mannerisms like "ah" and "uh" is likely to become all the listener hears. It reinforces distraction and forces the main idea into the background.

Express Ideas Vividly

The more vividly you can make your listeners visualize a scene or an incident, the more meaningful it becomes for them. Adding concrete details to the telling of a story heightens interest by making the ideas immediately clear and easy to grasp. If your language is vague, general and abstract, your listeners have to struggle for a clear picture of the ideas. They won't struggle long if the task is too difficult; their attention will wander. Vivid language builds sharply focused images of the ideas and adds an atmosphere of realism. This makes it easier for you to bring your topic closer to home. Chapter 15 discusses a number of stylistic figures that will make your language more vivid and expressive.

The effort to hold attention goes on throughout the speech. It is the principal purpose of transitions, while clarity is the most important result.

Using Transitions to Maintain Clarity

The language that relates a preceding topic with the topic that follows it is called a *transition*. Transitions are words, phrases, or sentences that make apparent the relationship between one section of the speech and another.

Transitions are variously described as "uniting" ideas, "joining" them, and "cementing" them. Although it may seem paradoxical, they also hold the same ideas apart. Transitions maintain the separateness of the two sections of the speech and show, at the same time, how the sections are related. The transition says, "The idea just discussed has a bearing on the one that's coming up right now. I'm supposed to show how the two are related to each other without mixing them up with one another." Thus, the principal job of transitions is to maintain clarity.

No one needs to be told to use transitions. Speakers seem to see instinctively that confusing gaps occur if they don't build good bridges when they move from one topic to the next. The trouble lies with the kind of transitions that speakers use. Expressions like "and," "ok," "also," "you know?" are virtually worthless as well as tiresome when repeated by speakers who want to indicate a movement of thought but don't know how.

In general, transitions appear in one of two forms. In the first, they merely indicate a sequence of ideas: "First, second, third." "Not only, but also." "Let me turn now to another point." These simple transitions signal a variety of operations: additions, contrasts, alternatives, causal relations, illustrations, sequence, and so on.[12] They may be used for simple connections.

For the most important connections (between introduction and body, between body and conclusion, or between main points) more elaborate transitions are needed. They should include a brief internal summary of what has gone before and should forecast the ideas that are about to come. The brief recap is the first span of a bridge between separate sections of the speech. The second span is a forecast that tells the audience what you intend to discuss next. When you combine these two devices, summary and forecast, you make it easy for your audience to keep in mind a clear and accurate picture of how your speech is moving toward its goal.

There is an example of a "summary and forecast" transition in the speech of Admiral Ronald Kurth that we cited earlier in this chapter. After discussing the relevance of Aristotle's *Politics* to conditions in the Soviet Union, Kurth briefy summarizes that portion of his speech and then gives a straightforward prediction of what is coming next. He says:

> At a minimum, then, Aristotle has at least two explicit messages in the current context of Soviet issues for Mr. Gorbachev. He must change the Soviet economy to a market economy as the basis for developing a middle class. Second, he must accept pluralism and give up Article 6 of the Soviet constitution which guarantees the primacy of the Party.

> Next, let us turn to that genius among our forefathers, James Madison, who in "The Federalist No. 10" argued so dramatically the pragmatic case for the effect of Original Sin in politics . . . Madison argued that . . . passionate factions may not be a minority, such as were the Bolsheviks. . . . Equally dangerous in Madison's logic was the potential tyranny of a majority faction who might seek to limit the rights of a minority of the citizens. Madison is here reminiscent of Aristotle and the latter's concern for the potential destructiveness of the *popular* will.[13]

In this way, good transitions make your audience "see" the same organization that your outline shows on paper. Transitions focus the audience's thinking and reinforce its memory—the same goals which the conclusion should satisfy.

Concluding the Speech

Eventually, everything must reach a conclusion. A chain of reasoning leads to a judgment; a decision or opinion is formed after investigation; a series of events reaches a climax; a speech comes to a close. Because the conclusion signals the end of the speech and brings it to an appropriate finale, it is just as important as either the introduction or the body. The one reaction you do not want an audience to have is, "What's the point?" Listeners cannot be amused (the way you intend), understand an explanation, or accept a line of argument unless they understand the central idea of your speech. Assuming that the body has unity and coherence, the conclusion can bring the main points and their supporting materials clearly into focus by reminding the audience of what you want it to know, to feel, to do. An effective way of making your message hit home is to use the conclusion to put the audience into the frame of mind that you want: thoughtful, amused, outraged, satisfied, or any other state of mind that best suits your purpose.

You can bring a speech to an appropriate close in numerous ways. Depending upon the subject, a *combination* of some of the following ideas might be the most effective way to end your speech.

Summarize the Main Points

When you conclude a speech to inform, you should draw together the principal points of your discussion. This gives the audience a unified and coherent overview of the subject. Your conclusion should include — at a minimum — a restatement of the subject sentence and the main ideas of the speech. In short, it should be a summary of what you have said. This restatement provides the audience with a smooth transition between the main body of the speech and the conclusion. The continuity of thought clarifies your purpose for the audience. Randall concluded his speech about the way dolphins communicate among themselves and with human beings as follows:

> We see, then, that dolphins have big brains, bright minds, sharp ears, and their own built-in version of a sonar system. Not only do they communicate rapidly and effectively among themselves but they graciously condescend, so it seems, to communicate with us even to the extent of learning some of our language.

> We like to consider ourselves expert communicators but we still have prejudices and people don't know very well how to touch each other and say, I love you. Maybe knowing something about dolphins will sharpen, highlight, and make more effective our research into the mysteries of human communication. Anthropologist Ashley Montague puts it precisely and simply when he says, "Dolphins have large brains. Possibly they will some day be able to teach us what brains are for."

Restate a Proposed Course of Action

Although informative speeches are obvious candidates to end with a summary as a conclusion, many persuasive speeches you hear will end with a restatement of the course of action the speaker wants you to adopt.

Susan Minielli of Ball State University ended her speech on boating accidents with a summary conclusion that reminded her audience of the problem (collisions and drownings), the cause (alcohol), and her three-part solution. She said:

> Over a quarter of our population goes boating each year. Unfortunately, many of these recreational boating outings end in collisions and drownings because of excessive drinking. These accidents are a result of the attitude of alchohol-acceptance and the effects of alcohol on the body. If states take action and license boaters, if we educate ourselves,

and if we exercise common sense when boating, the accidents will be reduced. And only then will recreational boating be truly recreational.[14]

Tell a Story

Stories, like most of the other devices for catching and holding attention (humor, quotations, and repetition), can be used anywhere in the speech to give the audience a vivid portrait of the point you want to make. A story in the conclusion is ordinarily given the additional task of characterizing or adding emotional color to the subject as a whole.

Alan Pessin is a correspondent for the Voice of America. On December 8, l989, he addressed the annual conference of the National Association of Government Communicators in Arlington, Virginia. His subject grew out of his experiences in China just before he was expelled from the country. To conclude his speech, he told a story that characterizes the courage and determination of those Chinese who are risking their lives to build a democratic society.

> The continuing commitment to reform among so many Chinese citizens, and their continuing desire to receive uncensored news, can be found in one last telephone call to the VOA Beijing Bureau during my tenure.
>
> This one came the day after I was ordered to leave—while I was packing the things from my desk, as a matter of fact. It began . . . with the caller asking whether he had reached the Voice of America. Thinking it was another obscene call, I almost hung up. But I didn't. The excited caller wanted to make sure he had **me** on the telephone and then, after a nervous pause, said, "Don't be discouraged."
>
> Here was a young man risking his freedom, perhaps his life, to call me to urge me not to be discouraged. I had only been expelled from China, sorry to leave but heading for freedom, family and friends. The young man on the telephone, who wisely identified himself only as a student at a university in Beijing, had just seen his friends gunned down, arrested or forced into hiding and his hopes for freedom impaled on the bayonets of the People's Liberation Army.
>
> And he was telling **me** not to be discouraged.
>
> I was lost for words. After a few moments, I finally managed to say, "Don't **you** be discouraged."
>
> He needed no time to collect his thoughts for a response. His instantaneous reply was, "We will **never** be discouraged."[15]

Use a Quotation

You can often find a quotation that will sum up, characterize, and give impact to a subject. Sydney H. Schanberg, an associate editor for *Newsweek* magazine, gave the commencement address at Nazareth College, Rochester, New York, on May 14, 1989. The theme of his speech was, "You can make a difference— if you stretch yourself." Here is his conclusion:

I leave you with a quote from Winston Churchill, who was speaking about his own young years and speaking to all young people. He said, "You will make all kinds of mistakes, but as long as you are generous and true, and also fierce, you cannot hurt the world or even seriously distress her. She was made to be wooed and won by youth."[16]

Ask Rhetorical Questions

Rhetorical questions can be asked at any point. They catch attention in the introduction, they reawaken interest during the course of the speech, and in the conclusion they help to focus the thinking of the audience on what you have been saying. On June 16, 1989, business executive James D. Griffin told an audience of young adults not to let themselves be diverted from their goals by those who would "snare the feet of greatness." His conclusion sums up his message with a series of rhetorical questions.

> You stand now at the very threshold of the future. Who will tell you that the door is now closed? Who will say it no longer can be done? Who will tell us that we lack the vision or the will? And who will stoop to snare the feet of greatness with pedantics and niggling? Who, I ask you, will point to a heroic woman who scaled Mt. McKinley on crutches, and then turn and say that you, on two legs, cannot follow her up that mountain of your own hopes and dreams?
>
> We are surrounded today by the gates and halls of our new Alma Mater. But soon we will leave. What will we be if some day we return? What will be then our troubles and triumphs? How will we stand when we cross this yard once again? And what will we have done to advance the twin causes of the beautiful and the good?
>
> These gates and halls stand silent before us, and they await our return.[17]

Develop an Analogy

Business executive John M. Griffin is interested in population shifts and the demographics of population centers. The purpose of his speech to the annual meeting of the Westfield Companies on June 16, 1989 was to persuade his audience to prepare for the impact of population shifts on the business community. He concludes his speech with an analogy that compares the need to prepare for change to learning to ski.

> Perhaps the moral of the story is: you can stand pat and get buried by a glacier—or you can learn to ski. The 1990s will be a time for many companies to plan ahead and to ski freely over the glacier of demographic change.[18]

Call for Action

The only time a speech will end with a call for action is when you support a policy claim. Otherwise, what kind of action would you call for? A speech to entertain: ''Laugh!'' A speech to inform: ''Understand!'' A factual claim: ''Believe!'' A value claim: ''Share my attitude!'' Speeches that support policy claims, however, by definition imply a need for action of some sort. The action you want the audience to take is always indicated, at least by implication, in the conclusion. Susan Minielli's conclusion that we quoted above is not only a restatement of her proposed plan to reduce boating accidents, it is a call for the adoption of her plan: state licensing of boats, self-education, and common sense.

Summary

The principal task of the introduction is to catch the attention of the audience. Several devices help you do this: rhetorical questions, quotations, stories, striking statements and humor. In addition to catching the attention of the audience, the introduction is also the place to state the subject and purpose of your speech, elicit the good will of the audience, establish your credibility, and supply the audience with any background it may need.

Catching attention is not difficult. It is harder—and more important— to hold the attention of the audience once you have caught it. The way to hold attention is to motivate the audience to want to listen: show the importance of the subject and occasion; create suspense; dramatize conflict; repeat significant ideas, express ideas vividly.

Transitions tie together the introduction, body, and conclusion, and the segments within these major parts. They form a bridge between consecutive ideas. They maintain clarity by showing where the speech has been and where it is going. The most complete transition briefly summarizes the ideas that have just been discussed and then forecasts what is to come.

The conclusion brings the speech to an appropriate end. Most often an informative speech concludes with a summary of the central idea and the major supporting points. Some policy speeches also will end with a summary conclusion that restates the plan of action proposed in the speech. In general, however, more effective conclusions of persuasive speeches will characterize the subject in some way. They tell a story, use a quotation, ask rhetorical questions, or develop an analogy.

When you argue in support of a policy claim, your speech, by definition, asks the audience to adopt the course of action you recommend. Therefore, the conclusion of a persuasive speech that supports a policy claim will usually include a call for action.

Key Terms

Attention	Importance of occasion
Subject sentence	Suspense
Good will	Conflict
Background material	Repetition
Quotation	Vivid expression
Story	Internal summary
Striking statement	Forecast
Humor	Rhetorical question
Importance of subject	Call for action.

Exercises

1. Examine one of the informative speeches at the end of Chapter 18. How effective do you think the introduction is? What alternative ways can you think of to introduce the subject to a college student audience?

2. Examine one of the persuasive speeches at the end of Chapter 19 and answer the same questions as in Exercise 1.

3. Select an informative speech made by one of your classmates and suggest how you might have tried to gain attention had you delivered the speech. Why is your method better than the one your classmate used?

4. Write a short paper explaining the conclusion of a recent speech you gave and why you concluded as you did. Explain either why that was better than some other possible conclusions or how you would improve the conclusion were you to give the speech again.

5. Listen to several speeches in your class and note the kinds of transitions used. Compare the speakers on how often they omit transitions, or use transitions that merely indicate sequence, and how often they make internal summaries.

Notes

[1] Gerald D. Stevens, "The Insurance Industry: Managing Now for the '90s" *Vital Speeches of the Day* 1 Apr. 1990: 375.

[2] Bryan Ciyou, "The Third Horseman," *Winning Orations* ed. Larry Schnoor (Mankato, MN: Interstate Oratorical Association, 1989) 26.

[3] Patti P. Gillespie, "Campus Stories, or the Cat Beyond the Canvas" *Vital Speeches of the Day* 1 Feb. 1988: 236.

[4] Ronald J. Kurth, "Can the Soviet Union Achieve Wisdom?" *Vital Speeches of the Day* 1 June 1990: 331.

[5] Robert K. Blechman, "Campus Comedy," *Readers's Digest*, Sept. 1984: 100.

[6] John Hope Franklin, "The Things We Know," *Representative American Speeches 1988-89* ed. Owen Peterson (New York: 1989) 165-66.

[7] Carl Sagan, "Thoughts on the 125th Anniversary of the Battle of Gettysburg," *Representative American Speeches 1988-89* ed. Owen Peterson (New York: Wilson, 1989) 113.

[8] For a discussion of the relation of motivation and incentives to cognition and performance, see Michael W. Eysenck, *Attention and Arousal* (New York: Springer-Verlag, 1982). In Chapter 6 Eysenck is interested in the influence of incentive and motivation on performance in general, but his discussion is readily applicable to the responses of audiences as well.

[9] George Bush, "National Drug Control Strategy," *Vital Speeches of the Day* 1 Oct. 1987: 740.

[10] Willard C. Butcher, "Action Time for the Trade Deficit," *Vital Speeches of the Day* 15 Feb. 1990: 273.

[11] Shannon Dyer, "The Dilemma of the Whistleblower," *Winning Orations* ed. Larry Schnoor (Mankato, MN: Interstate Oratorical Association, 1989) 64.

[12] For a suggestion of appropriate words and phrases to express each of these relationships see Wilma R. and David R. Ebbitt, *Writer's Guide and Index to English* (Glenview, IL: Scott, Foresman, 1982) 591.

[13] Kurth, p. 332.

[14] Susan Minielli, "B.W.I." *Winning Orations* ed. Larry Schnoor (Mankato, MN: Interstate Oratorical Association, 1989) 29-32.

[15] Alan W. Pessin, "Communications and Revolution," *Vital Speeches of the Day*, 1 May 1990: 331.

[16] Sydney H. Schandberg, "The Risk of Being Different," *Vital Speeches of the Day* 1 Sept. 1989: 702.

[17] James D. Griffin, "To Snare the Feet of Greatness," *Vital Speeches of the Day* 15 Sept. 1989: 735.

[18] John M. Griffin, "Demographic Opportunities for the '90s and Beyond," *Vital Speeches of the Day* 1 May 1990: 377.

Improving Oral Style

Until humans learned to use language for more than grunting threats at dangerous animals, there was no possibility there could be a Sophocles or a Shakespeare, a Demosthenes or a Churchill. In every major civilization, poetry, drama, and oratory have achieved high levels of artistic merit. The language you speak today has a potential for great beauty and power. It is both a tool and a weapon. Put to good use, it helped Winston Churchill hold a nation together. In the hands of Adolph Hitler, it tore the world apart.

Style has long been defined as the artistic use of language which provides clarity, assures correctness and propriety, and lends elegance to a speech. At times, style has been given greater importance than the canons of subject matter, organization, and delivery. You have already learned, of course, there cannot be a speech without *all* the canons.

Compare the outline of a speech to a human skeleton. Just as a human skeleton needs ligaments, muscles, and nerves in order to move, a speech outline needs the sinews and flesh of language to be complete. We can find at least one other similarity between the speech and the human body. The muscles of the body are either weak and flabby, or firm and strong. Language, too, is either weak and flabby or strong and firm. In this chapter, we shall see how to give life and strength to a speech by adding the firm, strong muscles of effective oral style.

> A word is not a crystal, transparent and unchanging; it is the skin of a living thought and may vary greatly in color and content according to the circumstances and time in which it is used.
>
> —Oliver Wendell Holmes

Language and Meaning

The substance of a speech is ideas, and the only way ideas can exist is in some form of language. You cannot transplant your ideas directly into the minds of an audience. The major way you *can* communicate is through language. By language we mean all of the visual and auditory symbols, verbal and nonverbal, that we use to transmit messages.

If your father clenches his teeth and looks straight at you when you do something he doesn't approve of, he gives you an unambiguous message without saying a word. However, oral language is the primary means of transmitting ideas in public speaking.

Language of any sort—written or oral, verbal or nonverbal—does considerably more than merely transmit words or their equivalents from source to receiver. Language has beauty and power because it also conveys values, attitudes, and emotional coloration.

The words you speak are symbols; that is, they *represent* certain things or ideas. If you use language competently, you have a sizable vocabulary

Language has the potential for great beauty and power. It helped Winston Churchill hold a nation together. The climactic conclusion of one of his speeches appears at the end of this chapter.

to describe a great number of items or concepts. Your understanding of each symbol (word) is called its meaning.

A listener's meanings can never be *exactly* the same as a speaker's. For a word to evoke an *exact* equivalent meaning in two people, their brains would have to be identical, cell for cell, synapse for synapse, and nerve for nerve. Their experiences with what the word names would have to be identical in order to have precisely the same understanding of it and exactly the same emotional attitudes toward it. How many people have had your exact experiences? How many people have you met who are exactly like you? No communication is ever perfect since meanings are not static entities. Franklin Fearing put it this way, "All communication contents are in some degree ambiguous."[1]

Of course, people's words and thinking both influence and are influenced by the cultural atmosphere in which they live. As a consequence, people who use words in common do have similar experiences and share many overlapping meanings for the words. While you and your audience will not share exactly the same experience, careful thought will usually allow you to express yourself successfully to a specific audience.

Language has four properties that determine how your listeners will understand you: denotation, connotation, syntax, and context. Denotations and connotations are characteristics of individual words; syntax and context relate to the construction of words into sentences. Understanding these properties will help you choose the best language to express your thoughts and to avoid confusion.

Denotation

As we mentioned earlier, words signify or stand for certain things or ideas. If someone doesn't understand what you mean by a particular word you can, in some instances, point to the item in question. You can't however, physically point to an idea such as a "monarchy" or even to a thing such as a "unicorn." A word, then, is a symbol that *denotes* (designate or stands for) a person, thing or idea. The word becomes a way of pointing to what it names. Words can thus refer to anything—even an imaginary creature. The word unicorn, for instance, "denotes a small, horse-like animal with a single horn in the middle of its forehead." Dictionaries are a reference tool for the commonly accepted denotations assigned to words.

Connotation

Your listeners share your denotations for many words. On one level (denotative), the audience will understand your use of the word "jungle" to mean "an area of land covered with dense growth of vegetation, typically in tropical regions." On another level, we attribute additional meaning to certain words—internalized, personalized, and attitudinalized meanings that cannot be shared exactly by any other person. Not everyone has lived in a "hobo jungle," nor been a high school teacher in a "blackboard jungle," nor fought for economic survival in the "corporate jungle." Even without having any of these experiences, everyone will have some kind of attitude toward jungles: like, dislike, indifference, or adventurousness. The same reactions occur in response to any word: "dogs," "cats," "houses," "hospitals," "police." These added meanings grow out of the personal experiences people have had and they reflect value judgments about what the word names. They are called *connotations*. Whether one likes it or not, the words of a speech will bring them to a listener's mind. They can either help your purpose or harm it.

The best way to avoid arousing unwanted reactions is to have as much insight into the audience as you can. Audience analysis gives you information about many of the attitudes your target audience is likely to have. Given that information, you can put connotative meanings to deliberate use. For example, everyone has the same denotative meaning for "abortion." No matter what words you use to define it, the denotation is "the termination of a pregnancy by artificial means." Depending on the attitude you want to evoke, you would define it either as "killing an innocent child," or "exercising a woman's right to control her own body." The connotative meanings for "killing," "innocent child," "right," and "control" will unquestionably influence the audience's attitude. Thus, connotative meanings give you the power to evoke a desired emotional response.

The purpose of informative speaking calls for audience understanding. Such speeches will, therefore, emphasize denotative language. Speeches to entertain and persuade will, on the other hand, frequently use connotative language for different purposes. But all language has some connotation.

A single word can encapsulate a whole complex of attitudes and reactions. When the word is honorific, it is called a euphemism. People are not poor, they are underprivileged. There is no poverty, only a low income level. When a word is *pejorative*, it is "name-calling": "pigs" for police, "ward-heeler" for politician, "raghead" for anyone who wears a turban.

In your effort to use precise language that expresses your values, you will have to decide how connotative to be. If you honestly believe that a negative attitude is warranted, it is not unethical to use a pejorative word. If you think a positive attitude is warranted, a euphemism is not excessive. It would be both unethical and excessive, however, to use either pejorative or euphemistic language to mislead your audience.

Syntax

Syntax is the way a sentence is structured to satisfy the grammatical customs of a language. It is sometimes seen as correctness. The relationships among the words give additional clues to meaning. Look at the following sentence: "The mud was cleaned up after being tracked into the house with a wet mop." The structure of this sentence raises a question about what it actually says. The sentence makes better sense when you say, "After being tracked into the house, the mud was cleaned up with a wet mop." The structure of the sentence, even if all the right words are there, can help or hurt communication. Use good syntax to insure clear, unambiguous communication.

Context

Syntactical meaning is determined by the way words are placed in a sentence. It is a function of grammar: the relationship of words to other words. Contextual meaning, on the other hand, is evoked by the subject matter. Many words are ambiguous. They have multiple meanings. Even when they are used in correct syntax, they can be misunderstood. Have you ever seen a dog run? Of course! It is an enclosure where dogs can exercise without the need of a leash. "No, No. Not the *noun* run. I mean the *verb*, like 'run across the street.'" Ambiguous words will say what you mean only when they are put into some clarifying context.

We have seen how people develop meanings for language. Let's look now at the criteria that tell you how to use it well. Good oral style is characterized by clarity, correctness, propriety, simplicity, originality, and vividness.

Clarity

Everyone has a personal way of using language; every profession or activity seems to evoke a distinctive style as well. Commentators and news reporters on radio and television use language in a distinctive way. Novels differ from poetry and plays; oral style is different from writing.

Clarity is the first aim of both writing and speaking. Speaking, however, has a special problem. Although comprehension is always vital, there is little need to grasp a written message instantly. Ordinarily, it is possible to examine a page at leisure, to think about the ideas, and to absorb them at a comfortable rate, or to reread a passage as many times as necessary. Oral communication, to the contrary, must be immediately clear. A listening audience has no time for leisurely consideration of ideas. Listeners cannot go back to rehear. If they pause to reflect, they break the chain of ideas, and are left behind. Consequently, oral style is more demanding than written style for it must make ideas *instantly* clear.

Clear language must be free from obscurity and confusion. To *provide* clarity, avoid its enemies: ambiguity, vagueness, meaningless qualifiers, abstract terms and general terms. To *preserve* clarity, use transitions and summaries between major points and ideas.

Avoid Ambiguity

One of the enemies of clarity is ambiguity. A statement is ambiguous when more than one meaning is possible and the context does not make clear which is correct. Ambiguity can produce amusing results:

"He told his father that he had been drinking too much."

"The boss fired those employees who were critical."

"I like football more than my wife."

These are examples of *grammatical* (or syntactical) ambiguity, they are ambiguous because of imprecise sentence construction. In another form of ambiguity, the context fails to make clear what the sentence says. For example, the lawyer who phoned his wife to say he would be late for dinner because he was delayed by a "bar" meeting was guilty of (deliberate?) ambiguity.

While the examples above are humorous, ambiguity can have embarrassing results. An early draft of the 1984 Republican party platform caused laughter in the media and glee among the Democrats. The troublesome language was a statement promising to "oppose any attempts to increase taxes which would harm the recovery." Does the statement mean that any tax increases which would *not* harm the recovery could be made? When you spend a great deal of time and effort preparing your speech, pay special attention to wording which might be ambiguous. You don't want to confuse your audience, and you probably don't want to cause a laugh at your expense!

Avoid Vagueness

When both the syntax and the context of an expression are precise, the likely causes of ambiguity are removed. Syntax and context are not as helpful with another enemy of clear expression—vagueness. Vagueness is found in words themselves, not their contexts. A vague word is one whose denotations are so broad even context will not clarify what you mean. You could oppose "gambling" but not church bingo parties. You might condemn "corruption" but accept an appointment in the treasury department after working on the winning governor's campaign. Similarly, if you want to discuss the political behavior of Edward Kennedy or Alan Cranston, don't talk about "some liberal politicians." The more specific you are, the more confident you can be that your meaning is clear. Using the wrong word is an obvious example of being imprecise. If you say incredible when you mean incredulous, your audience will be confused. *They* will have to decide what you really meant. The point of delivering a speech is to express *your* findings. Don't let vague language erode that opportunity.

Avoid Meaningless Qualifiers

Many words give the impression of qualifying or quantifying but they are imprecise. For example, the terms "fat," "thin," "tall," "short," "middle-aged," or "old" are so relative that they must be used with a defined scale. Some listeners will define middle-aged much differently from others. How much is "lots," or "very?" Whenever possible, make the information precise. "Joe is a six-foot, forty-five year old, 200 pound neighbor of mine. He owns three cars and each of them is worth more than $40,000." That says a lot more than, "I have a good-sized, middle-aged neighbor who owns several expensive cars." If you can't detail the information precisely, it probably doesn't belong in the speech.

Avoid Abstract Terms

It may be tempting to use abstract terms because it is sometimes easier than making clear distinctions among a number of overlapping cases. Abstract terms are vague because they refer to no tangible object. Of course, there are times when you must talk about abstractions, such as "justice," "honesty," "democracy," or "virtue." When you do, give clear examples of what you mean. For instance, "There must be justice, and I mean truly upholding the law with a fair trial, not submitting someone to a kangaroo court..."

Avoid General Terms

How many times have you heard speakers use phrases like: "Authorities agree...," "Statistics show...," "a noted scientist ...," "a large midwestern city...," "government sources...." Your audience will be much better informed if you use specific terms: *name* the authority, the city, the source; *describe* the research, *give* the audience the statistics that support the claim. They also might be more interested if they hear a name they recognize.

Provide Transitions and Internal Summaries

A good way to make audiences understand accurately is to let them know where they are, how they got there, and where they are going next. Review Chapter 14 on transitions and internal summaries.

Correctness

At some time in your life, you discovered that the way you use language is governed by a set of rules called "grammar." After years of speaking in sentences you have a personal grammar. "Her and I went to the country fair," or "Don't nobody be late for class" might be acceptable to some speakers but not to others. What you do is correct for you, and you accept it because you are used to it. If what others say fits your pattern, you accept that as correct too. At the same time, you probably recognize differences between your grammar and someone else's.

If correctness is all a matter of what one is accustomed to, why do rhetoricians claim that style should follow a "socially accepted" norm? If you speak the standard English language of educated Americans, you will be accepted as an educated person. If your language usage varies to any significant degree from this norm (except in very specialized situations), you are in danger of losing credibility with most American audiences.

As we will note later in this chapter, language need not be stuffy and formal, but for most public speaking situations an educated grammar (the kind usually used by network radio and television commentators, for instance) is the most correct grammar.

Propriety

Words in themselves are neither good nor bad in either a moral or artistic sense. The goodness or badness has to do only with the way they are used. In public speaking, propriety is a quality found in the language of a speech when all of the words are well adapted to the subject, audience and occasion. In daily life you constantly adjust your speech practices to different audiences. No two listeners are exactly alike: the boss, neighbors, casual acquaintances, total strangers, and old friends are all addressed differently. Automatically and unconsciously, audience analysis precedes your selection of words, sentence structure, and figures of speech. It is highly unlikely that a woman would talk to her husband in the same way she speaks to a sales clerk. You would never use the language of the *Congressional Record* in casual conversation.

Four kinds of usage cause problems of propriety: shoptalk, outmoded slang, taboos, and formal English.

Avoid Shoptalk

Shoptalk is jargon used as a private language foreign to anyone outside a particular activity. In spite of the way computers have grown in both popularity and use, there are still millions of people who don't know anything about them. When you talk to a group of that sort, bytes and megabytes, hard disks and floppies will be incomprehensible to them. If an audience is familiar with these terms, the jargon is no problem; in fact, it can make communication more efficient. Verbal shortcuts are useful for people in the shop, but the jargon of the trade is mainly useful for talking to the trade.

Avoid Outmoded Slang

Language is constantly changing and slang often represents its growing edge. Creative people, looking for fresh, sharp, colorful, or humorous ways to express ideas, invent new words and use old words in new ways. In Chapter 8, we quoted Carl Sandburg's definition of slang as ''language that takes off its coat, spits on its hands and goes to work.'' Cockney rhyming slang (feet are plates of meat) and musical ''rap'' are examples of how language constantly changes and grows. The resulting expressions either survive to become a part of the standard language, or they grow stale and die out.

The problem with slang is its short life. Middle-aged speakers who try to use young people's slang usually find that the expressions they are using are already out of date.

Slang should only be used when it is clear and does not obscure what it is meant to convey. Even when it is clear, it will be inappropriate if the occasion calls for more formal English.

Avoid Taboos

Certain tribes avoid naming their gods for fear of offending them, but they will still talk around them without using their names. Talking around subjects is a common way of avoiding linguistic taboos. Two terms with the same denotation often flourish side by side because one of them has connotations that make it improper in public discourse. Familiar examples are words that talk about reproduction and excretion.

One audience differs so greatly from another that it is difficult to know what any one group might call profane or obscene. Even so mild a word as "damn" or "hell" will offend some people, but others wouldn't flinch from language a lot stronger than that. The most practical rule is, don't take a chance. Why offend some of your listeners when you don't need to? Even if you can use profanity in private conversations without offending anyone, it is usually in bad taste in a public speech.

Profanity, vulgarity, and obscenity may shock and be effective, but they are more likely to be counterproductive. There is evidence to show that language which is considered obscene by a general American audience will make you seem more dynamic, but it will also decrease the listener's estimation of your trustworthiness and competence.[2] Whatever the taboos of an audience, if you violate them you are in danger of losing credibility.

Avoid Formal English

At the other extreme from shoptalk, slang, and linguistic taboos is formal English. This is the proper style for the speaking situation that is ceremonial in tone and in vocabulary. In a Supreme Court proceeding, business report, or research report, for instance, informality would be inappropriate. Articles in the professional journals of almost any academic field are very often written in formal English.

A style preferable for your purposes is general English. General English allows a large number of words and sentence constructions that formal English excludes, words and forms that are customarily found in the casual speaking of educated people. Since people are at ease in this language, you should feel quite comfortable in using it.

Dictionaries label some words "colloquial," as indeed they are, but that does not mean that they are inferior or incorrect. There is nothing wrong with saying "down on" if you think "hostile to" would sound stuffy.

General English is aimed at general listeners and readers: speeches, magazine articles, newspaper columns. This is the language that will be appropriate in virtually all of the speeches you will make.

Simplicity

A naive but common misconception is that "big" words are better because they are somehow more impressive than ordinary language. Speakers who act on this misconception often sound pompous when they think they are being dignified. Henry David Thoreau, whose own style is marked by economy and simplicity, said that long words have a paralysis in their tails. Far from being an elevated variety of English, self-conscious formality is pretentious and unnatural.

Former Representative Maury Maverick coined the term "gobbledygook" to label language that is pompous, wordy, involved, and full of long, Latinized terms. Gobbledygook destroys clarity. Columnist James Kilpatrick calls gobbledygook "bubble-gum prose." It leaves an indigestible, sticky residue behind. As an example, he quotes a blurb he read in *New Scientist* for a book on the role of pronouns in language.

> Starting out from the question of how semantically extremely attenuate forms such as pronouns can refer unambiguously to just one particular object, instead of being infinitely ambiguous, this study presents the outline of context-sensitive reference mechanisms and grammatically determined interpretation strategies.

Why not say, "This study gives advice on how to keep pronouns from being ambiguous."

Simplicity is not only a matter of using short, forceful words, but also the smallest number of words necessary to do the job. Language should demand as little effort as possible on the part of a listener. Therefore, economy is important. Ideas sometimes need complex language, but only what is necessary is useful. Show, tell, run, and eat say the same thing as reveal, narrate, operate, and dine, but they are all simpler and don't sound nearly as affected.

Originality

Originality in style is, in part, a skillful use of variety that helps to avoid monotony. It brings freshness and vigor to language by avoiding cliches, hackneyed phrases, and figures of speech that are tired from overuse.

William H. Whyte, Jr., built a composite business speech out of 60 badly overused expressions and constructions. It "lends a powerful straight-from-the-shoulder effect to ambiguity and equivocation," but it says nothing. Look at a brief sample of that speech:

> Yes, gentlemen, trying times. So you'll pardon me if I cast aside the glib reverberation of glittering generalities and the soothing syrup of sugarcoated platitudes and put it to you the only way I can: straight English.
>
> We're losing the battle!
>
> From every corner the people are being weaned from the doctrines of the Founding Fathers. They are being detoured from the high-speed highways of progress by the utopian highwaymen.
>
> Now, the man in the street is a pretty savvy fellow. Don't sell him short. Joe Doakes may be fooled for a while, but in the end he wants no part of the mumbo jumbo the global saboteurs are trying to sell him. After all, he is an American.[3]

Paradoxically, another way to be original is through imitation. Imitation can take all sorts of forms. The Greek orator Demosthenes reportedly copied Thucydides' history of the Peloponnesian Wars eight times so that he could master its style. In his November, 1765 speech at the Virginia House of Burgesses, Patrick Henry said: "Tarquin and Caesar each had his Brutus, Charles the First his Cromwell and George the Third—[Pause]—may profit from their example!"

Lane Kirkland, President of the AFL-CIO, composed this variation on Henry's theme when he attacked President Ronald Reagan in 1984: "Lyndon Johnson had his Vietnam; Richard Nixon had his Watergate; Jimmy Carter his Khomeini, and Ronald Reagan should—but doubtless will not—profit by their example."[4]

Vividness

Even clear, appropriate style can be improved by making it more *vivid*. A vivid style is one that heightens the impact of ideas because it deviates from common denotative usages and from ordinary sentence patterns. We will discuss a few of the most common figures of speech: simile and metaphor, overstatement and understatement, irony, antithesis, parallel structure, rhetorical questions, and climax.

Simile and Metaphor

These are the most common figures of speech. Both are formed by likening one object with another, but they do it in different ways. A simile ordinarily indicates the comparison with such a word as *like* or *as*. The Reverend Jesse Jackson spoke to the Democratic National Convention in 1984. (That speech is frequently titled "The Rainbow Coalition.") He carries out his theme with this simile:

> America is not like a blanket—that is one piece of unbroken cloth, the same color, the same texture, the same size. America is more like a quilt—many patches, many pieces, many colors, many sizes, all woven and held together by a common thread.[5]

A metaphor is also based on a comparison, but it says that one thing is not just *like* another, it says that it is the other. In one of the pointed and powerful metaphors Jackson used in the same speech, he said that graffiti are the "hieroglyphics of destitution."

Overstatement and Understatement

Overstatement and understatement are useful both for emphasis and amusement. Both of these terms will appear again in Chapter 20 when we discuss the use of humor in speeches.

Overstatement attracts attention to an idea by making a statement stronger than necessary to convey an idea. Eleanor Smeal, former President of the

Overstatement attracts attention. Eleanor Smeal used strong, vigorous language so that her audience would not mistake her intent.

National Organization for Women, spoke at the National Press Club in Washington, D.C. Near the end of her speech on the "feminization of power," she attacked President Ronald Reagan's nomination of Robert Bork to be a justice of the Supreme Court. Her ideas could have been expressed less forcefully, but this vigorous language makes the statement of her argument as strong as she wants it to be.

> A president whose administration has brought disgrace and dishonor to the Constitution he has sworn to uphold should not be allowed to appoint a Supreme Court justice who would provide the key point vote to dismantle human rights. This appointment could mean the reversal of *Roe v. Wade* which legalized abortion; the unraveling of affirmative action; the destruction of the Constitutionally-implied Right to Privacy; and the dismantling of the principle of one person, one vote. Bork, the man who carried out the order for the Saturday Night Massacre of Watergate, should not be further rewarded with a seat on this nation's highest court to carry out the Right Wing agenda of yet another failed Presidency.[6]

Hyperbole is the name given to the kind of exaggeration that is used for dramatic effect. It is an acceptable figure of speech and is not likely to cause confusion or lack of clarity. But hyperbole is noticeably different from a grossly exaggerated statement that is intended to deceive.

The vocabulary of advertising, for instance, uses the kind of exaggeration that destroys accuracy. "Big" isn't big enough, so advertisers use "gigantic," "colossal," and "supercolossal." As a result, manufacturers of toothpaste identify the smallest tube they sell as the large size. To exaggerate for emphasis has been called an American trait, but it fails to achieve its effect when it is overused, just as the habit of using too much spice makes normally seasoned food seem flat.

Understatement, on the contrary, calls attention to an idea by deliberately saying less than what might be said. To say that some out-and-out crook is "not the most scrupulous person I know," is to understate the case.

Irony

An ironic statement is one in which the intended meaning is the direct opposite of what the statement actually says. For example, an irate citizen of San Luis Obispo, California, has no liking at all for a proposed marina to be built in the nearby town of Morro Bay. She says:

> The famous heron/egret rookery in the trees right next door is already badly overcrowded; let's get rid of it. All those hundreds of people who come every year to watch the birds can just go into the State Park Museum and watch a video.

> With this development, a lot more people will be able to go out in the channel and bay in boats. If the seals, sea otters, pelicans, etc., now dependent on the bay don't like it, they can go somewhere else.

Morro Bay definitely needs more marinas and boats. In fact, with a little effort, it could be just like Marina Del Rey and Ballona Wetlands. You know, in the forward-thinking Los Angeles area. Down there, a person can walk from boat to boat and never touch the water. The white patches in the water aren't birds, they're Styrofoam cups. I say, let's go for it.[7]

Antithesis

Antithesis, the opposing or contrasting of ideas, is not only widely and commonly used today, it is among the oldest of the consciously practiced rhetorical techniques.

In accepting the Republican presidential nomination in 1964, Senator Barry Goldwater stated his conservative position with an antithesis that aroused quite a political controversy. "I would remind you that extremism in the defense of liberty is no vice! and let me remind you also that moderation in the pursuit of justice is no virtue!" In the speech of Jesse Jackson we quoted earlier; he said, "But just because you're born in the slum doesn't mean the slum is born in you."

Jesse Jackson skillfully used simile, metaphor, and antithesis to heighten the impact of his ideas in ''The Rainbow Coalition'' speech.

Parallel Structure

Parallel structure highlights and emphasizes a series of related ideas by phrasing them in expressions that are similar in language and construction. One of the best-known examples is the familiar set of phrases in Lincoln's Gettysburg address: "Government of the people, by the people, and for the people shall not perish from the earth." Jesse Jackson said, "Our time has come," ten times in the conclusion of his 1988 Democratic Convention speech.

In the State of the Union address, January 1990, President George Bush used the word "where" in 9 consecutive sentences in order to describe what he means by making our democratic system even better than it is.

> A better America where there's a job for everyone who wants one. Where women working outside the home can be confident their children are in safe and loving care, and where Government works to expand child [care] alternatives for parents. Where we reconcile the needs of a clean environment and strong economy. Where "Made in the U.S.A." is recognized around the world as the symbol of quality and progress, And where every one of us enjoys the same opportunities to live, to work and to contribute to society. And where, for the first time, the American mainstream includes all of our disabled citizens.

> Where everyone has a roof over his head, and where the homeless get the help they need to live in dignity. Where our schools challenge and support our kids and our teachers, and where all of them make the grade. Where every street, every city, every school and every child is drug-free, And finally, and finally, where no American is forgotten.[8]

Rhetorical Questions

A question is "rhetorical" when it does not ask the audience to give a direct answer (see Chapter 14); instead, it is meant to add vividness to an expression. A direct question, even one that requires no direct answer, attracts the immediate, personal attention of the audience to a degree that a statement often will not.

Climax

In every case, a speech should have a strong ending. It should be dressed in clear, appropriate, vivid language.

During the Battle of Britain in World War II, the English suffered a major defeat at Dunkirk. The courage and ingenuity of the English kept it from being a major disaster in human lives as well. In his speech reporting the evacuation of British and French soldiers trapped by the German army at Dunkirk, Winston Churchill brought his speech to a concluding climax with these words.

> The British Empire and the French Republic, linked together in their cause and in their need, will defend to the death their native soil, aiding

each other like good comrades to the utmost of their strength. Even though large tracts of Europe and many old and famous States have fallen or may fall into the grip of the Gestapo and all the odious apparatus of Nazi rule, we shall not flag or fail. We shall go on to the end, we shall fight in France, we shall fight on the seas and oceans, we shall fight with growing confidence and growing strength in the air, we shall defend our island, whatever the cost may be, we shall fight on the beaches, we shall fight on the landing grounds, we shall fight in the fields and in the streets, we shall fight in the hills; we shall never surrender, and even if, which I do not for a moment believe, this island or a large part of it were subjugated and starving, then our Empire beyond the seas, armed and guarded by the British Fleet, would carry on the struggle, until, in God's good time, the new world, with all its power and might, steps forth to the rescue and the liberation of the old.[9]

There is no doubt that all of the language devices we have discussed here can add vividness to a speech. But a word of caution: they can be used to excess. When they are, the style becomes not vivid but flamboyant, flowery, and weak. Like poor delivery, style can call attention to itself rather than to the substance of the speech.

Summary

The minimum requirement for effective speaking is good quality in substance, organization, and delivery. A truly superior speech will also be presented in a strong, handsome style. Human beings communicate through the verbal and nonverbal symbols of the language they use to communicate their ideas.

The way an audience will interpret a speech is determined by its understanding of what the words denote, by its connotations for those words, by the syntax of the language, and by the context in which the ideas are placed. The ability of language to lend emotion to ideas, when it is not used as a substitute for reasoning and evidence, will add great force to the style.

Good oral style makes ideas instantly clear and, at the same time, maintains a high level of attention and interest in the audience. The style that does this best is marked by clarity, propriety, simplicity, originality, and vividness.

The way to provide clarity is to avoid its enemies: ambiguity, vagueness, meaningless qualifiers, abstractions that are not defined, and general terms. To preserve the clarity of a speech, provide transitions and internal summaries between each major point and the next.

Propriety in style demands that language be suited to the audience, the subject, and the occasion. Using shoptalk unfamiliar to the audience, outdated slang, language that is taboo, or unnecessarily formal English will diminish the propriety of style.

Vividness is to style what seasoning is to food. The right spices in the right amount add zest and tang, but too much spoils the flavor. The spices of style are figures of speech: simile and metaphor, overstatement and understatement, irony, antithesis, parallel structure, rhetorical questions, and climax.

Key Terms

Denotation	Formal English
Connotation	Simplicity
Syntax	Originality
Context	Simile
Ambiguity	Metaphor
Vagueness	Overstatement
Meaningless qualifiers	Understatement
Abstract terms	Irony
General terms	Antithesis
Correctness	Parallel structure
Shoptalk	Rhetorical questions
Slang	Climax
Taboos	

Exercises

1. While at work, a student hang-out, a meeting of a departmental club, or some other special group, make a list of the words you hear that are not used in general society. Translate each of the words into language appropriate for a general audience.

2. Select an essay written in formal English style and convert one or more paragraphs into acceptable general English style.

3. Note examples of vague terms used in classroom speeches (meaningless modifiers, abstract words, general words) and show how they may be made more precise through illustration and definition.

4. Write down trite expressions in one round of classroom speeches and suggest a phrase that expresses each idea more vividly.

5. Select a speech from the Speeches for Study at the end of Chapters 13, 18, 19, and 20 and try to find at least two examples of each type of figure of speech. Say which is better and why. How might its vividness be improved?

6. Look for examples of the "enemies of clarity" in one of the speeches at the end of Chapters 13, 18, 19, and 20. Suggest how the statements could be made more precise.

7. In your next classroom speech, use two or three figures of speech to make it more vivid.

Notes

1 Franklin Fearing, "Towards a Psychological Theory of Human Communication, *Foundations of Communication Theory* eds. Kenneth K. Sereno and C. David Mortensen (New York: Harper & Row, 1970) 50.

2 Robert Bostrom, John R. Basehart and Charles M. Rossiter, "The Effects of Three Types of Profane Language In Persuasive Messages," *Journal of Communication* 23 (1973): 461-75; Velma Lashbrook, "Source Credibility: A summary of Experimental Research," paper read to the Speech Communication Association, Dec. 1971.

3 William H. Whyte, Jr., "The Language of Business," *Fortune*, 42 (Nov. 1950), p. 114, © 1950 Time, Inc. All rights reserved.

4 Lane Kirkland, "Free Trade Unionism and Collective Bargaining" *Vital Speeches of the Day* 1 Nov. 1982: 37.

5 Jesse Jackson, "The Rainbow Coalition," *Vital Speeches of the Day* 15 Nov. 1984: 78.

6 Eleanor Smeal, "The Feminization of Power," *Contemporary American Speeches* eds. Richard L. Johannesen, R. R. Allen, Wil A. Linkugel (Dubuque, IA.: Kendall/Hunt, 1988) 259.

7 Letter to the Editor, *The County Telegram Tribune* (San Luis Obispo, CA) 25 June 1990: A12.

8 George Bush, "State of the Union, 1990" *Vital Speeches of the Day* 15 Feb. 1990: 259.

9 Winston Churchill, "The Dunkirk Evacuation" *The War Speeches of the Rt. Hon. Winston S. Churchill* ed. Charles Eade (London: Cassell & Co.: 1967) III, 195-96.

chapter 16

Using Visual Aids

I. Types of visual aids
  A. Actual objects
  B. Models
  C. Pictures
     1. Photographs
     2. Drawings
  D. Symbolic representations
     1. Maps
     2. Graphs
     3. Charts
     4. Diagrams
     5. Flipcharts

II. Principles for the use of visual aids
  A. Large enough to be seen
  B. Simple as the facts allow
  C. At the audience's intellectual level
  D. Relationships indicated clearly
  E. Integral to the speech
  F. Not a substitute for your language
  G. Talk to the audience—not to the visual aid
  H. Put it out of sight when finished with it

The old adage that a picture is worth ten thousand words may be trite, but it makes a lot of sense. Millions of Americans spend hours watching television. As a result, they are more visually oriented. Television has conditioned them to learn with both their eyes and ears.

The interference that we described in Chapter 1 always threatens to block your message from the audience. Part of this interference exists in the barriers listeners set up against excessive verbalism—the use of too many words to the exclusion of other stimuli. Audiences easily fall into daydreaming when words alone don't establish quickly enough how your subject matches their interests. Physical discomforts add to the distractions. The audience is probably accustomed not only to watching TV but also to switching channels instantly at the first sign of boredom. As a result, attention spans have shortened and the ability to listen is more limited![1] There is ample interference to overcome. Visual aids offer one solution. Visual aids also bring about greater understanding of relationships and processes than is usually gained from verbal explanations alone.[2]

Visual aids offer a number of significant advantages. They make it easier for you to choose and to structure your ideas and materials. A photo or diagram may catch and hold the audience's attention, making it easier for you to present your ideas with clarity and coherence. Visual aids let you cover ground more efficiently. They reduce the amount of time you need to communicate your materials. The audience's memory of your ideas will have passed through more than one sense. They are another vehicle for introducing change, curiosity, and humor into your speech. Audiences like visual aids because of their interest value and their variety. This good attitude rubs off on both you and your subject.[3]

It is true, of course, that when you deliver a speech, the audience receives clues to your meaning through two senses—sight and hearing. Your listeners both see and hear you, which gives them a much fuller perception of your intensity, humor, emotion and shades of meaning than it would otherwise get. What happens, though, when you add more than just yourself to what the audience sees? If what you add is orderly, appropriate, and relevant material, the audience gains more knowledge about your subject. Visual aids add to the information the audience receives visually. The weather segment of the evening news on television offers a good example. Think about the graphs, charts, animated drawings, radar pictures, and satellite transmissions that you see. Not only do these visual aids help you to get a clearer understanding of the weather, they also add to its interest value.

Let's highlight the two essential qualities of a successful speech again: *clarity* and *interest*. Both can be enhanced through visual aids. Students frequently ask "When I make this speech, is it OK if I use a map [or a chart, or some other visual aid]?" Our answer is, "If the visual aid you want to use will help to make your speech more interesting and clear, not only is it OK, but you *should*." You owe it to your audience to explore every avenue that might make your speech more effective—easier to understand.

In this chapter, we will describe and illustrate a number of different kinds of visual aids you can use to make your speeches more interesting and understandable. As we discuss them, keep in mind that whatever you use as a visual aid must be easily visible, relevant and properly used. We will have some practical advice for you as we move along through the chapter. First, let's take a look at the different classes of visual aids.

Types of Visual Aids

A large variety of materials and devices can be useful if they are appropriate to the particular task you want them to perform. They can be grouped like this:

1. Actual objects
2. Models
3. Pictures
4. Symbolic representations

Actual Objects

In explaining an object, you can display the object itself to help your audience visualize what you are talking about. Putting aside considerations such as size, the actual three-dimensional object will often be a more useful visual aid than any representation of it. For example, Angie is a member of an ensemble of amateur musicians who play recorders. In a speech telling about this early form of flute, she showed the audience a number of actual recorders of various sizes and demonstrated their pitch ranges and tonal qualities. The speech would have been almost impossible without some kind of visual aid. The actual objects she was talking about were probably the best aid she could have used for this subject.

Conversely, it is doubtful you would bring an eight-foot python to class to help you explain how constrictor snakes get their food. For a variety of reasons, even if specimens, samples or artifacts are available, they are not always the best to use. As one writer puts it, "They are too large, too small, too expensive, too dirty, too dangerous, too delicate, or they come out only at night."[4] In cases like these, you have to choose some other form of visual aid.

Models

A model is a three-dimensional representation of something that exists in nature (like the solar system), or has been constructed (like a locomotive engine), or will be constructed (like a new hospital). Although a model is in a sense an imitation, it does not have to be an exact replica. The size, relative to the original object it represents, is not important. Some must be larger to be useful (like a model of a molecule of water). Other models obviously must be smaller (like a model of a constellation). Models can also be the same size as the actual object (like a model of a piston and cylinder in an internal combustion engine). The important job of the model is to represent relationships. Globes are models that are available in numerous sizes. Although they do not show physical properties of the earth accurately, they represent it in a way that would otherwise be difficult to visualize.

Two-dimensional representations, like pictures and graphs, can fool your eye. Three-dimensional models avoid this drawback. Besides being three-dimensional and representing objects in a comfortable viewing size, models have the additional advantage that they can be simplified to omit unnecessary details. For example, an architect's model of a hospital would omit the details of the operating rooms, but the audience would still benefit from viewing the model.

In addition to a model that represents only overall structure, two other kinds can be useful. A *working model* has parts that move to show how something operates (for example, how the moon revolves around the earth).

You probably used visual aids instinctively on numerous occasions. If the visual aid clarifies your meaning for the audience, incorporate it into your speech.

A *cutaway model* shows the interior of the object. It can also be a working model and show, for instance, how something like the interior parts of the human larynx move.

Unless you have access to the appropriate model for your speech, it will probably cost you too much time and money to make one. If a model is not available and if it is not simple and inexpensive to make, it would be better to choose other kinds of visual aids. Suppose you work for an architect and can borrow a model of a shopping center. That model was designed to be viewed by a few people standing around it. It might not be useful in a classroom where the audience is seated in front of it. A model, like any visual aid, must be used only if it helps to make your communication interesting and clear.

Pictures

Petroglyphs (designs carved on rocks) and the prehistoric paintings found on cave walls show that human beings used pictures to communicate long before they learned how to write. No matter how much more sophisticated we may now be, pictures are still useful. Pictures help to clarify the fuzzy or erroneous notions people have about things and ideas. Moreover, abstractions are often easier to grasp when they can be visualized literally by the eye rather than figuratively in the mind.

Photographs   The kind of picture most used is a photograph. Whether it is black and white or color is not important. It is more significant that the selection of photographs be made with a critical eye. Here are some criteria that will help you to choose.[5]

1. *Authenticity*. Photographs should be accurate representations of the subject. For political or commercial purposes, people are often made to look far better or worse than they do in real life.

2. *Simplicity*. Photographs should be uncluttered and clearly feature the subject of the speech. You shouldn't have to point out what you are talking about from a jumble of objects in the photograph.

3. *Relative size of items*. Photographs should include familiar objects to give a correct perspective on the size of an unfamiliar object in the photograph. Pictures of the tiny frogs of the Amazon are held in someone's hand. Archaeologists (and honest fishermen) put a six- or twelve-inch ruler in their photographs to give perspective.

4. *Camera work*. Photographs should be technically good. It doesn't help much if you have to say, "I know this isn't very clear, but you can see Bigfoot just at the edge of that tree."

Drawings   You have probably said many times when you were trying to explain something, "Wait a minute. Give me a pencil and a piece of paper. Now, here's what I'm talking about." Then you drew a sketch of the golf hole you double-bogied or a map showing the best way to get to your house. Drawings are a good way to make yourself clear.

The claim has been made that drawing on the chalkboard during a speech often helps to visualize an idea better than presenting a finished picture because the thought grows as the drawing develops.[6] This is true, but the sketching must be done quickly so that it will not distract from the speech. Unless you have a modest degree of skill in sketching, it is wise to make drawings beforehand, as a part of speech preparation, rather than putting an impromptu, time-consuming and perhaps clumsy piece of work on the chalkboard. A series of drawings made in advance can be revealed at appropriate times during your speech.

Symbolic representations

Some of the most useful (and most frequently used) visual aids are those that explain relationships and operations symbolically rather than directly the way models, pictures, and drawings do. Among these are *maps, charts, graphs,* and *diagrams.*

Maps   The most obvious use for maps is to clarify geographic relationships. This entails more than showing someone how to find Charleston on a map of West Virginia. The variety of maps and the kinds of information they can give is literally astonishing. As you know, a map is a representation on a flat page of all or some part of the earth's surface, usually showing such features as countries, bodies of water, cities, mountains, and roads. There are also many specialized maps. *Physical maps,* for example, show not only the outlines of land masses and bodies of water but, depending on their size, scale and purpose, can also show altitude, temperature, precipitation, vegetation or any other significant physical data. *Political maps* show the boundaries of nations, states, and other political entities and usually include a number of physical properties as well: mountains, rivers, cities, deserts, and bodies of water. These examples are too familiar to need illustration here. Any good map will clearly identify the physical properties and political boundaries of an area.

Other kinds of maps can be equally useful. A student from China spoke on the industrial development of Manchuria, the northeastern region of China. She used an *economic* map to illustrate data important to the economy of the area, and to show the products and industries found there.

In the same speech, she also used a *relief* map to show the topography of Manchuria. Relief maps show the irregularities in the surface of the earth. They do this either by suggesting various altitudes with colors or other pictorial means, or by three-dimensional surfaces on the maps themselves.

Graphs   A graph is a series of points, a line, a curve or an area that compares differences in one variable such as income and one or more other variables like age and gender. Complicated numerical data and the relationships among them are often the most difficult kinds of materials to make clear. It is easy to say clearly that there are 40,000 people living in a town. You would not confuse anyone if you said that there are several churches in the town, each representing a different denomination. But it would be difficult, using oral language alone, to compare the number of members in each denomination with the number of people who do not attend any church. You would end up with more specific numbers than your audience could retain. One very helpful way of handling this kind of material and clarifying complex relationships among quantitative data is to use graphs. Graphs are useful to maintain clarity when you want to discuss relationships.

Any graph should be simple, legible, and accurate. Failure to meet any one of these criteria will defeat your purpose in using it.

1. It should be *simple*. Your audience should be able to comprehend the graph at a glance. Too many data and too much detail are confusing and may actually tempt the audience to stop trying to understand you.

2. It should be *legible*. To be legible, the graph must be neat, and it must also be large enough for everyone in the audience to read easily. Lines, bars, and printing should be bold and clear.

3. It should be *accurate*. The data included on a graph should, of course, be correct, but it is equally important to construct the graph to correct proportions. Otherwise, it will distort and misrepresent the very relationships it is supposed to clarify.

There are many common types of graphs, each having advantages and applications. We will discuss four of the most useful kinds. The *pie graph*—also called a *sector* or *circle*—is a common representation. It is nothing more than a circle with segments sized to show the proportion each element contributes to the whole. In February 1990, President George Bush sent to Congress his proposed budget for the following fiscal year. A pie graph (Figure 16.1) would help the audience visualize the proportional breakdown of the sources of revenue and of expenditures.

A variation of the pie graph is a *pictorial graph*, or "pictograph." Instead of using pie segments to represent the income and expenditures proposed for the federal government in 1991, simplified drawings are used to symbolize each item. This is visually interesting and suggests a three-dimensional quality. Figure 16.2 uses a pictograph to illustrate the same numbers found in the pie graph.

Another versatile and often-used way of representing relationships among numerical data is the *bar graph*. It can be used in several different forms. A "100 percent graph" is simply a single bar that shows what percentage each of the components contributes to the whole.

Multiple bar graphs also help present statistical information. The number of elements and relationships that can be shown in one multiple bar graph is limited by how much an audience can take in without confusion. For

Figure 16.1 **Pie Graph**

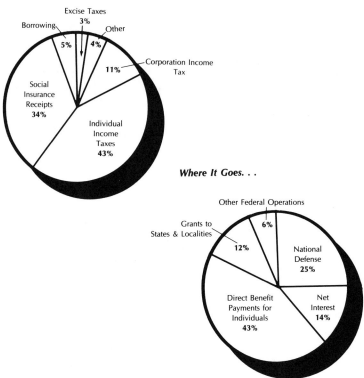

**Fiscal Year 1991 Budget Estimate
The Federal Government Dollar**

a speech comparing the enrollment by curriculum to the total student
population at California Polytechnic University, Jeannette could prepare
the multiple bar graph shown in Figure 16.3. Remember that an audience
doesn't have time to study the graph at leisure; it must be clear at a glance.

Perhaps the most precise graph of all, and the form most useful in
showing not only relationships but trends, is the *line* or *curve graph*. Any
factor can be tracked through a specific period of time. One of the values
of this kind of graph is that it demonstrates the similarities and differences
among a number of factors. Figure 16.4 shows unemployment rates by age
and sex. You can track the percent of women unemployed and how it
changed from 1970 through 1989 and also compare those rates with the
rates for youths or men. Again, avoid visual confusion and complication
on the graph. If the audience has to spend too much time figuring out what

Figure 16.2 **Pictograph**

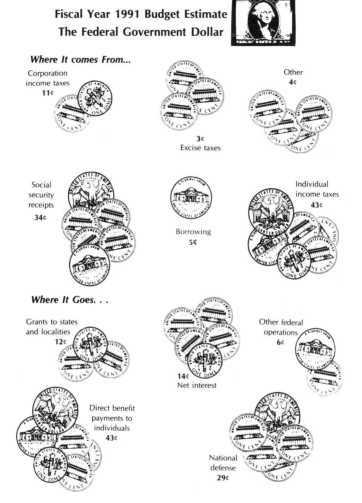

**Fiscal Year 1991 Budget Estimate
The Federal Government Dollar**

Where It comes From...

Corporation income taxes
11¢

3¢
Excise taxes

Other
4¢

Social security receipts
34¢

Borrowing
5¢

Individual income taxes
43¢

Where It Goes. . .

Grants to states and localities
12¢

14¢
Net interest

Other federal operations
6¢

Direct benefit payments to individuals
43¢

National defense
29¢

the graph represents, they will either give up or will stop listening to the rest of your speech.

Charts A chart is a form designed to provide or record information quickly and simply. It differs from a graph in that a chart shows relationships among two or more variables, whereas a graph makes no such comparison with anything outside the one variable it represents. There is almost no limit to the number and variety of charts. The term is used to refer to so many different kinds of visual representations that it can sometimes be confusing. A chart is a navigator's name for a specialized kind of map. It can be what a business man calls a graph of sales information. An engineer may call a technical diagram a chart. The great majority of such visual aids, however, can be sorted into a relatively small number of groups.

Figure 16.3 **Multiple Bar Graph**

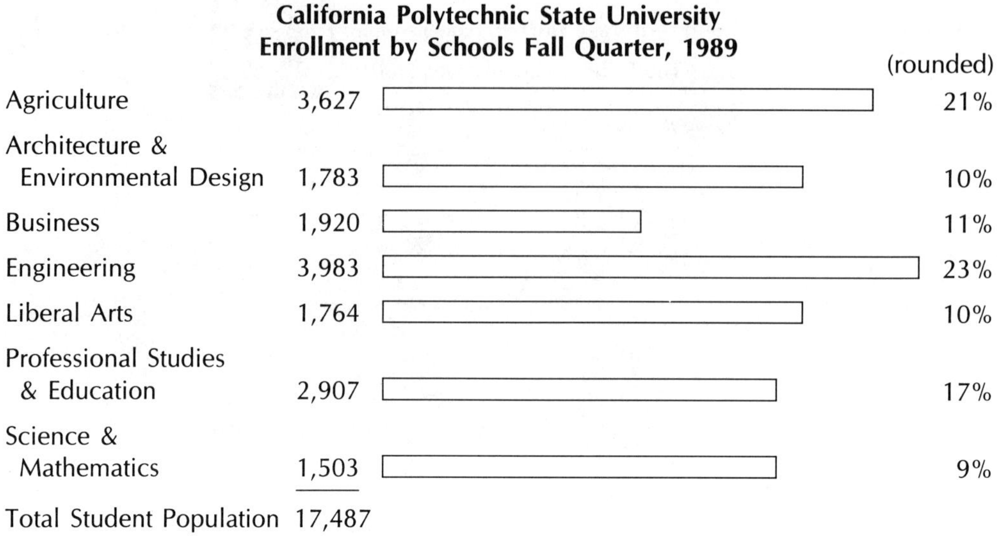

California Polytechnic State University
Enrollment by Schools Fall Quarter, 1989
(rounded)
Agriculture 3,627 21%
Architecture & Environmental Design 1,783 10%
Business 1,920 11%
Engineering 3,983 23%
Liberal Arts 1,764 10%
Professional Studies & Education 2,907 17%
Science & Mathematics 1,503 9%
Total Student Population 17,487

Figure 16.4 **Line Graph**

Percent of civilian labor force
20
15
10
5
0
Youth 16 to 24
Women 25 and over
Men 25 and over
1971
1973
1975
1977
1979
1981
1983
1985
1987
1989

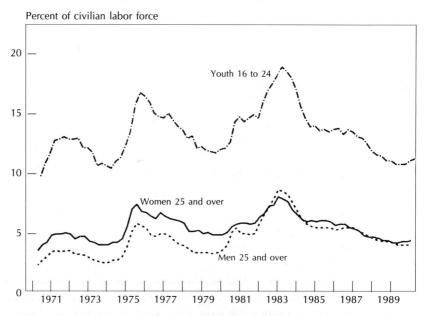

Unemployment Rates by Age and Sex Youth unemployment rates are higher than rates for adults. Rates for adult men and women converged in the 1980s.

A wide variety of information can be outlined in tabular form for easy comprehension by the eye. Arrivals and departures on an airline schedule or profit-and-loss figures of a business are two examples that are easily represented in *data* or *tabular charts*. They are used for quick and easy reference, like logarithmic tables. They are handy for such tasks as transposing Fahrenheit degrees of temperature into Celsius, or the English system of measurement into metrics, or fractions into their decimal equivalents.

Figure 16.5 **Data or Tabular Chart**

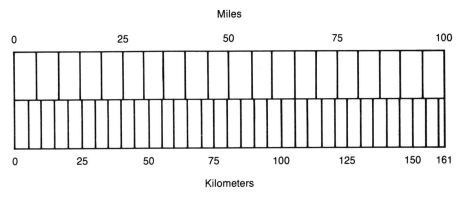

Transposing Miles to Kilometers

It is frequently difficult for an audience to visualize a large number of chronological facts and the relationships among them. While memorizing names and dates may not be a good way to study history, knowing how the major figures in a significant era relate to one another chronologically can be important. A *time chart* (Figure 16.6) helps to clarify and visually represent overlapping time periods.

When the relationship discussed is functional rather than quantitative or chronological, a *flow chart* helps to show how a system operates or how an organization is structured. A student used the flow chart in Figure 16.7 to explain how the editorial staff of a newspaper operates.

Two variations of the organizational chart are useful. They are called the tree chart and the stream chart. Both resemble an organizational chart, but they approach their information from opposite points of view. A *tree chart* portrays a number of offspring originating from a central root source. A ''family tree'' is an obvious example. This type of chart can be used to show any similar set of relationships: the multiple effects from a single cause, the by-products derived from a single mineral, or the different industries that have been generated by a single invention. (See Figure 16.8.)

A *stream chart*, on the other hand, does just the reverse. It is meant to show how a number of figurative tributaries flow together to form a common stream: how different elements contribute to a common goal—for example, the source of raw materials to produce steel or tires.

Figure 16.6 **Time Chart**

Significant Rhetorical Theorists of Ancient Greece

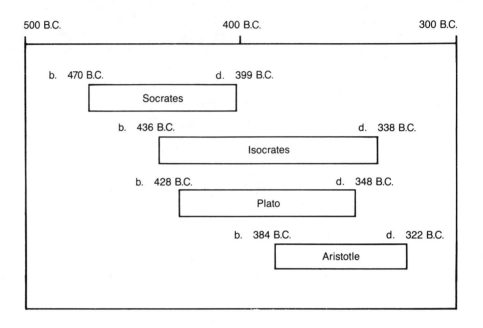

Figure 16.7 **Flow Chart**

Editorial Process of a Newspaper

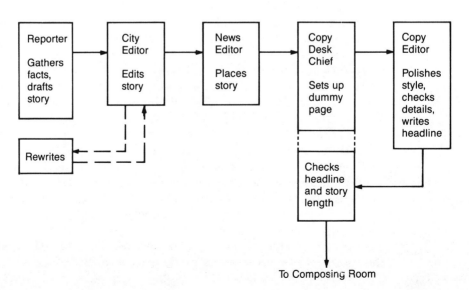

Figure 16.8 **Tree Chart**

Adaptive Radiation

Evolution from a common ancestor of several divergent forms adapted to distinct ways of life.

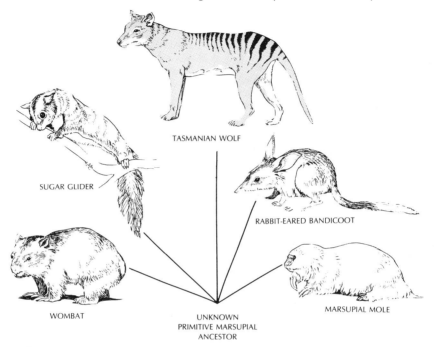

TASMANIAN WOLF

SUGAR GLIDER

RABBIT-EARED BANDICOOT

WOMBAT

UNKNOWN
PRIMITIVE MARSUPIAL
ANCESTOR

MARSUPIAL MOLE

A chart of any sort must be simple and clear. It should concentrate on one central concept and summarize important points rather than trying to convey a large number of details.

Diagrams A diagram is a sketch or drawing that explains something by outlining its parts and/or how they function. Figure 16.9 is a diagram illustrating the principal organs of the speech mechanism.

Like charts and graphs, diagrams appear in a wide variety of forms and are put to multiple uses. The purpose for which the diagram is intended will determine the amount of care given to producing it. A set of engineering plans for constructing a communication satellite to orbit the earth would be much more detailed than a rough guide for building a fence. Engineering construction plans for communication satellites would be useless for a classroom speech. A schematic diagram of one important part would be much more informative. In a talk about the basic operation of an internal combustion engine, for example, a schematic diagram will help to show the relationships among the various parts and functions of the engine.

Of all the ways of representing an object or an idea, a diagram is the sketchiest. When you draw rough lines on a sheet of paper to represent

Figure 16.9 **Diagram**

The Principal Organs of Speech
(ribs, diaphragm, and thoracic muscles not shown)

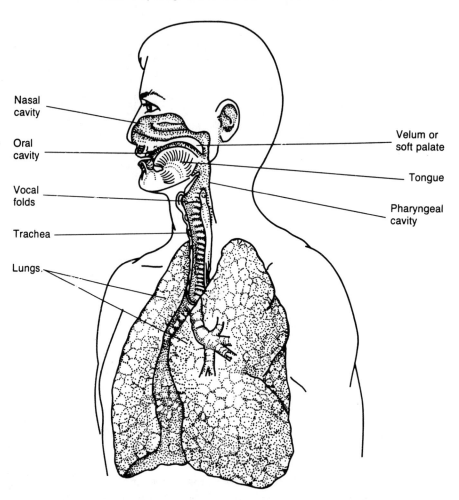

Nasal cavity

Oral cavity

Vocal folds

Trachea

Lungs

Velum or soft palate

Tongue

Pharyngeal cavity

the streets in your neighborhood, you don't intend to draw an aerial map. Even the most elaborate set of blueprints for a house is not a picture of the house itself, any more than a map is the actual territory it represents. Remember, therefore, that because diagrams are more abstract than other representations, they confuse your audience unless you make them clear.

Trying to handle a number of pictures, maps, drawings or any of the other representations at the same time can be troublesome. A good way to keep control over them is with a *flipchart*.

Flipcharts In a speech about the Anasazi, Joseph used four sketches he had made of prehistoric drawings on the walls of the Canyon de Chelly in Arizona. Each of his sketches was about 24 inches by 30 inches in area. He had them clipped together at the top and fastened to an easel. At the proper time, he simply flipped the page back over the top of the easel to disclose the next picture. A flipchart is used very frequently by sales representatives, architects, and lawyers in formal situations called *presentations*.

Principles for the Use of Visual Aids

When all is said and done, the only meaning a speech has is what the audience thinks the speaker means. When you use visual aids properly, they can help the audience understand more clearly and precisely what you mean. Happily, a little common sense is all it takes to use visual aids effectively. They will do what you want them to if you follow these simple principles.

The Visual Aid Must Be Large Enough to Be Seen

If it is too small, it will be of no help. Either the audience will be distracted from the substance of the speech by the effort to see the aid or, more likely, it won't bother to try. In either case, the utility of the aid is lost.

Make the Visual Aid as Simple as the Facts Allow

Your speech must supply necessary elaborations of detail. Trying to make a graph say everything will make the graph say nothing. It will be so complicated that it won't make sense. Visual aids must be understood very quickly or they are useless.

Aim the Aid at the Audience's Intellectual Level

The number and type of labels that are used to clarify the elements of charts, graphs, or diagrams are determined by the needs of the audience. If there are too many labels, the visual clarity of the aid will be lessened; if there are too few, the aid will not make sense. Ideally, the visual aid would be both simple and clear.

Indicate Relationships Clearly

The criteria of simplicity and clarity should also be applied to your language as well as to the visual aid. The language of the speech and the visual aids that support it should work *together* to bring your ideas sharply into focus in the minds and imaginations of the audience. Be sure that *you* are comfortable explaining the relationships symbolized on your visual aid so that the audience can easily grasp the connection.

The Visual Aid Should Be Integral to the Speech

Avoid using pictures, models, or any other aids unless they make a necessary contribution to clear communication of the central idea of the speech. No matter how attractive, a visual aid that does not support the central purpose of the speech draws attention away from it. The same restrictions apply to visual aids as to any other elements in your speech. If an aid is irrelevant to the audience's understanding, choose another vehicle to convey your meaning.

Don't Substitute the Visual Aid for Your Language

The language of the speech should be as vividly descriptive as if there were no model, map or diagram. Visual aids are just that, aids. They are intended to add a *visual* dimension to the delivery of ideas and supporting materials. It defeats their purpose to use them as a substitute for clear explanation.

Talk to the Audience and not to the Visual Aid

There is a tendency to turn away from the audience and to give your attention to the aid. This may help to focus the eyes of the audience on the aid, but it has the undesirable added effect of breaking your eye contact with the audience (see Chapter 17) and distracting the audience from the substance of the speech. Although it seems obvious, remember not to block the audience's view of the visual aid. We mention it only as a reminder not to be careless about where you stand or where you position the aid.

Once Through with the Aid Put It out of Sight

When you have moved on to another part of the speech, the continued presence of an earlier visual aid can prove to be a distraction. If it is possible without creating a distraction, put it away. Close the flip chart when you finish with it, turn the picture over, put the graph behind the speaker's stand, turn off the slide projector.

Summary

Public speeches communicate through both hearing and sight. One way to increase the quality of the visual element of communication is with visual aids.

Visual aids are of four types. (1) Actual objects are useful when they are available and can be safely and easily handled. (2) Models are often better because they can be constructed to show precise relationships. (3) Pictures, both photographs and drawings, are useful provided they are authentic, simple, of good quality, and show the relative size of the objects pictured. (4) Symbolic representations include maps, charts, graphs and diagrams.

Following a few simple rules will improve the effectiveness of visual aids. Make the aid large enough and as simple as the facts will allow. Design the aid for the intellectual level of the audience. Clearly indicate the relationships of the material represented. Use the aid only if it is an integral part of the speech. Don't use the aid as a substitute for good oral explanation. Talk to the audience, not to the aid. When an aid has served its purpose, put it out of view of the audience.

Key Terms

Actual objects	Line graph
Working model	Pictograph
Cutaway model	Tabular chart
Photograph	Time chart
Drawings	Flow chart
Maps	Tree chart
Pie graph	Diagrams
Bar graph	Flip chart
Multiple bar graphs	Presentations

Exercises

1. Prepare a five-minute informative speech in which you use visual aids to clarify the main purpose of the speech. Be sure that the subject you choose needs visual aids and that the aids are essential to the whole speech, not to just a part of it.

2. Listen to three or four speeches by members of your class and note how they used visual aids or didn't use such aids. Write a short paper on one of the speeches explaining how the speech might have been improved by more or fewer visual aids, or why it was well done in the use (or absence) of visual aids.

3. Get the official map to your college campus, the diagram of the organization of the company you work for, or some similar official map or chart. Come to class prepared to discuss its possible usefulness and weakness as a visual aid for a speech.

Notes

[1] Walter A. Wittich and Charles F. Shuller, *Instructional Technology* (New York: Harper & Row, 1973) 18-27.

[2] Wittich and Shuller, 33-3.

[3] Jerrold E. Kemp and Don C. Smellie, *Planning, Producing and Using Instructional Media* (New York: Harper & Row, 1989).

[4] A.J. Romiszowski, *The Selection and Use of Instructional Media* (New York: Wiley, 1974) 89.

[5] Adapted from James S. Kinder, *Using Instructional Media* (New York: D. Van Nostrand, 1973) 58-59.

[6] Kenneth B. Haas and Harry Q. Packer, *Preparation and Use of Audio Visual Aids*, 3rd ed. (New York: Prentice-Hall, 1955) 144.

chapter 17

Delivering the Speech

I. Methods of delivery
   A. Speaking from manuscript
   B. Speaking from memory
   C. Speaking impromptu
   D. Speaking extemporaneously

II. Using your voice to communicate meaning
   A. Speak loudly enough
   B. Emphasize important words
   C. Make clear distinctions among ideas
   D. Make words convey feelings
   E. Use standard conventions of pronunciation
   F. Speak in a conversational manner

III. Using physical action to communicate meaning
   A. Look directly at the audience
   B. Use appropriate posture
   C. Move with purpose
   D. Make gestures natural
   E. Use appropriate facial expression

IV. Dealing with anxiety
   A. Don't blame yourself
   B. Realize the importance of experience
   C. Choose situations with a high potential for success
   D. Concentrate on the message
   E. Prepare thoroughly
   F. Adopt a conversational attitude
   G. Consciously play the role of a confident speaker
      1. Walk briskly to the platform
      2. Look directly at the audience
      3. Use a good attention factor in the introduction
      4. Control the rate of delivery
      5. Keep your nervousness to yourself

All communication acts — spoken, written, recorded, or filmed — are alike in many ways, the most obvious being that they all use some form of language. However, *oral* communication is unique. In some sense, every form of communication is adapted to its audience, but a speech must make an immediate and very direct adaptation. Its face-to-face oral quality gives it an immediacy that writing and other forms cannot have.

The vocal and physical aspects of delivery, therefore, are more than mechanical tools for converting a written page or an outline into sounds and actions. They are a vital part of the communication itself. Delivery is as much a part of a speech as subject matter, organization, or language. From the moment you select a subject and begin your preparation, you should think of the speech not as an essay delivered orally but as a special interaction between you and your audience that combines ideas, sounds, and actions.

To help you understand better what delivery brings to communication, we will look at some overall methods of delivery with a focus on the extemporaneous speech. We will then examine how your voice and your physical actions communicate meaning. Finally, we will discuss some ways to control the anxiety which may interfere with conversational delivery.

Methods of Delivery

The vocal and physical elements of speaking are, in a sense, the raw materials that you manufacture into an effective style of delivery. But then comes the question, what kind of delivery is best?

Four different methods of delivering a speech are commonly recognized. These differ from one another according to the kind of preparation the speaker makes for delivery. If the language of the speech is thoroughly prepared in advance, the speech can be delivered either from manuscript or from memory. On the other hand, if the language is not chosen before the moment of delivery, the speech will be either impromptu or extemporaneous.

Speaking From Manuscript

Since the audience judges what is required for an effective speech, it is impossible to know in advance precisely how a speech ought to be delivered. However, you have a much better chance of accomplishing your purpose when you speak in simple, direct, straightforward language to listeners with whom you are making close visual and psychological contact. With this kind of delivery, it is much easier to make any necessary adaptations to the occasion and to the idiosyncrasies of the audience.

A person in a position of great responsibility (such as the U.S. Ambassador to the United Nations) can't afford to make a mistake, no matter

A manuscript speech is a necessary precaution for a person in a position of responsibility who cannot afford to make a mistake.

how small. A manuscript is a necessary precaution for this type of speech. When very strict time limits are placed on a speech, (for example, radio and television presentations), or when a situation such as a commencement ceremony requires a polished speech, it might be delivered from manuscript. Unless you face these specific constraints, your general rule should be, don't use a manuscript. If you do find yourself in a situation where you must speak from a manuscript, your delivery should have the qualities of good conversation.

Speaking from Memory

In preparing to deliver a speech from memory, you would ordinarily write out a manuscript and practice from it until you knew it by heart. This kind of delivery has few of the advantages and all of the disadvantages of the manuscript method. Unless you are a reasonably accomplished actor, you will find it difficult to deliver a talk from memory and to maintain close contact with the audience at the same time. Even if you are a good actor or recite well, you will contend with the same lack of flexibility that burdens the manuscript speaker. There is another disadvantage to speaking from memory: If you forget, you are lost. Categorically, we say *never* memorize a speech. If the occasion demands that kind of preparation, prepare a manuscript and use it instead.

Speaking Impromptu

An impromptu speech may be defined as one for which you have made no immediate preparation. You are unexpectedly called upon to speak and have to say things on the spur of the moment. You imagine yourself swaying masses of people and crushing opposition—the epitome of impromptu eloquence. But, you know that was a daydream. Such skill is not impossible to attain, but it requires commitment and dedication. Henry Ward Beecher, one of the most famous preachers of the nineteenth century, delivered a splendid talk that seemed to be completely impromptu. When he was asked how long he had worked on it, he said he had been preparing for the talk for 40 years.

Except when the occasion absolutely demands it, you should never speak impromptu. Take every opportunity to prepare as thoroughly as time will allow. If at all possible, take a few moments to think through what you will say and to jot down a few notes. If you must react at once, remember that the major functions of a speech are to introduce an idea, develop it, and conclude. If you do this, even the most hastily prepared talk will have the quality of order.

Speaking Extemporaneously

In speaking extemporaneously, the ideas, organization, and supporting material of a speech are *thoroughly* prepared in advance. The only part of the speech that is *ex tempore* (''out of the time'' meaning at the actual moment of delivery) is the language. The delivery is also practiced; the speech has been talked through several times. You do not write out the speech (although you should prepare an outline), nor do you make any effort to memorize the language you will use. Ideally, each time you practice the speech you will use different language and work toward a more precise and clearer statement of your ideas. When you deliver the speech, you will be so thoroughly familiar with the subject matter that you can ''ad lib'' the language.

We believe that extemporaneous delivery has the greatest number of advantages and the fewest disadvantages of the four methods. It can have all the spontaneity and immediacy of casual conversation without the disorganization that usually characterizes impromptu speaking. And it lends itself to direct visual and psychological contact with the audience. Unlike a manuscript or memorized speech, it affords flexibility in meeting the specific and yet shifting demands of an audience.

Using Your Voice to Communicate Meaning

Here's a brief synopsis of the physiological process of voice production. Muscles of the chest and abdomen must be tensed and relaxed to the right degree at the proper moment and for the right length of time to provide air at the proper pressure. The vocal folds must be lengthened and shortened, tensed and relaxed with great speed and precision to produce desired pitches. The resonating cavities and articulators that can be changed in shape must be modified at a rapid rate and at precisely the right moment to form the different sounds of speech. —Miraculous that we can talk at all, isn't it?

Actually, this complex mechanism works so rapidly and each element is so thoroughly integrated with every other that an attempt to isolate and improve any single part of the process should be guided by a highly skilled professional. Looking for solutions to speech problems in "diaphragmatic breathing," "lower pitch," or "more careful articulation" is a gross simplification. In a public speaking class, only the most general problems can be considered. Happily, these are the only problems the average student needs to be concerned with in the process of becoming an effective extemporaneous speaker.

The vocal process is made up of four elements of sound: loudness, rate, pitch, and quality. There is little you can do, or probably need to do, about the pitch range or the quality of your voice. If you think your pitch is "too high" or your voice quality is "raspy" remember these are a part of your speaking personality. They make you different from others, but not uncommunicative. They may even be helpful attributes.

Loudness, on the other hand, needs to be, and can be, adapted to the audience. You must be heard to be understood. In a similar way, rate may interfere with communication. If you talk too slowly you may lose the attention of the audience. If the speech is too fast, and lacks pauses, you will be difficult to understand. Most student speakers can adapt to loudness and rate problems. Here are some suggestions for using your voice to communicate meaning.

Speak Loudly Enough

Nothing you say will make any sense if your audience can't hear you. But to make the members of an audience "hear," you must make them *listen*. This requires that your voice be more than merely audible. Speak loudly enough not only to be heard but also to command attention in spite of the many normal distractions to be expected. To hold the attention of an audience, you must be able to contend with such competitors as a noisy air conditioner in the back of the room or a group of children playing ball outside an open window.

Emphasize Important Words

Writers have an advantage that speakers lack: they can let their readers understand ideas at leisure. But when you speak, you have an advantage that writers don't: You can use your voice to say instantly what you mean. You do not have to depend on such relatively crude signs as commas, periods, exclamation points, and question marks to carry shades of meaning. With your voice, you can give a whole range of different emphases to a single phrase.

In any sentence some words are more important than others. The less important ones can even be omitted without losing the basic meaning. To save both space and the reader's time, newspaper headlines are telescoped to the shortest form that can still make sense. Sometimes an obvious verb will be left out: "Midwest Flood Damage $100 Million." Such words as "a", "and", or "the" are seldom used: "Clouds, Fog Lift for Pleasant Day." To say more is unnecessary; to say less would be unintelligible.

But even after all the "unnecessary" words have been cut out of a newspaper headline, those that remain are not of equal importance. The *Los Angeles Times* ran a story with the headline, "Today's Fathers Not Afraid to Show a Caring Attitude." While all of the words may be needed, some carry a larger burden of the communication than others do. The headline is talking not just about fathers, but about *today's* fathers. The word "today's" would tend to get more stress. "Afraid," is significant, even more so than "Not," but the words "to" and "a" would get very little stress. The words "Caring Attitude" are central to the thought conveyed. Therefore they are very important and heavily stressed. No one can say, of course, what the "correct" reading of the headline is, but one way of using your voice to give an accurate sense of what the headline says would call for something like the following relative degrees of emphasis: "**Today's** *Fathers Not* **Afraid** *to show* a **Caring Attitude**."

You are the only one who knows exactly what you mean; you are the one who must decide which of your words carry the burden of your meaning. You select the important words and give them meaningful emphasis.

Emphasis is likely to be identified at first thought with loudness. One way to let people know what is important is to make it loud. When Mom and Dad say, "Come in the house, right now," the kids often wait until the call gets loud enough to show that the parents mean business. However, sophisticated people soon learn that loudness is the simplest form of stress. Effective emphasis is created through *variety* in *all* the elements of vocal delivery: pitch, rate, and quality as well as loudness.

Make Clear Distinctions among Ideas

"Catholics make up approximately 5 percent of the population of West Virginia compared with 30 percent in Wisconsin." In this sentence there are at least two and possibly three opposing sets of ideas. Five percent is certainly not the same as 30 percent, and West Virginia is not to be confused with Wisconsin. There is also an implied distinction between Catholics and non-Catholics among the populations of the two states. The only way you can make your listeners hear these differences is with your voice, and the only way your voice can make the ideas distinct is through variations in pitch, loudness, time, and quality.

The same principle applies not only to words that communicate a contrast, but also to those that express ideas in a series. In a Midwestern area, the National Weather Service once chose the wrong person to read the midday forecast on a local radio station. He knew all the names of the different meteorological phenomena, but his voice patterns were so unvaried that they made "clouds," "fog," "rain," "clear," and "warm," sound the same. His monotonous tone made all those words sound like synonyms. Variety would have made the words in this series distinguishable from one another.

Make Words Convey Feelings

Many words imitate the sound that they name. (This is called *onomatopoeia*, or "echoism.") For example, ducks quack, geese hiss, sparrows chirp, hens cluck. Insects buzz and hum. The word "boom" imitates the sound it names. The fact that words often imitate sounds can add color to speech.

Echoism, however, is only part of what we mean by making words sound like what you mean. A major function of words is to communicate not only the ideas you have in mind, but your feelings about those ideas as well. Through vocal quality you can make "war" sound heroic or outrageous, "peace" sound glorious or weak. Your voice can help you show the goodness or badness you impute to ideas, their rightness or wrongness, their ugliness or beauty, their merit or lack of it.

Use Standard Conventions of Pronunciation

Pronunciation is the sum of all the audible characteristics of a word: the individual sounds, the order in which they occur, their duration, the stress given to syllables, and so on. But you don't have good pronunciation until it is acceptable to your audience. In other words, it is quite possible for you to have very precise pronunciation and still have it be "wrong." A problem occurs when pronunciation is inappropriate—when it fails to meet the expectations of your audience. For example, if you pronounce the word can't as "cain't," your enunciation of each sound could be precise and you could be clearly understood, but your pronunciation would be wrong because it is not accepted by the vast majority of educated listeners. Acceptable pronunciation follows the standard usage of the educated members of a speaker's audience.

Dictionaries are the most obvious authority for the accepted pronunciation of words. But we say accepted rather than correct because as long as a language is spoken, it changes. Dictionaries report what is current usage at the time they are printed, and printing a word does not freeze its pronunciation for all time. But since language changes occur slowly, a dictionary's report of standard pronunciation can be safely accepted.

Speak in a Conversational Manner

Probably nothing in speaking contributes more to effective delivery than a conversational style. Even when you use inappropriate pronunciation or grammar, if your delivery is spontaneous, direct, and conversational, you are likely to be judged more effective than if you lacked this relaxed style.[1]

Most Americans do not, as a rule, read aloud very often or at any great length. When they do, they often sound like children first learning to read. Even when they read fluently, the words of inexperienced and untrained readers sound crated for delivery and boxed-in with stiff patterns. Repetitions of pitch cadences, unvaried tempo, unchanging degrees of loudness, and a dull quality of monotony all conceal much of what should be conveyed. Reading patterns almost always attach themselves to the recitation of memorized words as well. One mark of a poor actor is an inability to speak in a spontaneous, conversational mode.

Your speaking is an extension of your personality. Obviously, pronunciation, pitch, loudness, time, and quality have to be adapted to the size of an audience and the requirements of the subject matter, but your delivery should ideally be like the animated conversation that goes on among friends.

Making Your Delivery Conversational

- Speak as if talking to a group of friends.
- Speak and look directly at your listeners.
- Prepare carefully but make delivery spontaneous
- Show that you are enthusiastic about your subject
- Make your ideas intelligible to your audience

Using Physical Action to Communicate Meaning

Everything you do in public speaking or in private conversation says something. "Everything" includes not only your words, but the way you use your voice and the "silent language" you transmit with your body.

Each of these media, the linguistic, the vocal, and the physical, is a language and is interpreted by an audience as having some bearing on what you say. The more of these languages you put to use at the same time, the more likely your message will be to get through accurately. Of course, all of the languages must be saying the same thing: all of them must be carrying the same message. Otherwise, they will not only fail to make your message clear, they will actually obscure it by counteracting and contradicting each other. You want to make sure that there is unity in the messages carried by your words, your voice, and your physical actions. All of the audible and visible cues you give the audience should be saying the same thing at the same time.

Look Directly at the Audience

Looking directly at the audience involves something more than not looking at the floor, out the window, or head down into your notes. It means more than sweeping the audience with an occasional glance. It means looking directly into the faces of individual members of the audience. Of course, when you talk to a large group, or speak in a large auditorium, you are too far from the audience to look directly into the eyes of each listener. Look at individuals sitting in different areas of the audience. You will give the impression that you are speaking directly to each person sitting near those areas.

Your own experience will tell you that listeners will not respond well to a speaker who does not look at them. You have met people who avoided your glance. What was your reaction to them? The question is not whether someone who refuses to look you in the eye is shifty or untrustworthy; the important idea is that you tend to react negatively to someone who does not look at you.

There is another good reason for you to look directly at your listeners. The audience itself is an important source of information — and speakers need all the help they can get. As a rule, people respond overtly to what they see and hear, and those responses tell you what effect you are having on them. It would be wasteful not to take advantage of the feedback the audience gives you. Only by making direct visual contact with individual members of the group can you tell who is alert and friendly, who is bored, who is unconcerned, or who is just not listening. Only then can you make immediate and helpful adaptations to the audience.

Use Appropriate Posture

It is futile to try to distinguish between you and your ideas. Therefore, the way an audience rates you as a person will influence how it will respond to your ideas. One of the things that affects an audience's reactions to you as a person is posture. Consequently, you should stand before your audience in a manner that indicates stability and assurance. Your posture should be poised but not stiff, relaxed but not sloppy.

Experienced speakers sometimes lean on a speaking stand, put their hands in their pockets, or even sit on the edge of a table. But when speakers are this casual, it usually means that they and the audience know each other pretty well. Whether such posture is acceptable depends more on the degree of formality in a given situation than it does on the "rules" of public speaking. Being overly casual is likely to work to the disadvantage of beginning speakers, because they usually don't know the audience well and audiences expect strangers to treat them with at least semi-formal respect. A second and perhaps more important reason for not being too casual is that you are likely to dramatize your relaxation in an effort to dispel or disguise nervousness. Instead of covering up your anxiety, you emphasize it, and this detracts from your effectiveness.

Even so, you can communicate assurance by controlling your posture. Stand straight, balance your weight on both feet, and look directly at your audience. The results will be far better than anything you can do by way of draping yourself over the lectern, crossing your ankles, slouching with

Stand before your audience in a manner that indicates stability and assurance.

your hands in your pockets, sitting on the edge of a desk, or pacing back and forth in front of your audience. Proper posture will help keep your nervousness from interfering with your communication. You may not think so, but your audience will. That is the important point. Conscious decisions about posture in any specific situation should always be determined by what is appropriate to the audience, the occasion, and the substance of your speech.

Move with Purpose

In general, avoid movement that is not necessary. Pacing back and forth on the platform is never necessary and is rarely useful. Many an anxious speaker has used this kind of wandering as a means of working off excess energy. But when there is nothing to justify it, stalking around during the speech detracts from the communication. Physical movement can be used to signal an intellectual movement to a new idea or a change in the mood of the speech. But such movement should always have a purpose.

An important detail of movement is the way you get from your seat to the place where you will speak and back to your seat again when you have finished. An audience will hold you responsible for everything you do from the moment you leave your seat until you sit down again. That is to say, your speech begins, not when you utter your first words, but when you first stand up. Similarly, your speech does not end with your conclusion; it goes on until the attention of the audience is no longer on you.

Under these conditions, it is only reasonable to conduct yourself in a manner that will not detract from the general effectiveness of your speech. It will help to preserve your credibility if you neither race nor shuffle to the front of the room, but walk to and from the platform with firmness and poise. Give the impression that you want to speak and are ready for the occasion. When you have finished speaking, maintain the atmosphere of dignity and competence you have built by returning to your seat quietly and deliberately.

Make Gestures Natural

Another kind of bodily action is gesture. Gesture is distinguished from the kind of movement just discussed by the fact that it involves movement of the arms, hands and head but does not carry the speaker from one part of the room to another. Gestures made with the hands and arms are of two kinds: those that emphasize ideas and those that are used for description. There is no set vocabulary of gestures. You can emphasize an idea by pointing with your finger, or you can pound a word home with your fist. You may spread your hands to show size, or extend your arm to show place.

To be effective, gestures must seem spontaneous and natural. Yes, gesturing is natural for everyone, but it is not usually habitual for a beginning speaker in a formal speaking situation. Try to carry over into public speech the same free movement of hands, arms, and head that you normally use in private speech and the same mobility of facial expression. Some speakers quite naturally gesture more than others. Those rare persons who do not gesture at all, even in private speech, should maintain the poise of private speech.

Although most speakers use some movement of their hands and arms, their gestures in more formal speaking situations are unmotivated, choppy, and incomplete. Their natural inclination to gesture is inhibited by the formal circumstances. One very good way of overcoming this kind of problem is role-playing. Deliberately and consciously act the part of a competent and effective speaker. You have a clear image of how that sort of person would behave, because you've seen a lot of examples in movies, television, and real life. Imitate speakers you like, including those in your own class. Given time and experience, you will develop your own style. You will find that when you are enthusiastic about your idea and have a will to communicate it, your personal speaking habits will provide you with a spontaneous and varied group of gestures that are natural to you.

Use Appropriate Facial Expression

Facial expression in delivery is as significant as the gestures you make with your hands and arms. Listeners interpret your actions as clues to what you are saying, and audiences tend to read your face as closely as they listen to your words. Unfortunately, it's easy to give them the wrong clues. They may think you are bored or cynical, for instance, when you are not. How often have you had someone ask you what was the matter when nothing was wrong? It's up to you to give your listeners the right clues.

Dealing with Anxiety

If you are like most speakers, you will have some anxiety about the public speaking situation. It may interfere (or seem to interfere) with your conversational delivery. If so, you are not alone, because about 75 percent of the people in your speech class believe that this is an important problem.[2] A group of 3000 Americans were interviewed in 1973, and 41 percent of them said that they were more afraid of speaking before a group than they were of other common fears, such as heights, loneliness, or ugly bugs.[3] Even seasoned professional entertainers, actors, and lecturers are not immune to "stage fright." Indeed, many successful speakers and performers realize that nervousness is a natural part of getting ready for a public presentation. It is much like the athlete who has to be "psyched up" to have an outstanding day. Being tense and nervous before a speech is perfectly normal. It is something you can expect.

Anxiety, of course, can be very troublesome to a speaker even though it is expected. Anxiety may mean butterflies in the stomach, stumbling over words, vocalizing pauses (injecting ''uh'' and ''er'' without regard to meaning), trembling hands and knees, or being unable to look directly at members of the audience. And the symptoms can differ from one speaking situation to another. In your church group you may feel no nervousness, but a classroom speech may become a problem. Nervousness may also differ with the topic or the nature of the communication required.[4]

But please, put any anxiety you have in proper perspective. Anxious speakers frequently think that audiences expect more of them than they do. Furthermore, audiences do not detect as much of the speaker's anxiety as the speaker does.[5] Sometimes an audience won't perceive your nervousness at all. Again and again we have heard students comment on their nervousness only to have the other students say that they didn't notice anything.

Here are some practical suggestions to help you deal with anxiety.

Don't Blame Yourself

Speakers who find themselves displaying anxiety will frequently make the problem worse by becoming angry with themselves. But the physical manifestations of nervousness cannot be controlled easily. If you accept the fact that they are perfectly natural, you may be able to stop blaming yourself and thus reduce the psychic feedback. You cannot will away the anxiety no matter how much pressure you put on yourself. As a matter of fact, paying attention to the problem can make it worse.

Realize the Importance of Experience

Just as unhappy experiences can condition you to fear public speaking, so can favorable experiences condition you to enjoy it. Eliminating as much of the mystery as possible will help you to attain this goal. It is best to know what effective public speaking is and to study the methods of organizing speeches, supporting them, and delivering them. In the locker room, the hallway, or at the dinner table you are continually making speeches. It is your *perception* of a speaking situation rather than the situation itself that makes it threatening. Making a good speech requires nothing you cannot master. You can have the kind of experiences that build confidence. Each favorable experience will reinforce the others.

Some people have such serious anxiety that it is genuinely disabling. They need professional help.[6] But for most people, a well-developed program of speech preparation and presentation, such as the course you are now enrolled in, is very effective in reducing the problem.[7]

Choose Situations with a High Potential for Success

There are studies indicating that students who suffer from anxiety have a tendency to choose very simple or very difficult tasks.[8] Choosing a very

You have been making speeches for years — in the hallway, at the dinner table, etc. The same direct, involving, enthusiastic communication used in informal situations makes the most effective public speeches.

simple topic for a speech ("My Summer Vacation," "How to sew on a button," "How a tennis match is scored," etc.) might make you feel better but it won't give your listeners much information. It's not clear why many anxious speech students choose topics that are more difficult for them. But, it stands to reason that such a practice should be avoided as surely as you should avoid speaking on a trivial topic. Choose a topic you know a lot about and in which you have considerable interest. Add additional information from a study of the topic. Make yourself an expert on an interesting and worthwhile topic. Choose a topic you know well to start with. That will help to maximize your success.

Concentrate on the Message

We are convinced that the most important way to deal with anxiety is to focus your attention on the communication task before you rather than on any emotional problems you have. Concentrating on the message you want to convey will help you take your mind off the personal anxiety you feel.

Prepare Thoroughly

It seems obvious that anxiety will attack you if you aren't sure of what you want your speech to do or whether the speech will do it. In the presence of these uncertainties, you will be insecure about how the audience will react. Careful preparation is the only realistic solution to this problem. Study your speech subject well. Understand your topic and build a broad background of information around it.

There are certain laxities that effective speaking does not allow: "I'm not too sure about this, but I think it is pronounced . . . " "I understand that Professor Kernaghan has a different view on this, but I couldn't find his book in our library." "I had to work late last night, so I didn't have a chance to check all the facts." These confessions merely say that you are not expert on the subject. Listeners ask, "Why should I listen?" Confidence in speaking grows from knowing that you are well prepared and seeing that your audience realizes you are qualified to speak.

Thorough preparation includes a careful analysis of your audience. The more you know about your listeners, the more familiar they will become to you and the less threatening. Believe this! It's the best advice the present chapter can give: when you are sure of your audience and sure of your subject, you will be confident of your ability to meet the demands of the speaking situation.

Adopt a Conversational Attitude

It is helpful to think of public speaking as conversation. People speaking to a group of friends in informal surroundings have little trouble saying what they want to say. If you think of public speaking as something enormously greater and more formal than private conversation, you burden yourself with pressures that are not part of the informal situation. The more you can think of public speaking as conversation, the easier public speaking will be. The same direct, involving, enthusiastic kind of communication that is so enjoyable in a friendly get-together is what makes public speaking effective.

Consciously Play the Role of a Confident Speaker

There is much value in deliberately adopting a pose of good adjustment to the speaking situation. Visualize yourself as a confident speaker.[9] Actors have long recognized that audiences tend to do and feel what they see being done and felt. When they see someone in pain on the stage, they "feel" pain. When the actor is happy, they "feel" happy. This reaction is called *empathy*. It is useful to a public speaker. If listeners perceive an alert speaker, they will tend to be alert. The speaker, seeing a favorable audience response, tends to become more confident.

Here are a few specific actions you can practice to help give you the appearance and the feeling of emotional control.

Walk briskly to the platform   Walk directly and resolutely to the speaker's stand and put down your notes. Don't slouch or shuffle along the way. Don't fumble with your papers or clothing.

Look directly at the audience   When you reach the speaker's stand and have your notes assembled before you, look directly at the audience for a brief time before beginning your speech. Think of this as a moment when you "meet" the audience and make your first friendly contact with them. During the speech, concentrate on looking directly at the members of the audience. Speakers who seem unable to look directly at their listeners signal their anxiety.

Use a good attention factor in the introduction   Your introduction may set the tone for the reaction you will get to the rest of the speech. For this reason, you will want to get off to a good start. Make sure to plan an opening that will arouse the interest of the audience; then deliver it as you planned it. Don't let any anxiety you feel rush you into the main body of the speech so that you lose the interest value of the attention factor. Review Chapter 14 for more information on attention factors.

Control the rate of delivery   When nervousness strikes you, your first wish is to get the unpleasant experience over with as soon as possible. This reaction is understandable because the human organism always tries to avoid unpleasant stimuli. But, it could hurt your effectiveness. To avoid this reaction, control the rate of your delivery. Talk more slowly than you might be inclined to, especially at the beginning of the speech.

Keep your nervousness to yourself   Don't tell your audience that you are nervous. Far too many speakers try to break the ice by saying something like, "Well, I hope you're more relaxed about this speech than I am." Or, when they fumble with words or have muscle spasms, they look self-conscious or apologize or giggle. You might be able to gain sympathy this way, but you won't win respect and you won't get support for your ideas. Listeners can feel sympathy for a speaker in distress, but they will not follow one who finds it necessary to lean on them.

    If you are obviously nervous, your listeners know it without having to be told. When you have difficulty, empathy makes the audience suffer with you. Furthermore, there is reason to believe that feeling sympathetic makes an audience uncomfortable. If you fight out the problem, your audience will react favorably to your perseverance. Many will admire you for doing what they feel they cannot do.

Summary

    A public speech must make an immediate and direct adaptation to an audience. Therefore, the vocal and physical aspects of delivery are vital parts of communication.

There are four methods of delivering a speech: from manuscript, from memory, impromptu, and extemporaneously. Of these, extemporaneous speaking is by far your best choice except when you cannot avoid another method.

There are six principles for using your voice to communicate meaning:

1. Speak loudly enough
2. Emphasize important words
3. Make clear distinctions among ideas
4. Make words convey feelings
5. Use standard conventions of pronunciation
6. Speak in a conversational manner

Physical action is as much a part of your speech as ideas or voice. An audience judges you and your ideas by what it sees as well as by what it hears. Consequently, controlled physical action is an important part of effective delivery. Perhaps the most important visual aspect of communication is eye contact; look directly at your audience. Stand before the audience with a relaxed but not too casual posture. The way you move to and from the speaking position helps to show your enthusiasm, but you should not pace around the room during your speech. Gestures should be full and complete rather than choppy and undeveloped, defined rather than vague. Facial expression should express what you think.

If you have problems with nervousness (and probably 75 percent of all people do), remember that you never actually look or sound as bad as you think you do; the symptoms of your anxiety are frequently not even noticed.

There are several ways you can relieve the tension of communication anxiety: (1) Don't blame yourself; (2) Realize the importance of experience; (3) Choose situations with high potential for success; (4) Concentrate on the message; (5) Prepare thoroughly; (6) Adopt a conversational attitude; (7) Play the role of the confident speaker.

Key Terms

Manuscript	Pronunciation
Memorization	Conversational manner
Impromptu	Eye contact
Extemporaneous	Posture
Meaning	Movement
Loudness	Gestures
Emphasis	Facial expression
Clear distinctions	Anxiety
Feelings	Stage fright

Exercises

1. There are many opportunities to observe, analyze, and evaluate the part that vocal behavior plays in communication: The public platform, the pulpit, the theater, legislative assemblies, and the like. Observe one of these instances of communication and write a 500-word paper analyzing and evaluating the effectiveness of the part played by the use of voice in helping the speaker or performer communicate.

2. Make a recording of your own speech. Listen to the recording and evaluate how effectively you use your voice to communicate.

3. Prepare and deliver a speech in which you consciously prepare some gestures to use at certain points in the speech. Does this help your speaking?

4. Prepare and deliver a speech on how to do something requiring physical action: for example, hitting the backhand tennis shot, playing the guitar, or making a quilt. Don't use any visual aids. Communicate your information only with words and physical action.

Notes

[1] Barnett Pearce and Bernard J. Brommel, "Vocalic Communication in Persuasion," *Quarterly Journal of Speech* 58 (1972): 305.

[2] Raymond Ross, *Speech Communication* (Englewood Cliffs, NJ: Prentice-Hall, 1974) 91-92. Estimates of the percentage of beginning speakers who have a problem serious enough to require special therapy vary between 5 and 20 percent. Gerald M. Phillips, "Reticences: Pathology of the Normal Speaker," *Speech Monographs* 35 (1968): 42; James C. McCroskey, "The Implementation of a Large-Scale Program of Systematic Desensitization for Communication Apprehension," *Speech Teacher* 21 (1972): 260.

[3] *London Sunday Times* 7 Oct 1973.

[4] Linda C. Lederman, "High Communication Apprehensives Talk About Communication Apprehension and Its Effect on Their Behavior," *Communication Quarterly* 31 (1983): 233-37; Judee K. Burgoon and Jerold L. Hale, "A Research Note on the Dimensions of Communication Reticence," *Communication Quarterly* 31 (1983): 238-48.

[5] Joe Ayres, "Perceptions of Speaking Ability: An Explanation for Stage Fright," *Communication Education* 35 (1986): 275-285; Ralph R. Behnke, Chris R. Sawyer and Paul E. King, "The Communication of Public Speaking Anxiety," *Communication Education* 36 (1987): 138-41.

[6] For a summary of the major clinical approaches to serious speech apprehension, see Susan R. Glaser, "Oral Communication Apprehension and Avoidance: The Current Status of Treatment Research," *Communication Education* 30 (1981): 321-41.

[7] Michael Weissberg and Douglas Lamb, "Comparative Effects of Cognitive Modification, Systematic Desensitization, and Speech Preparation in the Reduction of Speech and General Anxiety," *Communication Monographs* 44 (1977): 27-36.

8 Kim Giffin and Shirley Masterson Gilham, ''Relationship Between Speech Anxiety and Motivation,'' *Speech Monographs* 38 (1971): 70-73; John A. Daly, Anita L. Vangelisti, Heather L. Neal, and P. Daniel Cavanaugh, ''Pre-Performance Concerns Associated with Public Speaking Anxiety,'' *Communication Quarterly* 37 (1989): 39-53.

9 Joe Ayres and Theodore S. Hopf, ''Visualization: A Means of Reducing Speech Anxiety,'' *Communication Education* 34 (1985):318-23.

Part Five

Types of Speaking Situations

Speaking to Inform

We are living in a period of "information explosion." The rate at which knowledge is increasing is startling. Although breakthroughs in science and technology are the most publicized, other areas of research make interesting and significant discoveries as well. In 1990, anthropologists found the bodies of hastily buried Confederate soldiers in the graveyard of a church destroyed in the Battle of Brandy Station during the Civil War. Because of recent scientific advances, researchers were able to identify who these soldiers were, where they were from, their social class, and the kind of work they did.[1] The expansion of knowledge in all fields has made both storing and retrieving information a problem of logistics.

The wealth of available information must first be organized and then communicated to be useful. One means of communicating information is the informative speech. In Chapter 5, we defined the purpose of the informative speech as giving an audience an understanding of a subject it would not otherwise have. Sometimes this means that a target audience knows little or nothing about a subject; at other times the listeners may know a lot but you want to give them a new way of looking at it. Experienced professionals attend workshops and professional meetings for similar reasons—they get new information and also learn of new ways to look at what they already know.

Informative speeches have a variety of names: "demonstrations," "instructions," "explanations," "oral reports," and "descriptions." In business, the popular term is "presentation" and probably includes visual aids, a flip chart, and/or slides, but it is an informative speech nonetheless. Although the names and emphases may differ, they are all essentially the same. The purpose is to present the audience with information it would not have had without the speech.

Understanding is a product of the transaction between you and your audience. We have said several times throughout this book that what an audience understands you to say—not what you intended to say—is, in fact, what you did say. In order for your intention and the audience's understanding to be as nearly identical as possible, your speaking has to have those twins we have mentioned so often before: interest and clarity. Your speech has to be interesting enough to make people *want* to listen to you and clear enough for them to understand you accurately. The remainder of this chapter is organized around five steps that should help you make this happen.

1. Determine the specific subject of the speech
2. Organize the body of the speech
3. Add supporting materials
4. Prepare the conclusion and the introduction
5. Practice the delivery

Determine the Specific Subject

Choosing a subject is the important first step in preparing a speech of any kind. (Review Chapter 5 for advice on how to select a topic.) Your first choice will probably be both broad and vague (mental illness, drugs, pesticides, deforestation). Consequently, before you can make an outline, and even before you begin to gather materials, you need to establish what the specific subject will be. To do this, you first limit the scope or breadth of your topic and then you formulate a precise statement of your specific subject.

Limiting the Subject

There are two ways of limiting a speech subject. The most common solution is to narrow the focus to a particular segment of the topic. On some occasions, however, you might want to paint the subject with a broader brush. In that case, you can select a number of aspects of the broader subject and narrow each of those to suit your discussion. Let's see how these two limiting processes work.

Narrowing the scope of a subject   Determining the scope of a speech usually means limiting or narrowing the subject so that you can develop your ideas in sufficient detail within the time limit of your speech. Keep in mind what your listeners want or need to know. This will help you eliminate extraneous information and focus on the information which best satisfies the needs of your audience.

Your first reaction to a narrowed topic may be that you won't have enough to say. If you prepare for your speech correctly, you will probably find that you have too much material!

Here are some ways to narrow your topic:

1. *Limit the subject in time.* The general subject "pesticides" might be narrowed to a discussion of "The controversy over the urban spraying for medflies in Southern California." A music major who grew up in New Orleans might narrow the subject of music to "The origins of Jazz." A discussion on drugs could be limited to the current medical information on the consequences of using marijuana.

2. *Limit the subject in space.* Deforestation is far too broad a subject for a single speech. It can be the source of a successful speech subject, however, if you limit your discussion. For instance, "The deforestation of the Brazilian rain forest" would be sufficiently focused by geographical area to be an effective speech topic.

3. *Narrow the subject to a subproblem.* Select part of a larger problem as the specific topic of your speech. Instead of discussing energy conservation, for example, Owen isolated the subproblem of the economics of solar energy.

4. *Discuss a portion of a process.* Janice is a prelaw student and also an Army veteran assigned to the office of the Judge Advocate General. She wanted to talk about the administration of justice. She made a very interesting talk on the differences between a court martial and a civilian trial.

It is not necessary to narrow a subject by all of these methods, but here is an example of a single topic limited by all four methods.

General subject: International diplomacy

Narrowed in space: Central America

Narrowed to a subproblem: Nicaraguan presidential election

Narrowed in time: February 1989

Narrowed to a portion of a process: The role of foreign monitors to insure an honest election

Treating a series of narrowed aspects of a subject   Sometimes the speech situation is such that you might not want to narrow the scope. Since you still have the same limits on time available, the number of points and the breadth of those points must be restricted even if the scope is broad. For example, an anthropology major wanted to show that the cultures of Native Americans are very diverse and do not fit the stereotypes they are given. He chose three frequent misconceptions and three tribal groups (Algonquin, Iroquois and Blackfoot) to illustrate the errors in the stereotypes. Here is the outline of the body of his speech:

Statement of Purpose: To show the diversity in Native American culture by showing three tribal groups that do not fit their stereotypes.

I. Indians are nomadic people who follow the hunt — Algonquin
   A. Lived in organized villages with streets
   B. Had extensive agricultural plots
      1. Corn
      2. Pumpkin
      3. Tobacco
      4. Sunflowers
      5. Squash
   C. Dishes like succotash, hominy and corn pone come from agricultural tribes such as the Algonquin.

II. Indians organize around individual tribes and tribal groups — Iroquois
   A. Iroquois Confederacy in what is now New York State
      1. Mohawk
      2. Oneida
      3. Onondaza
      4. Caguga
      5. Seneca
      6. Tuscarora
   B. Democracy to make decisions on matters affecting all tribes

1. Tribal chiefs held seats based on numbers of members
2. Emphasis on diplomacy and speeches
3. Benjamin Franklin—"It would be a very strange thing if six nations of ignorant savages should be capable of forming a scheme for such a union . . . and yet that a like union should be impracticable for ten or a dozen English colonies to whom it is more necessary."

III. Indians are very warlike—Blackfoot
   A. Combat before white man's weapons was more of a pastime
   B. "Counting Coup"—touching or taking something from an enemy
   C. Horse raiding—most common kind of war action—stealth, surprise, quick escape
   D. Taking an enemy weapon rated highest—"namachkani," Blackfoot word for war honor (means "a gun taken")
   E. Killing frequently not even recognized for an honor

Formulating a Statement of Purpose

Once you have limited your subject, a clear statement of purpose will help you select materials and organize the ideas of your speech. The most common procedure for making a statement of purpose is to formulate an infinitive phrase that identifies your goal in speaking, specifies the subject of the speech, and sets its precise scope. It identifies exactly what idea you want to clarify for your audience. For instance:

> To inform the audience of the current economic limitations on the extensive use of solar energy.
> To inform the audience about the differences between a military court martial and a civilian trial.
> To inform the audience of how Native American culture diverges from its stereotypes.

The written statement of purpose is used as a guide for your speech preparation. It will help you to decide what material belongs in the speech and what does not. You can always find many interesting ideas and tempting pieces of material to put into a speech. The problem is one of selection: including those items that are essential to the specific purpose and rejecting those that are not. Once it is formed, the statement of purpose should be used as a rigorous standard by which to identify necessary materials and to eliminate those that are unneeded.

Organize the Body of the Speech

The earliest writers on public speaking recognized good order as an essential ingredient in effective communication. We say "good" order and "effective" communication because, no matter how badly you may jumble your ideas and materials, you will still communicate something. Without careful organization, you have very little assurance that what you mean to say will bear much resemblance to what your audience thinks you mean. If a speech is to make the impression you want, its parts should be so related that the speech as a whole is easy to understand and easy to remember.

An effective speech normally has an introduction, a body and a conclusion. Organize the body of the speech first because it contains all the essential material implied in the statement of purpose. The introduction and the conclusion are important to the extent that they help you to say clearly what is in the body.

Organizing the body of a speech is a process that takes place in two steps: first, you determine the major points and how many of those you will cover. Second, you decide the best order for arranging the parts.

Determining Major Points

Dividing the subject into parts is necessary because the whole idea of the subject cannot be communicated at once. The component ideas must be given to the audience one at a time. Analyzing your subject will tell you what these components are and will help you judge what kinds of information are needed to satisfy the demands of the occasion.

This analysis is accomplished by looking at the subject to determine what its major divisions are. What are the component parts? Some divisions come quite naturally out of the established understanding of the field: Executive, Legislative, Judicial; animal, vegetable, mineral; before, during, after; string, brass, woodwind, percussion; etc.

If you wanted to discuss current medical information about the consequences of using marijuana, as Kathleen did, you could divide the speech by the parts of the human body affected: heart, lungs, brain.

Greg saw the opportunity for another interesting and worthwhile kind of informative speech on the same controversial subject. In his analysis, he looked for the issues that caused the differences of opinion in the matter. The purpose of his speech was to give the audience a clear understanding of the arguments on both sides of the debate over the legalization of marijuana.

You can see that this analysis is different from the standard sort of informative analysis that would lead to main points like animal, vegetable, mineral. Instead, it is the analysis we described in Chapter 7 as the one you would use for a persuasive speech.

The body of Greg's speech looked like this:

I. Do law makers have the right to interfere with an individual's free choice to protect him/her from harm?
   A. For legalization
   B. Against legalization
II. Can marijuana be useful to society?

A. For legalization
B. Against legalization
III. Do the costs of laws making marijuana legal outweigh the benefits?
A. For legalization
B. Against legalization

Notice that these issues (as you would expect in a policy speech) are related to the stock issues. The first is an issue over need for a change; the second asks about desirability, and the third is related to workability. If you made a speech of this sort about a disputed claim of fact or value, the stock issues would not be relevant.

Determining the major points in the body of the speech is the first part of analysis. But, what if your analysis doesn't give you a nice neat package of three or four points? What if it seems to say there are ten points? Then the second part of informative analysis becomes important: determining how many points should be in the body of your speech.

Determining the Number of Points

Research on information processing has long shown that the number of individual pieces of information the mind will retain is quite limited. The popular formula says, "Seven, give or take two." Some researchers say fewer, others say more.[2] Whether five, nine or twelve, the important point to remember is that there is a real limit to human retention. In a short speech of less than ten minutes, it makes sense to keep the number of points in the body of a speech between two and five. More than this number gives the audience too much to remember. You probably can't get more speaking time, so choose another topic if your initial choice requires more explanation.

Another problem you may encounter is that while the number of points fit the requirements, each one is too lengthy. The four divisions of a symphony orchestra fall in the two to five point range, but each (String, Brass, Woodwind, Percussion) must be narrowed or there will be far too much material. Think of all the different instruments that come under each of these: violin, cello, drum, flute, xylophone, triangle, etc. Narrowing becomes a problem of redefining the points.

If the number of main points is too many or if the scope of one or more of the points is too great, you need to return to the methods of limiting the subject. So, the segments of the symphony orchestra become the *major function* of each of the four segments of a symphony orchestra. Or, *the issues* in the legalization of marijuana become *the most widely contested issues.* You may have noticed that the three issues Greg identified are not the only ones. What about the morality issue? What about marijuana as a stepping stone to drugs like cocaine? It's clear Greg limited the issues on which he spoke.

The number of main points in the speech is also controlled to a large extent by the time you have available for speaking. Allow at least a minute to develop each of the major headings in the body of your speech. Thus, if your speech is to be 5 minutes long, four points in the body would be a maximum since you also need time for an introduction and conclusion. Even in a seven-minute speech, three points are not too few. If you have more time, it is much wiser to concentrate on extending the development of a few points rather than on increasing the number.

Patterns of Arrangement

Once your analysis has identified the main points of the subject, the next step is to decide how to arrange the parts into a pattern that will maintain interest and impart a unified body of information. Look for the organizational pattern that will best help your audience understand and remember what you say. There are several methods of arranging an informative speech to achieve clarity and retention. We are going to describe the six most common ones: chronological, spatial, topical, definition, comparison and contrast, cause and effect.

Chronological pattern   Many subjects fall naturally into a historical or chronological sequence of presentation. Helen was an avid horsewoman who wanted to speak about the American quarter horse, so she narrowed her subject to the development of this breed. The outline of the body of her speech looked like this:

Statement of Purpose: To inform the audience about the major steps in the development of the American quarter horse

I. Spanish horses were brought to Mexico and the Southwest in the 16th century
   A. They were of Arabian ancestry
   B. They had been selectively bred to provide
      1. Cow sense
      2. Stamina
      3. Speed

II. American Colonists developed horses and brought them to the Southwest in the 19th Century
   A. They were of two types
      1. Work horses
      2. Thoroughbreds
   B. They had their own special characteristics
      1. Work horses—strength
      2. Thoroughbreds—speed

III. The American quarter horse is a crossbreed of these types
   A. They were unique
      1. Thoroughbred's speed
      2. Spanish horse's small size and cow sense
      3. Work horse's strength and stamina

B. They served several purposes
1. Cow ponies
2. Raced short distances

Spatial pattern Another common pattern of arrangement is by location. This pattern shows the relationship of one point to another in space. The following example is appropriately organized in a spatial pattern. It explains the parallel between altitude and latitude. This example is particularly interesting because two geographical principles are at work in one speech and it helps a listener to understand *why* and *how* as well as *where*.

Statement of Purpose: To inform the audience of the parallel relationship between the plant life of a region and the region's altitude and distance from the equator

I. Tropical forests flourish near sea level and near the equator
   A. Climatic conditions
   B. Typical plants
II. Deciduous forests occur in temperate zones at low altitudes
   A. Climatic conditions
   B. Typical plants
III. Coniferous forests grow far from the equator and at higher altitudes
   A. Climatic conditions
   B. Typical plants
IV. Mosses, lichens, and low herbaceous growths are characteristic of the far North and areas above timber line
   A. Climatic conditions
   B. Typical plants
V. Ice and snow cap both polar regions and the highest mountains
   A. Climatic conditions
   B. Typical plants

Topical pattern Any method of partitioning that divides a subject into its component parts can be called a topical pattern. In this sense, both the chronological and the spatial patterns of organization are special forms of topical arrangement. The topical pattern is considered as a separate method of organization to accommodate natural or traditional classifications that are neither chronological nor geographical. We have mentioned several of them already: animal, vegetable, and mineral; political, social, and economic; executive, legislative, and judicial; strings, percussion, woodwinds, and brass. Any subject that can be analyzed into component parts can be organized by the method of topical arrangement. Here is an example of topical partition developed for an informative speech by Rene.

Statement of Purpose: To inform the audience of the most important threats of stress to the human body

I. Threats to the cardiovascular system
   A. Heart attack
   B. Hypertension

    C. Migraine

  II. Threats to the digestive system
    A. Ulcers
    B. Constipation
    C. Diarrhea
    D. Cancer

 III. Threats to the immunity screen
    A. Infections
    B. Allergies
    C. Cancer

 IV. Threats to the skeletal—muscular system
    A. Tension headaches
    B. Backaches

Pattern of definition   A fourth method of division is by definition. Speeches intended to answer questions like "What is radioactivity?" or "What is a depression?" or "What is a Socialist?" can often use as a system of main heads one of the methods of definition discussed in Chapter 8.

Statement of Purpose: To inform the audience of the essential nature of jazz

  I. Jazz is a form of popular music indigenous to the United States
    A. Jazz originated in New Orleans
    B. Jazz began just after World War I

 II. Jazz differs from other popular music
    A. It differs from spirituals
    B. It differs from western music
    C. It differs from folk music of the hill country

 III. Jazz takes several forms
    A. Dixieland
    B. Blues
    C. Progressive jazz

The pattern follows the rules of formal definition. It first puts jazz into a general class: American popular music. Then, it differentiates jazz from other types of American popular music. Identification of genus (classification) and species (differentiation) are the only essential steps in organizing the topic by the pattern of definition. However, explaining some of its diverse forms helps to identify exactly what jazz is.

Pattern of comparison and contrast   For clarifying ideas, speakers often use the similarities and differences between two items or concepts when an audience is familiar with one of them and not familiar with the other. Comparison and contrast are not only useful forms of supporting material, they also can be used as an organizing principle for an informative speech. Both comparison and contrast can be used separately in defining, supporting and organizing, but here is a speech in which the materials are organized by both comparison and contrast:

Statement of Purpose: To inform the audience of the nature of white-collar crime

   I. Like many other forms of larceny it does not physically threaten the victim.
     A. Theft is nonviolent and engenders no fear
     B. Shoplifting is nonviolent and causes no fear

  II. Like confidence games, it often depends upon being trusted

 III. It is different from many other crimes
     A. It is defined in a different sense
       1. The criminal is defined in terms of a class: "a person in business, government or a profession"
       2. The definition emphasizes the method by which the crime is committed, not the fruit of the crime: "fraud ... committed ... in the course of one's occupation"
     B. It is different from crimes of violence such as murder and rape
       1. It does not physically injure a victim
       2. It is not directed at individuals
     C. It is different from robbery and burglary
       1. It does not engender fear
       2. There is no physical threat

Pattern of Cause and Effect   When you want to explain what caused an event or when you want to explain the consequences of some event, you can use a cause-and-effect order. You would employ this pattern to explain either the causes for the demolition of the Berlin Wall or the effects of radioactivity on the human body. Although either can be used separately, in the following example, Marsha used both cause and effect in the same organizational pattern to clarify the subject more fully.

Statement of Purpose: To inform the audience about one of the major threats to our environment—acid rain

   I. Two main kinds of damage result from acid rain
     A. Damage to the world's fresh water supply
       1. In Canada 14,000 lakes have lost almost all fish
       2. 25% of the lakes in the Adirondacks cannot support fish
       3. By the year 2000, half of the streams in Pennsylvania will not support fish
       4. More than half of the drinking water reservoirs in Massachusetts are losing their ability to neutralize the acid
     B. Damage to crops and forests
       1. Half of the trees above the 850 meter [2800 foot] level in northeastern New York have died over the last 25 years
       2. Within the next 10 years, the sugar maple industry will lose $40 million
       3. Billions of dollars worth of crops will be destroyed

  II. The principle cause of this damage is burning fossil fuels
     A. Pollutants are released
       1. An estimated 25-30 tons of sulfur dioxide per year from electric power plants, ore smelters and chemical plants

   2. An estimated 15 tons per year of nitrogen oxide from autos
      and industrial furnaces
   B. Transformed in the atmosphere into sulfuric and nitric acids
   C. Returns to earth with the rain

Using Multiple Patterns of Arrangement

In organizing an informative speech, you want a method of arrangement
that pulls together the elements of the subject, most naturally expresses
the sequence of ideas for your listeners, and makes it easier for them to
understand.

You need not always use a single method of partitioning. It is quite
possible that your ideas will become clearer if you combine two (or even
more) of the methods. In some instances, the subject lends itself to multiple
levels of arrangement. Looking back at the speech defining jazz, you will
see that the first main head suggests a chronological development, the
second appears to be developed by contrast, and the third could very well
be developed with definitions by example.

We have already noted that the chronological and spatial patterns are
also topical. We could add that cause and effect must be chronological since
causes must occur before effects. So, both cause to effect and effect to cause
are chronological sequences. These naturally occurring multiple orders are
not as significant as those you choose deliberately. Finding several
rationales for your organization and making your audience aware of them
enhances the audience's sense of organization of the speech. The following
example illustrates this principle.

Statement of Purpose: To explain the legal process of extradition

I. Extradition is the surrender of an alleged criminal by one governmental
   entity to another
   A. In international practice, it can be likened to other treaty arrangements
   B. It differs from other instances of forcible removal
      1. Banishment
      2. Expulsion
      3. Deportation
II. There are two kinds
   A. International—between countries
   B. Interstate—within the United States
III. It has a long history
   A. Known in ancient and medieval times
   B. Developed chiefly after the eighteenth century
      1. Belgian law of 1833
      2. United States statute of 1848
      3. Netherlands act of 1849

The basic pattern of organization is clearly *topical*. But each of the
subordinate headings is developed in its own way, not necessarily the same

as the main pattern. The first main heading is a definition, but it is developed by comparison and contrast; the second main heading is given a topical development; and the third main heading is developed chronologically. Thus, not only does the speech have an overall pattern, but each of the points is organized by a separate pattern. Taken together, the multiplicity of patterns (because each is appropriate) is valuable in strengthening the unity of the speech.

In contrast, notice the lack of order in the following outline:

Statement of Purpose: To inform the audience of the essential nature of atheism

   I. Early Greeks
      A. Two meanings for atheism
         1. Believing in foreign or strange gods
         2. Believing that there are no gods
      B. The original Greek word was "atheos."

  II. Atheism and Communism
      A. Associated with international socialist movement
      B. Part of the state philosophy of some communist countries

 III. Atheists and agnostics differ in their beliefs
      A. Neither is convinced of the existence of God
      B. Lack of evidence convinces atheists that God does not exist
      C. Proof one way or another needed for agnostics to believe

 IV. Atheism today

The first main point appears to promise a chronological development. The second point shifts ground, however, and appears to be a topical heading of the central idea. The third point introduces yet another pattern in the form of comparison and contrast. The fourth point returns to the original chronological pattern. The result is a mishmash of tangled ideas. Even if each main point individually is made clear, the listeners will probably have only a confused notion of what atheism is. Imposing multiple patterns of organization on a speech is an advantage only when they are compatible and the variations contribute to a coherent and unified framework.

Add Supporting Materials

After you have established the organizational pattern of the body, you are ready to develop these main points by adding supporting material. Listeners usually grasp an idea more readily when it is associated with some object, person, or event that they already know or can easily visualize. The more vividly your examples, statistics, definitions, and quotations revitalize experiences that listeners have had, the better are your chances of making your speech interesting and clear. For this reason, it is a good rule of thumb to use at least one supporting detail for every important idea you bring into a speech.

Variety in supporting detail is a further help toward building interest. If you use statistics or hypothetical examples exclusively, or nothing but quotations, you may lose the attention of an audience because your materials lack variety. Even supporting material which lacks variety is preferable to having no material at all but try to introduce variety whenever you can.

Prepare the Conclusion and the Introduction

When you have organized your ideas and materials into the body of the speech, you have a unified and coherent view of what you want your audience to understand. Then you prepare the conclusion, which essentially summarizes the major ideas in the body. Finally, with a clear understanding of what the speech will say, you can prepare an introduction that will appeal to the interest of the listeners and let them know what the speech is about. The speech follows the rules of the old preacher who said: ''First I tell 'em what I'm gonna' tell 'em. Then I tell 'em. Then I tell 'em what I told 'em.'' Chapter 14 explains in some detail a variety of ways of developing the introduction and the conclusion.

Practice the Delivery

Until it is delivered, a speech is a growing thing, representing your increasing awareness of the subject and the target audience. For this reason, it will continually change while you are working on it. You will shift points around, replace one example with a better one, or consider new ways of partitioning the ideas.

Perhaps because so much emphasis in education is put on written communication, it is easy to think of a speech as something to write out and read. There is a temptation to prepare a careful outline and then to stop revising it and begin practicing the delivery. But a speech is not ''an essay standing on its hind legs.'' Consequently, it should be tried out *orally*, in parts and as a whole, from the early stages of preparation. As soon as you have drawn up the first rough approximation of your speech, begin to ''talk it through.'' But the revisions don't stop there. As you hear things you don't like, change them, and improve them. The outline should be developed in the atmosphere of oral, not written, communication. With this kind of preparation, the speech will become part of you; more and more it will grow into a communication that reflects your ideas, your knowledge, and your individual personality.

Summary

There is an information explosion in the world today. To be useful, all this information must be organized and communicated effectively. Therefore, skill in informative speaking is both necessary and desirable. To insure that the information you give will be interesting and clear, follow five steps in preparing an informative speech:

1. Select and narrow the subject, and formulate a statement of purpose. The more conventional methods of narrowing a subject include: limiting it to a specific segment of time; limiting the subject to a particular area (space); narrowing the subject to a subproblem in a larger controversy; or discussing the subject as single portion of a process. One or more of these methods may be used. A speech topic may also be narrowed by discussing limited treatments of selected aspects of the whole subject. Narrowing the whole gives a limited scope to the subject by developing in detail a very restricted view of it; narrowing the discussion to specific aspects of the subject gives a broader view without sacrificing concreteness and detail.

2. Determine the main points and organize them into the body of the speech. Organizing the body of a speech involves determining the main points, limiting them for the purposes of the speech, and choosing the best pattern of arrangement. The number of points needs to be kept between two and five so that you will have time to develop them adequately and the audience will be able to remember them. One or more of several patterns of organization may be used to impose a clear and reasonable sequence on the ideas of the speech, both in the main points and in their subheadings: (1) chronological, (2) spatial, (3) topical, (4) definition, (5) comparison and contrast, and (6) cause and effect. Multiple patterns of arrangement can be used to strengthen the unity of the speech.

3. Add the supporting details. Use a variety of supporting materials to bring your ideas sharply into focus for your audience (Chapter 8).

4. Prepare the conclusion and the introduction. For specific information of these points, see Chapter 14.

5. Practice the delivery. Familiarize yourself thoroughly with the ideas and materials of the speech by ''talking it through'' from the early stages of preparation. With the ideas firmly in mind, you will be able to deliver the speech with fluency, vigor, and conversational spontaneity.

Key Terms

Interest	Chronological pattern
Clarity	Spatial pattern
Scope	Topical pattern
Time	Pattern of definition
Space	Comparison and contrast
Subproblem	Cause and effect
Portion of a process	Multiple patterns
Statement of purpose	Preparing delivery
Number of points	

Exercises

1. Organize and deliver a five-to seven-minute informative speech on a topic selected from the subject matter of a course you are now taking (other than your public speaking course). Prepare the outline, and give your instructor a copy before you deliver the speech.

2. Select one item from the following list (or one supplied by your instructor) and prepare two statements of purpose for informative speeches on that subject. In the first instance, narrow the scope and limit the subject by using one of the methods explained in this chapter. In the second statement of purpose, do the same using another of the methods. Formulate a subject sentence for each statement of purpose.

Literature	Medical care
Biology	The national forests
The Middle East	College athletics
Summer jobs for students	Student government
Farming	Sports

3. Illustrate with a brief outline each of the six methods of partitioning the body of an informative speech.

4. With four of your classmates, select a subject for a symposium (each speaker delivers a speech on one specific phase of the general subject). Divide the subject into five subtopics. Have each speaker deliver a five- to seven-minute informative talk on one of the subtopics. The symposium topics might be:

   a. The basic beliefs (nature of man, God, and the relationship between the two) of the five largest non-Christian religions of the world.
   b. The main responsibilities of the five major executive officers of your state.
   c. The five most prevalent types of crime in your city.
   d. The philosophy of writing of five contemporary novelists.

5. Write a paper (no more than three double-spaced typewritten pages) evaluating either the "Genetic Profiling" speech or the "Country

Western Music,'' speech at the end of this chapter. How highly would you rate the speech for organization, interest, and usefulness of information.

6. Write a paper (no more than three double-spaced typewritten pages) evaluating how well the "Battle of the Bugs," speech, found at the end of this chapter, explained the issues in the controversy.

Notes

1 Edwards Park, "Around the Mall and Beyond, *Smithsonian 21* (June 1990) 18-22.

2 George A. Miller, *The Psychology of Communication* (Baltimore: Penguin Books, 1969) 14-44.

Speeches for Study

"Genetic Profiling"
Brenda Dempsey
Eastern Michigan University

1   Mary Stuart was twenty-three, happily married, and pregnant. A prenatal test showed it was a boy. But instead of the impending happiness which usually surrounds expectancy of a child, something was missing. You see, Mary's brother had been born with the crippling disease of Dishend's muscular dystrophy, a genetically inherited disease, which is passed on to boys from otherwise healthy mothers. Statistically, Mary stood a great chance of passing that disease to her unborn son.

2   Traditionally, couples in that type of situation had one of two choices; either to choose simply not to have children, or to take the risk, oftentimes asking themselves in the end, "Why me?" Well today, that very question is being changed. The May 25, 1986 issue of *U.S. News & World Report* explains that through a process called genetic profiling, we're able to locate those genes which make us susceptible to disease, allowing us to effectively predict what health risks lie ahead for us ten, twenty, even forty years ahead.

3   How could prospective parents like Mary, or even ourselves, develop healthy habits from this, so that we could possibly prevent a disease, so that it never develops? I realize that lately there has been some controversy surrounding the ethics of genetic profiling. However, most people will be receiving these profiles by the year 2,000, according to Michael McGuinness, Director of the United States Office for Disease Prevention and Health Promotion. What is vital, then, is that we understand the applications of genetic profiling, so that like Michael McGuinness we too can unlock the secrets behind the question of, "Why me?" and instead have a say in the answer of "Why not me?"

4   Now with that in mind, let's take a look at what genetic profiling is, some of its current applications, and finally what uses lie for us in the future.

5   Now the idea of looking at our genes for some type of answer is nothing new. But until recently, we had no idea exactly what we inherited from our parents. At the most we had what you could call "guess" genes. Now all that has changed. Through genetic profiling, we are able to locate those genes which make us susceptible to disease. And unfortunately we're all susceptible. Dr. Albrey Malenski, Director for the Center of Human Genetics at Boston University School of Medicine explains in the April 21, 1987 issue of the *New York Times*, we're all susceptible. Every healthy person has between four and eight harmful genes. Now that doesn't mean that we're going to contract any disease, just that the presence of those genes in our bodies make us more susceptible to one type of disease or another. To locate a defective [gene] a gene probe is performed. The process begins by extracting DNA from a sample of our blood. [Figure 1] Now as you can see, DNA looks like kind of a spiral ladder, with each section of this ladder having a specific function being called a gene. Of these genes there are thousands of code messages, as shown by the coded sequence on the rungs of the ladder. The sequences are passed down from generation to generation. You'll remember from one of your basic biology classes, it's the genes that make us who we are, why we have brown hair instead of blonde, or blue eyes instead of hazel, but most importantly, why we are more susceptible to one disease over another.

6   Now if there is an error or a misspelling of this coding sequence, or two wrongs not making a right [we have a problem]. To locate that defective gene then, this DNA matter is broken, [Figure 2] and as you can see, that break will cause the DNA matter to unsettle. Now the researcher will then take one strain of our human DNA, and combine it with one strain of artificial, radioactive DNA. And it will combine that human DNA [until it] also becomes radioactive, then a defective gene has been located.

7   Well, while this process here effectively pinpoints where that defective gene is, other genes are still a warning step. The March 1987 issue of *Changing Times* explains that in that situation, researchers have to settle for a chemically detectable marker. That's a gene located near the faulty gene and will be genetically inherited with it. While it is not the defective gene itself, just a marker, there is still a ninety-five percent chance that if it possesses the marker it also possesses the defective gene.

8   The April 21, 1987 issue of the *New York Times* explains that it is this technique that is allowing for the rapid explosion of important genetic findings. An explosion so fast, it seems researchers are joining the gene of the week club, allowing us to take a great leap forward in understanding ourselves.

9   So, now that we know what genetic profiling is, let's take a look and see how it is used. By doing so we can see how that intricate art of genetics is being brought to the level of the common man. And, in these past five years alone, researchers have racked up an impressive list of accomplishments, finding genetic markers to nearly fifteen different diseases. Gene probes, sometimes performed even before birth, are now available to those who suffer from everything from cystic fibrosis to the fragile exintron, including

hemophilia, sickle cell anemia, even adult polysistic kidney disease which affects over half a million people in the United States alone.

10   The February 1988 issue of *Scientific American* explains that gene probes are also available to those suffering from mental illnesses, such as Alzheimers or Hodgkins' Disease. While there are still no effective cures for these diseases, this early diagnosis is helping to prevent many of their traumatic effects. And it is this philosophy of prevention, through early diagnosis, that is giving this science its strength.

11   The idea of knowing our susceptibilities beforehand, thereby allows us to make creative choices as to how we live our lives, to possibly prevent the disease so that it never develops. Explains Ori Friedman, Chairman of Cooperative Research, "If I were predisposed to alcoholism, I wouldn't take my first drink."

12   Now that type of philosophy is widespread, not only interpersonally, but in the community as well. For example, when researchers found a genetic marker for dyslexia, which is a reading disorder that affects over fifteen million Americans, well, plans were made immediately to screen children at an early age, and then offer remedial training for those diagnosed [with this disease]. You see what happens many times as well, is that a dyslexic child will be wrongly labeled as being mentally retarded or a slow achiever. However, through this early diagnosis, they hope to not only reduce these traumatic effects, but eliminate that logic error. After looking at what this science has achieved in the past five years alone, when we look to the future of genetic profiling, we can see that it can't be anything but bright.

13   Right now researchers are on the threshold of finding genetic markers to defeat diseases like schizophrenia, arthritis, diabetes, even AIDS. The May 10, 1987 issue of the *New York Times* explains that researchers have now found a genetic link to AIDS, explaining why one person is more susceptible to contracting that disease over others.

14   But perhaps the biggest breakthrough, which impact will be reaching us within the next two years, is in the area of heart disease, particularly arterial sclerosis, which is a plaque build-up within our arteries. Right now arterial sclerosis often goes undiagnosed, at least until the person suffers a heart attack, or their arteries have been irreparably damaged. But in 1983, Drs. Michael Brown and Joseph Goldstein, geneticists at the University of Texas Health Center discovered that arterial sclerosis was genetically linked with one in four of us at risk of contracting some type of cardio-vascular disease. Not only did that breakthrough earn them a 1985 Nobel Prize in Medicine, but it also made it possible for widespread screening of arterial sclerosis with the next two years.

15   Well, that early diagnosis is allowing us to make such choices. Whether or not we should eat more bran cereal in the morning, or whether or not we should change our diet and exercise habits, possibly being able to prevent the buildup of these fats in our arteries altogether. Ori Friedman explains, that if this type of experimentation and success continues with such fervor, soon we will no longer have to treat just the symptoms of disease, we'll be treating the causes of disease itself. And in the distant future, being able to genetically correct a disease, by replacing a defective gene with a healthy one.

16   It is simply amazing that we are now reaching the ultimate vision of every physician since Hippocrates. The ability to prevent disease through early diagnosis. And by understanding what genetic profiling is, and how it is currently expanding our horizons of medicine, we can see that for people like Mary Stuart, there are answers to some of those difficult questions.

17   Concerned for the health of her child, Mary attended one of the over 1,000 genetic counseling centers across the United States, one of which is located right here in Tempe, and found that her child was not predisposed to muscular dystrophy. For people like Mary Stuart, and even ourselves, well we're getting new meaning to the phrase, patient, heal thyself.

Reprinted with the permission of the American Forensic Association from *1988 Championship Debates and Speeches* eds. John K. Boaz and James R. Brey (Annandale, VA: Speech Communication Association/American Forensic Association, 1988) 136-39.

"Country Western Music"

Arnold Rosenthal

California State University, Northridge

1   You've heard it said that the kind of music we call jazz originated in the United States, and it did. But there's another kind of music that was born and raised in America. It's country music, country western music to be more specific: music of the common man, truck driver music, cowboy music, hillbilly music and honky-tonk music.

2   In all its guises and forms, bluegrass, heart songs, western ballads, delta white soul, Memphis honky-tonk and, of course, the pop hybrid known as the Nashville sound, country music is growing astronomically in popularity and there's no sign that its popularity is going to stop. Today, for example, people like you and me spend $400 million a year to buy recordings of it. That's a fifth of the $2 billion spent in annual record sales.

3   It seems to me that anything in our culture that commands that much interest and is worth that much money is worth knowing a little something about. So let's look at the origin of country music, its popularity and present appeal, and the underlying significance of one of America's authentic art forms.

4   When people started to settle in our country, they brought with them, among other assets, their music. These settlers lived in separate communities many miles from each other and connected by poor roads. For the most part they had to entertain themselves. The most significant form of entertainment they had came from themselves. It was their music. The music they brought with them has changed very little since then and is referred to today as "folk music" or "rural music." This music told stories about their trials and tribulations and was handed down from generation to generation. It was either sung with no accompaniment or with instruments brought with them from where they had come.

Slide of original instruments

5   These instruments consisted of guitars, mandolins, violins, banjos, flutes, a washboard, spoons, or even two sticks of firewood. I mean anything they could get their hands on could be used as an instrument. Here's an example of one of these folk songs . . . "Down by the Riverside" as done by Peter Seeger:

Taped recording

6   Folk music remained pretty much the same until 1917 when America entered World War I. As a result of the war, cultural exchanges took place among the soldiers who had come from all over the country, bringing with them, of course, their own special brands of music. At the same time, radio was coming into its own, and beginning to experiment with recorded music. It is essentially these two events, the war and radio, which brought about a metamorphosis of folk music into country music.

7   Country music's first superstar came in 1927. He was Jimmie Rodgers, the Singing Brakeman from Meridian, Mississippi. He worked most of his life on the railroad. It's interesting to note that he was most influenced by workgang blacks. In fact, his first hit song, "The Blue Yodel," reflects this influence. This is what it sounded like:

Taped recording

8   The early thirties witnessed not only the depression but a definite turning point in country music's history. It was now apparent that a country boy, singing about his kind of life, could fall into some big money if he merely learned a few tricks.

Slide of cowboys

9   The cowboy movies began bringing big money to former hillbilly singers such as Gene Autry, Roy Rogers, and Tex Ritter. They carried cowboy music into the nation's big cities. Western swing, heavy on the fiddle, and made for dancing, developed in Texas with a Mexican influence.

Slide of newer instruments

10   There were new instruments and new techniques for playing them: the steel guitar, drums, bass fiddle and the electric guitar, just to mention a few.

11   World War II brought country music not only to people of this country, but to people all over the world. For example, in Japan and in Europe today, country music ranks high as one of the most popular forms of entertainment. By the time the war ended, the Grand Ole Opry had become an institution and country music had branched out to the point that it had borrowed the ears of the nation and the world.

12   If Jimmie Rodgers was the first big solo singing star in country music, then Hank Williams was the second. He was more fortunate than Rodgers in that he came along when the nation was hungry for entertainment and had the money to pay for it. Williams was born in 1923 on a tenant farm in Mt. Olive, Alabama. Typical of so many country musicians, the strong early musical

influences on him were the fundamental churches and the southern black street singers. And here's one of his most remembered songs, "Cheatin' Heart":

Taped recording

13   Country music was sailing right along, doing its own thing, having a ball, until Rock 'N' Roll changed everything. Rock snuck up and hit before anybody knew what was going on. It was the beginning of an era that is only now coming into full bloom. In the fifties, in other words, the kids took over and their leader was a snarling ex-hillbilly singer by the name of Elvis Presley:

Slide of Elvis Presley

14   Elvis had been raised on a farm near Tupelo, Mississippi and was country, jazz, blues, and gospel, all rolled into one. He thumped bass fiddle on stage at the Opry at one point and wailed Assembly of God songs back home at another. After hacking out a living as a truck driver, he got to Memphis in 1954 and a recording contract with Sun Records. He recorded this song and the world was ready for him:

Taped recording — "Mystery Train"

15   The country boom, of course, has reverberated far beyond its historic home in Nashville, Tennessee — you hear it in Bakersfield, California, which is known for the scruffier, less-polished sound of Merle Haggard and such other stars as Buck Owens and Freddie Hart. There is another Nashville satellite — Austin, Texas, where Willie Nelson, Jerry Jeff Walker and Michael Murphy are exponents of what might be called progressive country, which has a strong hint of rock.

16   But, Nashville remains the Capitol. The Grand Ole Opry has now moved into a new $15 million auditorium at the Disneyesque Opryland, U.S.A., boasting such country artists as: Tammy Wynette, Dolly Parton, Charlie Rich, Charley Pride, Johnny Rodriquez, Waylon Jennings, Tom T. Hall, George Jones, and Johnny Cash.

17   Country music is a growing phenomenon. With durable syndicated programs like "Hee Haw" and "The Porter Wagoner Show," as well as several annual specials, network TV is hardly ignoring the trend. But the most dramatic illustration of all lies in pop radio. In 1961, the number of stations playing nothing but country stood at a mere 80; now there are over a thousand.

18   Country music has always been the cry of the common man. Today, however, country music is taking on a new sound and a new diversity of messages as well. This year we are celebrating our 200th anniversary, our Bicentennial, and I can't think of anything more American than America's musical art form: Country Western Music, U.S.A., music of the people, by the people, and for the people. In fact, I've gotten into the act myself by writing my own country song and this is how it goes:

19   Well, I'm the world's first Jewish country singer,
     That's what I'm gonna be,
     From Hollywood to Nashville,
     We'll have a Jew . . . Balee,
     I can sing them country songs like all them stars do,

Cause if Charley Pride can make it, Johnny Rodriquez, too,
There ain't no reason on Heaven or Earth
Why Arnold Rosenthal can't make it too.

Printed with the permission of Arnold Rosenthal.

"The Battle of the Bugs"
Steve E. Chapman
Colorado State University

1   In the arena of insect pest control, we have in the far corner the chemical
companies and in the near corner are the proponents of biocontrol which
include environmentalists, entomologists, and health officials. Both groups
have been strongly fighting over the controversy of whether chemical control
of insects should be replaced by biocontrol. Biocontrol methods include the
use of predators and microbes of the insect pests. Predators can include other
insects, birds, fish, rodents, and the microbes can be viruses, bacteria, funguses,
and protozoa that attack the insect pest.

2   In this speech I hope to present you with the issues at the heart of this
controversy. These issues are: Is there a significant problem with using
chemicals to control insects? Are the chemical companies to blame for these
problems? Will the alternative of biocontrol eliminate such problems? And
finally, will the benefits of using biocontrol justify the costs of their
implementation?

3   Let us start with the first issue on whether there are significant problems
associated with using chemicals to control insects. Both sides agree on the
problem that chemicals can cause health problems. The persistent chemicals
such as DDT, chlordane, and dieldrin have been documented by the EPA and
many health organizations to cause nervous system disorders. The disorders
have especially been found in people who apply and are in frequent contact
with such chemicals. Both sides, however, are waiting on the results of possible
long term health effects associated with chemical use.

4   The chemical companies and biocontrol proponents also agree on the
problem that sustained use of a certain chemical can cause resistance in a
population of insects. Resistance is the ability of an insect to detoxify a chemical
rendering it harmless to the insect.

5   As you can see there are problems associated with chemical control, but
are the chemical companies to blame for these problems? The biocontrol
proponents say that they are while the chemical companies say they are not
to blame. The biocontrol proponents back their claim that the chemical
companies are at fault by research done by Stephanie Harris of the Public
Citizen's Health Group. She stated that the estimated cost of research and
development of a single pesticide can cost up to 15 million dollars, with only
a fifteenth of that amount being used for studies on toxic effects on animals

other than insects. Proponents say that this amount is grossly inadequate and that more money should be set aside for testing of new chemicals for possible health hazards. Their reason being that chemically related health problems can cost a person tens of thousands of dollars in medical treatment. Dr. Capinera, an entomologist at Colorado State University, also stated that chemical companies are not worried about resistance since they can just sell users stronger and more expensive chemicals to combat the insect pests.

6   On the other hand, chemical companies say they are not to blame. Dow Chemical Company says that all their chemicals are explicitly labeled with safe and proper ways of applying them along with any warnings of potential hazards to the user. They say that if the users follow the directions on the label the health hazards would be practically eliminated. On the question of resistance, Dow Chemical said that chemicals only cause resistance in insects if used more often and in higher dosage than stated on the instructions for their use. The chemicals are developed to be applied a certain way to eliminate this problem of resistance.

7   So now that we have both sides pointing fingers at each other, will the alternative of biocontrol eliminate the problems associated with chemicals? The biocontrol proponents say that it will solve the problems of health hazards and resistance and the chemical companies are forced to agree. Research and testing have shown that biocontrol agents act only on specific insects in which they kill. An example is the protozoa *Nosema locustae* which can only infect and kill grasshoppers and cannot live in any other animal. Biocontrol agents would also eliminate the problem of resistance. An analogy to this problem would be like a tiger killing a rabbit, if the tiger is hungry enough there isn't anything that rabbit can do. In other words, there is no way to defend against an attack.

8   Finally, this leads us into the issue of will the benefits of using biocontrol justify the cost of their implementation? This issue is a highly contested one with the biocontrol proponents saying it's effective and economically feasible while the chemical companies say that it will be neither. Biocontrol proponents back up their claim by saying that the benefits are long range control of the pests. The predators and microbes can remain in the system that they are applied to for a long period of time and produce successive generations. An example would be wingless ladybird beetles which remain in the area since they can't fly away and feed on aphids, a major pest of good crops. This would by far offset the initial high cost of implementing many biocontrol agents since it only has to be done once. Chemical companies, however, claim that biocontrol is not effective since most pests, especially aphids, can reproduce under cooler temperatures where biocontrol agents can sometimes not function. Hence, an outbreak of pests can easily happen in cool temperatures. The chemical companies also stated that biocontrol agents can be wiped out by environmental conditions such as weather or seasonal changes. They would then have to be reestablished and if it has to be done seasonally could make the costs very prohibitive.

9   In summary, this controversy over whether biocontrol methods should be used to control insect pests instead of chemicals has both sides agreeing

that chemicals can cause health problems and resistance. However, they wholeheartedly disagree on who's to blame. The biocontrol proponents are pointing their fingers at the chemical companies for the cause of these problems, but the chemical companies are blaming the chemical users for not carefully reading the labels. No matter who's to blame, biocontrol proponents say biocontrol would solve the problems of health hazards and resistance and the chemical companies are forced to agree. However, they disagree on the cost of using biocontrol. The proponents of it say that it is effective and cost efficient since it gives long term control. On the other side, the chemical companies argue that it won't work and is too expensive since the whole system depends on the weather which is too variable. In all, the controversy of whether biocontrol should replace chemicals can go into extra rounds with both sides bringing in new research and evidence every day to prove that their side is right.

Printed with the permission of Steve E. Chapman.

Speaking to Persuade

All speeches, even those that are intended to inform and entertain, influence people in some way by altering their beliefs, values, and actions. In addition, on radio and television you are told daily how you should act or what you should buy. Professors explain ideas but they also show preferences and expect you to choose one accounting system as better than another for a given use, one explanation of America's entry into World War II over another, one interpretation of the poetry of Langston Hughes as better than another, and so on. Your parents have preferences about what career you choose. Clergy of every faith have ideas about how you should lead your life. Politicians tell you why you should accept the policy they believe is best for both the nation and you.

It is difficult to think of communication that is not, in one sense or another, persuasive. As we said in Chapter 5, the essential difference between persuasive speeches and speeches to inform or entertain is that persuasive speeches try to resolve controversy while the others suppress it. This difference is largely dependent on audience attitude toward the topic. In this chapter, we will examine speeches aimed at persuading audiences.

The Nature of Persuasion

When an audience believes that the claim of your speech is controversial, persuasion is necessary. Persuasive speeches differ from other kinds of speeches because they intend to resolve controversy. Not all persuasion is the same. Persuasive situations vary in the objectives called for and the kind of proofs demanded.

The Objectives of Persuasion

Speakers often address audiences that don't know much about the subject or don't have strong views on it. Frequently, even when audiences have strong views on the subject, they agree with the speaker. In addition, individual audiences may well contain a variety of people who agree, disagree, are uninformed, or are uninterested. That is why the concept of the target audience which we introduced in Chapter 6 is so important.

Defining your target audience helps you identify the specific objective of your persuasion. For instance, you might want to persuade your listeners that student body fees should not be increased. Most of your audience will agree with you, but you want that group to carry their belief into action. Those people then become your target audience, and your objective is not to convince them that their belief is correct. You want to *activate* them. In another audience, a large segment might be uninterested in the question. If they are your target audience, you can *motivate* their interest by showing how a raise in fees affects them. Still another audience might be hostile to your purpose. These listeners believe that many worthy projects are hampered by a lack of funds. They want to agitate for an increase in student body fees. If you choose them as a target audience, you want to slow them down, encourage at least some of them to think about the negatives of such a cause. Perhaps you can even *convert* a few to your point of view.

In some cases, a target audience is quite small. People with radical political, social, or religious views frequently talk to hostile audiences but address their persuasion to the few in the crowd who may be willing to consider their proposals. There was a time in our society when, in most circles, you couldn't mention abortion, birth control, two people living together outside marriage, homosexuality, equality for African Americans, equal rights for women, or native American rights. Still speakers spoke on such topics—even went to jail for what they said. They spoke the unspeakable, but a few people listened. They had a limited target audience.

Russell Means offers an example. He is the cofounder of the American Indian Movement. He is an activist, even a radical, by our society's

Russell Means chose to target those members of the audience susceptible to his ideas. He was not interested in tailoring his message to a more general appeal.

standards. In 1980 he spoke during the Black Hills International Survival Gathering at the Pine Ridge Reservation in South Dakota on the theme ''For the World to Live, 'Europe' Must Die.'' By this he means a European way of thinking which he contrasts with an American Indian way of thinking. In effect, he calls for a complete change from European (Christian, Capitalist, Marxist) values. He objects to using written language and he objects to industrial development. He claims that value terms such as ''victory'' and ''freedom'' are used to justify ''butchery'' and ''dehumanization.'' Here is a segment of that speech:

> All European tradition, Marxism included, has conspired to defy the natural order of all things. Mother Earth has been abused, the powers have been abused, and this cannot go on forever. No theory can alter that simple fact. Mother Earth will retaliate, the whole environment will retaliate, and the abusers will be eliminated. Things come full circle, back to where they started. *That's* revolution. And that's a prophecy of my people, of the Hopi people and of other correct peoples.
>
> American Indians have been trying to explain this to Europeans for centuries. But, as I said earlier, Europeans have proven themselves unable to hear. The natural order will win out, and the offenders will die out, the way deer die when they offend the harmony by overpopulating a given region. It's only a matter of time until what Europeans call ''a major catastrophe of global proportions'' will occur. It is the role of American Indian peoples, the role of all natural beings, to survive. A part of our survival is to resist. We resist not to overthrow a government or to take political power, but because it is natural to resist extermination, to survive. We don't want power over white institutions; we want white institutions to disappear. *That's* revolution.[1]

There were probably quite a few in Means' audience who agreed with him and many who did not. His views are not a majority opinion among Native Americans. They would find very little support in a general audience of Americans, but Means would not change his position. His target was only those few who were susceptible to his ideas.

We have spoken here of how the objectives of persuasion change as a speaker moves from one target audience to another. Sometimes, however, persuasion has to be adapted to more than one target audience at a time. You might want to *activate* those in an audience who already support your position and to *motivate* the uninterested and uninformed to care and to learn about the issue. Therefore, you need a careful definition of your objectives. Your arguments and values need to be thoughtfully selected so that *both* target audiences can be addressed at the same time.

Persuasion, therefore, has a variety of objectives—reinforcing or activating those who agree, making the uninterested see the importance of your proposal, modifying those who disagree, and, occasionally, offending some to appeal to those few in an audience who may be willing to listen.

Persuasion Uses a Variety of Proofs

Every sentence uttered expresses a belief and thus entails a claim. And every claim implies that there are arguments to support it. Every argument involves three varieties of proof: (1) the contention that the claim is a *reasonable* conclusion from adequate evidence; (2) the intention that it be consistent with the *beliefs* and *values* of the audience, and (3) because explicitly or implicitly the phrase "I believe that . . ." is inherent in every claim, the suggestion that the speaker is a *credible source*.

How much an argument will emphasize one kind of proof over another will depend, again, on the target audience and the situation. Actuating listeners who already agree with you is largely a matter of reinforcing values they already accept. When an audience knows little about the subject or your position on it, you must depend more on the reasonableness of the argument and the adequacy of the evidence. In some cases, your high credibility with the target audience will be the most persuasive element. However, all three elements of proof—reasonable argument, relevant or appropriate values, and a credible source—are part of every argument.

The Limitation of Objectives

The dramatic picture of a speaker who meets a hostile audience and within the course of a half-hour address converts it into an audience of friendly partisans is a myth. It is much more realistic to recognize that under certain circumstances any attempt to persuade will be unproductive. Sometimes, the difference in beliefs and values between you and a potential audience makes persuasion virtually impossible. In other instances, an audience cannot give the desired response. People who can't pay their rent won't give money to some project a speaker supports. In such cases, remember the prayer of St. Francis of Assisi. He asked God to give him the courage to change what he could, the patience to live with what he could not, and the wisdom to know the difference between the two.

The way to maximize the degree of your success when you speak to these kinds of audiences is to make a realistic appraisal of your potential to persuade; that is, focus on the limitation of objectives. How do you know what your potential is? How limited must your expectations be?

We have said that some persuasion is designed for audiences that agree with you but need to be reinforced in their beliefs or moved toward doing something about them. In such cases, you will affirm values that you and the audience share. The audience analysis of Dave's speech on cancer that we used as an example in Chapter 6 is just such an analysis. That speech was informative—intended to make his classmates aware of the symptoms and causes of cancer. Suppose, however, Dave had wanted to persuade them to have themselves tested for cancer. No one claims to be in favor of cancer, so there is no issue there. An issue might arise over whether cancer is a potential threat to the young people in the audience. The evidence in Dave's analysis shows that many types of cancer are more prevalent among older people than they are in people his age. His target audience may have an "it can't happen to me" attitude. So, he must emphasize evidence of the early onset of cancer and its severity. In order to activate his audience, he must call into play the values he and the audience share: survival, health, and happiness. He must reinforce these and relate them to the prevention of cancer, and show that testing is the means to achieve that goal.

Perhaps, instead, he perceives still another problem: a young listener thinks, "cancer is more likely to happen to others, not me. My survival is not at stake. My health is not threatened. My happiness is not endangered." In that case, he might shift the emphasis the audience puts on those values: survival, health and happiness. For example, what of the social values? Of family, for instance. The young listeners can be alerted to the threat that cancer poses to their parents. Or the audience may be asked to consider the welfare of society and cancer's threat to social stability. This is not a matter of appealing to values the listeners oppose, but of basing argument on values they hold but have not yet recognized as being related to this subject. Any persuasive speech will, therefore, call for a limitation of objectives and, consequently, of what proofs will be applicable.

When the target audience is opposed to your position, it is even more important to limit your objectives. Trying to move people too far and too fast from a strongly held position can produce an opposite reaction. Moreover, the values that have the highest priority in someone's value system are the most difficult to change. People who oppose abortion because it violates the value of life are likely to see life as central to their value system. If they also have a strong commitment to divine law that they believe forbids abortion, you have an impossible task if you try to change them. In such a case, the most you can hope for is to make them aware of your position. Argument and evidence can sometimes bring hostile listeners to recognize an opposing point of view but only rarely will they agree with it.

Analysis of the audience and the subject will help you define a reasonable goal. Knowing your specific goal helps you determine the appropriate proofs and the best organization for the speech. Then you have the best chance of meeting that goal. We will look now at how organization is influenced by your specific objective and how the placement of arguments helps to maximize the objective you have chosen.

Organizing Persuasive Speeches

Chapter 14 will help you with introductions and conclusions. Our principal concern in this chapter is the organization of the *body* of the speech. We will mention only briefly the general structure of a persuasive message.

Persuasive Organization in General

The general structure of a speech to persuade is the same as that of any other speech. It has an introduction, a body, and a conclusion. The introduction plays the same role it does in any other speech. It catches the attention of the audience, provides any needed background, elicits the good will of the audience, and enhances credibility. It also has a subject sentence that tells the audience what the speech is going to be about. In many instances, as in informative speaking, the subject sentence in the introduction will state the claim clearly. At other times, only the general subject is identified in the introduction. The nature of the subject and the audience may make it expedient to withhold for a time the specific claim. The body of the speech advances the arguments and the evidence that support the claim. The conclusion brings the speech to a forceful and appropriate close. It may do this by summarizing the main arguments that support the claim but, more frequently, the conclusion will characterize the subject in some way that makes your appeals to the audience's beliefs and values emphatic and vivid.

Choosing the Best Pattern of Arrangement

As we said in Chapter 18, the pattern of arrangement used to organize informative speeches is designed to achieve understanding and clarification. Understanding and clarification, however, can also persuade. You may want the audience to understand how central cities are renovated and use Minneapolis as an example. Suppose a listener says, "Minneapolis sounds interesting. I think I will be sure to visit there on the way to the Black Hills next summer." Then your informative speech has been persuasive. We are interested here, however, in the way to organize the speeches you give when you *intend* to persuade. First, we will show you how informative patterns of arrangement can be used to organize persuasive speeches. Second, we will describe some patterns that are special to persuasion.

In every case, you will quickly see that what most clearly distinguishes any one of the patterns from the others is whether and to what degree you delay in stating the specific claim of the speech and what complexity your speech entails.

The claim must always be *explicit* at whatever point in the speech it does appear. This is true for two reasons. First, an audience is rarely as interested in a proposal as you are and is probably not inclined to pay as much attention. Second, audiences tend to hear what they want or expect to hear. Consequently, the claim must be quite explicit. It is particularly important to make a clear and precise statement of the claim in the conclusion. This leaves the audience with a correct understanding of what you want it to think or do.

Let's see how a speech would look in each of the four patterns of persuasive organization. They are called the *claim-to-proof* pattern, the *problem-solution* pattern, the *motivated sequence*, and the *reflective* pattern.

The claim-to-proof pattern   The claim-to-proof pattern is the persuasive adaptation of the patterns you have already studied in Chapter 18 on Informative Speaking. In the claim-to-proof pattern, the claim is stated in the introduction of the speech and then supported by a series of arguments in the body. The speech concludes with an appeal for acceptance of the claim. The audience is told from the beginning exactly what claim you propose to argue. It is the persuasive equivalent of the topical pattern used for many informative speeches. Each topic in the body is an argument that responds to a specific issue. Remember that an issue grows out of the clash of opposing claims.

Michael wanted to alert his audience to the dangers of radon gas and urge them to have their homes tested. He organized his speech by the claim-to-proof pattern.

Introduction

I.   You may be poisoned in your home by an invisible enemy

II. Radon gas is a problem in 25% of American homes

III. You should have your home tested for radon gas

Body

I.   In larger quantities, radon gas lodges in the lungs and causes lung cancer

II. It cannot be detected by the normal senses

III. Very few people are taking the inexpensive and easy steps to test and correct the problem

Conclusion

I.   You should buy an inexpensive charcoal collector and test your home for radon gas

Only rarely is an audience strongly opposed to a proposal. A lack of interest is a much greater danger than hostility. Consequently, most speeches can be organized in the claim-to-proof pattern. The audience needs to know what the proposal is as soon as possible so that your claim can be reinforced throughout the speech. Stating the claim early also reduces any concern the audience may have about where the speech is going.

Presenting a claim early makes it easier to be clear. The central issue is introduced immediately and is constantly before the listener, and its relationship to individual arguments can be continually reinforced. Moreover, if listeners know beforehand what your position is, there is nothing to gain from withholding the statement of the claim even if they disagree. In such a case, using the claim-to-proof pattern would be a sign of candor. It would build credibility by showing that you have nothing to hide, and it might tend to lessen somewhat the audience's objections to the plan.

Although the pattern illustrated by our example is topical, any of the other informative patterns may be used. Definition is a means of arguing, for instance, in value claims. When you argue that the people's democracy of China is not a true democracy because democracy is a form of government involving free elections, free speech, and established rights for individuals you are organizing by definition. Such a speech is also a form of comparison and contrast. The cause and effect pattern has obvious persuasive utility when you argue, for example, that automobiles are the major cause of air pollution.

Sometimes, a persuasive speech can be based on narration, the telling of a story. That is the chronological pattern. The claim that the National Park Service should abandon its policy of permitting forest fires to burn themselves out might be organized by telling the story of the fires in 1989 at Yellowstone National Park. In such a case, you would point out what might have been avoided if fire containment had been practiced at each stage of the narrative.

The problem-solution pattern   In the problem-solution format, your first task, as usual, is to get the attention of the audience. Next you present a problem that needs to be solved. Finally, you recommend a course of action and show how it will solve the problem. The audience is not told what solution will be proposed until after the problem has been explained.

The drug problem increasingly worries most Americans and its continuing severity has caused some people to look for alternate solutions to police action. In Chapter 18 we used the example of Greg's informative speech explaining the issues in the debate over the legalization of marijuana. In a later persuasive speech, he argued that drugs be legalized in the United States. Here is the outline of that speech in a problem-solution pattern.

Introduction

  I. Story of a woman who turned to prostitution to support her drug habit

Body

    I. Drugs are a major problem in America today
      A. An increasing number of people are using drugs
      B. Despite millions in government expenditures, drugs are readily available
      C. The cost of illegal drugs leads to increased crime

  II. Since present methods have failed, it is time to try a new solution: legalization

 III. Legalization would break organized crime and cut the personal crime rate

IV. Legalization would not increase drug use

V. Legalization would permit concentration on rehabilitation

Conclusion

I. Americans are intelligent people who understand that when something doesn't work, try something new

II. The War on Drugs isn't working. Let's join Mayor Schmoke of Baltimore, Conservative Columnist William F. Buckley, Former Secretary of State George Schultz and a growing list of intelligent and knowledgeable people and ask for a legalization of drugs

The motivated sequence   One popular variation on the problem-solution pattern is the "motivated sequence" developed by Alan H. Monroe.[2] This organizational format builds audience motivation into the structure of the speech. It organizes the materials of a speech around five steps:

1. Attention: In every speech, the first step is to catch the attention of the audience.

2. Need: A problem is identified and explained by showing how an existing condition fails to meet the needs of the audience.

3. Satisfaction: A plan of action is proposed to alleviate the problem and satisfy the audience's needs.

4. Visualization: The proposed plan is described in a way that gives the audience a vivid picture of the benefits it will bring.

5. Action: The final step is a call for personal involvement.

The motivated sequence is particularly useful when your persuasive purpose is to activate. It does not develop the complex arguments you would need if opposition were strong. It tries to make the audience visualize the benefits it will get from your plan and then it makes a direct appeal for action. The need step and the visualization step are parallel and opposite. The satisfaction step and the action step are also parallel, the action step being the culmination of the need step. Thus, once you know the need and the satisfaction (problem and solution) the other steps follow from it. This symmetry makes it easy to use.

Prudencio was concerned about the increasing incidence of teenage suicide. He knew that pressure to succeed and an unhappy home life were part of the cause, so he wanted to emphasize how those in his class could help. He organized his speech by the motivated sequence method.

Introduction

I. [Attention] Bob Buchanan, 17, outstanding student, athlete, student body leader, hanged himself last week

Body

I. [Need] This is a growing problem in America
   A. Increase among teenagers
   B. Caused by the pressure to succeed and an unhappy home life

II. [Satisfaction] We need to take the pressure off children and show them we love them

III. [Visualization] A happy home life where the Bob Buchanan's of the world don't feel threatened

Conclusion

I. [Action] It's up to each of us to help our own family members to take the pressure off teenagers and show them love

The reflective pattern Like the problem-solution pattern and the motivated sequence, the reflective pattern withholds presentation of your specific claim until later in the speech. The pattern describes a problem situation and its causes, then it suggests several possibilities for solution. Next, each of these is evaluated. Finally, the best solution is proposed. The persuasive-reflective pattern is modeled on the same pattern as group discussion (see Chapter 21). It looks like a thoroughly objective approach to a subject; its purpose, however, is to persuade. Far from being objective, everything it says is intended to move the audience toward accepting the course of action it advocates. It is more open in discussing other alternatives and is the most complex of the organizational formats we have discussed.

Remember Greg's speech on legalizing drugs? Andrea thought that the problem was so compelling it required a more comprehensive examination. She used the reflective thinking pattern to argue not for legalization, but for an expansion of current programs as the best solution to the problem.

Introduction

I. Drugs are a serious problem in America

Body

I. The drug problem is a complex one
   A. Increasing drug use in the inner city
   B. Decreasing casual middle and upper class users
   C. More serious crimes
   D. Growing costs of enforcement
   E. Rehabilitation is doing little

II. The causes are complex
   A. Lack of hope among unemployed people in the inner city
   B. As the War on Drugs succeeds in making it harder to get drugs into the country, the prices go up
   C. Campaigns like "Just Say No" and the threat of enforcement work only on casual users

      D. As the price goes up addicts commit more serious crimes to support the habit

      E. There are inadequate funds for rehabilitation

  III. We need a solution that will get at the causes of the problem: provide hope, increase rehabilitation and control the price

  IV. What might we do

      A. Continue the present program but that is a proven failure

      B. Legalize drugs but that would send a message to people that drugs are not dangerous and drug use would increase

      C. Continue the current restrictions in a modified form and

        1. Increase funds for rehabilitation

        2. Give drugs and drug substitutes to some addicts under carefully controlled conditions

        3. Fund an inner city jobs program

Conclusion

  I. Plan C is clearly the best because it gets at the causes. It could be funded by the eventual savings in the War on Drugs and the costs of crime

  II. It's time for Congress and the President to look at this problem more analytically and develop a plan to attack the causes

    An audience that is hostile to a claim may very well reject the claim once you have stated it. The problem-solution, motivated sequence, and reflective patterns help to prevent this by presenting the idea gradually, thereby letting you develop and support a position before the audience has any reason to reject it. It follows that when an audience is opposed to your position and knows the arguments that support its own view, it is better for you not to associate yourself too early with something the listeners oppose.[3]

    If the audience does not know exactly where you stand, the problem-solution, motivated sequence, and reflective patterns give your analysis of the case and the arguments that support it a chance to have a persuasive effect before the audience begins to think of counter-arguments. Even if you cannot achieve your primary purpose, it is possible to mediate some of the opposition and to make the audience more susceptible to later persuasion.

    The reflective pattern is particularly thorough and, therefore, should be useful when the audience believes it has little knowledge of the subject and wants to know more. It is designed to create understanding first and to discuss issues later. This pattern approaches the subject in such a way that the audience understands what kinds of decisions it must make before it makes them.

    The reflective pattern has another and perhaps more important advantage. It clarifies your analysis of the subject for the audience. The audience is thereby conditioned to that analysis, and other speakers will find it difficult to undo its persuasive effect. To do so, they must not only contradict the prior conclusions, they must counteract your analysis as well.

Audiences that are better educated and interested in the subject are the best candidates for the reflective approach since it is more complex and introduces other points of view.[4] The disadvantage lies in its complexity. It requires an audience with some sophistication, one that is willing to follow the complexity of the pattern.

Determining the Placement of Arguments

Once the problem of general arrangement has been solved, a more specific question arises: "What order should individual arguments follow?" Some say that putting the strongest argument last will give the speech a greater impact. Others, to the contrary, will claim that it is better to put the best argument first to give the speech a strong start. The research that has been done on the question has produced mixed results. Here again, as in virtually every case, the decision depends upon the audience. However, some general (though tentative) principles are worth considering.

1. If the ideas in a speech are sufficiently unrelated, the speech will appear to lack a unifying theme. It becomes something like a grocery list. The listeners' comprehension — and probably your credibility — are damaged by a disorganized message.[5]

2. When one argument depends on another, it must obviously follow the one on which it depends. That is why stock issues are a popular way to prove a policy claim (See Chapter 7). It makes sense to present arguments associated with the need for a change first, and the arguments that show the desirability of a plan second. Only then can you argue for the feasibility of your proposal. It is useless, for instance, to argue that some federal medical plan will alleviate the shortage of physicians in rural areas before the audience believes that such a shortage exists. And it is equally futile to support the feasibility of such a plan before showing that it will, in fact, alleviate whatever shortage might exist.

3. Although there is substantial disagreement over the relative importance of the first and last positions, arguments presented early and late seem to be remembered better than those presented in the middle of the speech.[6]

4. The best evidence seems to suggest that if an audience agrees with you, and knows little of the opposing position, showing only one side of the controversy has a stronger (but only temporary) effect. Showing both sides, however, produces better long-range effects because it prepares the listeners to resist counter-persuasion.[7] A vendor selling a combination vegetable peeler and hair dryer shows only one side of the case because the article has to be sold at that moment or not at all. But the undecidedness that characterizes many persuasive situations gives the audience an opportunity to see-saw. In general,

therefore, it is best to answer the principal opposition arguments because this helps to inoculate against future counter-persuasion. Even audiences that favor your position need to be immunized against later counter-argument.

5. Generally, it is better to refute opposition arguments after presenting those that support your position.[8] When opposing arguments are heard first, they tend to build opposition in the listener's mind. Then not only must you overcome the opposition, but you must also counteract any mechanisms the audience uses to let it ignore or avoid listening to the supporting arguments. An audience is more attentive before it makes a decision. Thus, even if the opposition arguments are refuted, the audience is less likely to "hear" the arguments that support your position, and listeners will be poorly guarded against future attempts to contradict your claim.

There is an exception to this principle. When listeners have firm arguments against a proposal, it is probably best to deal with those arguments as soon as possible after the claim has been stated. Otherwise, the audience may rehearse them throughout the speech and ignore the arguments that support the claim.

Summary

Every speech can be thought of as persuasive because all speeches try to influence belief and action. However, the speech to persuade is different from others because it aims overtly at resolving controversy. Although your general objective is to persuade, you need to identify a target audience to determine your specific objective. This target audience may be defined as whatever portion of a group you believe you can effectively reach. It is related to whatever limitation you impose on your persuasive objective.

Speeches to actuate are aimed at listeners who agree with you but need motivation to act. Other speeches address uninterested listeners. In these speeches, it is essential to make the importance of the subject clear. Hostile audiences probably can't be changed very much, but their hostility can be muted and you can at least encourage them to examine your position.

An accurate and realistic view of persuasion recognizes two important concepts: (1) that every persuasive speech uses a variety of proofs that are reasonable, appeal to the beliefs and values of the audience, and suggest that the speaker is a credible source, (2) that there are often narrow limits to what a persuasive speech can achieve.

A persuasive speech, like any other, has an introduction, a body, and a conclusion. Each part plays its familiar role. Four organizational patterns are useful in persuasion: claim-to-proof, problem-solution, motivated sequence, and reflective. They differ primarily in how early in the speech the specific claim appears and how complex the analysis is. The claim-to-proof pattern is developed like the patterns for informative speaking. The claim is in the introduction. In the other three formats (problem-solution, motivated sequence, and reflective) the specific claim is introduced later in the speech. The complexity of the claim, the attitudes of the audience, the level of your credibility, and the presence or absence of opposing speakers are all factors that help to determine your choice of persuasive order. No matter what order you use, the claim should be made explicit at some point in the speech, and the speech should answer opposition arguments.

Most speeches can safely be organized by the claim-to-proof pattern. In fact, many speeches do use this organization. The problem-solution and the reflective patterns are useful when an audience is opposed to your position. The reflective pattern is most useful when an audience doesn't know much about the problem and is prepared to follow a more elaborate analysis of the subject. The motivated sequence combines problem-to-solution and motivation. It is easy to use because of its symmetry but is not so useful for complex arguments.

The placement of arguments in the speech can help to reinforce agreement and to diminish opposition. (1) Organization is necessary; disorganization will damage your credibility and your audience will not be persuaded. (2) Arguments that depend on one another should be placed together. (3) The arguments that come first and last are remembered best. (4) If an audience agrees with you or knows little of the opposition arguments, a speaker can be successful showing only one side. Showing both sides and refuting opposition arguments has better long range effects. (5) It is better to refute opposition arguments after your own arguments are introduced except where listeners have strong objections to your proposal.

Key Terms

Specific objectives
Activation
Motivation
Hostile audience
Agitation
Target audience
Proofs
Limitation of objectives

Organization
Intention
Claim-to-proof
Problem-solution
Motivated sequence
Reflective pattern
Withholding the claim
Placing arguments

Exercises

1. Organize and deliver a five- to seven-minute persuasive speech. Turn in a copy of your outline, a brief analysis of your audience, and a short statement of what values you will use and why you will use them. Also include a statement of what organization you will use and why you chose it.

2. Write a brief analysis of one of your classmate's speeches and evaluate the method of organization. Could you improve the speech by changing the order? How and why? How well was it adapted to the classroom audience? What persuasive order did the speaker use?

3. Formulate a policy claim from one of the general topics listed at the end of Chapter 5. Sketch the outline of a persuasive speech on this claim for each of the three methods of persuasive organization discussed in this chapter.

4. Examine one of the persuasive speeches at the end of this chapter and write a short paper evaluating its persuasiveness for a student audience.

5. Examine the first two persuasive speeches at the end of this chapter and compare and contrast them for organization, supporting materials, beliefs and values, credibility, and language.

6. Former Governor Lamm's speech, found at the end of this chapter ("Rationing Health Care") is very controversial. It created a storm of protest when it was first delivered because of his suggestion that some people must be denied medical services. For a moment put aside whether or not you agree with his argument. Write a paper of no more than three double-spaced typewritten pages analyzing how well you think he would do in adapting his controversial ideas to an audience you know well.

Notes

[1] Russell Means, "For the World to Live, 'Europe' Must Die," *Contemporary American Speeches* eds. Richard L. Johannesen, R.R. Allen, Wil A. Linkugel (Dubuque, IA: Kendall/Hunt, 1988) 121.

[2] Douglas Ehninger, Bruce Gronbeck, Ray E. McKerrow, and Alan H. Monroe, *Principals and Types of Speech Communication* (Glenview, IL: Scott Foresman, 1986) 153.

[3] A.R. Cohen, *Attitude Change and Social Influence* (New York: Basic Books, 1964) 11-12.

[4] Erwin P. Bettinghaus and Michael J. Cody. *Persuasive Communication* (New York: Holt, Rinehart and Winston, 1987) 149.

[5] Bettinghaus and Cody, 141-42.

[6] Bettinghaus and Cody, 147.

⁷ Loren J. Anderson, ''A Summary of Research on Order Effects in Communication.'' *Concepts in Communication*, eds. Jimmie D. Trent, Judith S. Trent and Daniel J. O'Neill (Boston: Allyn & Bacon, 1973) 129-30; James C. McCroskey, Thomas J. Young and Michael D. Scott, ''The Effects of Message Sidedness and Evidence on Inoculation Against Counter-Persuasion in Small Group Communication,'' *Speech Monographs* 39 (Aug. 1972): 205-12.

⁸ Anderson, 130.

Speeches for Study

''An Ounce Worth Pounds''

Mike Stolts

University of Wisconsin, Eau Claire

1   Camp Kingsmont is in many ways very much like other summer camps. Children have rowboat races, swim and shortsheet their counselors' beds. But they also endure extensive calisthenics classes and three mile jogs, attend group sessions on how to balance their nutritional needs and struggle through a strict, reduced calorie diet. Camp Kingsmont is an adolescent weight loss camp, and all 350 of its yearly clientele are obese children.

2   Obesity is rapidly becoming a serious problem, diminishing the lives of millions of American children. Children who are 20% over the ideal weight for their body's build and are considered medically obese and in need of help. John C. McCable, chairman of Blue Cross and Blue Shield of Michigan says, ''Obesity is challenging malnutrition as a major American health problem, and fat children become fat adults.''

3   Children who are obese face tremendous obstacles. Physical health, emotional well-being—the very quality of a child's life—are endangered by childhood obesity. The health of America's children should be foremost of our concerns. Obesity is potentially the most dangerous, yet possibly the most preventable childhood health problem.

4   In order to understand and combat childhood obesity we must first realize how widespread and dangerous the problem is. Then we will examine why more children are becoming obese. Finally, we will determine what we as parents, future parents, educators and citizens must do to ensure that future generations do not grow up obese.

5   It's ironic that at the very time when 60% of American adults exercise regularly, their children are in the poorest shape ever. Dr. Robert Wharton writes in *Children Today*, November-December, 1984, ''Obesity is one of the most chronic problems in childhood, affecting between 5 and 30 percent of

children." This means that there may be as many as 12 million obese children in the United States today."

6   That number has risen tremendously in the last 20 years. Dr. William Dietz reports in *Science*, April 4, 1986, "Obesity increased by 54% among 6 to 11-year-old American children and by 39% among 12 to 17-year-olds over the past 15 to 20 years."

7   More children are fat now than ever before, and they are fatter now than ever before. But the extent of the problem means little until it is placed within the context of the long-term health problems caused by obesity. Obesity is not just a condition children grow out of. Childhood obesity dramatically affects a child's physical health. The *National Children and Youth Fitness Study*, conducted by the Department of Health and Human Services, reported that 28% of children studied had higher than normal blood pressure, 40% had high blood cholesterol levels and 98% had at least one risk factor predisposing them to heart disease. We usually think of middle-aged, overweight adults as being at risk of heart disease. Now we must realize that 10-year-old children face the same risk—if not now, almost certainly in the future. Dr. Kelly Brown reports that 80% of all obese children become obese adults. *Consumers Research Magazine*, April, 1985, links obesity to heart disease, diabetes, certain cancers, and premature mortality. Obesity kills, and children are not immune.

8   Obese children also suffer emotionally. In an age that glorifies fitness, obese children face discrimination and even hostility by their peers. Bonnie Waltzkin writes in *Parents Magazine*, November, 1983, ". . . studies have shown that most preschoolers believe that a fat child is ugly, stupid, mean, lazy, dishonest, and naughty. The hurt obese children feel from this teasing was poignantly demonstrated just recently. Twelve-year-old Nathan Farris shot and killed a classmate and then killed himself at their DeKalb, Missouri, junior high school. The *Kansas City Times* reported on March 3 that Nathan was the object of relentless teasing because he was fat. Nathan threatened to bring a gun to school to stop the teasing. On March 2, 1987, he carried out that threat and two children died. Nearby, a poster depicted life's peaks and pits. According to the *Times*, "One of life's pits, on the poster, was, 'People make fun of you because you're overweight.'"

9   Childhood should be a time of innocence, happiness, and play. But for too many children, running, jumping and playing are exhausting, if not impossible, because they are obese. Before we can solve the problems of childhood obesity, however, we must try to remember why children become obese.

10   Unfortunately, it is difficult to know why individual children become obese. Genetics, family behavior and personality all may play a role, but, it is fairly safe to say that children become obese by eating too much and not exercising enough. The explosion of junk food availability is one aspect of the growing problem of childhood obesity. Keeping candy and chips around the house makes it easy for children to fill up on high calorie snacks. Even one candy bar a day can make a difference. Dr. William Dietz has determined that as few as 50 extra calories a day can lead to obesity in children. A Snickers bar has three times that or more.

11   But even eating too much of "good" foods can be a problem. Overeating is taught early on by telling children to clean their plates. A clean plate is then rewarded with a high calorie dessert. This gives children the idea that it is OK to eat too much. Such patterns are set before children can watch and control their eating behavior.

12   The problem of overeating is compounded by the lack of exercise children get at home and school. Physical education has been on the decline in many states due to budget cuts, time constraints, and teacher shortages. The Presidential Commission on Physical Fitness and Sports reports that elementary schools teach physical education only 20 minutes per week on the average, and that two-thirds of 5th through 12th graders in this nation do not have daily physical education.

13   Another factor leading to inactivity is the TV set. The American Academy of Pediatrics reports that children watch approximately 25 hours of TV per week. They add, "Television viewing increases the consumption of high caloric density snacks and increases the prevalence of obesity.

14   Children today eat too much of the wrong kinds of food and can't or don't exercise enough to burn excess calories. That has resulted in a generation of obese children who face many physical and emotional problems. We must take time to examine what we can do to stop this—not just as parents or future parents, but as older brothers and sisters, aunts, uncles, cousins, or just responsible members of our communities.

15   The key to stopping childhood obesity is in preventing it from ever occurring. This can be done by seeing that children do get enough exercise and that they don't eat too much. Obviously, the causes and cures of obesity are much more complex than these few simple steps, but these steps can help in preventing obesity.

16   The first thing we can do is go to our local school boards and ask that grade school physical education be made a daily requirement. The Presidential Commission on Physical Education and Sports has determined that children need at least 20 minutes of continuous physical exercise each day for healthy growth. That exercise will burn excess calories and slow or even prevent weight gain. Studies in Florida, Michigan and California have demonstrated that daily physical education promotes weight loss and enhances physical conditioning.

17   Much more must be done at home. Dr. Robert Wharton recommends that we end the "clean plate syndrome." Instead of telling children to clean their plates, we should say, "When you feel you have eaten enough, you may go out and play," or "I would like you to try some of each food, but only eat as much as you feel comfortable with." This will promote responsible eating behavior and enhance the child's sense of self-control.

18   We should also limit the amount of time children watch TV. TV watching is extremely passive, so we should break up long stretches with periods of activity to help keep metabolic rates active. Healthful snacks, such as fruits and vegetables are also infinitely preferable to candy and chips.

19   We as parents or future parents must be involved in preventing obesity in our children. Dr. Leonard Epstein suggests in *Consumers Research Magazine*, May, 1985, that we incorporate exercise into children's daily

activities. Where safe, children should walk to school instead of being driven. He also says, "Don't reward good behavior with food; use parent/child activities instead." Doing things with children will cut out some calories, burn more, and strengthen family bonds.

20   Finally, we should watch our own diets. Children learn their eating patterns from us, so we should act consistently with what we teach. We should keep high calorie snacks out of the house so neither we nor our children can fill up on junk food. When we eat sensible portions of good foods, we teach our children to do the same.

21   Most of us here are not yet parents, but in the event we have families, we can use these guidelines to help prevent children from becoming obese. Childhood obesity is not healthy. It is not natural, and it's not necessary. A few ounces of prevention on our part can mean pounds for our children— pounds that will never weigh down their bodies or their spirits.

22   Healthy, fit children face an excellent chance of remaining healthy and fit all their lives. For today, freedom from obesity means children can run, jump, and play as they ought, and summer camps, like Camp Kingsmont, can concentrate not on dieting and exercising, but on swimming, boating and prankstering, the fun parts of summer camp.

Reprinted with the permission of the Interstate Oratorical Association from *Winning Orations* ed Larry Schnoor (Mankato, MN: Interstate Oratorical Association, 1987) 127-30.

"Outfoxing Mr. Badwrench"

Kristin Amondsen

Bradley University

1   For over five years now, after *60 Minutes*, we've seen a kindly man with greying temples in a clean pressed mechanic's uniform, come into our living rooms and proudly state, "Quality care for your car is what I provide for you." But when we go out—looking for Mr. Goodwrench, we invariably encounter his alter ego and we end up dropping our keys in the hands of someone I'd like to call Mr. Badwrench. Because in America today, according to Lauren Petite, Commissioner of Consumer Services in Chicago, auto repairs are still the biggest consumer complaint. And you know what? I know you're not surprised. Because according to the U.S. Office of Consumer Affairs, auto mechanic fraud is our country's number one consumer problem. So let's take a look at how we're taken. First, let's take a look under the hood: how bad is auto mechanic fraud? Secondly, we'll examine two important parts: examine two reasons as to why it exists. Then let's run a safety check: let's check the harms of this problem. And finally, we'll run a major overhaul to stop the breakdown. The breakdown of our consumer/mechanic relationship.

2   Sloppy and needless auto repairs cost us over 30 billion dollars annually. How widespread is mechanic fraud? In a study of 836 major chain store repairs, conducted by diagnostic centers at the University of Alabama in 1985, 25% of the repairs were found to be unnecessary. And one firm actually had a 47% rate of unnecessary repairs. But the U.S. Department of Transportation uncovered an even more disturbing fact. They found that at least 53 cents out of every dollar paid, for auto repairs, was spent unnecessarily because of inflated prices or needless work. Are you questioning the ethics of your so-called trusty mechanic yet? Well, the Colorado Public Interest Research Group did. They intentionally loosened a drive belt on a '71 Volkswagen. They then brought the VW to eight repair shops in Boulder. Only one of the shops solved the problem and charged the appropriate fee. Well, four other shops did fix the problem. But they also did costly and unnecessary tune-ups. Another type of dishonesty that makes us suffer is the overcharging of labor.

3   Take for example Roberta Grey of San Francisco. Well, Roberta took her red Datsun into a repair shop for a number of repairs. The shop made it clear that they charged $35 an hour for labor. One might assume by looking at Roberta's $350 labor bill, that ten hours of hard work was put into her Datsun. However, the shop only put in 6.4 hours. Now, logically speaking, Roberta's bill should have only come to $224; however, she spent an unnecessary $136. This is a perfect example of the auto repair industry's old con game. It's called a Flat Rate Fiddle ... and it's perfectly legal. Basically, what *Flat Rate Manuals* do is list various repair operations for a car. They then state exactly how long a repair should take. *Flat Rate Manuals* are published by auto manufacturers for mechanics to follow when doing repair work. Now, in Roberta's case, the *Flat Rate Manual* stated that her repairs should have taken ten hours. These manuals give our mechanics written permission to steal from us. And unfortunately, most repair shops do usually take advantage of this opportunity. The New York State Consumer Commission found during the investigation

of some 408 repair shops, that 56% of them were grossly overcharging their labor. The New York State Attorney General's Office has estimated that motorists of the state alone are being over charged 73 million dollars annually just through the use of *Flat Rate Manuals*. But the overcharging of labor isn't enough for "Mr. Badwrench."

4 It's been discovered that numerous mechanics will go much further. According to the June 18, 1984, issue of *U.S. News and World Report*, some mechanics will go as far as to paint your old automobile parts to look like new, and then proceed to put them back into your car, and better still: squirt fluid on shock absorbers before telling the motorists that they're leaking. Other examples include: barbecue sauce being poured on an alternator to cause a burning smell, a seltzer tablet being dropped onto the battery to make it foam, and one mechanic in Colorado went as far as to stick a blade in the toe of his shoe in order to slash tires. But why is this occurring? Well, often the mechanic has the incentive to sell you extra parts because he's receiving a commission and according to Sandy Mitchell, the New York State Assistant Attorney General, auto repair is so ripe for abuse because consumer ignorance is so widespread.

5 Let's face it. How many of you know which gizmo goes where, does what and how much it costs. But current studies show that often times, not only can the consumer be ignorant, but so can the mechanic. According to the National Institute for Automotive Service Excellence, about half of all mechanics in our nation can't even completely diagnose and repair even one area of your car. Now obviously, this symbolizes a bit of incompetence. The organization also stated that out of over 500,000 mechanics in our country only 28,000 passed all competency tests. That means that less than 6% of our nation's mechanics have passed industry sponsored competency tests. In comparison to some mechanics, I could probably repair your car better (and believe me, that's not saying much!). Think about this. Auto mechanic fraud has cost us billions of dollars unnecessarily. If we don't take any precautions before allowing our mechanics to work on our cars, chances are that Mr. Badwrench could be repairing your car unnecessarily and/or incorrectly.

6 But there are precautions we can take to run a major overhaul, to stop the breakdown of our consumer-mechanic relationship. The first thing that we can do is to find a competent mechanic. According to Lillian Borgeson, auto repair specialist, this can be achieved by finding a mechanic with credentials from the National Institute for Automotive Service Excellence or dubbed the ASE. This is the only nationally accepted organization that tests a mechanic's competence. Now in order to receive a certificate from the ASE, the mechanic must have at least one year of experience with the hardware. And must also have passed a three to four hour competency test. And that's not all. In order to assure the ASE that their skills are up to par, ASE mechanics have to pass new updated tests every five years.

7 Secondly, we as consumers must be a lot more careful in not only selecting our mechanic, but selecting our repair shop. There's a similar organization to the ASE that awards credibility to automotive repair shops; and those shops that pass the tough AAA test are awarded the right to display

a red, white and blue sign with the AAA seal of approval. It would be worth your time and money to look for that seal.

8   And finally, we can establish a checklist. In order to avoid the Flat Rate Fiddle situation, look for a mechanic or a repair shop that charges by the clock hour instead of the victimizing *Flat Rate Manuals*. Chances are that your labor will be a lot more down-to-earth. And what can you do to avoid the questionable repair shops? You can check the Better Business Bureau to learn complaint histories of particular repair shops. That way you can avoid one with a record. And before you have anything done with your car, it's a good idea to write down all of the symptoms in advance and then get a written estimate from more than one repair shop. Larry Coorigan from Atlanta found this to be helpful.

9   Larry was having trouble with his Mustang's electrical system. Taking it to one repair shop, he was told that it would need a new alternator, and that the tab would come to $135. However, seeking a second opinion, the mechanic of the [next] garage found the battery cables were simply corroded and solved the whole problem for just $3.

10   And what can you do to prevent your mechanic from painting and selling your own parts back to you? Ask your mechanic to give you back your old parts that are to be replaced before he even does the job.

11   And you know what? You don't have to do any of these things. If you want to have more auto mechanic fraud horror stories to tell . . . by all means don't. But chances are, you'll have more in the future. Because with every dollar we spend, we're telling Mr. Badwrench that it's good to be bad. If we close our wallets and start spending some common sense, we can say goodbye to Mr. Badwrench . . . and get the monkey wrench out of our lives.

Reprinted with the permission of the Interstate Oratorical Association from *Winning Orations* ed. Larry Schnoor (Mankato, MN: Interstate Oratorical Association, 1987) 29-32.

"Rationing Health Care: The Inevitable Meets the Unthinkable"
Richard D. Lamm
Former Governor of Colorado

1   I have come to the conclusion that the United States has to challenge all its basic institutions. Not overturn—but challenge: to keep what is necessary and efficient and to prune what is unnecessary and inefficient. Many of our institutions have become bureaucratic, inefficient, wasteful, and risk-adverse. A dynamic society should always re-examine its ends and its means.

2   It seems to me beyond argument, and perhaps even an aphorism, that man can't live by bread alone and that society can't live by health care alone. We have other desperately important values that we must invest in: education, infrastructure, retooling America, etc.

3   Our whole economy in the United States is tilting toward health care. In 1950, governmental spending for health care was 45.9 percent of that spent on education. By 1984 it was equal to all government spending for education. We have many important things to do with our limited societal resources, but one of these values, i.e., health care, seems to be receiving virtually all the funding it wants and needs and at the expense of other important societal values. Like the fading southern family in William Faulkner's novel that ''takes sick and ceases to work,'' we are treating our illnesses at the expense of our livelihood. We spend more than a billion dollars a day for health care, while our bridges fall down, our teachers are underpaid and our industrial plants rust. This cannot continue.

4   There is something fundamentally unsustainable about a society that moves its basic value-producing industries offshore, yet continues to manufacture artificial hearts on-shore. We have money to give smokers heart transplants, but not enough money to retool our steel mills. We train more doctors than we need and fewer teachers. On any give day, 25 percent of our hospital beds are empty, our school rooms overcrowded, and transportation systems painfully inadequate. We are great at treating sick people, but do very little to treat our sick economy.

5   We are not succeeding in international trade. Our trade deficit has exploded to $130 billion a year while the cost of health care has been compounding at a 10.2 percent rate since 1950, two-and-one-half times the rate of inflation. Our goods contain an ever escalating health care cost component that adds to their increasingly uncompetitive price.

6   I believe one of the major challenges of America's future is how do we more wisely invest our scarce resources. To do this we have to be realistic, we have to ask heretical questions, to question sacred cows. We cannot simply stand back and let one segment of our economy, no matter *what* it is, grow at two-and-one-half times the rate of inflation and not scrutinize it with great vigor. We must question its basic assumptions. We must probe its every justification.

7   When you look at where America is spending its ever more limited dollars, one soon comes to the health care industry. It is the third largest industry in America and now takes $.11 out of every dollar spent in America. One governor called it ''the PAC man of his budget'' because it eats up all of his flexibility to do other things with state funds. Like the man who carries a first aid kit, the weight of which gives him blisters—which is why he is carrying the first aid kit in the first place—our health care system has become part solution, part problem. We wouldn't want to be without it, but it has become a heavy burden. It is definitely interfering with the public's ability to invest in other public goods and with private industry's ability to re-tool itself. Health care insurance now costs U.S. corporations approximately $125 billion a year, slightly in excess of 50 percent of their pre-tax profits. That is money they need desperately to re-tool and re-industrialize. Corporations now recognize that they themselves have been largely at fault. By simply paying health care providers what they charge without any attempt to monitor the utilization or quality of services rendered, they were heading toward bankruptcy.

8   So when thoughtful observers started looking at health care and asking heretical questions, they came up with some interesting observations. There is little correlation between how much money is spent on health care and how healthy a society is. We are too easily seduced into thinking that health care means doctors and hospitals, when actually the great advances in health have been made in the area of sanitation, pasteurization, chlorination, vaccination, and refrigeration. Public health officials have saved far more lives than hospitals have. If we look at how we could improve the health of the average American, we would find that by far the greatest cause of premature mortality and morbidity is smoking too much, drinking too much, eating too much, and not wearing seat belts. Those are all four things that are under individual control, and three of them are things we do with our mouths. The mouth is by far the most dangerous organ of the human body. It becomes clear that there are many paths to health and, certainly, doctors and hospitals are some of them. But public policy makers have a wide variety of other tools available to improve health in the public. I am convinced that we could bring more health to America with a dollar-a-pack tax on cigarettes than we could by adding another $100 billion to health care spending. Give me some of those empty hospital beds to lock up drunk drivers and I will save more lives than the hospitals will. Resources have a variety of possible uses, yet this society seldom asks about the most cost effective alternatives.

9   I respect and honor doctors and hospitals, but they do not have a monopoly on promoting health in a society. But even when you look at that aspect of our health that is brought to us by doctors and hospitals, we have to question very closely what we are getting for our money. America has no better health outcome than many industrialized countries that spend far less than we do. The United States spends $1500 per capita on health care; England spends $400 per capita on health care; Singapore spends $200 per capita on health care; and we all have the same mortality rates. Now I recognize that that is not the only yardstick to measure health outcomes, and it does not fully dispose of the issue, but neither can it be ignored. The United States has an extremely expensive, inefficient health care system that needs to be questioned much more closely than it has been. We can no longer allow sacred cows to feed on our economic landscape.

10   We are not wealthy enough to continue to base our health care system on these assumptions: 1.) that there are infinite resources available, 2.) that the health care system is the only way to deliver health, and 3.) that fee-for-service medicine came down with Moses on the tablets. Like Abraham Lincoln we must say, ''As our case is new, we must think and act anew, we must disenthrall ourselves.''

11   This conference asks one of the basic heretical questions: do we ration health care. Linus, in ''Charlie Brown'' once said, ''There's no issue too big that you can't run away from it.'' But, alas, we can no longer run away from the question of rationing because it is here now, has been with us, and the sooner we recognize that, the sooner we will be able to reduce the harshness of its operation. Avoiding the problem avoids the solution. *The Painful Prescription* set this forth brilliantly and is much quoted: The Oregon health

decision people, in what was a marvelous contribution to the current dialogue stated, "Oregonians can no longer count on being able to get all the health care they may need. Rationing of health care is inevitable because society can not or will not pay for all the services modern medicine can provide. People in the state must search their hearts and their pocketbooks and decide what level of health care will be guaranteed to the poor, the unemployed, the elderly, and others who depend on publicly funded health services."

12   They point out that:

—*We already ration chronologically*, i.e., many publicly funded and charitable health programs have such limited resources that it is very wise to get sick early in the fiscal year.

—*We ration economically*. The rich obviously have better access to health care than the poor even when the poor have the best of circumstances.

—*We ration geographically*. Certain areas in which people live have far less access to health care than other areas.

—*We ration politically*. If you need an organ transplant, your chance of success is directly proportional to your access to the media or to some highly placed politician.

—*Related to the above, we ration by disease*. If you have an interesting disease, you are more likely to get health care than if you have an uninteresting disease.

—*We ration by prognosis*. If you have a fatal disease, watch the number of visits by doctors and nurses diminish.

—*We ration by employment*. Certain employees or unions have much better health insurance benefits than others.

In short, rationing is not a future possibility. It is a present reality.

13   The Greeks say that to know all to ask is to know half. Certainly, if we start asking the right questions, we vastly improve our chances of coming up with the right answers. If we ask ourselves how to avoid rationing, I believe we do society an injustice, if we ask, how do we make rationing as compassionate and sensible as possible, using it to increase rather than decrease medical care, then it will be a very positive endeavor. Rationing can be described in the same words as Mark Twain said of Wagner's music: "It's not as bad as it sounds."

14   But it is extremely important that we are honest with ourselves and honest with our constituents. In the past we have spent a destructive amount of time pretending there isn't a problem instead of a constructive amount of time looking for a solution. The price of avoidance has been enormous.

15   I have had numerous instances in the last year, after getting back from spending a week looking at the English health care system, of people telling me with shock and horror in their eyes how cruel the English system is. They cite as their evidence such things as the refusal of kidney dialysis to people over 55 years of age.

16   I am not a proponent of the English health care system, but I do have to admit that it is far less cruel than the United States health care system. The Robert Wood Johnson Foundation in 1982 found that about 12 percent of all Americans, or one in eight, have serious problems with access to adequate

health care. They found that, in that fiscal year, 1,000,000 families had at least one member who was refused health care. The literature is replete with numerous examples. One more will suffice. The National Medical Care Expenditure survey found that in the South, insured persons receive three times as many days of hospital care as uninsured, and 54 percent more physician ambulatory care than the uninsured.

17   Once we ask the Copernican question, how can finite resources ever keep up with infinite needs, then we are on the path to being able to analyze our problems and come up with some rational solutions. One clear lesson in life, as individuals, as well as public policy makers, is that our wants exceed our resources. This is particularly true in the area of medicine, where medical miracles outrun the ability of the public to pay for them. Infinite needs have run into finite resources. Once we admit that, it allows us to develop a strategy for spending our limited public dollars.

18   I suggest that even with rationing we can deliver more health care, more efficiently, to more people than if we continue to ignore and avoid the problem. We can have a "rational" rationing system rather than an "irrational" rationing system: A recognition of limits usually makes us allocate what is available more efficiently.

19   What, then, is my prescription for a rationing system that is both an efficient reallocation of resources and compassionate? Before attempting to answer I must ask myself whether we Americans have the political will to ration explicitly. A frustrated Lee Iacocca said recently that he's convinced that "if Americans really understood how deep in the hole they are (with the budget deficit), and what they are doing to their kids' futures, they would not only accept sacrifice, they'd demand it." Through a fascinating process of public debate in town meetings all over the state, the citizens of Oregon found that there was a consensus on these issues: that rationing exists now; that it is unfair; and that it is inevitable for the future.

20   Upon whom would fall the task of explicit rationing? A health czar? With battalions of health economists and cost-benefit studies and cost effectiveness analyses? Not in America.

21   Lester Thurow proposes a mental exercise for doctors in which every time they order an expensive procedure they would have to pick an American worker to be sentenced to a period of slavery long enough to pay the medical bill for that procedure. Victor Fuchs suggests that physicians have always practiced within constraints and that as long as this rationing has been implicit it has been tolerable. Rationing at the individual patient's bedside can continue to remain implicit if the patient/physician/family nucleus has accepted the economic, social, and moral importance of rational constraints.

22   Let me suggest that those systemic constraints must include, first and foremost, a reallocation of resources: Those of us who buy medical care must stop rewarding medical procedures and surgeries that are overutilized. We— and I mean state governments, business, Medicare—must rationalize what our benefits-design will be, what we will pay more for, and what we will pay less for. For example, should business benefits packages include mammography or organ transplantation? Should we subsidize the explosion in unnecessary

laboratory tests? Lab tests increased at an annual rate of 13.8 percent in hospital labs, and 15.6 percent in independent labs. For example, the average number of lab tests for perforated appendicitis increased from 5.3 per case in 1951 to 31.0 in 1971. For maternity care, the number rose from 4.8 per case in 1951 to 13.5 per case in 1971. It is estimated that a reduction to 50 percent of present levels would be reasonable to affect savings without reducing the quality of patient care.

23   We must stop training physicians in over-populated medical specialties in which invasive procedures and operations are excessively performed.

24   We must reduce our physician supply overall, and I suggest we start with reduced immigration of undertrained foreign graduates. The Graduate Medical Education National Advisory Committee (GEMENACO) estimated that there will be 145,000 more physicians than needed by the year 2000. Based on a GEMENACO report, Duke University's medical school announced a reduction in its class size of 13% over five years. Dr. David Sabiston, Chairman of the Medical Schools cited a 1978 report by the U.S. Department of Health, Education and Welfare that says each physician in practice increases the nations' health care costs by $300,000 annually. "Thus, with an average career spanning forty years, a single physician would create health care costs of some $12 million."

25   We must eliminate duplicative and excess hospital capacity. We must insist upon regionalization of highly tactical and expensive services. We have 100,000 to 200,000 excess hospital beds in the U.S. We should control the rise of intensive care units. The cost of ICU care has been the fastest-rising of all health care costs, increasing 30% a year, and ICU costs average 20 percent of total hospital costs and 10 percent of our total health care bill. And until recently, an estimated one-third of the people who occupied hospital beds didn't need to be there. The DRG system for Medicare and market forces are already helping remedy this problem. An excess hospital bed doesn't help anyone.

26   Flat-of-the-curve medicine — those medical practices that at the highest cost achieve little or no improvement in health status — must be reduced or eliminated. We must demand that professional societies and licensing authorities establish norms and standards for diagnostic and therapeutic practice that encompass both the costs and benefits of medical practices.

27   We must make the public a better participant in rationing. We may do this by requiring financial participation in medical care by those who pay. We must publish data on risks and benefits of procedures and surgeries, and on regional variations in practice.

28   We must do something about the litigation crisis and how it promotes defensive medicine. This is a subject of another conference, but we could clearly save and reallocate tens of billions of dollars by removing the litigation sword of Damocles that hangs over the health care system.

29   In order to remain compassionate in our rationing, we must guarantee that those who cannot pay have access to care.

30   There is an additional range of issues that must be addressed not merely by better management, but through public consensus on priorities and a

balancing of health care needs with the needs of our educational, transportation, and industrial systems, just to name a few.

31   We must look more maturely at many sensitive issues. Victor Fuchs does that in a number of areas, one of which is the assumption that we should ''spend any amount of money because a life is at stake.'' He rightly points out that it might sound good, but it is impossible to carry out. I could not agree more. I govern a state that last year had 101 plane crashes, many of them in our mountains. Many times we couldn't find these people or know whether there were survivors. Should I bring the State of Colorado to a halt and send all our resources out to find a plane because ''a life is at stake?'' We obviously can't do that. We must combine thinking heads with compassionate hearts and recognize that even where lives are at stake, there is a restriction on resources.

32   We need to talk much more candidly and openly about death and dying. We treat death as if it were optional, but alas, we cannot erase the hard fact of death. As Shakespeare said, ''We all owe God a death.'' And once we stop treating death as an enemy and recognize it as an inevitability, I believe we can save massive resources. Today patients with massive strokes are saved from death but live for years in a comatose state. Others with metastic cancer are subject to a myriad of studies and therapies that add little to longevity. We must look rationally at the phenomenal amount of resources we spend in the last few weeks and months of people's lives, often only to prolong their suffering.

33   On another sensitive subject, doctors often consider age as a factor when they treat patients. But is the public ready to use age as a factor when allocating scarce medical resources? I don't question the need to give both the young and the elderly access to preventive and primary care. But when it comes to limited resources that cannot be made available to everyone, I approach the problem with a very personal example in mind. Couldn't my 15-year-old daughter with 60.4 projected years ahead of her make better use of a limited resource such as an organ transplant than I could with 28.1 projected years ahead of me? Such a policy is not age discrimination but common sense: who should be our top priority for receiving limited organs?

34   The aged are not a static group. It is a status through which most of us go. We are locked in as males or females, black or white. Once a white male, always a white male. But we all age daily. In a marvelously egalitarian way, time takes its toll on all of us. When we give prenatal care to infants and vaccinate children we are, in a very real sense, improving the health status of the elderly.

35   Our health care resources can be used in many less dramatic ways with far greater benefit. The money we spent on the heart transplant for Mr. Schroeder could have been far more productively spent on the replacement of heart valves for 200 patients or the 40-50 percent of poor, pregnant American women who receive no prenatal care in their first trimester or the one-third of the kids in America who have never seen a dentist.

36   Are we going to wait until a politically active group of chronic heart patients—many of them smokers—wheel a bunch of artificial heart recipients before a congressional committee, their hearts literally and figuratively in their

hands, and plead for the taxpayers to save their lives by providing publicly paid-for artificial hearts? Is that how we want to set our health care priorities? Should taxpayers pay for transplants for those who have damaged themselves by years of physical neglect or self-abuse?

37   I am not a medical Luddite [opponent of technology]. I admire the miracles of medicine. But I contrast cornea transplants, cataract operations and hip replacements, which add tremendously to the quality of life for the elderly, to artificial hearts.

38   Our overwhelming fascination with new technology drives the media and public to demand that as soon as we develop it, it be put to use, whether or not we have any real idea of its cost-effectiveness. The National Institutes of Health called for greatly expanded federal research efforts to develop a fully implantable permanent artificial heart. Such devices, it said, "Could provide a significant increase in lifespan, with an acceptable quality of life, for 17,000 to 35,000 patients below age 70 annually." The group estimated its *annual* cost at up to $5 billion. This is a staggering price tag for the few people who would benefit. It will add significantly to the cost of health insurance premiums for all of us. It will eat into the budgets for Medicaid and Medicare. But it won't do a thing to prevent heart disease in the first place. And if we think we can add research on the artificial heart to other research programs and still pay for them all, we are tragically mistaken.

39   My criticism is not of high technology. On the contrary, I believe that high technology, if correctly applied, can save far more lives at a lower cost if we manage it correctly. My criticism is the mindless way in which we invent certain high technologies and then are forced to use them, at the same time foregoing many more high-benefit procedures and technologies that could save far more lives. An artificial heart is a high technology, low benefit invention because its cost is so very high and it only benefits a few people. Humana's budget for the artificial heart is almost exactly what it cost society to eradicate smallpox from the whole world.

40   The ultimate goal to which this society should apply its high technology is the understanding of the mechanisms which are the underlying causes of disease. Lewis Thomas writes that the diseases that were the greatest menace to human health when he was a medical student on the wards of Boston City Hospital 50 years ago were, "in the order of degree of fear they caused in the public mind, tertiary syphilis of the brain, pulmonary tuberculosis, and acute rheumatic fever. Also, of course, poliomyelitis." He points out that because of classical clinical research "all four have nearly vanished as public health problems, and the vanishing involved the expenditure of pennies compared to what we'd be spending if they were still with us." Now *that* is true high technology medicine. But just as we would never have cured polio by putting all our money in artificial lungs, so also we will not understand and cure heart disease if we put our money into artificial hearts.

41   In conclusion, I am reminded of a story in the second world war during the time of rationing when a man went into a restaurant and ordered a cup of coffee and asked for more sugar. The waitress cast a cynical eye on him and said, "Stir what you have." I believe that that is what America must do — stir

better the over $1 billion a day that we already put into health care. There is enough money there to buy an incredibly high standard of health care for all our citizens if we simply utilize our resources better. I believe that we can much better stir what we already have.

Reprinted with the permission of Governor Lamm.

Speaking on Special Occasions

Every culture honors certain occasions with speeches. The purposes may be informative, persuasive or entertaining, but what specifically identifies these speeches are the occasions at which they are presented. When young persons earn the Eagle Scout award, it is not enough just to receive the badge, someone has to say something about the event. When you graduated from high school, a commencement speech was the highlight of the program. When a business or civic group sponsors a dinner, a speaker is scheduled to address the gathering. Frequently, the speaker chooses to deliver a speech to entertain—usually called an after-dinner speech. Eulogies are delivered at funerals. From birth to death, speeches celebrate special occasions.

History records the custom of celebrating important occasions with speechmaking. So important was the practice that Aristotle recognized it almost 2400 years ago as a separate form of oratory. He called it epideictic. The speeches delivered on special occasions are similar to other speeches in all important respects: they have a subject and a purpose, they seek a specific response, they have structure and supporting details, and they require good delivery. Most importantly, however, they must meet the ceremonial requirements of the occasion.

The event to be celebrated may be happy or sad. The speeches are addressed to the young and the old, the rich and the poor. They may, like the after-dinner speech, be intended solely to entertain or they may be seriously persuasive. But they all commemorate the occasion.

These occasions provide speakers a time to remind audiences of the values they share as members of the society: honesty, salvation, bravery, goodwill. The emphasis is on instrumental values—those that define ideal behavior. The speeches tell of the character and conduct of heroes and heroines.

Because ceremonial speeches have great personal significance and a heavy emphasis on values, they frequently put greater demands on speakers for significant thought, language, or humor. There are many different kinds of special occasion speeches. Every group seems to have its own name for special occasion speeches (e.g.; testimony, counsel, hellos, knighting). Despite the diverse labels, all occasional addresses may reasonably be divided into four types: speeches of courtesy, speeches of tribute, speeches of good will, and speeches to entertain. Let's look at some distinguishing characteristics of these subtypes.

Speeches of Courtesy

Speeches of courtesy clearly indicate the ceremonial nature of some occasions. When the county attorney comes to your organization to speak, you don't just nod to her and expect her to get up and speak. She has to be introduced. When the outstanding player on your baseball team receives

Ceremonial speeches, such as the commencement address, place a heavy emphasis on values and are frequently marked by significant thought, language, or humor.

a plaque at the annual awards banquet, it isn't just handed to him. Someone makes a presentation and the baseball player is expected to respond. Unfortunately, these speeches are often trite and unprepared. Speeches of courtesy are important, however. Each one presents an opportunity for the speaker to find fresh, new ways to express the familiar values the audience expects to hear.

Introductions

Speeches of introduction are probably given more often than any other speech of courtesy. The task of the introductory speech is to present a specific speaker to a specific audience. The best person to make an introduction is usually someone who knows the speaker or at least the speaker's reputation. The purpose of the speech is to inform the audience about the achievements of the speaker and to invite the audience's attention.

The speech of introduction *must* do two things—and normally should do three. It must introduce the speaker to the audience by indicating the speaker's qualifications to speak on the subject. It must introduce the subject of the speech by showing its significance, timeliness and relevance to the audience. And finally, the speech should express the introducer's personal pleasure in both the speaker and the subject.

The audience is there to hear the speaker. Therefore, the introduction should be brief. Anything that is required can be said in no more than a minute or a minute and a half. It is traditional, after all, to introduce one of the most important people in the world with the briefest of introductions: "Ladies and gentlemen, the President of the United States."

You may be assigned to introduce one of your classmates during this course, and you may not know that person very well. You should schedule an interview to learn the title and subject of the speech, the speaker's qualifications, and the significance of the speech for the audience. Remember that you will have limited time—probably about half a minute. You must tell the audience the speaker's name and the subject of the speech. Try to add one significant fact about the speaker and one about the subject that the audience will find interesting and which will make the listeners more receptive to the speech. It is your job to help the speaker off to a good start. Make sure that is your goal.

Nominations

A speech of nomination is, in very many respects, a speech of introduction. It tells the voting audience what qualifications the nominee has for the office. If you are called upon to nominate someone for an office, ask yourself "What problems confront this organization that my candidate would be most qualified to solve?" "How does my candidate represent appropriate values?" "What specific examples of past conduct show that my candidate is ideal for this organization at this time?"

On December 24, 1988 President-elect George Bush called a press conference to announce that Elizabeth Hanford Dole would be Secretary of Labor in his administration. That speech served both to introduce her and announce his nomination of her for the Senate confirmation. The style makes it clear that the speech was extemporaneous.

> Well, I would say I'm sorry to impose on you on Christmas Eve day, but I'm not because I have a piece of good news to deliver before the holiday, and that is that Elizabeth Hanford Dole has agreed to be the Bush administration Secretary of Labor.
>
> The skills that will be required of America's work force will be increasingly great in the years ahead, and the work force itself is in dramatic change, with women especially continuing to enter the work force in ever larger numbers. In this environment, it is essential that we have a Secretary of Labor who understands the challenges out there and who has the experience, the stature and the ability to deal with them effectively. The point is that these changes are coming, and there is no getting around it. We need as the head of the Labor Department someone who understands changes and can help us as a nation to manage it well.
>
> I am absolutely certain that Elizabeth Dole will be such a Secretary of Labor. She is a woman of talent, integrity, great skill, and of course, tremendous experience. As you know, she served for five years as Secretary of Transportation in the Reagan-Bush Administration. Prior to that she was Assistant to the President for Public Liaison in the White House, and in that job had a lot of contacts, I might add, with the great labor leaders of this country. Prior to that she served for six years as a Commissioner of the Federal Trade Commission.[1]

Speeches of Welcome

A common courtesy in a group is to welcome new members or visitors. Meetings of professional groups (sales meetings, academic or professional conventions, etc.) offer good examples of this custom. The purpose of a speech of welcome is to make the visitors, most of whom are usually from out of town, feel more comfortable and to highlight the significance of the business they have come to transact.

A welcome need not be long. For example, under International Olympic Committee rules, the statement which formally opens the games is precisely prescribed; the name of the host city and the number of the Olympiad are the only changes made. In 1984: ''I declare open the Games of Los Angeles, celebrating the XXIII Olympiad of the modern era.'' The rule limiting what the chief of state of the host country can say is intended to keep politics out of the games. Although President Reagan changed the word order a bit when he delivered the statement in 1984, he did not say more than the sixteen words prescribed as a maximum.

In some situations—for instance, when a public official such as a mayor welcomes a professional organization—there are greater expectations. A welcome speech is expected to contain references to the significance of what these professionals do. If there is a special relationship between the group and the meeting place (if the group first met in that city, for instance), then that should be mentioned. The group is made to feel welcome because there is a significance to the group and its relation to the place where it is meeting.

You have probably experienced a welcome in the simplest form such as: "On behalf of the ski club I want to welcome our visitors Sue Johnson, Robert Rossi, and Heather Watcher to our group. We hope you'll feel at home with us and we will enjoy lots of good times together in the future, on the slopes."

Presentations

According to a story in the *Los Angeles Times*, the Soviet encyclopedia identifies 37 orders and 47 medals with which Soviet citizens can be honored. And that's only a partial listing. There are even medals for motherhood: first class for having eight or more children, second class for six or seven. In the United States, awards in great variety and large numbers are given for many accomplishments. Honorary degrees are bestowed and Nobel laureates are honored. Oscars, Emmys, Tonys, Obies, and Grammys are among the awards given to outstanding entertainments and entertainers.

Awards, of course, are not the only occasion for making a speech of presentation. When someone donates money to a cause, books to a library, or statues to public places, speeches are as inevitable as the photograph in the next day's newspaper. The speech always details the reasons for making the presentation.

Thus, the speaker's primary task is to give an audience reasons to respect and admire the person being honored. By implication, the speech also suggests that others might emulate the bravery, generosity, pioneering spirit, or whatever quality or conduct earned the award.

Soon after Lt. Col. John H. Glenn, Jr. (later Senator from Ohio) made his historic flight as the first American astronaut to orbit the earth, President John F. Kennedy presented him with the NASA Distinguished Service Medal. This ceremonial speech has historical significance because Kennedy not only commends Glenn for past action but states America's determination to go to the moon. The president said:

> Seventeen years ago today, a group of Marines put the American Flag on Mount Suribachi, so it's very appropriate that today we decorate Colonel Glenn of the United States Marine Corps, and also realize that in the not too distant future a Marine or a Naval man or an Air Force man will put the American Flag on the moon.
>
> I present this citation:
>
> "The President of the United States takes pleasure in awarding the National Aeronautics and Space Administration Distinguished Service Medal to Lieutenant Colonel John H. Glenn, Jr., United States Marine Corps, for services

set forth in the following: For exceptionally meritorious service to the government of the United States in a duty of great responsibility as the first American astronaut to perform orbital flight. Lieutenant Colonel Glenn's orbital flight on February 20, 1962, made an outstanding contribution to the advancement of human knowledge of space technology and in demonstration of man's capabilities in space flights.

"His performance was marked by his great professional knowledge, his skill as a test pilot, his unflinching courage, and his extraordinary ability to perform most difficult tasks under conditions of great physical stress and personal danger. His performance in fulfillment of this most dangerous assignment reflects the highest credit upon himself and the United States."

Colonel, we appreciate what you have done![2]

In a presentation speech, the speaker's primary task is to give an audience reasons to admire the person being honored.

Speeches of Response

Depending on the circumstances, any speech of courtesy can call for a response.

Although any speech of response can be impromptu, the recipient is not likely to be surprised by the presentation of an award. No one, for example, ever received an Academy Award as a complete surprise. Acceptance speeches by recipients—breathless and startled as they may seem—are not naive. They are more artful than impromptu.

The recipient should have a better response than a bashful grin and a mumbled "thanks." If you are given an award for something you did solely on your own, accept it with openness. Don't gloat, but don't grovel in false modesty. If the award comes as the result of a team effort, or if others had any part in its success, give them a generous amount of credit.

After President Kennedy pinned the medal on his lapel, John Glenn made a brief speech of response. The conversational quality of the speech and the lack of polish in the style suggest that it was not written out and memorized. Nonetheless, he shared the credit with others who had played a vital role in his achievement and said what he wanted to say with forthrightness, propriety, and modesty.

> I can't express my appreciation adequately to be here in accepting this when I know how many thousand people all over the country were involved in helping accomplish what we did last Tuesday and knowing how particularly this group here at the Cape and many of the group here on the platform, our own group of astronauts who were scattered all around the world and who performed their functions here at the Cape also.
>
> We all acted literally and figuratively as a team and it was a real team effort all the way.
>
> We have stressed the team effort in Project Mercury. It goes across the board, I think. Sort of a cross-cut of Americana of industry and military and Civil Service, Government workers, contractors. The—almost a cross-cut of American effort in the technical field, I think. It wasn't specialized by any one particular group.
>
> It was headed up by NASA, of course, but thousands and thousands of people have contributed, certainly as much or more than I have to the Project.
>
> I would like to consider that I was sort of a figurehead for the whole big, tremendous effort and I am very proud of the medal I have on my lapel here, for all of us—you included—because I think it represents all of our efforts, not just mine. Thank you very much and thank you, Mr. President.[3]

Speeches of Farewell

Custom and courtesy seem often to require that exits as well as entrances be ceremonialized. An officer or member leaving an organization is frequently expected to make a speech of farewell. A long-time employee of a company, who is given the traditional "gold watch" upon retirement, may make a speech of farewell as an appropriate response. It is customary for such a speech to express sentiments of pleasure, gratitude, and fondness.

Notable for its brevity and grace is the speech with which Abraham Lincoln said goodbye to his friends on February 11, 1861, when he left his home town of Springfield, Illinois for the White House. Note how he links his departure to his audience and to their values.

> My friends: No one not in my situation can appreciate my feeling of sadness at this parting. To this place, and the kindness of these people, I owe everything. Here I have lived a quarter of a century, and have passed from a young to an old man. Here my children have been born, and one is buried. I now leave, not knowing when or whether ever I may return, with a task before me greater than that which rested upon Washington. Without the assistance of that Divine Being who ever attended him, I cannot succeed. With that assistance, I cannot fail. Trusting in Him who can go with me, and remain with you, and be everywhere for good, let us confidently hope that all will yet be well. To His care commending you, as I hope in your prayers you will commend me, I bid you an affectionate farewell.

Speeches of Tribute

To a degree, all ceremonial speeches pay tribute to something or someone. But some of them make this their sole purpose. The speaker intends to arouse in the audience a high level of admiration for the person or event being honored and to reinforce the values that the person or event exemplifies.

Eulogies

Throughout recorded history, humanity has, in some fashion or another, paid tribute to its model citizens. One common form of eulogy, for instance, is the funeral oration. In it, praise is given to someone's life, character, and deeds. In Athens in 431 B.C., Pericles delivered one of the most famous eulogies, commemorating Greek soldiers who had died in the Peloponnesian War. It set a structure which virtually all eulogies in western society have followed: praise, lament, and consolation.[4] Traditionally, the funeral orator recites the deeds of the deceased that deserve admiration, examines the values those deeds exemplify, and shows how the audience can perpetuate those values in its own thoughts and actions.

Television cameras recorded the lift-off of the space shuttle Challenger on the morning of January 28, 1986. Seventy seconds later, the shuttle exploded before a horrified audience of millions. All seven crew members died in the explosion. At 5:00 pm that day (Eastern Daylight Time),

President Ronald Reagan presented a eulogy to the astronauts in place of his scheduled State of the Union address on national television.

Ladies and gentlemen, I'd planned to speak to you tonight to report on the state of the Union, but the events of earlier today have led me to change those plans. Today is a day for mourning and remembering.

Nancy and I are pained to the core by the tragedy of the shuttle *Challenger*. We know we share this pain with all of the people of our country. This is truly a national loss.

Nineteen years ago, almost to the day, we lost three astronauts in a terrible accident on the ground. But we've never lost an astronaut in flight; we've never had a tragedy like this. And perhaps we've forgotten the courage it took for the crew of the shuttle; but they, the *Challenger* Seven, were aware of the dangers, but overcame them and did their jobs brilliantly. We mourn seven heroes: Michael Smith, Dick Scobee, Judith Resnik, Ronald McNair, Ellison Onizuka, Gregory Jarvis, and Christa McAuliffe. We mourn their loss as a nation together.

For the families of the seven, we cannot bear, as you do, the full impact of this tragedy. But we feel the loss, and we're thinking about you so very much. Your loved ones were daring and brave, and they had that special grace, that special spirit that says, "Give me a challenge and I'll meet it with joy." They had a hunger to explore the universe and discover its truths. They wished to serve, and they did. They served all of us.

We've grown used to wonders in this century. It's hard to dazzle us. But for 25 years the United States space program has been doing just that. We've grown used to the idea of space, and perhaps we forget that we've only just begun. We're still pioneers. They, the members of the *Challenger* crew, were pioneers.

And I want to say something to the schoolchildren of America who were watching the live coverage of the shuttle's takeoff. I know it is hard to understand, but sometimes painful things like this happen. It's all part of the process of exploration and discovery. It's all part of taking a chance and expanding man's horizons. The future doesn't belong to the fainthearted; it belongs to the brave. The *Challenger* crew was pulling us into the future, and we'll continue to follow them.

I've always had great faith in and respect for our space program, and what happened today does nothing to diminish it. We don't hide our space program. We don't keep secrets and cover things up. We do it all up front and in public. That's the way freedom is, and we wouldn't change it for a minute.

We'll continue our quest in space. There will be more shuttle flights and more shuttle crews and, yes, more volunteers, more civilians, more teachers in space. Nothing ends here; our hopes and our journeys continue.

I want to add that I wish I could talk to every man and woman who works for NASA or who worked on this mission and tell them: "Your dedication and professionalism have moved and impressed us for decades. And we know of your anguish. We share it."

There's a coincidence today. On this day 390 years ago, the great explorer Sir Francis Drake died aboard ship off the coast of Panama. In his lifetime the great frontiers were the ocean, and an historian later said, "He lived by the sea, died on it, and was buried in it." Well, today we can say of the *Challenger* crew: Their dedication was, like Drake's, complete.

The crew of the space shuttle *Challenger* honored us by the manner in which they lived their lives. We will never forget them, nor the last time we saw them, this morning, as they prepared for their journey and waved goodbye and "slipped the surly bonds of earth" to "touch the face of God."[5]

Commemorations

Virtually any holiday celebrated in America—Labor Day, Veterans' Day, the Fourth of July, to name only a few—calls forth speeches of commemoration. Local politicians give speeches of commemoration when they plant a tree on Arbor Day.

The President of the United States is called upon to commemorate many events. Here is Jimmy Carter's commemoration of the Jewish New Year of Rosh Hashanah.

> As you solemnly review and judge your own conduct during the past year, we are all reminded that we serve God most faithfully by showing concern for our friends and neighbors.
>
> In a world made small by modern technology, all peoples and nations have become closer together, and the concern for others has become more important than ever. This is the wellspring of our nation's commitment to human rights, and it is why we are determined that all of America's words and deeds will honor that commitment.
>
> Among the Rosh Hashanah prayers recited in the synagogue is one which looks toward the day when mankind will be joined in universal brotherhood. This is a prayer to which all of us add our heartfelt "amen" as we wish each of you a happy and prosperous New Year.[6]

Speeches of Good Will

Not all of the advertising on television has the immediate purpose of selling a product or service. Instead, it is meant to win, hold, and build the prestige and friendly relations the sponsoring company has with its customers. Good will is so elusive, delicate, and important that corporations (insurance, oil and communication, among others) spend literally millions of dollars a year to maintain it.

One series of commercials on national television in the summer of 1990 were produced by Chevron Oil Company. They show shore birds walking in shallow water, an egret taking off, ducks and coots swimming by, and a large flock of birds flying off the water. The words tell the viewer that "This is one of the best little rest stops in Mississippi. It's a salt water wetland, the kind of a place nature might have made. A good spot to drop in, grab a bite, or just sit a spell. It was made by people who work in the nearby refinery. Do people need to create places where nature can spread its wings?" Then the words are said and printed beneath the Chevron logo: "People do." The commercial purports to be informative. It is also persuasive—not in selling Chevron products but in selling the image of the company. It is a good will commercial.

Business and industry are not alone, of course, in their desire to maintain a friendly image. The Federal government has long used the office of "good will ambassador" to help maintain friendly relations with foreign nations. Indeed, this has been an important part of the duties of all ambassadors throughout history.

In essence, a good will speech is designed to show how the organization or service represented by the speaker is working in the interests of the audience. A speech of good will is basically organized to appear as an informative speech. As such, it does not directly deal with issues. That is, the speaker does not acknowledge opposing arguments, but rather acts as if there were no issues.

A telephone company representative comes to a local service club or PTA to tell the members about the new advances in technology that will provide better services and save the customer money. The president of a university addresses the Chamber of Commerce on recent achievements of the university. The secretary of a local union speaks at a high school about a scholarship the union provides to an outstanding graduating senior. All of these speeches are informative in content and strategy, but they have purposes which go beyond merely conveying information. They build good will for the organization the speaker represents.

The method of preparing and delivering speeches of good will is not significantly different from that of informative speeches. The principal concern in preparing a speech of good will is to keep it informative in tone. If it begins to argue a controversial point, it will have quite a different purpose. To succeed, it will then have to meet the very different requirements of persuasive speaking.

Speeches to Entertain

On occasion, the purpose of a speech will be to amuse an audience. But a speech to entertain need not be devoid of serious ideas. It can have a very real and useful point. For example, a talk about the "glories" of growing up that describes the dubious advantages of maturity—with its debts, taxes, and responsibilities—would surely make a point. Nonetheless, it could amuse and divert an audience by approaching the subject from a deliberately offbeat, eccentric point of view.[7] What distinguishes a speech to entertain from a speech to inform or to persuade is the light touch with which the speaker takes up the subject. The success of a speech to entertain springs from the ability to use humor well.

However, a speech to entertain is not merely a collection of funny stories. As a speech it must have at least a semblance of unity and order. It has a central idea and the speaker "develops" it. Some of the audience's pleasure may come from the zany way the idea is developed, but it must appear to start from a reasonable base. In public speaking, digressions are normally inadvisable. In a speech to entertain, however, they are permissible provided they contribute to the humor. If you digress from your central theme, you must return to it. Even speeches to entertain must show the audience a sense of order.

Good transitions are as useful and necessary in a speech to entertain as in any other speech. Any audience deserves an orderly presentation. It is not sufficient to use "That reminds me of a story," as a transition to your anecdote. The audience will be listening to learn in what direction the speech is moving. Transitions should move from point to point, not joke to joke, so that the speech is well organized and flows smoothly. The stories and quips then fall into place as supporting material. In other words, the transitions emphasize the gist and not the jest.

A familiar occasion for speaking to entertain is the after-dinner speech. "The Wonderful World of College" was an after-dinner speech in intercollegiate forensics competition by Ian Fielding, an undergraduate student at California State University, Northridge. It illustrates this kind of speaking and can be found at the end of this chapter along with one of the most famous after-dinner speeches: Mark Twain's "Speech To The Insurance Agents."

The value of humor in public speaking is by no means limited to speeches to entertain. It is an asset to any kind of speaking. Therefore, it is useful to have some understanding of the types and uses of humor.

Humor as Supporting Material

Humor is as universal as language. It is found in the gentle teasing of a friend, in subtle quips understandable only to a few, in bitter satire that strikes at folly and vice. The things that cause amusement range widely, from the most intellectual delicacies of wit to the broadest form of slapstick, custard-pie-in-the-face comedy. In life's most serious moments, laughter relieves the tension. Grim jokes about war clearly indicate that individuals seek release and frequently find it in humor.

Types of Humor

The list of items that elicit laughter is long and varied. We will mention here six types of humor that seem especially useful in speaking.

Overstatement America as a nation has been credited with overstating situations as a characteristic form of humor. The tall tale, some say a product of the vastness of the continent that had to be conquered, is an important part of folk humor. Paul Bunyan and Babe his blue ox, are only one example. To be most effective, overstatement must have some imagination to go with it. Here's an example:

> No old-time cowboy would expect to amuse you by saying that the outfit for which he worked owned a billion acres of land, as gross an overstatement as this would be. He would say that they used the state of Arizona for a calf pasture; that it took three days to ride from the yard gate to the front gallery; that the range reached so far that the sun set between headquarters and the west line camp. The folk humorist did not say of a hero that he had the strength of ten either because of his pure heart or because of his impure whiskey. He detailed concretely what the hero would do: he would fight a rattlesnake with his bare hands and give the snake three bites to start with. The roughneck of the oil fields did not say that Gib Morgan built a derrick five hundred miles high. He said that the derrick was so high that it took a man fourteen days to climb to the top of it. A crew of thirty men was required in order to have a man on duty at all times. There were at any given time fourteen men going up, fourteen men coming down, a man at the top, and a man off tower (that is, off shift). There were dog houses built a day's climb apart for the men to sleep in on their way up and down.[8]

Understatement If one may believe them, the stories that are told about President Calvin Coolidge make him the champion understater of all time. "Silent Cal" wasn't much of a talker and what little he had to say didn't incline much toward elaboration. Mr. Coolidge returned from church one Sunday morning and was asked by Mrs. Coolidge what the minister had talked about. "Sin." "Well, what did he have to say?" "He's against it."

Irony Ironic humor occurs when the meaning is the opposite of the literal sense of the words. According to Abraham Lincoln:

> A politician of less than ideal quality so aroused the citizenry of a small town that they decided to tar and feather him and ride him out of town on a rail. As they put him on the rail, he remarked, "If it weren't for the honor of the thing, I would just as soon walk."

Unexpected turns Governor Mario Cuomo of New York who has frequently been mentioned as a possible Democratic candidate for president reportedly told a Washington, D.C. audience that the Devil came to him one night to offer him a deal. Governor Cuomo said, "He offered me the presidency in exchange for my soul. So I said, 'What's the catch?'"[9]

Play on words   William L. Churchill was Director of Public Relations for Trinity College in Hartford, Connecticut when a prankster turned on the lawn sprinklers during outdoor commencement ceremonies. "I watched in disbelief as graduates, faculty and families scrambled to escape the deluge. The shower was quickly shut off, but a colleague leaned my way and said, 'I can already see the headline in tomorrow's Hartford *Courant*: Trinity Soaks Parents One Last Time'" [10]

Burlesque   Humor that parodies or mocks established concepts of the society is called burlesque. "The Peter Principle" ("In every hierarchy every employee tends to rise to his level of incompetence") mocks the established wisdom of society and makes a social comment of its own. It is reinforced by its authors Lawrence J. Peter and Raymond Hull with a long glossary of support definitions like these:

> puller—an employee who has pull
>
> first commandment—the hierarchy must be preserved
>
> deadwood—an accumulation at any level in a hierarchy of employees who have reached their level of incompetence
>
> Peter's placebo—an ounce of image is worth a pound of performance
>
> Peter's corollary—in time, every post in a hierarchy tends to be occupied by an employee who is incompetent to carry out its duties [11]

Using Humor

The following suggestions will help to make the best use of humor in speaking.

Be objective   Overriding all use of humor should be a sense of objectivity toward the situations and people characterized in the humor. Listeners must feel that the weaknesses a speaker pokes fun at are the normal weaknesses of human beings. Outlandish techniques may be used to point up these foibles, but listeners can laugh more freely if the situations and people are rooted in reality (though drawn in caricature) and are impartially presented.

Show kindliness   Speakers are constantly tempted to be sarcastic, to ridicule some person, group, or idea. Sarcasm and ridicule are properly classed as forms of humor, and they are powerful weapons in the arsenal of an effective speaker. But they often strike an unintended sour note. [12] Barbed attacks may sometimes find favor with an audience, but the truth is that although they may please, they do so by appealing to base instincts. The speaker invites the audience to share a smug, contemptuous attitude. Speakers run the danger of offending their listeners or of having the audience realize that they have been cheapened by participating in a meanness of spirit. Pointing out incongruities is not in itself an act of unkindness. But to do so with bitterness is not likely to be perceived as humor. Good-natured satire and banter lack the bitterness of sarcasm and ridicule. These may be used in a spirit of good will.

Use good taste Good taste is difficult to define, and audiences differ in what they will accept. Therefore, the injunction to avoid jokes about nationality, race, religion, and sex is not necessarily good advice. A good rule to follow is that if any bit of humor is at all likely to offend, don't use it. On the public platform, therefore, avoid any humor that even hints at vulgarity or obscenity. The stock in trade of night club comedians is not acceptable for the kind of speaking we are discussing. The world is full of fine humor that can be drawn upon without invading areas that might be offensive. The cost of a laugh is too high if looking tawdry is the price.

Learn to laugh at yourself One way you reveal both objectivity and kindliness in humor is to laugh at yourself. Before speakers can find effective humor in the weakness of others, they must first sense the foibles in themselves. Humor directed at oneself is frequently the most effective kind.

Lee Iacocca, Chairman of the Board of the Chrysler Corporation, used self-deprecating humor in his introduction to a speech delivered to the American Society of Newspaper Editors in Washington, D.C. in 1986. At that time, rumors were circulating that he might be a Democratic candidate for president.

> Thank you, Joe (Stroud).
>
> I appreciate that, Joe, believe me. And my thanks to all of *you*. I don't always get such a nice reception here in Washington these days. Don Hodel [Ronald Reagan's Secretary of the Interior] thinks I've got a conflict of interest and Don Regan [Ronald Reagan's Secretary of the Treasury] won't ride in my cars. So this is a switch, and I like it. I don't like it enough to *move* here, but I *like it*. And I thank you.
>
> At the outset, I want to make it perfectly clear that I'm not running for anything — except maybe for my life! Hell, you've even got my title wrong in the program. I'm *not President* of Chrysler. I'm not president of anything. Everybody keeps trying to run me. And I wish you'd all stop it because you're making my campaign staff nervous as hell! (Although Joe Califan [well-known Democrat] did say I have the right stuff to take a shot at it because I can read cue cards without moving my eyes!)
>
> By the way, I understand that you had my personal choice for a running mate on your program. It would make a hell of a ticket, wouldn't it? Iacocca and Westheimer [Dr. Ruth, popular sex therapist]! I'd run all over the country telling people *what* to do, and she'd follow me telling them *how*![13]

Let the humor label itself   There is no joke that has to work as hard for a laugh as the one that is introduced with the suggestion that it is supposed to be funny. A speaker who seems to be working at being witty, will never make it. Humor that is worth using needs no identification. Then, too, some audiences are strangely perverse. When they are told something is going to be funny, either they expect too much or they set themselves (unconsciously or not) to resist. The most effective humor slides into the mind without announcement or fanfare.

Stop When you're ahead   Developing a taste for applause is too easy— and it is insatiable. It's hard to stop when you know you're doing a good job, the audience is responsive, and you feel that you could continue indefinitely. There is always the temptation to seek a positive response from the audience just once more. But one extra story or joke may be all it takes to push the humor beyond its peak of effectiveness.

Summary

Many speaking occasions are ceremonial; they respond to the demands of social custom. The skills and techniques appropriate to informative and persuasive speaking are just as applicable to speeches for special occasions. Because such speeches are highly ritualistic, they are always in danger of being stale. Try to find fresh ways of saying what tradition demands. Sincerity and civility help greatly to offset the debits of dullness.

The occasions for ceremonial speaking are frequent. Some of the most common are listed below.

An *introduction*, whether serious or humorous, prepares the audience for both the speaker and the subject.

A *nomination* presents a candidate for office and outlines the qualifications of the nominee for the position.

Speeches of *welcome* help visitors, either individuals or groups, feel that their presence is appreciated. They are often intended to give groups, such as political or professional conventions, a heightened sense of the importance of their meeting.

Awards are given to those who have earned them by meritorious behavior. Speeches of *presentation* describe the service or conduct that warrants recognition.

A *response* to a speech of courtesy expresses gratitude for the kindness, courtesy or honor bestowed. The speaker is obligated in both courtesy and justice to credit any others who deserve it.

A *farewell* speech is a graceful departure from tenure in an office or membership in a group.

Speeches of *tribute* are designed to inspire an audience with such sentiments as admiration and affection for a person, zeal for a tradition, or rededication to an ideal. *Eulogies* praise the dead and *commemorations* memorialize important events.

Speeches of *good will* are the means of building a favorable image for a group. Most commonly, they are used by commercial organizations to show how they are working for the benefit of the listener.

A speech to *entertain* has the purpose of amusing or diverting an audience. A familiar instance is the after-dinner speech.

No matter what the purpose of a speech, the ability to use humor is a valuable skill. If amusement is the goal, as it will be in a speech to entertain, humor will be the means of achieving it. In speeches to inform or persuade, even though laughter is not an end in itself, the interest of the audience can be heightened by using supporting details in humorous ways: through overstatement, understatement, irony, unexpected turns, play on words, and burlesque.

These suggestions will make humor more effective: (1) be objective; (2) show kindliness; (3) use good taste; (4) learn to laugh at yourself; (5) let the humor label itself; and (6) stop when you're ahead.

Key Terms

Introductions	Humor
Nominations	Overstatement
Welcomes	Understatement
Presentations	Irony
Responses	Unexpected turns
Farewells	Play on words
Eulogies	Burlesque
Commemorations	Objective
Good will	Kindliness
Entertain	Good taste

Exercises

1. You are going to introduce a student speaker in your speech class. Interview the student and prepare the introductory speech.
2. Prepare a nominating speech for a friend whom you think should be elected to the student senate.
3. The "Woman of the Year" from your state is visiting your campus. You are student body president. Prepare a speech of welcome for her.
4. A group of which you are a member (fraternity, sorority, Hillel, Newman Club, or the like) is making a substantial contribution to a medical research foundation. Prepare the speech of presentation.

5. You are being honored by the Rotary Club of your community for winning their annual student scholarship. Prepare a response to the presentation of the award.

6. Upon graduation, you, as valedictorian, will speak at the commencement exercises. On behalf of yourself and the other graduates, prepare a speech of farewell to the faculty and the campus.

7. Prepare a speech commemorating the anniversary of the death of someone such as John F. Kennedy, Martin Luther King, Jr., Woodrow Wilson, Franklin D. Roosevelt, or Susan B. Anthony.

8. Examine the speech at the end of this chapter by Ian Fielding, ''The Wonderful World of College.'' That after-dinner speech was intended for a college audience. Do you think it is a good after-dinner speech for such an audience. Why? Why not?

Notes

1   ''Excerpts From Bush News Conference With Elizabeth Dole,'' *New York Times* 25 Dec. 1988: 22.

2   John F. Kennedy, *Public Papers of the Presidents of the United States: 1962* (Washington, DC: U.S. Government Printing Office, 1963) 159-60.

3   *New York Times*, 24 Feb. 1962: 16.

4   George Kennedy, *The Art of Persuasion in Greece* (Princeton, NJ: Princeton UP, 1963) 155; Takis Poulakos, ''Historiographies of the Tradition of Rhetoric: A Brief History of Classical Funeral Orations,'' *Western Journal of Speech Communication* 54 (Spring 1990): 172-88.

5   Ronald Reagan, ''Address to the Nation, January 28, 1986,'' *Weekly Compilation of Presidential Documents*, 22 (February 3, 1986) pp. 104-105.

6   Wesley G. Pippert, *The Spiritual Journey of Jimmy Carter* (New York: Macmillan, 1978) 148.

7   This is very much like what journalist Andy Rooney does. Watch him some Sunday evening on the CBS television program, *60 Minutes*.

8   Mody C. Boatright, *Folk Laughter on the American Frontier* (New York: Collier, 1961) 97-98.

9   Charles B. Reed, ''Education Is What It's All About'' *Representative American Speeches 1988-89* ed. Owen Peterson (New York: Wilson, 1989) 150.

10 ''Campus Comedy,'' *Reader's Digest* May 1990: 27.

11 Laurence J. Peter and Raymond Hull, *The Peter Principle* (New York: William Morrow, 1969).

12 Christi McGuffee Smith and Larry Powell, ''The Use of Disparaging Humor by Group Leaders,'' *Southern Speech Communication Journal* 53 (1988): 279-92.

13 Lee A. Iacocca, ''If You Don't Listen, How Can You Take Any Action,'' *Contemporary American Speeches* eds. Richard L. Johannesen, R.R. Allen, and Wil A. Linkugel (Dubuque, IA: Kendall/Hunt, 1988) 198.

Speeches for Study

"Speech to the Insurance Agents"
Mark Twain
Delivered in Hartford, Connecticut at a Dinner
Welcoming Englishman, Cornelius Walford

1   Gentlemen, — I am glad, indeed, to assist in welcoming the distinguished guest of this occasion to a city whose fame as an insurance centre has extended to all lands, and given us the name of being a quadruple band of brothers working sweetly hand in hand — the Colt's arms company making the destruction of our race easy and convenient, our life-insurance citizens paying for the victims when they pass away, Mr. Batterson perpetuating their memory with his stately monuments, and our fire-insurance comrades taking care of their hereafter. I am glad to assist in welcoming our guest — first because he is an Englishman, and I owe a heavy debt of hospitality to certain of his fellow-countrymen; and secondly, because he is in sympathy with insurance, and has been the means of making many other men cast their sympathies in the same direction.

2   Certainly there is no nobler field for human effort than the insurance line of business — especially accident insurance. Ever since I have been a director in an accident-insurance company I have felt that I am a better man. Life has seemed more precious. Accidents have assumed a kindlier aspect. Distressing special providences have lost half their horror. I look upon a cripple now with affectionate interest — as an advertisement. I do not seem to care for poetry any more. I do not care for politics — even agriculture does not excite me. But to me now, there is a charm about a railway collision that is unspeakable.

3   There is nothing more beneficial than accident insurance. I have seen an entire family lifted out of poverty and into affluence by the simple boon of a broken leg. I have had people come to me on crutches, with tears in their eyes, to bless this beneficent institution. In all my experience of life, I have seen nothing so seraphic as the look that comes into a freshly mutilated man's face when he feels in his vest pocket with his remaining hand and finds his accident ticket all right. And I have seen nothing so sad as the look that came into another splintered customer's face when he found he couldn't collect on a wooden leg.

4   I will remark here, by way of advertisement, that the noble charity which we have named the Hartford Accident Insurance Company is an institution which is peculiarly to be depended upon. A man is bound to prosper who gives it his custom. No man can take out a policy in it and not get crippled before the year is out. Now there was one indigent man who had been disappointed so often with other companies that he had grown disheartened, his appetite left him, he ceased to smile — and life was but a weariness. Three weeks ago I got him to insure with us, and now he is the brightest, happiest spirit in this land — has a good steady income and a stylish suit of new bandages every day, and travels around on a shutter.

5 I will say, in conclusion, that my share of the welcome to our guest is none the less hearty because I talk so much nonsense, and I know that I can say the same for the rest of the speakers.

From *Mark Twain's Speeches*, with an introduction by William Dean Howells (New York: Harper & Row, 1951), 249-251. Copyright 1923, 1951 by The Mark Twain Company. Reprinted by permission of Harper & Row, Publishers.

"The Wonderful World of College"
Ian Fielding
California State University, Northridge

1 On September 15, 1952 my parents were married. On September 16, 1952 they began saving for my college education. By the time I was born nearly ten years later, and why it took ten years is another story entirely, my parents had accumulated $12,564.52. My fate had been sealed. I was going to college whether I wanted to or not. My only trouble was that I did not. By the time I was eighteen and ready to make my reluctant entrance into college, kicking and screaming all the way, my folks had amassed $189,214.87, all of it for my education. That may seem like an awful lot of money but several years earlier my parents had joined organized crime. Even so, Mom and Dad scrimped and saved and sacrificed, and for twenty eight years cheated on their income tax just so I could go to college. That's why I knew in the summer of my eighteenth year that I would have one heck of a tough time telling my father I didn't want to go to college. I knew it would hurt him, even shock him, but I had to tell him. It was a lovely funeral. That fall, out of respect for my father's memory and under threat of severe bodily injury from my mother, I entered college. I was hysterical, but I entered college.

2 Yes, college, that grand and venerable institution of higher education. Today, I'd like to discuss three aspects of college life: the academic part of college, college professors (God love'em), and social life in college. By doing this I hope we can all come to the understanding that there is life during college. It's bleak, but it's life nonetheless.

3 Before going any further, it's important to remember that there are reasons for going to college. The purpose, in fact, is threefold. First, you learn words like threefold; second, it gives you something for your resume besides your name and address; and most important of all, it teaches you how to make important decisions in case you ever happen to become an adult. And there are reasons for becoming a college professor, as well: a love of knowledge, a desire to teach, . . . sadomasochistic tendencies.

4 When I first entered college I was not a happy person. I remember very clearly when my first tuition payment came due. I was peeved enough just having to be there and I thought I'd show them. I took a brown paper bag,

filled it with tens and twenties, stormed into admissions and screamed, "Here you leeches, take my father's blood!" And they did. In fact, they wanted more.

5   After that rather humbling experience I thought it would be a good idea if I got clued in as to what was expected of me academically speaking so I went to see my advisor. She told me that I was going to have to work, I was going to have to study, I was going to have to apply myself. I hated that woman. I was shocked. I always thought that doing the work in college was optional, like P.E.

6   It also came as quite a surprise to me to learn that I had to select a major. After all, you can't get a B.A. in "undeclared." (God knows I've tried.) So being the smart alec that I once was, when my advisor asked me what I wanted to major in, I told her "Serbo-Croation!" Little did I know they had it. See what happens when you don't read the catalogue?

7   I quickly decided a different approach was in order. I realized that as far as academics went, I was in college to seek out knowledge, to seek out understanding, to boldly go where no man has gone before—the women's locker room. But I also wanted to study something lucrative. In other words, I wanted to go for the cash. I did a little research of my own and I found out that the highest paying jobs in America today are computer engineer, chemical engineer, petroleum engineer and Michael Jackson's agent. Little did I know that Speech Communication majors, which I was to become, have the best chance of being found asleep on park benches.

8   Once you choose a major and select all your classes like Mickey Mouse this and bonehead that, your next big obstacles in college are the tests. College tests can sometimes be just a wee bit difficult. But then, circumnavigating the globe on a pogo stick is just a wee bit difficult. I, however, have a helpful hint for when you do take a test in college: cheat. It's so simple. If that fails, then chances are so do you.

9   The tests you're subjected to in college and in fact the classes you take will very often depend on the particular professor and this brings us to our second fact of college life. In college there are good professors and not-so-good professors; just like with cars, there are good cars and not-so-good cars. So why is it that as far as professors go I always get stuck with Edsels? I'll give you an example. For my social science class, "The History of Everything," I had a lulu of a professor. The man was a terror. His classes made "Friday the 13th" look like a Sunday picnic. Nothing can be said about this man that hasn't already been said about Stalin, Mussolini and Toxic waste.

10   But don't let this one bad apple cloud your vision. For the most part professors in college do an excellent job, especially when you consider all the problems they face; namely, the students. Let's face it, as students we aren't perfect. (I come pretty close, however.) Professors have to put up with students who are complainers, whiners, smart alecs; students who are apathetic, indifferent, unconcerned—you know, your average business major. But professors do have one very effective weapon, it's called finals.

11   Up to now we've discussed some of the more "serious" aspects of higher education. Now its time to leave scholastic discipline and turn to the nonacademic side of college life. At many institutions it seems that this side

involves nothing more than sex, drugs and rock and roll. If this is true, then I'm going to the wrong college.

12   Before I began college, my mother said to me, ''You'll have fun. You'll make friends.'' She lied. I didn't. My first bright idea was to join a fraternity. What better place for an alcoholic pervert like myself? They turned me down— all seventeen of them. But I didn't despair, not much anyway. I figured I could always join a club. After all, there had to be something out there that would interest me. At just about any other university that would be true, but at my school—Hey U—the choices are rather narrow. The big organization on my campus is the Young Bedouin Society, which I couldn't join anyway because I don't have my own camel. I was getting desperate. Finally, I joined the Campus Crusade for Christ. I'm Jewish. They didn't care, those people will take anybody; not unlike the debate team.

13   I'm not disappointed, though, I've had a lot of fun in college even though my social calendar isn't filled to the brim. By the way, can anyone use 365 blank pages? I realized that whatever one's form of entertainment is in college, whether it's playing bridge at the dean's house or drinking a six pack and throwing up in the library (my personal favorite), college can indeed be fun, fun, fun. College should be fun, fun, fun. And when you consider the average cost of college is now sixty bucks a day, you better have some fun, fun, fun.

14   In the end, I'm glad I'm going to college. Soon I'll be graduating and ready to face that big world out there. I have no idea what I'll be doing, but I'll be ready to face that big world out there. I know that the money my parents set aside for my education has been put to good use: $15,000 for college and $179,000 for pizza and beer.

15   You know, I've often wondered why we're all here. Why are we all in college? It's not a difficult question to answer, really. Students are here because they wish to improve their lives. Professors are here because they enjoy teaching, they better, God knows it's not for the money. Finally, I'm here because if I wasn't, I'd lose my inheritance. Thanks Dad. Thanks Mom.

Reprinted with the permission of Ian Fielding.

Speaking in Small Groups

Much oral communication takes place in small groups: in business conferences, around the family dinner table, on an outing with friends. Some of these groups are formally structured, others are informal, and many are even unplanned. In this chapter we are interested in the more formal situations you might encounter at school or at work. If you have the opportunity to participate in a small group discussion, you will be a more effective participant if you understand the nature of small group speaking, the situations that arise, and the responsibilities of participants and leaders.

Small Group Speaking Defined

Small group speaking may be defined as *a process that involves a limited number of people interacting with one another about a problem of common interest in a situation wherein the group has the responsibility of making effective decisions.* To get a clear understanding of the definition, let's look at its important elements.

The group is *limited in size.* A group can be as small as two—for example, when two people are named as a committee to arrange a family gathering. Depending on the given task, the size of the group will grow. A somewhat larger group would probably be needed to plan an alumni reunion. But there is some maximum number beyond which a group can no longer be called small; perhaps ten would be a reasonable maximum.

The group is *interactive.* The appropriate number of members (ten or less) is not the only requirement for small group status. Ten members of an audience for a public speech would not be what we mean by a small group. In small group speaking, each participant must be actively involved in three roles: speaker, listener, and decision maker.

The group *makes decisions.* An intercollegiate debate team usually has only two members, and these speakers interact with each other and with the members of the opposing team. However, a judge who is a member of neither team makes the only significant decision. Debates, therefore, are not examples of small group speaking.

For other reasons, therapy groups also do not meet our definition of small group speaking. They have quite valid purposes, they are limited in size, and their members participate interactively, but any decisions made are personal and they are not applicable beyond the individual who makes them.

A final point: although our definition does not explicitly call for a leader, a small group of the kind we are talking about typically operates under the guidance and direction of one of the members.

The decisions groups make are not limited to matters of policy. Juries make decisions on questions of fact: to what extent did the government's case depend on entrapment? Church groups make decisions on questions of value: What modes of conduct are the best in race relations? Sexual mores? The role of women? There are "learning groups" whose members pool information on a subject. You may have participated in such a group when you prepared for final exams last semester. These are just a few examples from an unlimited number of groups and countless topics of discussion. Whatever the group and whatever the cause for meeting, small group speaking will have these characteristics:

1. The size of the group is limited.
2. Group members are independent but interactive.
3. The group has a decision-making responsibility.
4. The group typically has a leader.

In small group speaking, each participant must be actively involved in three roles: speaker, listener, and decision maker. If you know how to plan a discussion, how to be a good participant, and how to lead, you will profit from the advantage of group activity.

Decisions made by small groups are not necessarily better than those made by a single person, but the process has certain advantages. It permits pooling of information and it provides for correction of individual error.

Perhaps you've heard it said that a camel is a horse built by a committee. If you know how to plan a discussion, how to be a good participant, and how to lead, you'll be able to profit from the advantages of the group activity and, above all, to avoid building a camel when you want a horse.

Patterns of Group Decision Making

Different kinds of problems require different kinds of solutions. Thus, the decision-making process will vary depending upon the problem to be solved. Although there are numerous approaches, the foundation is the same: the group must first understand the problem it must solve (just as a speaker's first need is to understand the subject of a speech). Given this, the group can choose the pattern of discussion best suited to the problem at hand. We are going to look at three decision-making plans: division of labor, reflective thinking and the argumentative plan.

Division of Labor Pattern

The members of some groups are chosen because each of them has a special expertise or knowledge. For example, suppose you are asked as a class exercise to lead a group discussion to determine what your university's liberal education program ought to be. To avoid undue bias, you want your group to include a science major, a humanities major, an engineering major, a health major and a social science major. If a division of labor were your plan of operation, you would ask each person to prepare an ideal program in his or her specialty and to present it briefly to the group. Based on whatever criteria you select (size of the program, purpose, emphasis, etc.), you and the group would negotiate among yourselves to determine the final program. The organization of the division of labor procedure looks like this:

   I.   What contribution can each field make to the program?
        A. Humanities
        B. Sciences
        C. Engineering
        D. Etc.

   II. What criteria can we negotiate for a unified proposal?
        A. Size
        B. Purpose
        C. Emphasis on theoretical or applied
        D. Etc.

   III. What single program based on our negotiated criteria can be agreed upon?

In such a group, every person has a role to fill as an expert in a particular area. Each one serves as a resource person and a decision maker. This is not the same as group meetings conducted for an outside audience: for example, an informative symposium wherein each person presents specific information or a debate in which each speaker argues a position. Division of labor groups are not performing for an outside audience. They are truly interacting to find the best decision just as any other interactive small group would do.

Reflective Thinking Pattern

About seventy-five years ago, philosopher John Dewey defined a systematic method of thought by which an individual might arrive at better decisions.[1] Others have adapted it to the group situation. It is also the basis of the reflective pattern in persuasion discussed in Chapter 19. This plan develops the group decision-making process through the following five steps: (1) locating and defining the problem, (2) analyzing the problem, (3) establishing goals, (4) finding the best possible decision, and (5) putting the decision into operation.

Locating and defining the problem   You cannot be completely objective in looking for a solution to any problem. Your personal desires and knowledge will influence your ideas. But, neither do you want this personal element to push you to a solution without giving the problem thorough analysis.

Imagine (and perhaps you don't need to imagine) a university parking lot that fills up early. When you arrive for your 9 o'clock class at 8:45, either you can't get into the lot or you have to search so long for a place that you are late for class. You might respond with rage and kick the parking lot gate or you might change your habits and come at 6:30 to be sure of finding a place. Both of these are decisions, but they are not reflective. Reflective decision making requires analysis to locate and define the problem.

Suppose you are a member of a group formed to study the parking problem. First you must ask questions like these: What is the parking problem on the campus? Is it confined to certain lots? Certain hours? Certain people? Does it involve public transportation? Off campus street parking?

In this first stage of the discussion the group must be sure that its members share a common understanding of the problem. When you talk with others about any set of circumstances, communication often suffers for lack of common ground. Failure to clear away as many of the obstacles to communication as possible will do much to destroy a potentially good discussion. Consequently, it is necessary to locate and define the problem.

The discussion of definition in Chapter 8 is very useful here. The method to choose is the one that will best specify, through clarification of words and phrases, the nature of the problem under consideration. The participants in the group are searching for agreement; therefore, a series of dictionary definitions of the words that state the problem is not enough. Since the members of the group are the ones who discovered the problem, they are the only ones who can state it correctly. At the conclusion of this step of the discussion process, the group should be in agreement about the specific subject under discussion and should be prepared to analyze it with a minimum of confusion.

Analyzing the problem   Analysis is the second step. Its function is to find the cause of the difficulty. The thoroughness with which this essential step is conducted determines as much as any other factor the success of the group in establishing a desirable new policy.

The first step in analysis is a review of existing conditions. A doctor who sees you for the first time needs to examine you thoroughly to take your medical history, and to question you about your symptoms. Symptoms are the clues to the cause of an illness. This determination of causes is a vital step in any problem-solving process. When a group discusses a policy question, it can be compared to doctors in consultation. The members must make a thorough investigation of facts and be familiar with conditions past and present in order to penetrate to the causes of the problem.

What are the symptoms of your campus parking problem: Lots fill up from 8:00 A.M. to 3:00 P.M.? All lots? How many spaces? How many cars? What are the fees? What are the fines? What are the causes for the problem: Inadequate space? Inadequate public transportation? Student refusal to walk from outlying lots? Inadequate fine system for violators? From the information the members of your group have gathered, they should be able to list the symptoms and the factors which helped to cause those undesirable conditions.

Establishing goals   Before determining what solution will best meet a problem situation, a group must have some standard for judging or testing any proposal. What are the standards any acceptable solution to the parking problem must meet: Be fair to all? Not raise parking fees? Provide adequate parking within easy walking distance of classes? Clarify the parking regulations? Consider off campus solutions? Once established, the goals serve as standards of judgment for evaluating potential solutions. Indeed, this is the reason the symptoms and the causes are explored in the first place—to know better what kind of solution will be most satisfying. Through analysis of the problem, the group distills the criteria which tell what a good solution must be.

Determining goals is frequently a difficult step in discussion. It is not a common practice for people to think through their goals when they make decisions. If you are asked why you bought a certain pair of socks, aren't you likely to say, "Because I liked them"? Likewise you may support a certain political party, believe in stricter law enforcement, or want more government support for older citizens without clearly spelling out why.

But there is a why—a goal or set of goals—and if someone insists, you can usually explain. Your responsibility as a member of a group is to identify goals *before* you propose solutions. If all members do the same, progress will be much more systematic and far less time-consuming.

To determine goals, then, is to develop a yardstick to measure the many possible courses of action. If the analysis of the problem has been thorough, the goals will be more easily determined. The more thorough and realistic the goals of a group are, the better the chances it will choose the most desirable solution to a problem.

Finding the best possible solution   Determining the best policy requires an examination of the advantages and disadvantages of each potential, proposed, or likely course of action. Each is compared with the others to see which will come closest to achieving the goals that have been established. If these goals are realistic, the course of action that most closely fits their specifications will be the one that most effectively reduces the causes of the problem and thereby limits the undesirable symptoms.

All reasonable possibilities should be considered. That is to say, it is quite possible that the present policy (the status quo) might prove to be the most desirable. So, your group investigating the parking problem on your campus might agree that arriving earlier or walking from a remote lot is better than a large increase in fees to build a parking garage at the center of campus. It is possible, in other words, that any proposed change would be for the worse. At any rate, the status quo should always be evaluated in comparison with the alleged advantages of any proposed change.

Putting the decision into operation   The final step in the reflective thinking plan is implementation of the decision. In this part of the discussion, the group examines the decision to see what must be done and by whom. The problem-solving group must find the most practical way, in light of its criteria, to put the solution to work. Your group may have decided that the solution involves better public transportation so the city must be lobbied to change the bus schedule. It might also imply stricter enforcement of the parking rules (campus security) and a change in class scheduling (the University administration). How would your group approach these agencies and what methods of implementation will you suggest?

In summary, then, the reflective thinking plan of group decision making develops through the following steps:

I. Locate and define the problem: Clarify the limits of the problem and define all vague, ambiguous, or unfamiliar terms to the satisfaction of all the members of the group.

II. Analyze the problem.
A. Symptoms: Examine the status quo and its history to discover the nature and severity of the problem.

B. Causes: Examine the symptoms and their history to determine what cause or causes produced the undesirable elements of the situation.

III. Establish goals: Develop standards of judgment for the group. That is, identify and state the criteria that constitute the requirements for a good solution.

IV. Appraise the possible solutions.
   A. List the reasonable courses of action.
   B. Evaluate each to see how well it attains the stated goals of the group.
   C. Select the course of action that most closely achieves the goals.

V. Determine procedures for putting the chosen solution into operation.

Argumentative Decision-making Pattern

Any reflective thinking plan is concerned with evaluating the nature of the situation *before* possible decisions are advanced. In contrast there is some research and considerable experience to recommend using a pattern which we have called argumentative decision making. In the argumentative plan, potential decisions are advanced tentatively and then tested by the group. Each testing permits the members of the group to understand one another better and so to advance new decisions that are additions to, or modifications of, the original proposal. In this way, group decisions are built a piece at a time, but they begin with a proposal for decision, not with an analysis of the problem. This may not be the most desirable method for solving complex problems, but it is commonly used in everyday life.

This model has been described as a "spiral." When one person advances a decision, it is tested and altered until all have agreed upon it. It is then fixed and used as a basis for determining decisions about other questions.[2] Here's a sample of how it works: "Let's eat out tonight." "Okay, which restaurant?" "How about Shanghai House? They have Mandarin dishes." "No, I don't want Chinese food." "Okay, how about the Pit? You like BBQ ribs." And so on. Although this plan is less tightly organized than the reflective thinking plan, it is still systematic. It involves "reach testing" a proposed step forward from an agreed-upon position. If the step is approved, an advance is made; if not, the group returns to the earlier position and "reach tests" another idea.[3]

A more general argumentative pattern is described by B. Aubrey Fisher. His research revealed that an untutored group will naturally use four steps in making a decision.

1. *Orientation* Participants are tentative in advancing proposals and stating disagreement with others. They seem to be determining their positions in the group.

2. *Conflict* There is strong ideational conflict among members of the group. They seem to have established their social positions and the most vigorous testing takes place.
3. *Emergence* Argument tends to dissipate and movement toward consensus of opinion begins. There is some tendency to be more ambiguous, as in the orientation stage, because members who expressed strong opinions in the conflict stage are in the process of accepting the consensus.
4. *Reinforcement* Although the group has actually made a decision, its members need to reinforce the views which reflect their unity of opinion.[4]

Participation in Group Decision Making

No matter what pattern of group decision making is used, the members of a group must participate in its activities. In this section we will see how a participant can help to achieve the two objectives which are essential to effective group activity: cohesiveness and productivity.

Cohesiveness

Group members are individuals. They have their own reasons for being part of the group. They differ in how important a solution is to them. They differ in their relations to the other members of the group. Yet they must interact with one another. Their success as a group can be measured in part by the kind of cohesiveness the group develops. A group with considerable cohesiveness is one in which individuals are willing to work for the good of the group. You might call it "team spirit." It helps the group be more productive.

Productivity

Groups are judged by their productivity. If a committee that is supposed to come up with an idea for a homecoming float can't come up with a good theme, the committee will be judged negatively for it. Obviously, groups which provide new and imaginative solutions to problems get a lot of credit. But in some circumstances, even if a group doesn't come up with a good solution, it can be considered productive to some degree if it clarifies the issues which divide it.

Securing Cohesiveness and Productivity

To produce maximum cohesiveness and productivity in group discussion, each individual must participate efficiently and effectively. We will discuss four ways of securing this kind of participation: identify with your group, be supportive of others, be prepared, and follow the plan.

Identify with your group   If the group product is going to be worthwhile, the members have to identify themselves with the group. This is a time to put aside personal reactions and any negative attitudes you may have toward others in the group. It is also a time to control any tendency you may have to take charge. Even if you have a good solution, it must be developed as a group consensus if it is to be accepted outside the group. The more quickly you can identify with the group, the easier it will be for you to influence the other members. When all the members accept their responsibility to act this way, cohesiveness will develop and productivity will increase.

Be supportive of others   Some members will be more shy than others. Some will have less knowledge than others. As a member of the group you will want to help those who are less talkative become more involved in the discussion. You will also avoid any personal put-downs even when someone is clearly wrong. Being supportive means that your comments should be related to the problem under discussion and the group's involvement in it. That means having respect for the others in the group. You may need to disagree but you should do so without personal implications.

Be prepared   The Boy Scout motto is as appropriate here as it is in any other speech situation. Unfortunately, some people do not take group speaking situations as seriously as they do formal public speaking assignments. Perhaps they assume (selfishly) that others will have studied the question so they need not know as much. Pooled ignorance doesn't make for a good decision. The computer platitude, ''garbage in, garbage out'' applies here. The productivity of the group and its cohesiveness will be increased when all the members are well informed. What all groups need starts with a single member—you.

Follow the plan   The reason groups adopt a plan of analysis is to provide a more systematic examination of the problem. It is easy for a group discussion to drift off on interesting tangents. But nothing destroys cohesion more than for each member to go off on a personal tangent and ignore the analytical process. Of course, we are not advocating a slavish adherence to any plan. Indeed, the argumentative plan advocates reach testing and to reach you need to try new ideas which may seem tangential. A certain amount of reach testing is necessary in any plan. But reach testing should always be done with a realization of its place in the analytical process.

If there is a division of labor, you as an individual need to accept whatever responsibilities are yours. You must also pay close attention to what others say so that you can detect when the group may be losing track of the discussion plan.

The above four guidelines for participating apply to everyone in the group but they bind with even greater force for those participants who assume leadership responsibilities.

Leadership in Group Discussion

It is usual to think of the person in charge of procedure as the leader of the group. In fact, however, such a person may not be the leader at all. Assigned to control the group, some people become mere figureheads, not leading the group but following the procedural and substantive suggestions of some other member. This other member is the real leader. In short, the real leader is the one who guides either the procedure or the substance of the discussion, or both. That may or may not be the person appointed as chair.

The leadership role is a function of the group; that is, the members decide who will direct their thought. Leadership may change hands as the discussion changes. The members of a decision-making group may accept the leadership of one person on one topic (or on one phase of a problem) and turn to someone else for leadership at another time. The members of the group decide how much authority they will give, to whom they will give it and for how long.

Furthermore, groups do not always have an assigned leader. Your instructor may ask four or five of you to conduct a group discussion on some problem of your choosing but not designate a leader. Your employer may ask you and a few other employees to see if you can solve a merchandising problem. Even though it is usual for a committee, board, or panel to operate under the guidance of a presiding officer, you will work in many problem-solving groups that have no assigned leader.

Whether or not a leader is assigned, every member of the group must be prepared to assume the responsibilities of the chair. If you notice, for example, that the group should move on to another phase of the discussion, don't wait more than briefly for someone else to make the suggestion; make it yourself. Perhaps someone else will emerge as leader, and you won't need to assume the procedural initiative, at least in that phase of the group's progress. Every member of the group should be prepared to act if the need for leadership arises.

Functions of Leadership

The functions of leadership are much the same as the four rules for securing cohesion and productivity. To be an effective leader, you will *identify with the group* and will show the others that you consider the group's goals important. You will *be supportive of others*. The most effective leaders are those who induce cooperative behavior in others by setting a good example themselves.[5] To be a leader you must *be prepared*, not only by studying the problem to be discussed but also by studying the other members of the group. A leader has to take a special interest in helping the *group follow the plan*. It is perhaps an oversimplified, but nonetheless useful, generalization that a good leader is one who does an outstanding job as a participant.

Specific Tasks of Leaders

An effective leader readily adapts to the requirements of the particular group-speaking situation and to the expectations of the group. However, three specific tasks will generally be required of you.

Getting the discussion started   The first of your three responsibilities, getting the discussion off to a good start, is probably the most difficult. Once it has been started and the group is functioning, the discussion tends to move along.

Your introduction of the discussion topic should be clear, brief, and interesting. You may give a short resume of the history of the problem, or you may show briefly the nature and importance of the question. This sort of beginning, if you choose it, is only to permit the participants a moment to collect their thoughts. No one needs or wants a long speech from you. Under no circumstances should you take the responsibility of analyzing the problem. If necessary, you should introduce the members of the group to one another by name.

This much is easy. It is a set of functions that must be performed but does not solve the vital problem of getting the discussion off to a good start. Most inexperienced groups have to be led into useful and worthwhile discussion. There are several ways of helping these less vocal groups to get under way.

One useful device for getting started is to ask a question designed to elicit an intelligent and relevant response. This opening question should ordinarily be directed to the group rather than to an individual. It would probably be unwise to put any one participant "on the spot" this early in the discussion. Moreover, the question should be general rather than specific. A specific question may require a specific piece of information which no one has immediately at hand.

Another useful maneuver is to quote a statement referring to the problem or to cite some specific instance or illustration of the problem and ask for comment. If the topic is a broad one, you may want to ask for some specification or limitation. In each of these cases, any member of the panel, even one minimally prepared, should be able to make a reasonable comment.

Keeping the discussion going   Once started, a well-informed group will usually move along quite briskly with a minimum of prodding. Once you get the discussion started, your major functions are to encourage general participation, to keep the discussion on track, and to guide the group away from hasty, unrealistic action. See that everyone participates and that no one monopolizes the time of the group. If several speakers try to speak at the same time, the one who has spoken less frequently should be given the opportunity to speak first.

One of your most useful devices is frequent, brief summaries of what the group has accomplished up to that point. These summaries help to avoid needless repetition, keep the discussion on track, and point out areas of agreement and disagreement.

Probably your most important function is to make sure the group thoroughly investigates the problem. Both evidence and argument must be submitted to rigorous testing. Guiding questions provide the best means of analyzing any conclusions reached. Differences of opinion are not to be stifled. Although you will want to point out and stress the areas of agreement that exist, it is also important that the differences be brought out; otherwise they can never be eliminated. Consensus is valuable only when it results from a realistic adjustment of honest differences.

Bringing the discussion to a close   Any meeting will eventually end, and the chairperson has the responsibility of closing the discussion. Usually, a summary is in order. When any issues need further discussion, the concluding comments should be in the form of a progress report, summarizing the agreements and disagreements discovered in the group.

Summary

Small group discussion is a common speaking situation. It usually involves a limited number of people interacting with one another on a problem of mutual interest where the group must make some kind of a decision. Participants have the advantages of being able to pool information and to correct individual error. To realize these advantages, it is necessary to plan.

There are three major patterns for group discussion. The "division of labor" pattern provides for each person to approach the problem from a personal point of view and then participate in negotiating a group decision. The "reflective thinking" pattern has five stages: (1) locating and defining the problem, (2) analyzing the problem, (3) establishing goals, (4) finding the best possible decision, and (5) putting the decision into operation. In the "argumentative" decision-making pattern, the members advance ideas about solutions so that they can be tested and modified by the group. It naturally occurs in four steps: (1) orientation, (2) conflict, (3) emergence, and (4) reinforcement.

Although the members of a group are individuals, they need to develop cohesiveness as a unit. They are expected to provide a solution to the problem under discussion, or at least to clarify the disagreements that prevent consensus. To help secure cohesiveness and productivity for the group you need to do four things: (1) identify with your group, (2) be supportive of others, (3) be prepared and, (4) follow the plan.

Leadership cannot be assigned. A committee chair is not necessarily a leader. Leadership emerges from the group. It will sometimes change from person to person as the subject changes. In general, leadership comes to those who do a better job of meeting the four requirements of participation. In addition, the leader must be prepared to undertake the specific tasks of getting the discussion started, keeping it moving along, and bringing it to a close.

Key Terms

Group size	Argumentative plan
Interactive	Operation
Decisions	Orientation
Division of labor	Conflict
Reflective thinking	Emergence
Definition	Reinforcement
Analysis	Cohesiveness
Goals	Productivity
Solution	Leadership

Exercises

1. Make an analysis of some personal problem using reflective thinking: How worthwhile do you find this method? What alternate possibilities do you think would be as effective? More effective? Why?

2. Form a discussion group with four or five other members of your class. Select a problem to discuss. Word it. Come to some common understanding of the terms of the question. Let each member of the group gather material. Present the group discussion in class a week after you have chosen the topic.

3. Observe the chair of some group to which you belong. Write a paper of no more than three typewritten pages explaining what techniques the chair used and how successful they were. To what extent was the chair the leader of the group?

4. Discuss in class how effective group discussion is in learning situations such as classrooms. Explain why they are as good as, better, or worse than lectures, films, or textbook reading.

Notes

1 John Dewey, *How We Think* (Lexington, MA: Heath, 1910).
2 Thomas M. Scheidel and Laura Crowell, "Idea Development in Small Groups," *Quarterly Journal of Speech* 50 (1964): 140-45.
3 B. Aubrey Fisher and Donald G. Ellis, *Small Group Decision Making* (New York: McGraw-Hill, 1990) 159.
4 B. Aubrey Fisher, "Decision Emergence: Phases in Group Decision Making," *Speech Monographs* 37 (Mar.1970): 53-66.
5 H. Lloyd Goodall, Jr., "The Skills of Leading Small Groups In American Business and Industry," *Small Group Communication: A Reader*, eds. Robert S. Cathcart and Larry A. Samovar, (Dubuque, IA: Wm. C. Brown, 1984) 425.

Part Six

Evaluating Speeches

chapter 22

Speech Evaluation

I. Why speeches are evaluated

II. The steps in speech evaluation
   A. Analysis
      1. Argument
      2. Value appeals
      3. Credibility
      4. Organization
      5. Language and style
      6. Delivery
   B. Synthesis
   C. Judgment
      1. Effect
      2. Artistic merit
      3. Historical significance
      4. Ethical worth

III. Preparing the evaluation
   A. Begin with judgment
   B. Relate judgment to synthesis
   C. Support synthesis and judgment with analysis

In previous chapters, we have examined a number of ways to make speeches effective. Everything we have said is related to increasing your skill in handling the substance, organization, style, and delivery of a message. In this chapter, however, we are going to look at speech making from another point of view—that of the listener. In other words, we want to show you a method whereby you can make a sound *evaluation* of speeches. We are still concerned with substance, organization, style, and delivery, of course, because those are the elements of every speech. They are what make it good or bad and, consequently, they also provide the only reasonable basis for evaluation.

When you evaluate something, you assess it; you determine what merit it has. In recent years there has been considerable diversification in the approaches to speech evaluation. Methods that were appropriate to literature, anthropology, or psychology, for instance, are now being applied to public speaking. In this chapter, we will show you how to evaluate speeches by the neoclassical standards.

Why Speeches Are Evaluated

Perhaps the best reason to learn to evaluate a speech is to improve your own speaking. By examining the techniques used effectively by other speakers, you will have a better idea of what techniques you should use. What may be effective at one time with one audience will not necessarily be effective in other circumstances. By observing how an audience responds to various techniques, you gain insights into what techniques are the most useful in specific situations.

Evaluating speeches will also lead to improved listening skills. Have you ever heard a speech and labelled it as good or poor without testing your conclusion by asking what, specifically, made it good or poor?

A thorough evaluation of a speech will also provide insight into the historical significance of the speaking situation. The interrelation of speaker, speech, and audience is extremely important. When Franklin D. Roosevelt said in his first inaugural address, "We have nothing to fear but fear itself," his statement had great significance for the depression-ridden people of the 1930s. Reading and analyzing that speech against the political and economic background of that era is much more revealing than reading it with no knowledge about people's problems and attitudes during the depression. Historical research is necessary to understand Roosevelt's audience and why he chose to say what he did.

The evaluation of speeches not only offers an understanding of some particular point in history, but more broadly, it gives insights into the nature of human beings in general. When you study speeches from a number of eras, you soon become aware that although issues change and techniques change, many attitudes remain constant. The arguments advanced during the late 1960s and early 1970s by opponents of the war in Vietnam are essentially the same as those advanced in the 1840s by opponents of the Mexican War. Effective public speakers, whether purposely or not, reflect the prevailing ideas of the times; they reflect, in addition, their own insights into all of human existence.

The Steps in Speech Evaluation

There are three steps in speech evaluation: analysis, synthesis, and judgment. In an analysis, the speech is taken apart so that its various elements can be individually examined. These elements, as we have said, are the substance of the speech (the arguments and their supporting materials, the value appeals, and the efforts to win credibility), the organization of the ideas, the style of the language, and the delivery. The individual facts you have gathered from your analysis are then *synthesized* around what seems to be the basic or central strategy the speaker uses. Finally, there must be a *judgment*, not merely a statement that a speech is good or bad, but an indication of strengths and weaknesses as you see them. If a judgment is based on intelligent analysis and synthesis, it will be worth the attention of others. No one expects that in a beginning speech class you will be an accomplished critic, but you can begin to develop evaluative skills.

Analysis

First, analyze the substance of the speech—the main ideas and the support used to substantiate the claims. Three elements in proof have been recognized since classical times: argument (*logos*), value appeals (*pathos*), and credibility (*ethos*). Although all three are viewed as equally important and involve the interrelation of audience, speaker, speech and occasion, the argumentative function is more directly related to the message than the others are; values bear most upon the audience, and credibility is attributed to the speaker.

Argument Perhaps the most complex part of an analysis lies in discovering the central claim and how it is argued and supported. The following is a section of an analysis of the argument in Elizabeth Stanton's address, "Lords of Creation," at the 1848 Woman's Rights Convention in Seneca Falls, New York:

> The content of Mrs. Stanton's speech suggests she did not assume her listeners readily agreed with her. Counter-refutation pervaded the entire address as she first attacked the assumption that man was intellectually, morally, and physically superior; then refuted traditional arguments against woman's rights; and, finally answered prevailing objections to

woman suffrage — particularly objections that women themselves might raise.

The graduate of Troy Female Seminary showed she was well versed in her subject. She referred to no less than seventeen women by name and deed to show it was "strange that man — with the pages of history spread out before him — is so slow to admit the intellectual power, the moral heroism of woman, and her identity with himself."

Mrs. Stanton also revealed she was practiced in the art of argument. Eight times she turned to the Bible, a source of authority often used by her opponents, to support her contentions. In the story of Creation, for example, she found evidence that man is not intellectually supreme, for did not the Evil One offer Eve the apple of temptation because he knew "man could be easily conquered through his affection for the woman, but the woman would require more management?" [1]

Here are some questions to consider in analyzing the argumentative dimension of the speech:

1. What appears to be the central claim the speaker wants to support?
2. Is the speaker aware of the issues that divide opinion?
3. What ways of looking at the issues does the speaker propose?
4. Does the speaker meet opposition arguments?
5. What form of reasoning does the speaker use in developing the arguments?
6. What kind of evidence does the speaker provide?

Value appeals   Your analysis also identifies the specific value system revealed in the speech. The value system the speaker appeals to is revealed by the words that carry value judgments: the positive and negative value terms in the speech. Your examination of these terms will help you determine the speaker's value system.

In his first inaugural address, President Woodrow Wilson called for reform of the nation's economy. In the following passage from that speech, the terms Wilson considers *good* are printed in italics and those he considers **bad** are printed in boldface.

But the **evil** has come with the *good*, and much *fine gold* has been **corroded**. With *riches* has come **inexcusable waste**. We have **squandered** a great part of what we might have *used*, and have not stopped to *conserve* the exceeding *bounty of nature*, without which our *genius for enterprise* would have been **worthless** and **impotent**, **scorning** to be careful, **shamefully prodigal** as well as *admirably efficient*. We have been *proud* of our industrial *achievements*, but we have not hitherto stopped *thoughtfully* enough to count **human cost**, the **cost** of *lives* **snuffed out**, of *energies* **overtaxed** and **broken**, the **fearful** *physical* and *spiritual* **cost** to the men and women and children upon whom the **dead weight** and **burden** of it all has fallen **pitilessly** the years through.

From an examination of the value words that carry Wilson's argument, you can see the value system underlying what he says. To paraphrase him: We must with candid and fearless eyes conserve our riches (the bounty of nature) through careful, efficient use of our genius for enterprise with due pride in our industrial achievements. We must reject the corrosion of fine gold through waste, squandering, overtaxing, the snuffing out of lives, and the great spiritual and physical costs. Further, we must discontinue our attention to worthless things. We must stop being impotent, prodigal, and selfish.

Wilson appeals to the Puritan values so basic in American society: a respect for nature and enterprise; a rejection of selfishness, waste, and false pride. Further examination will show that the emphasis of this passage is negative; that is, President Wilson uses the words of his value system to reject what he considers bad more strongly than to identify what he supports.

This illustration identifies the basis for some important analytical questions:

1. To what value systems does the speaker appeal?
2. What general warrant does the speaker emphasize at the most important points in the speech?
3. Are the values justified by the subject?
4. Do the warrants remain consistent throughout the speech?

Credibility   Credibility is established when an audience judges a speaker to be trustworthy and competent. Speakers can establish credibility by projecting good images of themselves and bad images of their opponents. When you analyze credibility, ask yourself not only what qualities speakers claim to possess, but also what qualities they ascribe to the opposition. In his 1982 congressional campaign, President Reagan argued that the American people should "stay the course." He characterized his opponents in the Democratic party as having a long history of errors in judgment. Supporting the Republicans ("staying the course") meant supporting the people who chose the rational solution to problems.[2]

Credibility is further classified as either direct or indirect. In direct credibility, the speaker's attributes and accomplishments and/or the defects of the opponent are referred to directly. When she accepted the vice presidential nomination of the Democratic Party in 1984, Geraldine A. Ferraro, spoke directly about herself:

> Tonight, the daughter of an immigrant from Italy has been chosen to run for Vice President in the new land my father came to love.
>
> Our faith that we can shape a better future is what the American dream is all about. The promise of our country is that the rules are fair. And if you work hard and play by the rules, you can earn your share of America's blessings.

Those are the beliefs I learned from my parents. And those are the values I taught my students as a teacher in the public schools of New York.

At night, I went to law school. I became an assistant district attorney, and I put my share of criminals behind bars. Because I believe: If you obey the law, you should be protected. But if you break the law, you should pay for your crime.

When I first ran for Congress, all the political experts said a woman could not win in my home district of Queens. But I put my faith in the people and the values that we shared. And together, we proved the political experts wrong.[3]

Although speakers often seek to build credibility by showing the audience directly that they are competent to speak on the subject, indirect credibility is developed more subtly.

In July of 1987 Eleanor Smeal spoke to the National Press Club in Washington, D.C. She opened her speech with a series of examples of wrong-doing by prominent persons to establish what she considered the problem of the day—the violation of established values. In so doing, she also indirectly told the audience what made her credible.

In business, in the church, in high government, in the military, scandal is the order of the day.

The Vatican bank officials cannot leave the Vatican because Italian authorities will arrest them for bank fraud.

The PTL Club mess of illicit sex, fraud, and greed would provide comic relief if so many had not been taken for so much.

The internecine electronic ministry wars make the hostile take-overs of the corporate world look almost civilized. Wall Street is rocked by arrests for illegal trading and drug deals.

The Wedtech incident gives new meaning to the concept of affirmative action minority set-asides. Who could have believed Meese and company, who have repeatedly attacked legitimate affirmative action to end discrimination against women and minorities, were willing to use it for their own ends?

Some 100 plus officials of the Reagan administration have resigned or are hanging on under a cloud of impropriety. This administration which promised to return the nation to old-fashioned morality and balanced budgets has instead established a *high level crook of the month club* and has made the U.S. the fastest-growing debtor nation. . . .

I believe the American people have had enough.[4]

Organization The structure of a speech helps you to see how well the speaker gives the message *unity*, *order*, and *coherence*.

The primary constituent of unity is *singleness of theme*. Are all the arguments and value appeals of the speech relevant to one main theme? If there are several themes, are they skillfully related to one another and well developed to give a sense of unity?

Similarly, *scope* is a function of unity. The impression of unity is not only created by the singleness of the speaker's theme but is influenced by the listener's perception as well. Is the speech limited to what the audience can comprehend and yet broad enough to engage listener interests?

Order in a speech originates in the sequence of ideas. The manner in which the central claim (the theme) of the speech is revealed is called *thematic emergence*. Does the main theme become clear somewhere around the middle of the speech? Is the cat let out of the bag one whisker at a time? Does the theme emerge at the beginning in an unequivocal statement to the audience? Determine what pattern is used to organize the speech: chronological? spatial? claim to proof? problem-solution?

Coherence is directly related to both unity and order. It can be checked by examining the transitions the speaker uses to link one thought with another. Ask yourself, to what extent do the transitions help a listener develop a clear and correct understanding of what the speaker says?

Thus, you analyze the structure of a speech to discover how its theme emerges, what order is used to organize the material, and what means are used to link one idea with another.

Language and style   Language is the fundamental ''hardware'' of a speech; it is the vehicle that transmits the substance of the speech and manifests the organization. In a very real sense, therefore, whatever you learn about a speech must come through analysis of the speaker's language. In addition, you analyze the language of a speech to discover how the speaker achieves the primary goals of style: clarity and interest.

An important aspect of stylistic analysis is evaluating the level of the speaker's vocabulary in relation to the audience's understanding. The vocabulary level of a speech is a factor in deciding whether the language will be readily accepted and easily understood. No audience wants to hear a speech that is insulting because of its simplicity or confusing because of its complexity. Imagine addressing an adult audience in the language of a first-level reader. ''See Puff. See Puff run. Run, Puff, run. Run, run, run.'' Or imagine the response of an audience addressed in the complex jargon of a field that it does not understand.

Syntax is potentially as serious a problem as vocabulary. Given words it understands, an audience can often do a reasonably good job of straightening out unclear sentences, but when syntax is awkward and unsure it will impair communication. This does not mean that simple sentences are always preferable. A well developed complex sentence can be just as clear as a series of short ones, perhaps even more so. Indeed, subtle ideas or shades of meaning may be lost in simple sentences.

Vividness in language—achieved through stylistic devices to decorate and to embellish ideas—probably does the most to add interest value to a speech. Consider the *level* of embellishment used. To a degree, you can determine how enriched the style is by comparing the language with that of other speakers in similar situations. Consider next what *kinds* of figures of style the speaker tends to use. The late President John F. Kennedy, for example, became well known for his use of antithesis ("Ask not what your country can do for you—ask what you can do for your country"). Some speakers make extensive use of metaphor, others do not.

In addition to humor (when it occurs) and vividness, any device that a speaker uses to heighten the interest of an audience can contribute to the success of the speech. For instance, *suspense* is created when speakers withhold information which would forecast their desired final outcome. As long as listeners are guessing, they are interested. Curiosity—the desire for information—is universal in people.

An interest in conflict also seems to be natural, as we pointed out in Chapter 14. Speakers create interest when the language they use suggests conflict or struggle. Since conflicts, like crime stories and jokes, have outcomes that listeners want to know, timing the revelation of the outcome creates suspense and further heightens the interest generated by conflict.

Delivery The facial expressions, gestures, vocal quality, and vocal emphasis of a speaker are all agents of communication that tell the listener what the speaker wants to say. The policeman holds up a hand to say "Stop." When a speaker smiles or frowns, speaks loudly or softly, or emphasizes one word over another, he or she says something to the audience.

In analyzing a speaker's delivery, you must judge whether gesture, facial expression, vocal quality, and loudness are coordinated with the ideas of the speech; whether they constitute emphasis or mere exhibition. Ask these questions:

1. Do the gestures, vocal quality, and other elements of delivery help to communicate the speaker's meaning?
2. Do they draw attention to themselves?
3. Is the delivery an aid or a hindrance in eliciting the meaning the speaker wants the listener to have?

Synthesis

When your analysis is complete, you know what the speaker has done with the various elements of the speech: the argument, value appeals, credibility, organization, style, and delivery. But you end up with a list of separate and independent items and your reactions to each of the different aspects of the speech. Some have greater significance than others. Isolated comments on argument or style or delivery give a jumbled notion of what your analysis discovered. You need to combine the series of isolated comments into a unified conception of the whole. The following four steps will help you to synthesize your analysis into a description of the central strategy and how the strategy was aided (or perhaps hindered) by the way in which the speaker developed it.

1. Describe the central strategy of the speech—the plan by which the speaker tried to move the audience toward the goal of the speech.
2. Determine what specific elements of the speech are used to support this strategy.
3. Note any elements of the speech that detract from the strategy.

For one speaker, an argumentative development may be the central strategy: the basic appeal is to reason; the speaker generates credibility by building the image of a "reasonable" person. Another strategy will emphasize the trustworthiness of the speaker, and other rhetorical elements will be subservient to credibility. Still another speaker may create a rhetorical strategy centered in the deeply felt values of the audience. This strategy reveals itself through the emphasis given to some particular value appeal throughout the speech and especially at critical junctures.

David Henry finds the metaphor of family as the central rhetorical strategy in Governor Mario Cuomo's highly regarded Democratic National Convention keynote address of 1984:

> Clearly, Cuomo's rhetorical strategy met the situational and audience challenges posed by the keynote setting. By first raising doubts about the accuracy of Ronald Reagan's vision of America as a "shining city on a hill," Cuomo was able to unite his diverse listeners around the shared values and experiences common to both target audiences [party members and "middle America"]. He did so by packaging his theme of progressive pragmatism or traditional Democratic principles in the metaphorical container of the family, thereby offering an appealing alternative to the president's preferred but allegedly misleading trope.[5]

Judgment

Judgment follows naturally from your synthesis of the data gathered in making your analysis, and it is the natural culmination of the evaluative process. But every decision requires some standard of judgment. Several methods of evaluation have been advanced by writers on rhetorical criticism. You are the best judge of which one you want to use in any particular case. The important thing is to understand the requirements of the standard you elect to use and to apply it consistently. These four are the most common: effect, artistic merit, historical significance, and ethical worth.[6]

Effect Some theorists maintain that a critic should only make judgments about the immediate and long-range *effect* of a speech on a listener and on society. Only the most naive evaluation of effects considers the merit of a speech to depend solely upon whether it succeeded in getting the audience to do what the speaker wanted. One speech, standing alone, may have little discernible effect, but the results of a series of speeches may be cumulative. A speech, moreover, may produce results that the speaker did not even intend but which, nonetheless, introduce noticeable changes into society. It may be that in a particular case a speech has no significant effect because no adequate means of persuasion are available to the speaker. Nor does counting votes after an election necessarily determine the more effective speaker.

Judging by effect is based upon an analysis of how well the speaker's strategy may have been appropriate to the situation and the audience. What characteristics of the speech situation might make the speaker's task more difficult? The reputation of the opponent? That was the case for Adlai E. Stevenson in 1952 when he (a little known Governor of Illinois) ran for president against Dwight D. Eisenhower, one of America's war heroes. In a more recent example, President Ford was better known than Jimmy Carter in 1976; he had been appointed Vice President by Richard Nixon. After Nixon resigned in disgrace, Ford became President and later pardoned Nixon. Furthermore, Ford was challenged in a bruising Republican primary by Ronald Reagan. All these factors may have been as important in his defeat as anything he or Carter said. Thus, to judge by the standard of effect you must assess the rhetorical situation at the time of the speech and consider how well the speech met that situation.

Despite its limitations, effects evaluation has strong support in the critical community.

Martin Luther King, Jr.'s "Letter from Birmingham Jail" was written in 1963 to refute a Letter to the Editor in the *Birmingham News* by eight leading caucasian clergymen calling on the civil rights protesters to work through legal means to solve their problems. Richard P. Fulkerson concludes his analysis of King's letter by pointing to its effectiveness.

> To lose the moral and social content of King's argument in critical analysis of nuances would, of course, be a mistake. Central to this examination is the attempt to bring about a more refined appreciation of King's text as an instance of rhetoric in the classical sense, a conspicuously compelling effort to persuade. It cannot be fully understood in isolation. As a public letter it stands in the context of its time and place, and it has a precise dialectical relationship to the document which provoked it. It is thus a very real effort to use language as a medium of social-problem solving, as a medium of change. Nevertheless, it also exists, especially for readers today, as a permanent articulation of human perception of an issue, which justifies examining it in all of its eloquent, rhetorical complexities. As an exercise in clarity and logic, King's essay well deserves the fame it has gained. Its structure makes it both readable and thorough. Its refutative stance makes it alive with the fire of heated but courteous controversy, and the dual nature of the refutation makes it simultaneously persuasive and logically compelling. Its stylistic variety and nuance portray a personality in print, manipulate a reader's emotions, and create a union of reader and rhetor.[7]

Artistic merit　Some speech critics insist that the proper measure of quality is not how effective a speech may have been but what level of artistic merit it achieved; in other words, how successfully it applied the principles of the art of speaking.

Every art form has recognized principles that govern the production of its artifacts. All of these rules, of course, are concerned with the way the substance of the art work is communicated. In painting, a visual art, the rules are related to line, form, color, and composition. In music, the rules have to do with tonality and harmony—all of the elements of sound: pitch, force, time, and quality.

For almost two thousand years, it was the practice to evaluate speeches by applying standards appropriate to *literary* criticism: the universality of the central idea, the unity of the structure, the level of the style. Students of Greek and Latin study the speeches of Demosthenes and Cicero primarily as exemplars of classical standards and only incidentally as masterpieces of influential public address. Thus, a speech may be judged by the established rules of the art of rhetoric embodied in the canons of invention, disposition, style, and delivery. If we look for examples of relatively modern speeches that have been judged by artistic standards, Abraham Lincoln's "Gettysburg Address" and Martin Luther King, Jr.'s "I Have A Dream" come quickly to mind.

Historical significance　Sometimes a critic will ask whether the speaker's analysis of the past is accurate. Others will ask whether later history supports what the speaker said. A critic making an evaluation on this basis determines the extent to which the ideas expressed in the speech reflect, lead, or trail behind the society.

Colleen E. Kelley examined the speech of Mikhail Gorbachev to a 1987 international forum on world peace held in Moscow. She found three dramas: "a nuclear free earth or no earth at all," "world peace through socialism," "from salvation to self preservation." Her analysis of how Gorbachev developed these dramas led to conclusions not only about the immediate situation but also about the future.

> It is still too early to determine what effect Gorbachev's discourse will have on controlling nuclear weapons and resolving conflict in the socio-political world arena. It is clear, however, that his vision goes beyond simple maneuvering to court world opinion. The rhetorical reality created by Mikhail Gorbachev in these three dramas transforms the role of the Soviet Union from a malevolent war monger to a benevolent agent of peace and world unity. Audience participation in any of the dramas results in believing, albeit for different reasons, that Gorbachev and the Soviets genuinely want to limit nuclear weapons and thus to produce a less-divided and more peaceful world.
>
> The situation motivating the Soviet call for de-escalation involves domestic and international crises: "Never before have the two issues—

the development of the Soviet economy and world security — been so intimately connected.'' These twin threats become the substance of Gorbachev's discourse and produce the powerful, complex motives in the three dramas: the Soviets must exist in a nuclear-free world to recover economically, and the world must be nuclear-free to ensure the survival of an international stage for peaceful world competition. It is precisely because he is so motivated, that peace may finally be given a chance under Mikhail Gorbachev.[8]

Ethical worth   Judgments are made by some critics as to the ethical worth of what the speaker says. An evaluation of this kind determines the merits of a speech by weighing the speaker's ideas on the balance of the critic's ethical norms.

Kenneth Burke makes an overtly ethical judgment in his analysis of *Mein Kampf*, Adolf Hitler's blueprint for Nazi action:

> Our job, then, our anti-Hitler Battle, is to find all available ways of making the Hitlerite distortions of religion apparent, in order that politicians of his kind in America be unable to perform a similar swindle. The desire for unity is genuine and admirable. The desire for national unity, in the present state of the world, is genuine and admirable. But this unity, if attained on a deceptive basis, by emotional trickeries that shift our criticism from the accurate locus of our trouble, is no unity at all. For, even if we are among those who happen to be ''Aryans,'' we solve no problems even for ourselves by such solutions, since the factors pressing towards calamity remain. Thus, in Germany, after all the upheaval, we see nothing beyond a drive for ever more and more upheaval, precisely because the ''new way of life'' was no new way, but the dismally oldest way of sheer deception — hence, after all the ''change,'' the factors driving towards unrest are left intact, and even strengthened.[9]

Preparing the Evaluation

Obviously, the form and depth of analysis will differ as situations differ. When you evaluate a classmate's speech, you will have far less time to consider, study, and prepare than when you have several weeks in which to pore over a text and check items in the library before you write a paper. However, the basic approach will be the same. A few general principles will be helpful as you begin to express your evaluative judgments.

Begin with Judgment

Evaluations are what your listeners or readers are most interested in. Avoid the ''laundry-list'' analysis (''He said this, ... then this, ... then this ...'') Center on two or three important evaluative statements about what you regard as good or poor in the speech.

Relate Judgment to Synthesis

Reveal in your evaluation what you see as the strategy of the speech. Reconstruct, if necessary, the situation that led you to your judgment. Show how individual judgments join to provide an overall impression of the speech.

Support Synthesis and Judgment with Analysis

To say merely that something was good or bad, or that it was central to the persuasive effort, is not enough. Your evaluation must show how arguments, values, credibility, style, delivery, or structure illustrate the strategy of the speech. Of course, you won't use everything you have discovered through your analysis but only what is necessary to support your judgment.

Analysis, synthesis, and judgment—the three elements of speech evaluation—are closely comparable to the elements of communication discussed in earlier chapters. Your judgments are like the specific purposes of a speech. They identify what you want the audience to know or to believe. Synthesis identifies major points and gives order to your evaluation. Your analysis provides the specific supporting materials necessary to understand your judgment. It is equally incumbent on speaker and critic to have something to say and to say it well.

Summary

Evaluating the speeches of others helps you to improve your own speaking and listening skills. It also gives you insight into the significance of the speaking situation and a better understanding of human beings and their concerns.

There are three steps to speech criticism: analysis, synthesis, and judgment. In the analysis stage you look for the central claim of the speaker and the arguments, evidence, values and credibility which support that claim. As a part of your analysis you will want to examine the structure of the speech to see if it has unity, order and coherence. You will look at the language and style for clarity and interest. And, when possible, you will analyze the delivery.

When you synthesize this analysis, you identify the central strategy of the speech and determine which specific elements of the speaker's technique provide the important supports for the theme and which detract from it.

Judgment is made on the basis of one, or a combination, of four standards: effect, artistic merit, historical significance and ethical worth. In preparing the evaluation you begin your statement with judgment. You then relate the results of your synthesis to the judgment. The analysis supplies the evidence that supports both the synthesis and the judgment.

Key Terms

Analysis	Coherence
Synthesis	Theme
Judgment	Scope
Argument	Language and style
Value appeals	Delivery
Credibility	Effect
Organization	Artistic merit
Unity	Historical significance
Order	Ethical worth

Exercises

1. Act as a critic for one of your classmates' speeches. In your oral criticism explain what you believe to be the two greatest strengths and the two greatest weaknesses of the speech. Give specific examples to support your judgement.

2. Listen to a speech by some local person (your minister, priest, or rabbi for instance) and write an evaluation of the speech.

3. With a group of classmates, prepare and hold a group discussion evaluating a speech delivered on television by some nationally known person such as the president or the governor.

4. Write an evaluation of a speech of historical importance, such as Abraham Lincoln's "Second Inaugural Address," Booker T. Washington's "Atlanta Exposition Address," or Franklin D. Roosevelt's "Declaration of War." Emphasize the ways in which the same speech delivered today might be differently received.

5. Listen to a speech by a person appearing on campus and write a paper on some phase of speech analysis assigned by your instructor.

Notes

[1] Elizabeth Myette Coughlin and Charles Edward Coughlin, "Convention in Petticoats: The Seneca Falls Declaration of Women's Rights," *Today's Speech* 21 (1973): 20.

[2] Cathy A. Sandeen and Malcolm O. Sillars, "Stay the Course," *Exitasis*, 7 (1983): 12-37.

[3] Geraldine A. Ferraro, "Acceptance Address," *Vital Speeches of the Day* 15 Aug. 1984: 645.

[4] Eleanor Smeal, "The Feminization of Power," *Contemporary American Speeches* eds. Richard L. Johannesen, R.R. Allen, Wil A. Linkugel (Dubuque, IA: Kendall/Hunt, 1988) 255-56.

[5] David Henry, "The Rhetorical Dynamics of Mario Cuomo's 1985 Keynote Address: Situation, Speaker, Metaphor," *Southern Speech Communication Journal* 53 (1988): 117.

[6] See Robert Cathcart, *Post Communication* (Indianapolis: Bobbs-Merrill, 1981) 26-30.

[7] Richard P. Fulkerson. "The Public Letter as a Rhetorical Form: Structure, Logic, and Style in King's 'Letter From Birmingham Jail'," *Quarterly Journal of Speech* 65 (1979): 135.

[8] Colleen E. Kelley, "The Public Rhetoric of Mikhail Gorbachev and the Promise of Peace," *Western Journal of Speech Communication* 52: 332-33. Copyright 1988 by the Western Speech Communication Association. Reprinted by permission.

[9] Kenneth Burke, *The Philosophy of Literary Form* (New York: Vintage, 1957) 188-89.

Index